Housing Policy Analysis

Also by Stuart Lowe

URBAN SOCIAL MOVEMENTS
PUBLIC SECTOR HOUSING LAW (*with David Hughes*)

Housing Policy Analysis

British Housing in Cultural and Comparative Context

Stuart Lowe

First published 2004 by
PALGRAVE MACMILLAN
Houndmills, Basingstoke, Hampshire RG21 6XS and
175 Fifth Avenue, New York, N.Y. 10010
Companies and representatives throughout the world

PALGRAVE MACMILLAN is the global academic imprint of the Palgrave Macmillan division of St. Martin's Press, LLC and of Palgrave Macmillan Ltd. Macmillan® is a registered trademark in the United States, United Kingdom and other countries. Palgrave is a registered trademark in the European Union and other countries.

ISBN 0–333–80178–4 hardback
ISBN 0–333–80179–2 paperback

This book is printed on paper suitable for recycling and made from fully managed and sustained forest sources.

A catalogue record for this book is available from the British Library.

A catalog record for this book is available from the Library of Congress.

10   9   8   7   6   5   4   3   2   1
13   12   11   10   09   08   07   06   05   04

Printed in China

Contents

List of Figures and Tables

Figures

Tables

Preface and Acknowledgements

This book arose from the demands of students taking my housing course for a single text that would guide them through it but also point them to the wider literature and web-based resources. The end product is unlikely to satisfy everyone and is by no means comprehensive (there is no chapter dedicated to housing finance, for example), but it does attempt to show both the big picture of housing and society and also as much of the important detail as space allows. Where there are gaps I have indicated other books and sources. It should not be too difficult, therefore, for students to navigate the housing literature, using this book as a foundation. Housing policy has been and remains one of the most dynamic and rapidly changing areas of public policy and I have tried to tell the story as it appears at this moment. What is likely to happen in the 'social' housing sector is particularly uncertain and I may have overstepped the line between fact and speculation. Only time will tell whether what I have suggested about the future of British housing comes to pass, although I have been guided by expert opinion.

As I have been writing the book two names in particular have constantly recurred as guiding stars. Jim Kemeny has helped in his writing and in our conversations to shape the conceptual basis of the book and Alan Holmans' numerous reports, articles, commentaries and (not least) his book, have been an endless source of detailed knowledge about British housing, especially the demographic underpinning of the subject. I hope I have referenced everything of theirs appropriately. Whether they approve of what I have written is another story, and I alone am responsible for this text.

A few others have helped by commenting on individual chapters. I am thankful especially to Janet Ford, Alison Ravetz and Steve Wilcox. I would also like to thank Paul Keenan for helping with the preparation of Chapter 2. May I also take this opportunity to thank my commissioning editor, Catherine Gray, for being so patient. Thanks are also due to Keith Povey for overseeing the final editorial work on the typescript and index. I am very grateful to my family and friends for their forbearance because writing a book of this type inevitably spills over into weekends and evenings. Most of all I wish to thank my wife Sue, who is a constant support despite her own hectic career.

York   STUART LOWE

The author and publishers are grateful to the following for permission to adapt and modify copyright material: J. Hegedüs, S. Mayo and I. Tosics for a table in *Transition of the Housing Sector in East-Central European Countries* (Budapest, Metropolitan Research Institute, 1996); Peter Malpass and Palgrave Macmillan for a table from *Housing Associations and Housing Policy* (Basingstoke, Macmillan, 2000); John Perry and Joseph Rowntree Foundation for diagram from *Housing Finance Review 2000/2001* by Steve Wilcox, published for the Joseph Rowntree Foundation by the Chartered Institute of Housing and the Council of Mortgage Lenders; Glen Bramley for a list from 'Housing Surpluses and Housing Need' in Lowe *et al.* (eds), *Housing Abandonment in Britain* (York, Centre for Housing Policy conference paper, 1998); Peter Kemp and his co-authors, and Policy Press for material from *Single Homelessness* (Bristol, Policy Press, 2000), from an article in *Housing Studies*, 16(1), 2001, and from *Private Landlords in England* (London, HMSO, 1996); Roger Burrows and his co-authors, and Joseph Rowntree Foundation for a table from an article in *Housing Finance Review 2000/2001* by Steve Wilcox, published for the Joseph Rowntree Foundation by the Chartered Institute of Housing and the Council of Mortgage Lenders; Ivan Turok, Nicola Edge and Policy Press for a diagram from *The Jobs Gap in Britain's Cities* (Bristol, Policy Press, 1999); Frank Castles and Edward Elgar for a table from *Comparative Public Policy* (Cheltenham, Edward Elgar, 1998); Chris Hamnett and UCL Press for material from *Winners and Losers* (London, UCL Press, 1999); Alan Holmans and Croom Helm for a table from *Housing Policy in Britain* (London, Croom Helm, 1987) and from an article in *Housing Finance Review 1999/2000* (York, Joseph Rowntree Foundation); and Routledge & Kegan Paul for a table from Steven Merrett, *Owner Occupation* (1982).

Every effort has been made to trace the copyright holders but if any have been inadvertently overlooked the publishers will be pleased to make the necessary arrangements at the first opportunity.

1
Housing Policy Analysis

CHAPTER AIMS

- To introduce the main themes of the book
- To explain the significance of the cultural and historical foundations of British housing and the role of globalization in shaping the housing policy agenda
- To introduce the key concepts of the policy analysis approach which is the disciplinary foundation of the book
- To show how knowledge of policy analysis informs and shapes the study of housing.

Introduction

It is no exaggeration to say that during course of the twentieth century British housing experienced a revolution. It was a quiet and long revolution, but its consequences transformed the structure and ownership of the nation's housing stock, impacted dramatically on the economy and in recent decades has exerted a strong influence over the character of what has come to be known as the 'post-industrial welfare state'. Although every country is in some way unique, some features of this development were very different from comparable nations in Europe and the wider group of OECD countries. This book is about what happened to British housing in the twentieth century, what the outcome was and, above all, why there was such dramatic change. The explanation requires not only a sensitivity to the historical and cultural context of the British case but also a discussion about the very nature of 'housing' itself and how it helps to shape the pattern of societies. The book is more, therefore, than an account of British housing, and one of its central arguments is that it is not possible truly to understand any one country in isolation from its more global context. If Britain is in some ways 'different' it must imply the questions 'different from what and why?'

A second key feature of the book is that the way of thinking about these issues is built up from a policy analysis approach, which is a sub-field of political science. Policy analysis focuses on the changing nature of institutional structures and on the way policy is made and implemented. Inside this approach is a 'new' institutionalist litera-ture, which lays considerable emphasis on the historical and cultural foundations of societies and the way nation states have been compelled to change under the impact of globalization processes. The book is inherently comparative in approach. This concern with institutions and the policy-making process grew rapidly in the latter decades of the twentieth century, stimulated by an increasing aware-ness that very few policies achieved clear-cut results and that there were routinely gaps between what policy-makers intended and outcomes at the moment of 'delivery'. Indeed, more often than not policies created perverse consequences requiring further interven-tion, or they quite simply failed. Students of housing know well the example of the notorious 1957 Rent Act, which deregulated large sections of the private rented sector (PRS) but failed to revive invest-ment. Instead it contributed to the further demise of the PRS and, as a result, the continuation of council house building through the 1960s. It is almost a law of policy analysis that intention and outcome rarely equate.

The main aim of this chapter is to outline the key features of the policy analysis approach and how it relates to the study of housing policy. The idea is to provide a conceptual map that will guide readers through the book. 'Policy mapping' is quite common in the policy process literature and is a useful metaphor for helping to make sense of complex issues as well as the contents of a book. As Hirschman points out, 'without models, paradigms, ideal types and similar abstractions we cannot even begin to think' (Hirschman, 1970: 338). It is import-ant, however, not to confuse the map with reality and to know that there are many different maps, and that they are made for different reasons.

Themes and Leitmotifs

Tenure Restructuring

Built into the book are a number of linking themes or leitmotifs, to use an operatic analogy. The first one derives from the key distinguishing feature of the British case, the dramatic re-structuring of the tenure system over the seven middle decades of the twentieth century (Figure 1.1). Britain began the twentieth century as a nation of private renters, the classic housing tenure of European industrialization. It entered the twenty-first century utterly transformed, having progressively become a nation of homeowners, with a large residual state housing sector. Most other comparable countries have not followed such a dynamic pathway. Some countries have had longer-term more stable patterns of owner occupation, notably the English-speaking nations of the OECD, normally also retaining a sizeable private rental sector. Other countries, mostly in Europe, have evolved a more pluralistic housing system incorporating a variety of providers of rental housing. In the latter

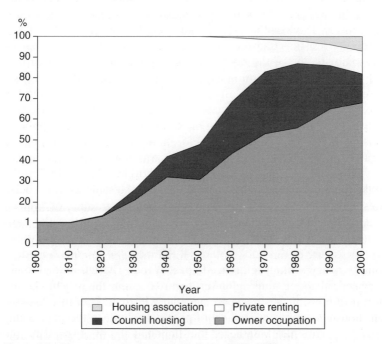

Figure 1.1   **Tenure re-structuring in Britain, 1900–2000**

countries there has been a drift towards home owning during the 1990s, but the change was been gradual and on average quite small.

The feature that is most different about Britain is the very long process of converting to being primarily a nation of owner-occupiers, a process that accelerated to what seemed to be its conclusion by the early 1990s. Excluding Britain (and Ireland, which is a related case) the average growth in home ownership between the early 1960s and the mid-1990s in the twenty-one nations of the OECD was 7.5 per cent. In Britain the figure was 26 per cent – in the USA no change, in Canada and Switzerland a decline of 2 per cent and Japan a decrease of 10 per cent (Castles, 1998: 251). If nothing else, such figures do not suggest the convergence of the industrialized nations, which is often spoken of in the comparative literature, and certainly not towards a home owning norm. The drift towards owner occupation has produced an OECD average of 60 per cent of households. Britain, at about 70 per cent, has completed its catch-up phase and has been stable at about that level for nearly a decade. The idea sometimes spoken of in the literature that Britain, especially in the 1980s, was leading the way towards a 'home owning' Europe is very far from the truth. There are a number of ways of explaining the modest growth of owner occupation in Europe over the last half-century. The idea that is least plausible is that 'catch-up' Britain was somehow irresistibly transferring her policies across the English Channel.

A major theme of the book revolves around the questions of how and why this quiet revolution happened in Britain and what its consequences will be for the twenty-first century, not just in housing but across the wider pattern of society. The long historical view shows that British 'peculiarity' was built into the situation at the very inception of housing 'policy', in the decades before and after the traumas of the First World War when the major question was how and in what form to provide rental housing for the European working classes. In Britain, unlike the other industrialized nations, earlier experiments with 'social' housing flourished into a full-blown building programme of 'council houses'. It is at this time and for closely related reasons that the roots of the home owning society are also to be found. That 'history matters' is a key feature of this book because it is impossible to explain modern housing policy without reference to past events. There is indeed something special about 'housing' in this regard because the very bricks and mortar of housing are in a sense peculiarly historical because the current housing stock consists only of properties built in the past. Many older properties have weathered the slings and arrows of social change in the twentieth century, changing tenure on several occasions, storing up the hidden and treasured memories (sometimes nightmares) of its occupants but remaining more or less the same building.

The Impact of Globalization

The second leitmotif concerns the impact on housing policy of the radical surgery that the British state underwent after 1970, under the impact of globalization. The post-war unitary state organized from Whitehall has given way to new forms of governance. What has happened in housing is one case of a much wider and deeper agenda in which the basic fabric of the state has been re-cast. In outline, the argument is that the creation of a global economy made a powerful impact on Britain with her long history of sea-faring and international trade, and legacy of Empire. The economy was very vulnerable to the expansion of the world economy with its powerful dynamic towards the creation of 'core, semi-periphery and peripheral' national clusters (Giddens, 1989: 520–1). The increasingly dynamic character of the global financial markets impacted sharply on the City. Under these pressures there was an intense strain on Britain's post-Second World War political consensus which irrevocably broke down during the 1980s, creating major fractures in the process of government that changed Britain from a unitary state centred on Whitehall to a much more fragmented system, captured in Rhodes' phrase 'differentiated polity' (Rhodes, 1997: 24). Here the discussion is not of government but of *governance*, of a political system founded on extensive self-governing policy networks increasingly detached from the democratic centre. Contracting out of service delivery, new public management, privatization of publicly owned assets, devolution, the abolition of the committee system and the election of powerful mayors and 'cabinets' to run local government, are all symptomatic of the collapse of the unitary state founded on the so-called 'Westminster model'.

Another set of questions flowing from this is the extent to which nations diverge or converge under the impact of globalization. If British housing is different from her European neighbours, what does this tell us about the power and influence of the global economic order? International capitalism is a powerful engine of change but it is equally important to recognize unifying cultural and historical forces that might connect different societies in ways that are not fundamentally economic. The English-speaking, home owning family of nations is a clear example of countries with a shared linguistic heritage and historical roots to Britain's imperial past (Castles, 1998). Globalization is a contested concept but the impact of worldwide economic processes are fundamental, and few social scientists dispute its significance even if there are many interpretations of its consequences. The point is to be clear about effects that are truly global and those that have other sources, and where they overlap. In practice, the result of globalization has often been to fracture otherwise stable political and social systems. As Giddens pointed out, globalization also has a dramatic impact at the level of the individual simply because old cultural certainties are less able to provide the source of people's self-identity. Facing a more open future requires individuals to make their own identity. As will be shown in Chapter 3, the concept of 'home' becomes, as a result of this, a crucial element in the response to globalization. At the very least the globalization agenda creates the realization of the *interconnectedness* of the personal, local, regional, national and international levels, and ultimately this may be its main significance.

The Nature of 'Housing'

A third leitmotif turns the spotlight onto *housing* itself. Mention has already been made of the significance of taking an historical approach to the study of housing. But there are other indications in the social science literatures that housing is not an easy field of investigation to character-ize. Most housing is built by private developers, at least in economically advanced societies, but how many houses are built and to what stand-ard, where, and who owns them (landlords or 'owner-occupiers)' are all matters of public policy. One of the 'odd' features of housing is that it stands uneasily between the public and private sectors. A large part of British council housing was built by private construction companies but has been owned and managed by municipal authorities. Housing is also unusual because it is normally 'consumed' (used) by individual 'house-holds' and so is inherently a place containing people's private worlds, where we build our psychic stability and cultivate and strengthen the manner in which we face the world beyond the front door. Schools and hospitals are very different entities, because they are used collectively.

It may be that this complex agenda makes the conceptualization of housing different from other forms of social provision. Kemeny, for example, has persistently pointed out that housing is a neglected part of the comparative welfare state literature, or at best has been thought of as marginal to the other great pillars of welfare – social security, educa-tion and health (Kemeny, 1995). The major scholars of welfare state development – Wilensky, Esping-Andersen, Heidenheimer, Castles and others – all for one reason or another marginalize housing or do not include it in their analysis, even though in some cases data was collected (Wilensky and Esping-Andersen both collected housing data). What is so different about housing that it should be neglected in this way? Part of the answer is that a very large part of the research programme on housing has been conducted by economists who, in the main, have thought of housing as an economic good rather than the product of social, cultural and political structure and agencies. Thinking about housing as a cultural/historical formation as well as an economic product and commodity is, however, very revealing not only of the difficulties in the welfare state literature but, more significantly for this book, to the nature of 'housing' itself – its bricks and mortar, the costs of building it, the idea of 'tenure', the theme of home-making and the question of how housing relates to welfare states, indeed wider society as a whole. Kemeny has argued that the marginalization of housing can hardly be because housing is insignificant and he concludes that, 'The neglect of housing by comparative researchers is paradoxically testimony to the importance of housing rather than its insignificance' (Kemeny, 1999).

Indeed, the importance of housing to everyday life could hardly be more obvious. It is the place where we keep our clutter and prized possessions, often experience our closest relationships and is a foundation of social and psychological well-being. As will be shown later in the book, the concept of 'home' is super-charged with symbolic and practical meaning. That housing is allegedly difficult to conceptualize may partly be that it is so socially and culturally embedded. Certainly the idea of 'home' has had relatively little consideration in the mainstream housing studies literature, despite being discussed elsewhere in the social sciences.

Thus there is an important inner agenda to this text, which is to think about housing not only from the outside, as an object of policy, but also to think about it literally from the inside out. Apart from the homeless everybody has some experience of housing as a shelter from the elements but much more significantly, in the words of the French phenomenologist, Bachelard, it is 'our corner of the world' (Bachelard, 1964). It is upon this foundation that the cultural and then historical approach to housing studies is built.

The Structure of the Book

- **Chapter 1** (Housing Policy Analysis) introduces the themes of the book and discusses the policy analysis literature and how it relates to the study of housing.

- **Chapter 2** (The New Governance of Housing) deals with the changing pattern of housing governance in Britain, particularly the dramatic programme of transfers of council housing to other landlords and the consequences of devolution.
- **Chapter 3** (Housing, Home and Society) is a discussion of the concept of 'home'. It was indicated above that it has been neglected and yet is clearly a fundamental concept in housing, if for nothing else to know what the awful experience of home*lessness* entails.
- **Chapter 4** (Housing Need) addresses the fundamental concepts and methods involved in the analysis of housing policy, beginning with a definition of housing need and going on to consider how many houses there need to be so that every household is adequately housed. What is an acceptable standard of housing, who is entitled to access to independent accommodation of their own, how are housing needs measured and what policy instruments are available to governments to ensure that housing is built in sufficient quantity (and standard)?
- **Chapter 5** (Housing and Social Exclusion) examines in detail the extreme end of the housing needs spectrum, namely, homelessness and other forms of social exclusion, which are caused by or contributed to by housing.
- **Chapter 6** (Tenure Re-Structuring) places the development of housing policy in its historical context, and asks the question how and why was the structure of British housing tenure changed during the course of the twentieth century? It begins by drawing attention to the public health origins of housing policy and highlights the dramatic impact on the progress of housing policy of the two world war (1914–18 and 1939–45).
- **Chapter 7** (The Sustainability of Home Ownership) With the UK having matured as a nation of homeowners in the early 1990s this chapter focuses on profiling this newly dominant tenure and whether homeownership is sustainable for all households, especially the more recent entrants. It builds on Chapter 6 to explain why the expansion of home owning has more or less stopped, before analysing the social composition of the tenure and the wider social consequences of the dominant place that owner occupation now has in British society.
- **Chapter 8** (The Residualization of Rental Housing) explores the profile of the rental tenures that have also undergone rapid change in recent decades. One-third of the population lives in rental housing and will continue to do so for the foreseeable future. The public and private rental sectors have both been subject to residualization over

many decades. The consequences of this are outlined and discussed, and the connection to their residualization and the maturation of owner occupation is made.

- **Chapter 9** (Comparative Housing) is a discussion of comparative housing. It begins by exploring the conceptual basis of the comparative literature and then focuses on the question of why Britain might be thought of as 'different' and how this affects wider society and patterns of welfare state development. Detailed attention is given to the situation not only in Western Europe but also to housing in East and Central Europe.

- **Chapter 10** (The Significance of Housing) brings together the core ideas of the book in a final summing up and shows the significance of housing to wider society. This raises a series of issues about the nature of housing and the impact that housing has on the development of welfare states in different countries. Housing, it is argued, is a key to understanding the nature of different societies.

This is the broad sweep of the book. It has been designed so that it does not have to be read sequentially because it works at several levels. The idea is to guide students about the key issues of contemporary British housing: the need for housing, homelessness, inner city housing, regeneration, the new governance of housing, tenure profiles, New Labour's approach to housing, etc. Key technical issues – how to measure housing need, the demographic context, the law on homelessness, the administration of housing policies – are also built into the structure of the text. Always, however, the broad themes are never far away because it is simply not possible to explain day-to-day issues or technical questions without bedding them into the big picture.

The rest of this chapter is a brief account of the key features of the policy analysis approach and how they relate to housing studies. It should be made clear before embarking on this brief foray into the policy analysis literature that it is a large and complex literature and after briefly introducing its scope and significance the main aim of the rest of the chapter is to highlight those aspects of it that are of particular significance to the housing case. Policy analysis is best thought of as an *orientation*, as a way of thinking about a subject matter. In the case of housing the policy analysis literature draws attention particularly to housing's relationship with globalization, the changing role of the state and the significance of culture and history. How all these elements connect is essentially derived from this literature. Policy analysis is the book's superstructure.

The Policy Analysis Approach

This section sketches in some of the main themes of the policy analysis approach and illustrates these with 'housing' cases and examples, many of which will be discussed in more detail later in the book. Policy analysis spawned a huge literature in the latter decades of the twentieth century, and the purpose of this section is to give a flavour of the general approach but principally to focus on the concepts and ideas that help explain issues, problems and questions involved in housing policy.

The policy analysis approach developed inside American political science after the Second World War. The founding father of the 'policy orientation', as he called it, was Harold Laswell and an indication of what was on his mind is evident in the opening words of one of his early post-war texts:

> The continuing crisis of national security in which we live calls for the most efficient use of manpower, facilities and resources of the American people. (Laswell, in Laswell and Lerner, 1951: 3)

Laswell goes on to say that there is a need in this effort to overcome divisions between the disciplines such as philosophy, natural science, biology and social science. He suggests that there has been a growing awareness of the 'policy process as a suitable object of study in its own right, primarily in the hope of improving the rationality of the flow of decisions'. A number of key themes in policy analysis are thus immediately apparent. It is not a social science discipline in its own right but is inherently inter-disciplinary. It has a problem centred orientation. It aims to improve the rationality of decision-making. As Wildavsky defines it:

> Policy analysis is an applied sub-field whose content cannot be determined by disciplinary boundaries but by whatever appears appropriate to the circumstances of the time and the nature of the problem. (Wildavsky, 1980: 15)

As we have seen above, Laswell's motivation for creating a policy 'orientation' was the intelligent application of different disciplines to improve society and to defend democracy, 'the special emphasis is upon the policy sciences of democracy, in which the ultimate goal is the realisation of human dignity in theory and practice' (Laswell, 1951: 14–15). His main contribution is really to see public policy as a form of *public education* in which citizens learn how to be active in society for their own improvement and the betterment of society as a whole. In later papers, Laswell shows that the policy sciences have an increasingly indispensable role in mediating and bringing rationality to complex decision-making. He developed the idea of 'think-tanks' for this purpose and set up Masters-level degree courses to train a new generation of policy analysts. He was concerned that policy-makers should be aware of their own value-systems. Thus Laswell distinguished between two sorts of knowledge: the idea of 'knowledge of' the policy process and 'knowledge in' the policy process. In other words, there is a distinction between those analysts who evaluate and think about the policy process as a whole and those who use such knowledge to develop techniques for improving the quality of policy-making and especially how policy can be implemented more effectively – for example, by manipulating behaviour through the use of performance indicators for workers and managers. The focus of this book is on the first, more general, approach although the two strands are not always clearly demarcated.

Metaphors of the Policy Process

In developing 'knowledge of' the policy process Laswell identified it with a series of consecutive stages and functions. Policy generation begins with 'intelligence' about a problem, 'promotion' of the issue, 'prescription' of what should be done, 'innovation' of a policy, 'application' of the policy in practice, 'termination' when the problem has been solved and 'appraisal' of the impact (Laswell, 1956). However, Laswell did not consider these stages as 'real' in the sense that they encompassed a beginning and end point. Rather he was concerned with the value-systems, institutions and wider social processes that shaped policy in the real world.

The policy cycle or stages approach should not, therefore, be thought of as a 'real-world' description but as a model or metaphor for developing knowledge about the policy process. But it is a common image of how policy systems works and is useful in the evaluation of case studies. The danger, however, is that it implies a 'top down' view of policy-making in which there is a high degree of rationality. It fails as a result to take into account the impact of street-level bureaucrats, does not adequately explain how policy moves from one stage to the next and does not easily account for the myriad and complex sets of policy networks that are at the heart of real-world politics. There is also a very subtle danger that by creating a discourse around rationality, cycles and stages, policy analysts forget the inter-disciplinary foundations of the subject. It can quite easily, and mistakenly, be imagined that policy analysis has some kind of scientific status. Indeed losing their disciplinary roots is one of the major problems with some of the applied 'social sciences' such as social and public administration, or indeed with 'housing studies'. As Kemeny has persistently pointed out such a focus insulates scholars of social administration or housing policy from the great raft of disciplinary ideas and knowledge and leads them to stand in danger of perpetually re-inventing the wheel, imagining their findings to be new, and unable to integrate their research findings into the wider disciplines (Kemeny, 1992).

There are also completely different metaphors other than policy cycles or stages for explaining or thinking about policy. The idea of *policy communities and networks* captures more readily the complexity of the policy process, and is used throughout this book. More extreme metaphors, such as the 'garbage can' model dispute that there are *any* rational boundaries to the policy process. Instead of policies leading to solutions, this explanation argues that there are a limited number of solutions which are mixed up with problems and, moreover, the nature of this garbage changes from time to time so that there is no settled contents. Policy, it is claimed, thus emerges as solutions and problems more or less randomly collide inside the garbage can (Cohen, March and Olsen, 1972).

Policy as 'Muddling Through'

The most widely read and significant critique of rationality and 'stageism' in the policy process, is that made by Lindblom. Rejecting the notion of policy as a series of stages, he sees policy as essentially incremental. Lindblom's famous article on the 'science of muddling through' (Lindblom, 1959) is probably the single most widely read policy analysis paper, and a key contribution to the literature. Lindblom argues that policy cannot be understood as a series of packaged stages but is essentially a process of *gradual change and accretion*. This early version was criticized for being a defence of the status quo, 'a champion of market systems and dedicated opponent of planning' (Hogwood and Gunn, 1984: 57). But in later work Lindblom elaborates his ideas, claiming that problems such as unemployment or the environment were the fault of structural problems in the American constitution, its system of government and the threat posed by corporate and business interests (Lindblom, 1979). Later still he warned of 'deeper forces' at work in US politics and the growth of political inequalities (Lindblom and Woodhouse, 1993). It is thus clear that Lindblom's incrementalist approach is not reactionary and he has maintained consistently that the essence of policy-making is 'muddle' (Lindblom, 1979).

Despite the complexities and widely varying views about the policy analysis approach it is possible to define its basic parameters. The first of these has already been alluded to. It is an approach which depends a great deal on the use of metaphors for describing and evaluating what is happening in 'reality'. The metaphor of the policy cycle is useful in that it identifies key moments and processes which are implicit in the policy process. As Hogwood and Gunn suggest before discussing their policy stages, 'In practice, of course, policy is a seamless web involving a bewildering mesh of interactions and ramifications' (Hogwood and Gunn, 1984: 26). In a similar vein Parsons argues the necessity for some form of division in the literature in order that it can be applied to particular policy fields. Acknowledging the danger of unwittingly using a 'top down' pedagogy, Parsons uses a threefold classification – meso-analysis, decision analysis and delivery analysis. Figure 1.2 is a schematic representation of Parsons' framework.

Knowledge for	Knowledge of
Meso-analysis	
Think- tanks	Agenda setting
Expertise	Non-decision
Professionalization	Deep structures
	Policy networks
	Boundary setting
	Globalization
Decision analysis	
New Public Management	Resource constraints
Cognition	Public choice
Agency theory	Institutionalism
Social psychology	Personality
Programme analysis	
Cost-benefit analysis	
Forecasting	
Delivery analysis	
Review	Outputs
Performance monitoring	Top down/bottom up
Termination	Street-level bureaucrats
Evaluation	Delivery systems
	Evaluation/feedback

Figure 1.2 **Parsons' division of the policy analysis literature**
Source: Based on Parsons (1995).

Parsons' text is based on the idea of *policy mapping* – of providing plans that offer various routes through the literature depending on the purpose and policy field under consideration. His book also incorporates Laswell's idea of 'knowledge for' and 'knowledge of' the policy process.

Meso-Analysis

Meso-analysis principally concerns explanations and theories of the various 'stages' or elements of the policy process. These range from the early identification of a problem and the decision that something needs to be done ('deciding to decide'), through an agenda setting process, making decisions about solutions, implementing the policy and the evaluation of the programme. The focal point of meso-analysis is finding out how a problem comes to be on the agenda and theories that are used to explain what is going on. The importance of this is that it provides two related bridging dimensions – a middle (meso) level – which stands between, on the one hand, the moment encapsulated in deciding to decide through to the delivery of the programme and, on the other hand, between the macro level (the broad boundaries) of the policy process and the micro level (of detailed implementation). These two dimensions are closely connected in reality, but knowing the distinction between them is useful in reading the policy analysis literature.

For the purpose of thinking about housing policy analysis and the discussion in this book the approach is to begin with the macro issues, the broad issues that are the stage set to the policy process, then think about the middle tier ('meso' level in the second sense) which focuses particularly on network analysis, and finally look at the micro level, that time when the policy is in the process of being delivered (when the key question is whether street-level action in fact delivers what the policy-makers intended, and with what further consequences).

Decision Analysis

Decision analysis focuses on explaining how a decision came to be made, particularly the value-systems that inform what took place. The emphasis in this literature is very much on the idea of 'knowledge in' the decision-making and implementation process. For example, the use and evaluation of new public management, forecasting theory, cost-benefit analysis or performance indicators to 'improve' policy-making in practice. There are thus two foci here – how decision-making relates to the other processes and the use of management techniques, programme analysis, etc. to manipulate and/or improve the efficiency and effectiveness in practice. As Parsons suggests, 'Decision analysis is concerned with the knowledge of the decision process and the use of knowledge in that process' (Parsons, 1995: 83).

Delivery (Implementation) Analysis

The third major building block in the policy analysis literature covers the rapidly expanding field concerned with what happens at the point of delivery of a policy programme. Implementation was quite often ignored or taken for granted in the orthodox management and administrative literature. It was simply assumed that the civil servants, housing officers, teachers or whoever were broadly speaking following directives given to them from higher up the management structure. Moreover, it was more or less assumed that a properly designed policy, or even one that had been mandated politically, would accomplish its intended effects. It was enough for rents in the private rented housing sector to be de-regulated (following control due to war-time circumstances) for private renting to regain much of its lost share of the housing market and at the very least that it would 'revive'. In practice, a great deal of the history of housing in Britain during the twentieth century concerned the successive failures of this policy. Intention and outcome were often, indeed, more often than not, very considerably different. This may be due to badly designed policy, but was significantly affected by the impact on it of those who have the final duties to deliver. The implementation literature thus challenges the notion of a top down policy process and re-focuses attention on the role of 'street-level bureaucrats' and other influences – social movements, the voluntary or third sector in social welfare, the legal process – in shaping – indeed, changing – the practical outcome of a policy. The research on how homeless people have been treated in Britain and how they experience the process of declaring themselves homeless to local authority officials is littered with evidence of very different treatment according to which local authority is involved. This is the case despite an increasingly detailed Code of Practice intended to smooth out inequities and a judicial system that is replete with detailed case law in how local authorities should treat homeless applicants. Delivery analysis is therefore concerned with the relationship between top down and bottom up models of delivery, how policy is finally administered, and also encompasses monitoring and policy evaluation issues.

It must be emphasized that the division of the policy literature into meso-level analysis, decision analysis and delivery analysis is artificial and that the concepts, theories and paradigms employed are inter-related. The art of policy analysis is knowing which elements of the literature to draw on and deploy in different policy fields, issues and problems. It is a rich and colourful palette. The approach in this book draws mainly from the meso level and the delivery analysis literature. The next section looks in a little more detail at some of these key elements of the policy analysis approach. It begins by asking questions about the broad influences which shape housing policy in the UK and transnationally. A link is then made between this and one of the core theoretical propositions of the meso-level analysis, the idea of policy networks. Finally, there is a brief introduction to the implementation literature and how it relates to housing policy analysis.

The Boundaries of Policy

In the policy analysis literature one of the seminal questions relates to what might be called 'boundary' issues (Parsons, 1995). They concern the extent and influence of economic development, demographic change and cultural/historical foundations, including the contested issues of globalization. At the heart of these broad-brush issues is a dispute between scholars who emphasize economic development against those who argue that political/institutional structures are the key to policy outcomes. These two camps, having been somewhat outmoded in recent years, have made a resurgence in the debates over globalization. Their arguments tend also to sustain a broad 'convergence' and 'divergence' explanation of global patterns of change. It is perhaps not surprising that an economic view, with an emphasis on market processes and trade between nations, created a unilinear model in which societies develop, albeit at different rates, towards industrialism (and post-industrialism), classically described by Wilensky as 'leaders' and 'laggards' but nevertheless converging towards a common end point (Wilensky, 1975). It might also be noted that the economics/convergence paradigm is methodologically closely associated with the use of large-scale quantitative data sets.

Against this view are ranged other scholars whose emphasis is on the seminal influence of political institutions and the policy process itself, the so-called 'institutionalists'. This approach evolved in the 1960s and 1970s to counter the arguments of structural-functionalists, stimulated particularly by the work of Herbert Simon. Simon developed the idea of 'bounded rationality', which argues that human behaviour is limited but not irrational. The institutionalist case arises from the fact of the manifest differences that exist between the nations in the scale of provision and purpose of public and social policies. This view does not reject the fact of the world economic order but focuses on why there are such significant divergences. The Scandinavian welfare state, or more generally the European social market approach, stands in marked contrast to the US free-market, minimalist state. The key to these differences is not fundamentally an economic issue – they are all advanced capitalist economies – but of decisions made inside the political/institutional networks. Such an approach is more focused on cultural and historical contexts, with an emphasis on more qualitative research methodologies.

'Economics Matters' versus 'Politics Matters'

An economy with sufficient development and a growth trajectory is, of course, the *sine qua non* of welfare provision and public policy in general. It is a widely argued case that economic affluence creates demand for public goods and services (Musgrave, 1959; Gemmeu, 1995). The counter-argument that affluent economies need to spend proportionately less because demand can be met from lower GDP share is probably a more plausible case (Wilensky, 1975). In a sense, the arguments are not necessarily contradictory when looked at in a more historical way. There is strong evidence, for example, of a phase of post-Second World War 'catch-up' by some European countries that reach a threshold of affluence when the delivery of modern welfare state services began. Beyond this economic ceiling, issues of political choice and historical/cultural influences inside the societies re-assert themselves (Castles, 1998).

One of the classic statements of the 'economics matters' thesis is found in the work of Wilensky, who used cross-national data from over sixty countries to compare levels of spending on social welfare. He argued that the cause of welfare state development was economic growth, which was associated with the ageing of populations. 'As economic level climbs the percentage of the aged climbs, which shapes spending directly' (Wilensky, 1975: 47). This finding produces a clear convergence outcome because all societies, irrespective of economic system, the partisan nature of its government or other social factors, will be patterned by this relationship and become more alike. In similar vein, Hofferbert argues that policy agendas are set in response to geographical or demographic factors or the existence of mass politics. These broad environmental factors act as filters, which shape trends in policy. Hofferbert thus argues that political processes are essentially peripheral influences on the development of policy (Hofferbert, 1974). The difficulty, however, with the filtering metaphor is that the policy environment does not just exist but is itself largely a creation of the policy process. More recently the impact of globalization has re-asserted the convergence view arising from the common trends in the organization of production and patterns of economic power, which transcend national boundaries.

The case against Wilensky and Hofferbert has been most directly made by Castles whose study of the twenty-one nations of the OECD revealed the existence of families of nations with distinctive routes through the modernization process, 'a fractured modernity in which continuing economic, social and political diversity promises a comparable diversity of national policy outcomes' (Castles, 1998: 93). Using a broad range of indicators in a multi-variate analysis Castles confounds Wilensky's argument, particularly the proposition that linked economic development via the ageing of populations to welfare state development. The key point to emerge from Castles' work is that as nations reach a threshold of modernity and continue to grow in affluence they adopt different means of provision, reflecting different ideological, institutional and cultural influences which continue to differ country by country.

That 'politics matters' is also evident in the renewal of interest in recent decades in the institutional parameters which impact on agenda setting and policy formulation. This approach is almost the polar opposite of the Wilensky/Hofferbert thesis in arguing for the centrality of institutions in determining outcomes (Ostrom, 1990). March and Olsen claim to demonstrate that policy agendas and solutions are shaped within the state and are relatively autonomous from wider environmental factors (March and Olsen, 1989). More than anyone Skocpol has emphasized the need to 'bring the state back in', although not in a narrow and dogmatic way. She compares 'strong' states – Sweden, the UK – with 'weak' states – classically the USA – showing in both cases the power of the institutional actors to shape policy and change. The point is not to abandon historical, cultural and economic parameters, far from it, but to add in the key influence of the political/institutional systems in creating long-term, stable and relatively insulated policy regimes (Skocpol, 1985). Political institutionalism thus acts as an important counter-factual to the economic determinism/convergence schools of thought that dominated the second half of the twentieth century.

New Institutionalism

New institutionalism has grown rapidly since 1985 and has produced an extensive literature. Standing at the heart of contemporary policy analysis it emphasizes the role institutions play in framing 'the rules of the game' that political actors have to encounter, and which they use to shape and promote their preferences. The term 'institutions' in this context refers to a wide range of organizations, social groups and settings and value-systems, encompassing relationships within and between agencies (government departments, central–local relations), elections and voters, political parties, the structure and organisation of key economic groups (such as trade unions) as well as social structures (social classes) and social norms and values. Traditional institutionalist approaches tended to focus only on the formal structures of the political system, and so were unable to account for policy change except in formalistic terms. Institutions in the wider sense are now recognized as being at the heart of the policy process, not only determining the policy process but to a large extent shaping the responses of politicians, policy-makers and the wide array of actors involved. The institutionalist literature has burgeoned to such an extent that it is possible to identify distinct schools of institutionalist thought (Hall and Taylor, 1996). Rational choice institutionalists draw mainly from the economic perspective and emphasize the idea that people seek to maximize their material well-being. This approach has been challenged from many directions, not least by those who follow Lindblom and Simon in believing that the essential quality of the policy process is that rationality of this type is at the very least 'bounded' and/or incremental and more accurately characterized as muddled. According to a more sociologically influenced institutionalist school, policy-making actors (agents) have identities and see reality from a point of view shaped by core social values, leading to shared definitions of what policy options are most likely to succeed.

The most important strand of institutionalist thinking, and the one that influences this book, is 'historical institutionalism'. The basis of this school is that history 'matters' and that without a fundamental understanding of the long view of the factors that influence policy change, it is difficult to make sense of the present. Theda Skocpol showed not only the need as she famously asserted, 'to bring the state back in', but also the necessity take an historical perspective. She showed how the institutions of the state over long periods of time became socially and culturally embedded into a society. State centred approaches were thus enhanced by scholars, who pointed to the role of the wider institutional context – the influence of social classes, of pressure groups and interest groups, and of deep cultural settings – in fashioning policy outcomes. Thelen and Steinmo argued that state centred and society centred approaches were bridged by historical institutionalism. They argued that this approach not only permits understanding of policy continuities within individual countries but also of policy differences between countries (Thelen and Steinmo, 1992). Historical institutionalism thus exerts considerable theoretical leverage in the field of comparative welfare state analysis – including, of course, comparative housing. It has the notable advantage of tackling the central dilemma of comparative studies: of avoiding *ethnocentrism*, that is to say of judging other countries from the standpoint of the institutional structures and cultural setting of one's own country. A rich seam of ideas and literature has emerged around this school. The idea of critical junctures, for example, showed how at key moments in time there is particular opportunity for policy change, although the influence of the social and political structures inherited from the past exerts considerable influence on what happens, on what Hall and Taylor refer to as the 'path dependency' of policy change (Hall and Taylor, 1996).

Another important strand within the new institutional literature, which is related to this historical emphasis, is *policy transfer*. As the world has become increasingly 'networked' under the impact of globalization, so it has been possible to look outside one's own country for ideas that appear to work. Through the process of diffusion and 'policy learning' the transnational policy communities increasingly create opportunities to exchange policies. The most well-known case of this is the alleged influence of the USA on patterning British workfare policies during the 1980s and 1990s (Wolman, 1992; Dolowitz, 1997). It does not follow, of course, that the intention of the donor country is benign or that policies necessarily adapt properly to a new cultural/political setting, so that the policy transfer literature once again draws attention not only to the unequal distribution of power between nations but also to the fundamental cultural/historical context. Workfare ideas were successfully transmitted to the UK because it was a politically and ideologically receptive host.

The case of British housing policy, and where it fits in relation to other comparable nations is, replete with ideas drawn from the historical institutionalist literature, and through this lens it is possible to see more clearly the forces that have shaped the direction of policy. The key to the whole approach is that political and social institutions are fundamental to what happened during the course of the twentieth century and that 'history matters', indeed in the case of housing it matters a great deal, even to the point where there is something 'different' about housing compared to other policy areas.

History and Culture

That 'history matters' is the case both in relation to specific policies and in macro-level analysis. In the narrow sense, practically all current policy is the product of, or closely related to, past policy, which inevitably impinges on its design and social purpose. Housing is inherently very 'path dependent'. As Hogwood and Gunn argue, policy can exist only in a 'policy space' which contextualizes legislation and policy programmes (Hogwood and Gunn, 1984). Parsons sums up the situation by suggesting that, 'it is existing policies which set the agenda for "new" problems and provide the discourse within which problems will be constructed' (Parsons, 1995: 231). In this sense, history matters more than might usually be the case in housing policy. The reason for this is that all current housing stock represents an accumulation of previous policies, building programmes and architectural styles. In Europe and most industrialized nations, housing is built to be relatively permanent, and this implies a range of policies concerned with its repair, renovation and, when needed, demolition. The idea of 'housing standards' is an endless discourse. The point is that no assessment of housing needs or standards can take place without reference to the historic housing stock and its accumulation of problems, improving standards and interaction with changing demographic structures. The wider issues of housing need – how many houses need to be built, where and of what type, and how many need to be upgraded to extend their life – are fundamental issues of the analysis of housing policy (see Chapter 4).

State intervention into housing had relatively early beginnings as a public health issue and took the form of powers for municipal authorities (dating back in Britain to 1835) to close and demolish insanitary dwellings (so-called 'plague spots'), and later on whole areas of slum property. Rebuilding slums and later on the provision of general needs working class housing was, however, not a simple case of an administrative development spawned by public health concerns. There were other issues, particularly patterns of central–local government relations, the social structures that supported private landlordism and crucially the experience of working class political movements in the latter part of the nineteenth century. The British experience soon diverged sharply from what happened in the countries of our near Continental neighbours. This early divergence between Britain and almost the whole of industrialized Europe is one of the keys to the 'peculiarity' of the British housing system. It might also be observed that state housing provision was targeted at the 'working classes' (almost all the British legislation used this term in its titles until 1945), whereas education was intended to be a universal provision and after the Second World War the health services were designed to be universal.

Thus a 'dwelling' is an inherently historical entity and this is one of the deep theory characteristics of this policy field. The bricks and mortar cannot fundamentally change but the manner in which it is occupied, its function and tenure can and does change quite frequently. It is something of a paradox that such an apparently fixed object can be subject to such dynamic social, legal and ideologically driven policy change. Housing tenure in Britain underwent nothing short of a revolution during the course of the twentieth century (see Chapter 6 for a detailed examination of this). Tenure (from the Latin *teneo*, 'I hold') is not simply a means of classification but contains major differences in property rights, financial benefits and significant connections to the patterning of a society's urban form and structure, and even connects to the shape of welfare state development. This is a broad agenda involving at the lowest level individual 'households' (indeed, individuals within households) and at the highest level to major issues of social formation. Many individual dwellings began life in the nineteenth century as the properties of private landlords, may have become owner occupied during the 1930s or 1950s (when sold by the owner to the sitting tenants), been subject to compulsory purchase by a local authority and sold subsequently to a housing association for redevelopment, eventually in the year 2004, over 100 years since it was built, finding its way back to being owned by a private landlord. The neighbourhood in which our house is situated might have been subject to equally dynamic changes. Location and neighbourhood are also key features of the housing policy matrix. A house does not stand on its own and its value, use and status are closely related to where it is.

The historical institutionalist approach draws attention to the 'long view' of history and the need for extreme sensitivity to a nation's cultural foundations. This is seen, for example, in the European context in the impact of the Reformation in patterning the cultural receptivity of different societies to welfare provision, and indeed in the structure of welfare states in different countries. The European Reformation split the church into two branches, Catholicism and the new Protestants. Their different doctrinal systems (the former being confessional and hence hierarchical, the latter emphasizing the personal bonds that relate humans to God and so more open to outside influences) and relationships to the secular world underpinned the emergence of very different political and organizational structures in society. These configurations continue to exert an important influence over society, even in an era when formal religious faiths have declined sharply. It is, for example, no coincidence that all the English-speaking 'home owning' societies are Protestant.

Another example of the seminal influence of 'history' is the early experience in Britain of industrialization, beginning in the mid-eighteenth century. It meant that Britain was the first in history to become urbanized on the basis of an advanced industrial economy. Astonishingly, by the time of the Great Exhibition in 1851, there were already ten urban areas in England with populations of over 100,000, accounting for 24.8 per cent of the whole population, and numbers continued to grow in frightening and unprecedented numbers (Burnett, 1986: 7). Urbanization impacted dramatically on people's changing social horizons. It created new opportunities and new pressures on relations between the sexes, impacted on fertility, divorce and the whole shape of domestic and family life. It also significantly re-divided society on the basis of social class. The key here concerns the extent to which different configurations of classes and trade-offs between classes impacted on policy outcomes. As will be shown in later chapters, this is very much the case in housing: for example, there were powerful political interests supporting private landlordism in mainland Europe but not in Britain where private landlordism was based on a tradition of small-scale ownership. Housing the new urban 'working classes' and the solutions to this problem contain the seeds of modern housing policy, a concept unknown until the last decade of the nineteenth century and then only barely and weakly perceived. In other words, the 'early start' in Britain to industrialization had major and enduring consequences for the way British housing evolved compared to other countries, even to our closest neighbours in Europe. The idea that societies evolve pathways through history ('path dependency') is a useful metaphor for understanding the progress of British housing policy.

The point of this discussion is to demonstrate that the historical/cultural influences on welfare state development and on the shaping of housing policy are crucial. The ideas common in the comparative housing and welfare state literatures – that economics is the dominant force in patterning social policies – or the opposing view – that political partisanship is crucial – are both suspect. What is abundantly clear is that *all* these forces and influences are important and that the process of development never stands still.

Globalization

The international nature of politics is by no means a new phenomenon. Marx famously exhorted the workers of the world to unite in the face of worldwide capitalism. The notion of global politics is implicit in Laswell's approach. He argued that the global character of political and economic activity impacted on the state and the levels of social and economic organisation below the nation state. In the 1980s and 1990s, the notion of 'globalization' captured the sense of an increasingly convergent world economic order owing to the speed with which ideas and people move across the face of the planet. As Giddens expressed it:

> The globalization of social relations should be understood primarily as the reordering of time and distance in our lives. Our lives, in other words, are increasingly influenced by activities and events happening well away from the social contexts in which we carry on our day-to-day activities. (Giddens, 1989: 520)

Giddens identified three factors which shape globalism: the growth of transnational companies, growing economic integration and the globalization of communications.

Although the extent of these interdependencies can be exaggerated, few serious commentators do not now take into account the impact of the world economic and political system. Being a generally over-theorized literature it is important for this purpose to be clear about the impact of globalization factors. There are good grounds for supposing that they are very considerable indeed. At the most obvious level there clearly is a range of genuinely global issues – global warming, AIDS, nuclear accidents, drugs – which transcend national boundaries. Above all there is the imperative of the world economic order to create stable trading and monetary conditions. This is the core globalization issue and its impact, particularly on a state like Britain – which is a trading nation heavily dependent on financial markets and has a historical legacy of Empire – is very significant. As Cerny and Evans argued, the institutions of the state have been compelled 'to conform to the anti-inflationary norms of the international financial markets' (Cerny and Evans, 1999). It was no coincidence, they argue, that the first major policy initiative of the first New Labour government, elected in 1997, was to cede control of interest rate policy to the Monetary Policy Committee (MPC) of the Bank of England, with a specific brief to meet inflation targets. The post-Fordist state is therefore not just about regulating and managing the political and economic system in the face of globalization but of *promoting* an open economy and polity in order to enhance the benefits for specific interests, but at the cost of what has been called a 'democratic deficit'.

One of the key features of globalization is thus the debate about the extent to which domestic policy agendas remain in the close control of governments compared to the past. This is the central paradox of globalization: it simultaneously creates a convergent economic order while dividing and fragmenting the nation state (see Chapter 2). This certainly does not mean the end of the nation state. Ironically under these conditions, it becomes bigger as it responds to these agendas through new layers of regulation and new interdependencies. One of the complexities of this process of internationalization is that the global polity is fragile compared to the nation state, creating compliance problems (McGrew and Lewis, 1992).

The impact of globalization on national policy directions is profound. For example, one of the key propositions of globalization theory is that welfare states are dismantled under pressure from competitive world markets. But the evidence does not support a significant reduction of welfare state expenditure, at least in the OECD countries. Even examples of ideologically driven attempts to redefine welfare entitlements according to the logic of 'free-market' economics and the global economy, such as the Thatcher and Regan administrations, did little more than contain the expansion in the rate of growth of state spending programmes (Castles, 1998: 322). Indeed, there may be areas of new spending implicit in the post-industrial settlement – such as improved standards of paid maternity and paternity leave – and the ageing of the population has significant implications in the field of health care. The New Labour 'project' is more sensitive to these pressures, but has essentially embraced the shift of social policy towards a more contract-orientated, post-industrial welfare state (Cerny and Evans, 1999). Policies such as ending free higher education and the introduction of 'workfare' programmes designed to reintegrate the unemployed into the private sector labour market are very symptomatic of their approach. Housing policy is no different, and following the sale of very nearly 2 million council houses during the 1980s and 1990s under the Right to Buy Policy, preparations are now in hand to transfer the housing stock of most major cities to housing companies and housing associations before 2010, and so wrap up the long history of municipal housing provision in Britain.

Housing policy is thus an exemplar of what Rhodes (1997) refers to as the 'hollowing out of the state'. This involved, through the 1980s and 1990s, the loss of functions by the central state to myriad agencies and implementation bodies, the introduction of New Public Management (NPM) methods, privatization of large parts of the publicly owned infrastructure, contracting out of services and a blurring of the distinction between the public, private and voluntary sectors, all leading to a situation in which, as Osborne and Gaebler put it, government 'steers rather than rows' (Osborne and Gaebler, 1992). Globalization undoubtedly underpins and accelerates the break up of Britain as a unitary state into a much more fragmented system – a 'differentiated polity' as it is described by Rhodes – in which government has substantially given way to governance to 'self-organizing, interorganizational networks characterized by interdependencies, resource exchanges, rules of the game and significant autonomy from the state' (Rhodes, 1997: 15).

The paradox of this situation is that the state is at one and the same time both bigger and more centralizing and yet increasingly differentiated. This is a complex agenda which will be referred to throughout the book, but it is very clear that it is no longer viable to think of Britain as a unitary state – based on the so-called 'Westminster model' – and that state centred narratives are of diminishing value. Increasingly we have to read the policy process as one bounded by the global economic order, 'stretching' and 'deepening', as McGrew and Lewis succinctly put it (McGrew and Lewis, 1992) and creating in the process new forms of inter-relationship between layers – global, national, regional and local. This returns us to our earlier point. It is not surprising to find economists pointing to convergence tendencies in spite of the evidence of fragmentation and divergence between nations. The nation state remains the most important focus of decision-making. As Parsons points out:

> Issues and problems may well be increasingly constructed in international and global terms, but decision-making and implementation still remain domains which must be analysed within the context of nation states. (Parsons, 1995: 243)

Nevertheless the extent to which policy agendas and the internal fragmentation of the state is influenced by globalization imperatives remains very high.

Policy Networks and Implementation Analysis

Policy Networks

The idea of policy networks became a key paradigm in the policy analysis literature during 1990s. It is important to dwell on it here because
the approach in this book is very much shaped by network theory. It is
at the heart of explanations about how the modern British state functions. Network analysis also helps explain some of the peculiarities of
the British welfare state and housing system. The basic point is that
network theory shows why state centred explanations are of decreasing
value. The British state in the early part of the twenty-first century is
a great deal more fractured and 'hollowed out' than conventional
accounts allow for. The 'new governance' comprises networks that are
delivering autonomously with resultant problems of 'steering' and of
accountability and services that are more fragmented, requiring greater
inter-organizational linkages and co-ordination, and the capacity of
the centre to regulate and manage this system is increasingly in doubt.
As Rhodes succinctly summarizes the situation, 'The state becomes
a collection of interorganizational networks made up of governmental
and societal actors with no sovereign actor able to steer or regulate'
(Rhodes, 1997: 57).

It follows that the development of housing policy needs to be read in
this context, a context in which the portrayal of the political system as
a unified and homogeneous state is no longer adequate. It should also
be noted that network theory is a powerful meso-level analytical tool
because, as it is used here, it links the macro- and micro-level environments to agenda setting theory and delivery analysis – the moments
before, during and after implementation takes place. Network analysis
is thus a key explanatory metaphor because it connects the 'inputs' and
'outputs' of the political system and is fundamental to understanding
the governance of Britain in the early years of the twenty-first century.

Policy network theory is built on an extensive foundation of case-
study and analytical literature, much of it written in the 1980s and
1990s. It is impossible to do full justice to this rich literature, but a brief
account of its origins and how it became embedded into UK political
science is followed by a discussion of its importance to a knowledge of
the contemporary purpose and structure of the British state.

Network theory originated in the US literature, arising from criticisms of the 'iron triangle' explanation of the relationship between the
President, Congress and external interests. Heclo (1978) used the idea

of 'networks' in order to free up the rigid and rather misleading accounts of the tripartite model of American politics. Previously Heclo and Wildavsky had made an analysis of the British Treasury, using the idea of 'policy communities' to explain the closed world of decision-making at the heart of the British government (Heclo and Wildavsky, 1974). In a similar way, Dunleavy used the notion of 'ideological corporatism' to explain how groups of key players were able to operate across institutional and departmental boundaries because they shared dominant values and professional interests (Dunleavy, 1981a,b). The most influential study which applied an early version of network theory was that of Richardson and Jordan, who characterized the British political system as a fragmented cluster of sub-systems which were impenetrable by 'unrecognized groups' (Richardson and Jordan, 1979: 174). The idea of 'networks' and 'communities' were used interchangeably in these studies and as Hall suggests, 'Communities are a stronger version of networks... networks may cohere into communities and communities may dis-integrate into networks' (Hall, 1977: 72). Marsh and Rhodes (1992) argued that policy communities have a number of distinguishing features: limited membership, exclusive access, shared value-systems, frequent interaction and resource exchanges managed by the communities' leaderships. At the other end of continuum are issue networks, which have large, diverse memberships, variable and uneven levels of contact, limited resources and unequal power. In between these tightly knit policy communities and loosely framed issue networks are a range of more or less coherently integrated and structured communities/networks. Professional networks, for example, are very much at the more exclusive end of the spectrum, characterized by internal stability, interdependence of the membership and a rather limited vertical articulation (Marsh and Rhodes, 1992). Closely related to the latter type are what Adler and Haas refer to as 'epistemic communities' – professionals, scientists and policy analysts who share common perceptions of a policy field – which are increasingly important in a networked globe, especially in policy transfer (Adler and Haas, 1992).

The importance of this type of analysis is to demonstrate how core areas of policy are shrouded from public gaze, in effect depoliticized, while other more open agendas are left in the political domain and subject to more conflict. For example, key interest rates in the economy are set within a very closed community with the Bank of England's MPC linked to Treasury officials and the commercial banking system. The housing policy arena, on the other hand, may be thought of as an inter-governmental network which has relatively limited membership but with a significant, but decreasing, degree of vertical integration – 'council' houses are owned and managed by local authorities but are subject to a complex funding regime which was vigorously contested during the 1980s, leading to a progressive 'tightening' of housing finance policy by central government – and a quite high degree of articulation, from the DETR officials in London to the tenants' representatives and estate managers in virtually every local authority in the country. But, as will be shown in Chapter 2, the governance of housing is changing dramatically as municipally owned council housing is broken up through the process of stock transfer to new owners. The organizational structure of social housing is thus loosening to a very considerable degree, implying much less vertical integration and more extensive forms of network. In effect, social housing, and housing policy more generally, is being manoeuvred into a quasi-private sector over which the centre will have much less steer.

Implementation Analysis

The final stage of the policy process – assuming that the policy cycle metaphor holds good – is the moment when the programme or service is finally delivered on the ground. Until the 1970s relatively little attention had been paid to implementation because, according to the rational model, the administrators would generally follow the guidance of their managers, who in turn followed the intentions of the policy-makers. Such a narrow view came under scrutiny following the failure of the US 'War on Poverty' and the realization that street-level workers and bureaucrats were unable to deliver the intended results and/or results quite unlike those the policy-makers had envisaged. Attempts were made to explain this as a failure of rationality (Dunsire, 1978) so that conditions for the production of perfect implementation simply needed to be more clearly specified (Hogwood and Gunn, 1984). This meant better communication down the line and a higher degree of compliance by administrators.

This essentially top down, managerialist approach was commonplace in the literature of the period. The first widely read study was Pressman and Wildavsky's research on an economic development programme in Oakland (USA) which showed that an *implementation deficit* arose due to the lack of inter-organizational integration, inadequate funding of the programme and the poor training of the front-line staff (Pressman and Wildavsky, 1973). In a later series of studies Wildavsky developed the theme of implementation as an evolutionary/learning process (Wildavsky, 1980). But the original text was explicitly top down, with agenda setting and policy initiative firmly located at the top of the chain of command.

The problem with the rational/hierarchical view was given further impetus by Lipsky (1980), who argued that 'street-level bureaucrats' were incapable or unwilling to respond to clients. It was thus apparent that there was in reality no easy connection between policy and outcome. Implementation is often hampered by conditions on the ground, underlying economic conditions, lack of resources and lack of clarity about what is intended. Policies can be complex and are bounded by circumstances and rarely start, as we have already seen, from a *tabula rasa*. Some policy is little more than political ploy. Indeed, as Edelman made abundantly clear, a great deal of 'policy' is symbolic rather than really substantive. This, he argued, is because of the necessity to manipulate voter preferences through control of the political discourse – 'words that succeed but policies that fail' (Edelman, 1977). As Parsons suggests:

> The policy-maker may therefore think that a policy has 'solved' or a condition has been improved when in 'reality' all that has happened is that symbols have been manipulated. The public is reassured by such actions and policy-makers have enhanced or maintained their legitimacy. (Parsons, 1995: 181)

In the 1980s NPM techniques – performance monitoring, performance related pay, etc. – claimed to have addressed these problems and provided professionals with a renewed sense of their worth. The evidence, however, suggests that NPM has tended to erode trust between managers and workers and has spawned a new industry of reporting, appraisal and 'audit explosion' (Power, 1994).

Bottom up approaches to implementation accept that it is inevitable that professional and street-level bureaucrats have a major impact on policy outcomes. Policy and practice are not that different and in reality the delivery stage has considerable, if not in some cases a decisive impact on outcomes – which may be quite different from the intention of the designers of the policy. In reality, policy-making is still in progress. Lipsky described a paradox in which street-level professionals operate inside complex bureaucracies and so, 'feel themselves to be doing the best they can under averse circumstances' (Lipsky, 1980: xii) but also having a significant degree of discretion in how they treat their clients. They have a considerable power to manipulate the lives of people who they control. Lipsky argued that these professionals clearly have a political role in shaping the delivery of policy, and that their superiors often have difficulty controlling their front-line workers.

Nevertheless, owing to lack of resources, uncertainties about their own job security and often under pressure of overload, street-level bureaucrats often feel alienated and under-valued. Hill argued that Lipsky appeared to be inconsistent when he portrayed them as either as spearheading service delivery or as grudging cogs in a complex bureaucratic machine (Hill, 1997). The answer seems to be that resource constraints compel front-line workers to operate defensive practices to their own benefit. The tendency is to stereotype clients because this leads to much easier and quicker solutions. Informal rules and procedures based on the discretion of front-line staff gradually come to shape what in fact is delivered to the public. NPM, which claims to be able to enforce greater compliance and limit these delivery problems, appears to have much less effect in changing these cultures than was at first imagined (Hood, 1995).

Barrett and Fudge suggested the idea of a 'policy/action continuum in which an interactive and negotiative process is taking place' (Barrett and Fudge, 1981: 25). The bottom up authors stress the idea that it is difficult – indeed, in some cases, not desirable – to predetermine outcomes. Elmore's notion of 'backward mapping' suggested that outcomes should be measured by their impact on individuals rather than pre-determined criteria (Elmore, 1979). Street-level bureaucrats are frequently in conflict with each other, so that there rarely is an unambiguous result. Moreover, different issues or problems are more or less amenable to 'solution'. Parsons (1995) questions why it appeared to be easier to put a man on the moon than provide decent accommodation for homeless families. Political salience, resources and the management process all contribute. Fundamentally human rather than technological problems are more complex and less easy to solve. Implementation, therefore, has to be read in the context of the type of problem, its political salience and the complexity of the policy networks.

Moreover, as we have seen previously, the British state has fractured since the 1970s, under the impact of globalization and internal 'hollowing out'. This factor is crucial in reading the implementation literature because if the axis of the policy process is subject to significant drift towards the 'bottom end' the implementation level is of increasing importance. Given the salience of networks inside the 'differentiated polity', as discussed above, this raises serious questions about the degree of accountability that remains in the political system, with the implication of a significant shift towards a polity that is largely unaccountable. The influence of the 'street level' may be to increase the degree of fragmentation in the system and widen the democratic deficit.

Conclusion

The policy analysis approach, when it is applied to any area of public policy, necessarily creates a wide-ranging and complex mix of issues and layers of analysis, from the personal to the international. Translated to 'housing' the agenda moves through concern with the meaning of 'home' for individuals and families to comparisons between different nations' housing systems and the impact of globalization. It is a broad agenda, and incorporates a variety of 'middle-range' theories and conceptual tools that span the macro and micro layers of society and the policy process. The idea of 'theories of the middle range' is particularly associated with the seminal work of the American sociologist Robert Merton, who devised an analytical approach opposed to either the excesses of empirically empty grand theory or theoretically empty data gathering (Merton, 1957). In the policy context Parsons neatly sums up this way of thinking:

> Meso (from the Greek '*mesos*': middle, or intermediate) analysis is a middle-range or bridging level of analysis which is focused on the linkage between the definition of problems, the setting of agendas and the decision-making and implementation processes. (Parsons, 1995: 85)

Meso analysis, as it is used in this book, has two inter-related meanings. On the one hand, it refers to the organizations, networks and inter-governmental bodies that are the agency and structure of the policy process. On the other hand, it refers to a number of linking themes that thread their way through the book. These may be thought of as leitmotifs – themes that recur and are developed throughout the text – that link the various sections of analysis. A key to the 'peculiarity' of the British case is found in the early history of industrialization and urbanization, which also leads to the sensitivity of Britain to the impact of globalization. The reasons that lie behind deconstruction of the unitary state in recent decades are founded on this long history. The idea that British housing is in some way 'different' from the comparable nations of the OECD is inherently comparative and derives from the historical institutionalist approach. Without grounding in the theoretical literature there would be a risk that this analysis would be mistaken for an argument that the British case is an 'exception'. This sort of ethnocentric approach is not uncommon in the housing studies literature, as will be seen later in the book, and it is must be made clear here that 'difference' derives from an institutionalist perspective in which the focus is on the historical and cultural factors which cause path dependency. The maturation of Britain as a home owning society and the emergence in the early years of the twenty-first century of a quasi-privatized social housing sector are explicable by an analysis that engages with comparative analysis deriving its theoretical leverage from historical institutionalism.

The third leitmotif focuses on the nature of 'housing' itself: the fact of its fixed location, its high cost, its economic place predominantly in the private sector, its social embeddedness, its role as the locus of home-making, all make housing a somewhat 'different' pillar of welfare. As Torgersen describes it, housing is the 'wobbly pillar under the welfare state' (Torgersen, 1987). If 'housing' is different in this way, a set of questions that are implicitly comparative are added to the agenda. It may be that these differences are what lie at the root of the charge made by Kemeny (1995), that housing has been a neglected part of the comparative welfare state literature.

Chapter 2 begins this exploration of British housing by focusing on the consequences of the break up of the unitary state, a debate which originates in the globalization thesis. Britain has evolved in a very short space of time from a unitary state to a fragmented polity. What does this mean for the governance of housing?

FURTHER READING

Beck, U. (1999) *What is Globalization?*, Bristol, Polity Press.

Castles, F. G. (1998) *Comparative Public Policy: Patterns of Post-War Transformation*, Cheltenham, Edward Elgar.

Giddens, A. (1989) *Sociology*, Oxford, Polity Press.

Hill, M. (1997) *The Policy Process in the Modern State*, 3rd edn, London, Prentice-Hall/Harvester Wheatsheaf.

Parsons, W. (1995) *Public Policy: An Introduction to the Theory and Practice of Policy Analysis*, Aldershot, Edward Elgar.

Rhodes, R. A. W. (1997) *Understanding Governance: Policy Networks, Governance, Reflexivity and Accountability*, Buckingham, Open University Press.

2

The New Governance of Housing

CHAPTER AIMS

- To show the impact of globalization on the collapse of the post-war unitary state
- To show how the 'governance' of housing has changed dramatically in recent years and is one example of the changing nature of the state
- To show how devolution has impacted on housing policy
- To describe the break up of traditional council housing by stock transfer and other forms of new ownership and control
- To highlight the 'democratic deficit' involved in these processes
- To evaluate how these changes have impacted on housing officers
- To consider changes to the governance of building societies.

Introduction

The aim of this chapter is to describe the changing pattern of housing governance in Britain; how housing is owned and managed, how its various elements inter-relate and how these changes relate to wider political developments – because, of course, they are not unique to 'housing' but are part of a much larger political project. The default for much of the discussion is the English case but the devolution agenda highlights the significant and arguably growing differences between the constituent nations of the UK. Detailed accounts of the differences in housing governance between these countries is beyond the scope of this chapter. The aim is to provide a broad steer about the direction and pattern of the current position.

Governance is not just about government but incorporates the activity of a wide variety of non-state actors. The idea of governance has many meanings in the political science literature, but here it refers to a rather eclectic mix of factors. A principal feature is the need to be sensitive to the boundaries between public, private and voluntary sector agencies. A key here is the *process* of networking between these organizations, especially in the negotiation and allocation of resources and in defining shared purposes. Networks are the engine room of the modern British polity. Finally, these inter-organizational networks have a significant (but *not* total) degree of autonomy from the state. The nature of this balance is captured by Rhodes: 'Although the state does not occupy a sovereign position, it can indirectly and imperfectly steer networks' (Rhodes, 1997: 53). Governance is the result of assembling these elements into one concept.

The Origins of New Governance

How do we apply the idea of 'governance' to the field of housing? The two main developments in the broad pattern of housing in the early years of the twenty-first century were the final maturation of home ownership as the dominant housing tenure (nearly 70 per cent of households) and, secondly, the break up of the historic stock of local authority 'council' housing, either by its sale to individual sitting tenants through the Right to Buy (RTB) terms in the Housing Act 1980 (and later developments), or by transfer of the stock to a variety of companies, agencies and bureaux. In 1979 there were nearly 6 million council houses in Britain accommodating very nearly a third of the population. By 2010 there may be less than 1 million, although it is difficult to predict when and in what manner the dispersal of the local authority stock will conclude. It is very likely that by 2004/5 council housing in England will be a smaller proportion of social housing than that owned by a variety of quasi-private, social businesses, so called 'Registered Social Landlords' (RSLs). The implication of this for housing governance is very dramatic indeed, and is the main focus of this chapter.

The chapter begins by sketching a conceptual framework, briefly explaining the significance and provenance of the idea of governance which, so it is argued, is sourced in the process of globalization. The chapter then analyses the housing consequences of devolution, the nature and purpose of the stock transfer companies and the impact of the 'new financial regime' of the late 1980s on the housing association movement and, finally at the implications of these changes on street-level bureaucracy. A leitmotif of the chapter is the issue of *accountability*: to what extent are social businesses truly 'social'?

Globalization and Social Transformation

Globalization is the vital context in which much of what has happened to housing policy in recent decades has to be set. Indeed, it is probably the most important concept being debated in the whole of the social sciences at the moment. Its significance is that the consequences of globalization have invaded every aspect and tier of human life, from the truly global scale of economic organization down to the way individual people experience life in the early years of the twenty-first century. The language of globalization is on the lips of almost every politician, social commentator and academic and is intensely discussed because it is a new concept, almost non-existent, certainly in housing text books, until the early 1990s. Its sudden appearance as a key social science concept is highly symbolic of one of its main messages, that the *velocity* of world-wide communication has increased dramatically in recent years. In the modern world, an idea does not need years of dissemination before it is broadly accepted or rejected but on the internet can spread round the world instantaneously. It does not matter as Giddens suggests 'whether you live in Beijing or Seoul or Africa, many people can get the same sources almost immediately, usually using electronic technologies' (Giddens, 1999).

The key processes which make globalization so significant have been summed up by Held *et al.* in four themes:

- *Stretching* of economic, political and social activities aross geo-political frontiers
- *Intensification* or growing scale of the inter-connections between trade, finance, migration and cultures
- *Velocity* of all these processes, which has increased dramatically so that ideas, capital, information and people relate to each other much more quickly
- *Deepening*, meaning that the effect of quite small local events can potentially have big repercussions elsewhere in the world: 'In this

sense, the boundaries between domestic matters and global affairs can become increasingly blurred' (Held *et al.*, 1999).

It is difficult to portray briefly the implications of the globalization process. One example is the huge acceleration of currency and 'invisibly traded' financial commodities moving round the globe at breathtaking speed, in the order of 100 times higher now than it was only in the mid-1980s. Much of this intensification of activity is not of manufactured goods but of traded services. A measure of this is given in what Quah calls the 'weightless' economy. He calculates that the total volume of trade of all types has increased by about five times compared to 1970 and that the vast majority of this increase is due to weightless trading of services, particularly currency dealing mainly through electronic, 'virtual' means (Quah, 1999). It is important, however, to realise that much of the significance of this change is not essentially economic but is at root a combination of economic, social, cultural and political processes. The point is that, taken as a whole, very few corners of the world are now unaffected by globalization processes.

A fundamental factor here is the recognition that these processes do *not* imply a simple convergence of everything to some common endgame. Globalization does not mean the end of the nation state and the take over of the world by multi-national corporations, far from it. Rather it means that nations have to respond to globalization pressures from within their own historical, cultural and political domains. New layers of governance have been laid down across the globe, new elite networks use the global highways to strengthen their power bases and often these networks are supra-national, they are above the level of national boundaries. In a prodigious review and analysis of this, spanning three lengthy volumes, Castells argues that a new form of capitalism has emerged that is much more flexible than before and has created a 'network society' in which the power of a new 'techno-economy' interacts with social movements (that resist the imperatives of global power-mongers) resulting in macro-transformations of worldwide society and politics. The key to the network society are electronically processed information networks (Castells, 1996, 1997a, 1997b). In these circumstances, the role of the nation state has changed and is being 're-articulated, reconstituted and re-embedded at the intersection of globalizing and regionalizing networks and systems' (Held *et al.*, 1999). The power of the nation state is not in this sense diminishing or declining. In some spheres, notably in the less economically developed parts of the world, statehood has increased under these circumstances. New forms of global governance – for example, in the case of the Kyoto Treaty on global warming – are fundamentally based on strong, sovereign nation states. The paradox of apparent weakening and strengthening under the impact of globalization represents a process of readjustment and re-articulation, of the role of the state under these new conditions. In fact, with the collapse of the Soviet Union and the British Empire, almost for the first time in history the nation state is the *principal* from of geo-political organization, at least for the time being.

A key to understanding globalization is thus to realise that it is not just an expansionary force but is crucially a *deepening* force which sometimes causes breaks which cut across existing boundaries (increases in ethnic/culturally based 'nationalism') and brings a new awareness that, say, inner city decline in Newcastle and squatter settlements in São Paulo are fundamentally the subject of common economic and political processes. Globalization brings new possibilities for local social movements to articulate and make sense of their problems. Moreover, and an especially important point in relation to Chapter 3, which is a discussion of the concept of 'Home', globalization is about changing the terms of personal identities; as Giddens so poignantly puts it, 'It's an "in here" phenomenon. Our lives, our personalities, our identities, our emotions our relationships with other people – these are being reshaped by globalising processes' (Giddens, 1999). It is not surprising that the television is cluttered with 'make-over' programmes in which people's rooms and gardens are transformed using 'this year's colours' or even that the voyeuristic 'Big Brother' commands more votes than the Labour government, because they are all essentially about the same question: 'how should we live?' In a world bombarded by new choices and new risks, how do we make sense of our own self-identity?

Globalization is thus about the changing nature of relationships opened up by new communication networks and new power bases. They have re-patterned the way the world works and how people in different parts of the world, sometimes never having met, relate to each other but equally with our closest partners.

The 'Hollowing Out of the State' and Governance in Britain

How has globalization impacted on the particular circumstances of the British state and housing governance? First and foremost has been the necessity for the British state to spearhead the radical rebuilding of the British economy through the creation of a 'competition state' (Hutton, 1995; Cerny, 1999). In the 1980s, this took the form of economic re-structuring mounted by the Thatcher governments in response to the neo-liberal agenda of restraining the powers of government in favour of the market. The Blair 'project' to create a stakeholder society has responded to the same pressures and taken forward the same agenda, albeit in rather different language and policy initiatives. The basic requirement of all this is the deconstruction of the post-war unitary state based on the now antiquated 'Westminster model' of government. This is the orthodox explanation of how the British polity operates: the sovereignty of parliament, cabinet/prime ministerial government, accountability via the electorate, an institutionalized opposition, majority party control over the executive. A key feature in the new pattern of governance is the loss of control over the executive wing of government, which is constitutionally the core of the Westminster model, and also the parallel rise in demands for inclusion and greater participation.

The new governance thesis is neatly captured through the process of 'hollowing out' the state. As described by Rhodes, it involved the privatization of key public assets (the largest of which has been the sale of council houses), the loss of central and local government functions to agencies and quasi-governmental bodies arranged as networks and policy communities, loss of functions to the European Union (EU) and, the loss of discretion of public servants through the imposition of new public management (Rhodes, 1994). The public sector has become particularly vulnerable to experiments in new ways of service delivery involving the use of agencies, quasi-markets, contracting out and the use of special purpose bodies. The implications of this are to reduce control over implementation and a loss of accountability. Beyond the hollowing out thesis lies a more general set of arguments about the changing nature of the British state under the impact of globalization. The broad outline of the switch from a unitary to a fragmented state is described in Table 2.1.

These processes straddle the political spectrum and all the major political parties are caught up in the consequences of globalization. Paradoxically, as we have seen above, globalization does not create convergence in the political and cultural layers of society but demands for greater inclusion and a 'new' form of politics appropriate to the twenty-first century. Without really empowering the people this reform agenda has been delivered by New Labour through constitutional restructuring in the form of the establishment of the Scottish Parliament, the creation of Welsh, Northern Irish and London Assemblies, the strengthening of English regional government through new Regional Development Agencies (RDAs) (with the probability of future regional assemblies in

Table 2.1   **The fragmentation of the state, 1940s–2000s**

	1940s–1970s	1980s–2000s
Structure	Unitary state; the 'Westminster model'; strong central–local orientation	Fragmented state; devolved assemblies; weak local government
Character	Bureaucratic; centralized; classic Weberian hierarchies	Quasi-governmental agencies; policy networks; centralization of major policy instruments
Methods	Control of policy-making and delivery; multi-layered tiers of authority; macro-planning	Contracting out; new public management (NPM); public/private/ voluntary networking; meso- and micro-focus
Culture	Interventionist state; Beveridge welfare state; Keynesian demand management	Stakeholder society; business orientation; neo-liberal ethos

Source: Adapted from Cerny and Evans (1999).

some parts of England), the reform of the House of Lords and the abolition of the committee system in local government in favour of a more executive-style governance. As Cerny and Evans observe, 'For Tony Blair the constitutional reform project has represented a means of achieving stakeholder politics through a constitutional method rather than through economic interventionism' (Cerny and Evans, 1999). Thatcherite economic liberalization and Blairite constitutional reform are part and parcel of the same political imperative.

The key point, however, is to come to terms with the fact that globalization is the vital agenda for the modern state. Cerny's idea of the 'competition state' argues that the central state and government restructure but also *loosen* control, in order that business elites, especially financial services, can enter the global economy proactively rather than defensively (Cerny, 1999). The state thus needs to break up its antiquated, unitary and vertically integrated structures. Rhodes' idea of a differentiated polity fits well with the competition state thesis. Global financial elites have been constructed through the creation of supranational networks and their influence on the British economy and system of governance is inescapable.

As shown above, the result is that political structures are shaken and fragmented into different configurations, with an emphasis on networks. Both internally and externally globalization leads to a state of divergence rather than convergence, more so at the political than the economic levels. In this context the British state has become more flexible and its structures more fragmented, more 'hollowed out' by privatization, devolution, the creation of policy networks, etc. Networks are now pervasive features of public service delivery and this raises major issues about the scale of the 'democratic deficit' left behind by these largely unaccountable agencies. Moreover, in this context it is easier to explain the ideas of New Labour, which illustrate the radical readjustment and realignment of social democratic politics to the new realities of globalization. Globalization may be likened to an earthquake, which sends out shock waves across the social and political landscape, causing institutional and ideological fracturing. In these circumstances, governments 'steer' but no longer 'row'. The centre, of course, retains high significance, particularly in directing the broad dimensions of public spending (within the agenda of the counter-inflationary, workfare state) but delivery and increasingly policy direction is the domain of policy networks operating across the political terrain. It is with this in mind that the development of housing governance since the late 1980s should be approached. It becomes a matter of empirical investigation what precisely the outcome is in this field of policy.

The New Governance of Housing

The forces that have been shaping the deconstruction of the unitary state and the issues they raise of governability and accountability are well illustrated in the case of housing. The post-war unitary state was represented in housing by a strong central apparatus with policy emanating from the Ministry of Housing and from 1971 the Department of the Environment (and under New Labour the housing division of the Department of the Environment, Transport and the Regions (DETR), then the Department of Transport, Local Government and the Regions (DTLR) and currently a function inside the Office of the Deputy Prime Minister (ODPM)). This old system had a strong vertical transmission via the local government associations to individual authorities. The relationship was one of 'power dependency' because central–local relations were negotiated to a large extent (Rhodes, 1985). The centre needed the local tier for delivery and the local level needed the resources and direction of the centre. This system also had an element of horizontal integration through the gradual professionalization of housing management (although it remains at a very low level), the activity of the building industry with its strong regional character, a limited role for tenants' associations and, after 1974, in the housing association movement via a strong element of voluntary involvement. One key outcome of the negotiated element of the power-dependency model was the relatively high degree of discretion afforded the authorities. This impacted on the council housing building programmes, the considerable variation in the treatment of homeless households round the country, the level of tolerance towards tenants' involvement and so on, all of which reflected local patterns of party political control, the long-run policy stances of the authority and the influence of key street-level bureaucrats especially Chief Housing Officers.

Developments in the governance of housing since the 1970s is rendering this post-war pattern of municipal ownership and management almost unrecognizable. It is conceivable (although unlikely) that by 2010 there will be *no* local authority owned 'council housing', as it was known throughout most of the twentieth century. The constitutional reforms of the Blair governments have been, as we have seen, the other side of the coin of Thatcher's deregulation of the British economy in the 1980s, and in many respects in the case of housing both have pursued similar policy agendas. One of the debating points among housing practitioners, activists and students of housing following the election of the Blair's first government in May 1997, was why New Labour appeared not to have a housing policy and changed very little from the previous administration. It was not until the publication of the housing Green Paper in April 2000, nearly three years after they were elected, that the shape of New Labour housing policy became apparent (DETR, 2000a). The reason for this delay is easily explicable in terms of this wider analysis. There was fundamentally little to chose between the two governments, the Labour government if anything more vociferously espousing the transfer of council housing into what, in effect, is a new housing private sector.

The Blair project should be read, therefore, as the continuation of the much larger aim of turning the unitary state into a competition state. Blair's constitutional reform was the centre-piece of this strategy. The reform of local government via the abolition of the traditional committee system and its replacement with powerful elected Mayors and Cabinets shows the commitment of the Labour government to create a slim, entrepreneurial-style polity in line with the imperative to provide conditions for harmonization between the public and private sectors. The election of Ken Livingstone as the first Mayor of London clearly backfired and reveals how vulnerable the central executive has become to spillover and 'mistakes' (Cerny and Evans, 1999). Political and constitutional reform as instruments of political modernization both loosen the ties between the central executive and the rest of the country and have apparently unpredictable results. This type of new local governance is matched with the development in the social housing sector with what Mullins and Riseborough have called housing 'social businesses' (Mullins and Riseborough, 2000). This entails the continuation – indeed, acceleration and elaboration – of the break up of traditional council housing. The same processes have almost completely re-patterned what had previously been the much smaller housing association, voluntary 'movement', as this too has been drawn into a new era of entrepreneurship. How these events have unfolded and been shaped, and with what consequences for social housing, is the main focus of the next sections. The first stage is to consider briefly changes to housing governance arising from devolution (not including Northern Ireland, because the situation there is too complex for an overview chapter).

Housing Change in Scotland

Housing policy in Scotland has throughout the twentieth century, and indeed before then, taken very much its own course compared to the rest of the UK. It has its own legal foundation and statutes arising from a different, more adversarial history of tenant/landlord relationships and a tenure structure that embraced a higher proportion of social housing than elsewhere in the UK. Housing conditions are significantly worse in some parts of this stock. In the campaign leading up to the elections for the Scottish Parliament housing was a major issue, and in the new constitution it is a matter wholly managed by the Scottish Parliament, although as Lynch shows there is an important difference between the Parliament and the Executive. In effect the Executive, made up of the elected ministers (MSPs) and civil servants, is the *de facto* government, while the Parliament is simply the total of the elected MSPs and is essentially a scrutinizing body (Lynch, 2002). The main potential for conflict with Westminster concerns the administration and reform of housing benefit, which remains on the list of matters reserved to Westminster (via the Department of Work and Pensions and the Office of the Deputy Prime Minister). In the system of powerful parliamentary committees (which are akin to Westminster select committees but have additional powers to initiate legislation) housing was initially under the auspices of a committee overseeing social inclusion and the voluntary sector (the Social Inclusion, Housing and Voluntary Sector Committee), but within a year was remitted to the new committee on Social Justice. Having been given a high profile at the outset 'housing' appeared to slip down the agenda and disappeared from the titles of ministries, committees and departments (Taylor, 2002). But the Housing Scotland Act 2001 signalled major reform, with the abolition of Scottish Homes (see below) and its replacement with what in effect is a regulatory body, Communities Scotland.

Hitherto, one of the main differences between England and Scotland was that the Scottish equivalent of the English Housing Corporation, Scottish Homes, was not only the source of finance and appraisal of performance in the housing association sector, but also owned a very large tranche of stock in its own right. This is because when the Housing Corporation (HC) was restructured in 1989 (Tai Cymru set up in Wales, Scottish Homes in Scotland, leaving the HC in control of funding and monitoring English housing association stock), Scottish Homes was formed by the merger of the Scottish HC and Scottish Special Housing Association. Scottish Homes began voluntarily to dispose of its stock of 74,500 units to alternative landlords in 1991/2. As this stock was directly owned by the state it was more amenable to transfer through financial pressure from the centre (see below).

The thirty-two local authorities also were involved in transfers but initially only of small amounts of run-down housing usually incorporating an element of Housing Association Grant (HAG) from Scottish Homes to help the new cooperative owners refurbish the stock. As Taylor has pointed out, this pattern of action was very different to what was happening in England, where the first phase of transfers occurred through whole stock transfers (LSVTs) to new housing associations. These, however, were not issues principally arising from devolution but were part of the quite different pattern of policies and responses in Scotland. New Labour's New Housing Partnership (initiated in 1997) in Scotland sought to extend 'Community Ownership' and paved the way for Scottish local authorities to consider whole stock transfers for the first time.

The most influential force that seems likely to shape the future of housing in Scotland, and that suggests further divergence from England and Wales, is the different political culture that is already apparent arising from the proportional representation electoral system (Thain, 1999). Whereas English and UK politics is locked into a two-party system, often producing long periods of one-party government, the Scottish Parliament seems set to be based on coalition politics. The first government elected to the new parliament was a coalition between Labour and the Liberal Democrats. The problems of bringing Scottish housing up to European standards are considerable, and already there is all-party agreement on the general direction of the housing strategy focusing on ways of levering in private capital. The major plank of this policy is the transfer of local authority stock to Community Ownership (see below).

Housing and the Welsh Assembly

The Welsh Assembly has considerably fewer powers than its Scottish sibling – but the new Welsh administration is developing its own housing strategy in the context of the National Assembly's 'Better Wales' campaign. The housing function falls within the portfolio of the assembly Minister for Finance, Local Government and Communities. Most housing issues are dealt with in the Local Government and Housing Committee, set up in March 2000. The Housing Directorate officers deal with policy and strategy in relation to the local authorities and RSLs, incorporating the functions of Tai Cymru (funding/performance monitoring of housing associations), creating a powerful core housing executive. A National Housing Strategy for Wales is currently being developed, encompassing all the housing tenures, emphasizing sustainable home ownership, a functioning PRS and high-quality social housing.

In theory, the room for manoeuvre in Wales is less than in Scotland, not only because the key issue of housing benefit is reserved to Westminster but because the Welsh Assembly does not have powers to raise additional finance (as the Scottish Parliament does). In practice, there are financial constraints in both countries. Early statements by key politicians indicated concern about the (historically) poor quality of Welsh housing and social exclusion. Compared to Scotland, there has been in Wales virtually no attempt to lever in private finance through stock transfer, but it seems probable that this will change. Local authorities have been asked to outline their position on private finance and transfers in their Housing Strategy and Operational Plans. Generally the tone of the Welsh approach has been to develop close links between the Assembly and the local authorities, partly because the politicians are drawn from a common pool with strong roots in traditional municipal politics. This would seem to presage the emergence of a distinctive 'Welsh' housing policy, which at the moment takes the form of resisting council house stock transfer. But this seems likely to change arising from evidence of the poor performance of local authorities in delivering improvements in housing (Audit Commission, 2002). As in Scotland, it is the Whitehall Treasury that will drive through its agenda of encouraging stock transfer as the way to lever in private finance, apart from anything else because they have agreed to write off debts arising from the negative valuation of most of the Welsh social housing stock (Williams, 2002). This is an idea familiar in the competition state thesis, of increasing central control over finance but loosening in terms of delivery.

Housing Governance in the English Regions

In England, a variety of changes in the formal structures of government pre-date devolution in Scotland and Wales. In 1994 the regional offices of the Departments of the Environment, Transport, Trade and Industry and Employment were merged into single Regional Government Offices and in 1999 Regional Development Agencies (RDAs) were established in nine locations. At the same time voluntary Regional Chambers (so-called 'Regional Assemblies') were established to bring together the business community, the voluntary sector and local authorities to oversee the RDAs. Each Region also spawned a number of related bodies, notably Regional Housing Forums that supported the production of Regional Housing Statements (required since 1999). Drawing on local authorities, housing associations, the Chartered Institute of Housing, the National Housing Federation *et al.*, and in some cases involving private sector business interests, these Forums have tended to reflect HC capital funding priorities (Cole, Robinson and Slocombe, 2001) and have become increasingly strategic. In particular, it has been acknowledged that local housing markets do not necessarily follow administrative boundaries, and this needs to be accounted for if integrated planning is not to be deficient.

The publication of the 2002 White Paper on the provision of directly elected Regional Assemblies for some parts of England added a new dimension to this emerging and rather poorly integrated network of bodies (DTLR, 2002). It was indeed to provide greater co-ordination between the disparate interests of economic planning, land use planning and housing providers in both the public and private sectors that these quite powerful elected Assemblies had been proposed. In the housing case, a key problem is how to tackle inter-regional disparities (low demand in the north, lack of supply in the south) and enable both a more integrated approach to regional planning but also greater sensitivity to local needs. The new governance of housing in England has been characterized by a complex, poorly integrated set of policy networks, with the result that, as Cole, Robinson and Slocombe suggest, 'housing interests are struggling to inform and influence the development and content of other related regional strategies' (Cole, Robinson and Slocombe, 2002). This, they argue, is due to the lack of synergy between Regional Housing Statements and other regional strategies, which in turn results from the focus of the housing agencies on social housing while not integrating with the dominant private housing market and housing producers. As will be shown throughout the book, this is a key characteristic of housing – that it is primarily a private sector function and in the public sector prone to cuts and constraints because of its capital-intensive form of provision: as Torgersen (1987) described it, 'a wobbly pillar under the welfare state' (see Chapter 10).

At the moment, though, the regional Government Offices have strong leverage over housing, because they control both the level of the housing associations' development programme (ADP) and are also responsible for the co-ordination of the local authority Housing Investment Programme (HIP). Through the Joint Commissioning process (from 1997) the regional package of spending for both the authorities and the RSLs is linked. In this way, a strong steer is given to the social housing programme. But the uneven treatment of private sector housing in the context of regional governance in England is a persistent problem, causing lack of integration between housing policy and regional economic development strategies.

The proposal in the White Paper that elected English Regional Assemblies (most likely in Yorkshire, the north-east and the north-west) take on the responsibility of housing should improve, in theory, the profile of housing as a key to the health of regional economies and draw together the disparate housing/planning structures. The aim of Regional Assemblies in housing policy terms would be to enhance the interface between the public and private sectors and so encourage private investment supported by public subsidy in the social inclusion and regeneration agendas. Such assemblies would clearly challenge the local authority level of local governance and possibly have the effect of renewing the drive towards stock transfer in those urban authorities that still retain housing. They would be the regional face of the competition state, designed to give a regional steer to economic activity while opening up and loosening delivery. As it stands, the wider housing network made up a variety of powerful stakeholders, notably the large, investment-orientated housing associations, contributes to a loosely framed housing policy network, with a high potential for inter-organizational rivalries, communication breakdowns and muddle.

The Transfer of Council Housing to New Landlords and Managers

The process of breaking up council housing has occurred in two main forms. The initial method was the individual Right to Buy (RTB) under the Housing Act 1980 and subsequent developments of it, which to date has depleted the council stock of the UK by approaching 2 million properties, out of the 6 million in 1980. In England, RTB sales were nearly 1.5 million dwellings up to the year 2000. In Scotland, there were 356,000 RTB sales between 1980 and 1998 under the Scottish version of the legislation (from the 1980 Act and then the Housing (Scotland) Act 1987).

The second source of council house depletion was through partial stock transfer of individual estates or parts of estates (the most usual route in Scotland until recently) or most commonly in England by whole stock transfers. Indeed, in the early years of 2000 stock transfer was having a much bigger impact in reducing the scale of council housing than the RTB, with the government permitting the transfer of some 200,000 council houses per annum under stock transfers, against 50,000 RTB sales in 1999 (RTB sales are bound to decline as stock is transferred out of local authority ownership). In England, the cumulative 'loss' of some 450,000 LSVT plus RTB sales has depleted local authority housing stocks by nearly 2 million, currently accounting for less than 15 per cent of dwellings, less than half its high point in the mid-1970s (Figure 2.1).

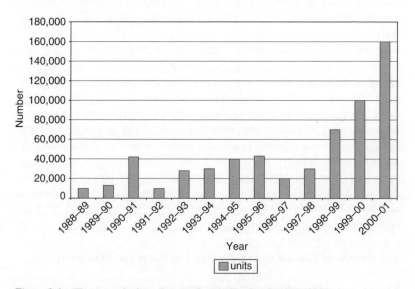

Figure 2.1   **The record of stock transfers in England, 1988–2000**
Source: ODPM (Office of the Deputy Prime Minister) Housing Live Statistics.

The record of stock transfers was very different in England compared to Scotland. In both countries, transfers have occurred in two main phases involving changes in the form and purpose of the transfer agencies. In England, the first stage of so-called Large Scale Voluntary Stock Transfer (LSVT) was not initially a purpose-designed government policy but arose from officer-led initiatives to take the housing stock out of the restrictive, centrally imposed financial regime of the late 1980s. For the first six or seven years this involved only rural and suburban 'leafy suburb' authorities with housing of relatively high quality and values. Chiltern Council in Buckinghamshire in 1988 was the first council to transfer its whole stock, 4,650 properties, to a purposely set up housing association. The opportunity to do this came through a permissive legislative framework arising from Section 32 of the Housing Act 1985 (by which local authorities could dispose of land and buildings). Between 1988 and March 1998 260,000 properties owned by sixty-eight authorities were transferred in England. LSVT authorities raised over £4 billion of private finance for the purchase and renovation/repair of these houses, an average of over £9,000 per property in capital receipts (Nevin, 1999: 3).

In England, the LSVT initiative was primarily officer-led, which suggests a second level of motivation. Housing was and remains very under-professionalized (see below) with less than 10 per cent of officers qualifying to be members of the Chartered Institute of Housing. Through LSVT, officers had opportunities to enhance their career prospects, providing the kind of control over the organization previously unavailable to functionaries of a municipal authority. Under-professionalization was an important motivation behind the initial LSVT move: moving into a less constrained more business-oriented environment held major attractions for senior officers, but less so for more junior staff. The idea of 'bureau shaping' shows how key managers can enhance their prestige and incomes through control of privatized agencies. Through reorganization, such as separating budgetry control from day-to-day management, key managers can build a power base from which they enhance their own careers and status (Dunleavy, 1981a). The lack of opposition to the disposal of council housing through stock transfer is quite plausibly explained by the notion of 'bureau shaping', owing to the low level of professionalization in housing. The development in this way of 'social entrepreneurship' inside social housing management was an early symptom of a new business-oriented ethos striking at the heart of the notion of accountable public services, and was a prelude to New Labour's social market, 'stakeholding'.

In Scotland, there was a parallel but rather different story. Here, the picture was of greater diversity in the earlier period, most transfers being small scale (Taylor, 2000). In the local authority sector the emphasis between 1986 and 1996 was on partial transfers of poor-quality housing to facilitate major repairs. It was only after the announcement of the New Housing Partnership in 1997 that whole stock transfers came in any serious way onto the Scottish agenda. Glasgow had started transfers of its housing to a variety of co-ops, housing associations and even private developers a decade earlier, using the injection of HAG to facilitate refurbishment. Other authorities followed, although there were a variety of schemes, funding packages and owners. Up to 1997 a modest total of 23,000 units were transferred but the average HAG expenditure was considerable, working out at about £26,000 per unit (Taylor, 1999). There was only one case of a whole stock transfer – Berwickshire trans-ferred its 2,000 units to a new housing association prior to local govern-ment reform in order to retain local control of the stock.

A second strand, as we saw above, involved Scottish Homes transfer-ring nearly 40,000 of its stock of 74,500 properties to ninety alternative landlords. As with the local authority transfers, these were relatively small-scale, ranging from only fifty to 2,500 units, often through a ten-dering process. Because Scottish Homes' stock was mainly in good condition, these deals mainly involved refinancing packages, borrowing from the financial markets rather than HAG. The aim of this transfer strategy was to enhance tenure diversification as well as levering in private finance for refurbishment.

Through the New Housing Partnership initiative, the Labour govern-ment made funding available for Scottish local authorities to undertake feasibility studies leading to whole stock transfer, and indicated the possibility of being willing to service residual debts on stocks with nega-tive values. The Scottish Housing Green Paper, published in February 1999 (over a year ahead of the English Green Paper), underpinned this by again discussing the benefits of community ownership of housing as a means to social inclusion (Scottish Office, 1999). Community-based associations and co-ops, it was argued, could radically re-orientate local social control as well as serving the purpose of the urgent need for repair and refurbishment of the stock. £278 million was allocated for the period 1999–2002 through the New Housing Partnerships Advisory Group (made up of representatives from Scottish Homes, The Scottish Federation of Housing Associations, the Chartered Institute of Housing and the Scottish local authorities). About half this finance was allocated to deal with the residual debt of the seven front-runner authorities that successfully bid to make whole stock transfers – Aberdeen City, Comhairle Nan Eilean Siar, Dumfries and Galloway, Glasgow, Orkney, Scottish Borders and Shetland.

In fact, there have only been three successful transfers to date, including a chaotic and heavily contested saga in Glasgow where a successful ballot of tenants took place in March 2002 but the handover of the stock itself to the new agency Glasgow Housing Association (GHA) was fraught with controversy, mainly over funding issues. GHA has been given a grant of £300 million by the Scottish Executive to assist the stock transfer process but conditional on a further stage of transfer from GHA to smaller bodies.

If all the proposed transfers had gone through successfully, some 150,000 properties would have been transferred to new landlords by March 2002, nearly a quarter of the remaining council housing. In fact, including by far the largest case, (Glasgow) the figure at the time of writing was about 105,000.

The motivation for most of the English transfers was the drastic decline in public sector capital investment and the huge backlog of repair and maintenance that was unable to be funded. The Westminster government's 'new financial regime' under the Local Government and Housing Act 1989 imposed a strict centrally determined rent setting system designed to compel local authorities to charge 'market' rents and stopped authorities spending capital receipts and 'cascading' interest from receipts into repair work. Refinancing the stock through LSVT and partial transfers circumvented this system. New landlords are not subject to public sector borrowing controls and are thus able to borrow from the private markets for repair and modernization. The main stumbling block to transfer remains the question of residual debt. It has been estimated, for example, that even with present levels of support for transfers in Scotland there will still be £2 billion of debt, requiring an annual charge of £46 million. The Treasury has indicated a willingness to service this, but it is not at all clear whether this money will be 'new' or found by reducing other housing investments, such as HAG. Housing policy has a more consultative and open stance than in the past, but it seems clear that the main plank of housing policy in Scotland is for the Executive to encourage stock transfer, with few real alternatives. Devolution in Scotland has thus paradoxically led to a tightening of control, as Taylor observes: 'New legislation creates imperatives for more social sector uniformity, and under more centralised control than in the past and than in England. There is a measure of increasing difference in the Scottish housing system' (Taylor, 2002: 21).

However, it is equally clear that both Scotland and Wales are con-strained by their resources base and so long as the Treasury supports the option of stock transfer and is prepared to write off residual debt, and that housing benefit is controlled and funded from London, other areas of policy will mainly have to be funded from local budgets. (Wilcox, 2002). As a result, it is increasingly difficult to sustain a pos-ition that housing policy has been devolved; Westminster continues to exert a strong steer.

In England the agenda has been much more overtly about the creation of 'social entrepreneurship' inside social housing management and was an early example of a new business-oriented ethos striking at the heart of the notion of accountable public services. In effect, LSVT was a prelude to New Labour's social market, 'stakeholding'. Social housing that was transferred was no longer subject to oversight by democratically elected representatives, albeit through an impoverished local mandate, but instead was managed by boards and management committees made up of differing combinations of local councillors, company managers and a minority representation of tenants. There is thus an issue as to the exact nature of these transfer bodies, although it is clear that most of them are private or quasi-private companies. A key question here is that of the legitimacy of these boards, largely unelected and with very little direct public accountability. This came to prominence in the 1990s through the work of the Nolan Committee on local public spending bodies (Nolan Committee, 1996) and was echoed in the governance enquiry set up by the National Federation of Housing Associations (1995). Mullins and Riseborough's research into housing associations found a paradox at the centre of this new world of social businesses. On the one hand, associations were urged to respond to the lessons of the Nolan Committee by becoming more open and transparent, notably to strengthen the role of tenants, while at the same time there were strong pressure from the private financiers to create slim executive bodies able to respond quickly to commercial imperatives and business opportunities (Mullins and Riseborough, 2000: 92).

This streamlining of social housing undoubtedly dovetails into the newly modernized local authority governance, with centralized execu-tives, cabinets and executive mayors, in parallel with a reduced role for local councillors, whose role is to act as conduits of information in a clearly top down system. The paradox of creating social businesses but expanding the citizenship agenda is far from being resolved. Insofar as it is, the imperative to operate through 'modern' slim-line bureaux clearly trumps open government.

Local Housing Companies and Other Transfer Vehicles

A new and decisive phase in stock transfer in England began in the mid-1990s. Until then no *urban* authorities had transferred their whole stock. The problem for them, compared to the leafier suburbs and rural authorities, was that their much larger stock had lower, and in many cases negative values, and the properties were in a worse state of repair, sometimes very much worse. The difficulties arose from the inadequacy of the rental stream to service both debt charges (the residue of the capital borrowed to build the houses/flats) and mount an effective renovation and maintenance programme. If the sale of the property generated low receipts, then the local authority would be left with the liability of servicing the remaining debt but with no stock to do it. Moreover, officers and particularly councillors were more sensitive to the problems of the democratic 'deficit' caused by the transfer of council housing to publicly unaccountable bodies. A number of new ideas began to be discussed which would enable local authorities to have influence over transferred stock and solve the problem of funding the transfer. The normal housing association model was not suitable once attention began to focus on negative-value urban stock.

Previous experience through the Conservative' government's 1995 Estate Renewal Challenge Fund had addressed the problem of urban authorities with negative-value housing stock. Funding was put in by the government to relieve the debt burden and enable transfer of estates through competitive bidding. The idea was that the local authority would continue to have a role after transfer. Such 'local housing companies' were promoted as an alternative form of transfer vehicle (Wilcox *et al.*, 1993) and were subsequently written into the Housing Act 1996. The key to their success was that, assuming landlord borrowing would not count against the government budget deficit, transfer to a housing company would release, over a period of twenty years or so, tens of millions of pounds of additional local housing investment. Moreover, the cost to the Treasury of providing residual debt subsidy would be offset by other savings, notably the capital receipt from the transfer, ending of public sector borrowing consents, etc. (Wilcox, 1997: 133). New Deal for Communities projects were also allowed to operate partial transfers in this way in pursuit of the government's regeneration ambitions.

Following ideas raised in the Housing Green Paper (DETR 2000a) a number of alternatives to LSVT and Local Housing Companies (LHCs) for council housing have been put forward, largely in response to tenant ballots which turned down transfer, leaving few options except to make the most of what could be gleaned from the 'old system' housing investment programme. The first main option is Private Finance Initiatives (PFI), which enable improvement of stock by levering in private finance without changing its ownership. This avoids the costs of buying out the stock but as yet is confined to eight 'pathfinder' schemes. The second option is an idea specifically promoted in the Green Paper, of 'arm's-length companies' which would be set up to manage the housing stock (which would still be owned by the council) and would gain freedom to borrow and invest according to how well they performed in relation to the government's Best Value performance appraisal. The 2000 Comprehensive Spending Review (CSR) budgeted £160 million for 2002/3 and £300 million for 2003/4, and so prepared this route for a limited number of authorities. This combination of public money and freedom to borrow from the private market may well become an attractive alternative for some authorities. The danger, however, is that this type of route, under Best Value discipline and Treasury constraints, may be regarded as a second-best solution when the alternative of whole stock transfer is for some reason (the poor quality of the housing) blocked off. A spectrum of transfer and investment options has thus emerged (Figure 2.2).

Perry estimated that with the government's planned transfer programme of 200,000 houses per annum a pragmatic assessment (taking into account negative ballots, etc.) would reduce the current 3.2 million English council housing stock to about half that level. Where along the continuum of other options the remaining 1.5 million or so dwellings fall remains to be seen, although the use of arm's-length companies seems likely and already has funding attached to it, and presumably does not negate the possibility of a stock transfer at some later date. The rejection of transfer in a ballot by tenants of Birmingham City Council in the

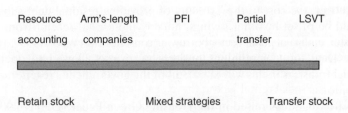

Figure 2.2   **The spectrum of investment options for English local authorities**
Source: Perry (2000).

Spring of 2002 also suggested that the final break up of council housing may not be such a smooth transition as the government hoped, and has undoubtedly put the brakes on transfer in other large cities.

Whatever the outcome of the next phase, it is abundantly clear that the ownership and management of council housing has already become very different from the late 1980s. The re-financing of the existing transferred stock in England has attracted private finance in the order of £3.6 billion for the transfers with approaching £8 billion in investment into the repair and renovation of these dwellings.

The market for private finance could in the end amount to between £30 and £40 billion by 2010, although there are a number of potential problems. First, the price of transfers and their increasing complexity has meant the withdrawal of some of the lenders from this market. Second, low demand in some areas of the country could be a stumbling block to smooth transfer, as in the case of Birmingham, where 30,000 demolitions were proposed at one stage. Third, and by far the biggest question that hangs over transfers policy, is the question of housing benefit. Restrictions on eligible levels of housing benefit in the private sector threatens future private investment because it raises doubts about returns on capital. It would, however, make no sense for the government to threaten the success of transfers because of the apparently unconnected issue of housing benefit. It is a key issue at the heart of this stream of policy and is the sensitive spot (and possibly Achilles' heel) of 'social businesses', expected to keep rents affordable, dependent on housing benefit to do so but needing a secure an income stream to attract private investment. The outcome of this difficult public/private mix remains to be seen.

The benefit of this revolution in the historic position of council housing is in drawing down huge sums of private finance, allowing unprecedented programmes of renewal and repair to be conducted. The transfer of properties into what are essentially private or quasi-private companies raises questions, as we have seen, of accountability. Moreover, as Perry pointed out, these companies and non-profit agencies will in future come to have considerable financial strength and development potential as their debt profile matures, 'but outside the democratic framework within which their housing stock was originally built' (Perry, 2000: 34). Against the individual RTB, which takes this housing entirely outside the social rental sector, these new social businesses at least have the benefit of retaining a heritage of public rental housing, albeit in dramatically different forms compared to twentieth-century 'council housing'.

The Changing World of Housing Associations

In the late 1980s housing associations were a minor part of the social housing scene, albeit with a long and varied history dating back to the thirteenth century, when the organization that is now the St Lawrence Housing Association provided accommodation for 'two female lepers' (Best, 1991).

As Figure 2.3 shows, spending on social housing fell sharply through the 1980s and 1990s and in the latter decade the vast majority of social housing construction was by housing associations (and following the Housing Act 1996 RSLs alongside other company landlords, LSVT associations, co-ops and housing management bodies). These were dramatic times for the 'traditional' associations who had built up their stock since 1974 through the use of the so-called 'flexible' Housing Association Gran (HAG) system, a form of subsidy that wrote off capital debts to allow the associations to provide low-rent accommodation. A new system, introduced in 1989 undermined this position by

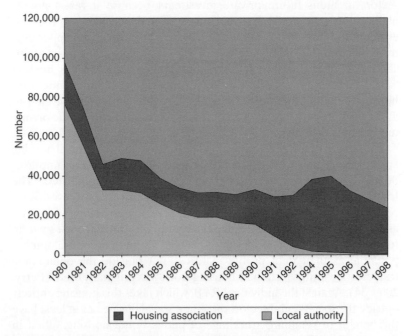

Figure 2.3 **Local authority and housing association completions, Great Britain, 1980–98**

fixing the amount of HAG at less than building costs, so that the associations had to borrow (increasingly) from private lenders to make up the difference (Malpass, 1990).

This new system exposed the associations, as was intended by the government, to the risks of the capital markets while at the same time increasing government's control over the level of grant given, and indirectly over rents. Associations now had to offer assured tenancies, taking them out of the fair rent system, and thus preparing the way for rent increases to fund the new borrowing and capital fund for long-term repairs. As Malpass suggests:

> RSLs compete with each other within a highly structured quasi-market, in which the Treasury, the DETR, the Housing Corporation and the local authorities all have considerable influence over what gets built, where and for whom. (Malpass, 2000: 222)

The nature and scale of the housing association movement has thus changed dramatically since the heyday years of the voluntary movement after the Housing Act 1974. In 1989, at the time of the introduction of the fixed HAG system, the National Federation of Housing Associations had 3,500 member organizations.

Table 2.2 shows that the number of English associations had fallen to just over 2,000 by 1998. The decline since 1989 was through a combination of mergers between medium and larger associations trying to strengthen their financial base and the deregistration of smaller organizations unable or unwilling to compete in the new era dominated by private finance.

In March 2000 there were 2,067 RSLs in England. The vast majority of these were small associations: 80 per cent owned fewes than 100 self-contained properties, which made up less than 3 per cent of RSL stock. Nearly 30 per cent were so small that they did not employ full-time

Table 2.2 **Size distribution of RSLs, March 1998**

Size of association	England	Scotland	Wales
Up to 100 dwellings	1,626	37	60
101–1,000	236	118	13
1,001–2,500	100	37	
Over 2,500	122	6	21
Total	**2,084**	**198**	**94**

Source: Malpass (2000: 11).

staff. By contrast, the largest twenty English associations (1 per cent) each had over 10,000 properties, making up 25 per cent of the total. 8 per cent of RSLs owned 80 per cent of the stock in 1999/2000. The largest associations tended to buy and develop property outside their local geographical areas so that smaller local associations found themselves outbid for new programmes by outsiders, often with central offices hundreds of miles away. As Malpass pointed out: 'It represented a leaking away of local accountability', making local interest in participation on management boards less likely (Malpass, 2000: 253). This concentration of stock into the hands of an elite of large associations is bound to continue over the next five – ten years, owing mainly to stock transfers from local authorities and the ability of the biggest associations to develop on a national scale.

Although RSLs are not-for-profit bodies, the ambition of the highly paid executives who drive the agendas of the leading organizations are very akin to private sector developers, with whom they often collaborate. These powerful associations are not simply being driven by government policy but are able to choose what they became involved in and distinguish between government funding streams and other revenue-based sources of income, and increasingly funding from other activities. The argument that these organizations are essentially agents of central government (Cope, 1999) is much less plausible in this highly networked universe. These are powerful players that are not simply reacting to government directives but increasingly able to shape them. It is a policy community characterized by inter-organizational linkages, lobbying and intense networking. Mullins and Riseborough observed in their research that there was a strong element of social purpose and an ethos of respect for the history of voluntarism among the leading players, but that this should be read as defining their 'territory' rather than shaping their strategies and management styles, in which commercial judgements and business efficiency were endemic (Mullins and Riseborough, 2000: 85).

It is readily apparent, as the Nolan Committee (1996) pointed out, and other commentators have observed, there is a conflict of accountability between the commercial imperatives of the companies and the voluntary and representative ethos of the associations. As Kearns has pointed out, there are conflicts between the unpaid but increasingly onerous role of committee members and well-paid, full-time professional managers. 'Voluntary governance has to be both feasible and enjoyable to be sustainable' (Kearns, 1997: 64). Without due attention to this key feature of the governance of the new social housing businesses there is a danger that the structure could implode, leading eventually to the complete disenfranchisement of tenants.

Other Governance Issues

New Public Management and the Housing Inspectorate

The fragmentation of central and local state relations has, as we have seen, been supported by the emergence of new managerial paradigms. Public choice theorists posited the idea that bureaucratic intervention made problems worse and a variety of management theorists have claimed that performance can be enhanced by appraisal, cost-benefit analysis and the enhanced use of 'human resources' (Drucker, 1954, 1990; Peters and Waterman, 1982). Central to the new managerialism has been the shift of organizational power away from administrators and professionals and towards 'managers' and 'accountants' (Miller and O'Leary, 1987). The aim of new management was to engineer shifts in behaviour and the culture of organizations. In housing, New Public Management (NPM) was a strong theme from the 1980s onwards, running in parallel with the break up of the public housing stock. Externalization of services, requiring local authorities to find new service management agencies while they retained a mainly planning and enabling role in setting standards, defining local needs and managing local competition for contracts, has been endemic. The adoption of private and quasi-private solutions to the break-up of council housing has been matched by new managerialism in which the default assumption is that public sector management is less efficient, although evidence of improvement under the new system is scant.

The result is that public housing services have been required to meet financial and other measurable goals, while the involvement of local communities has been given a low priority. Part of the drive towards greater scrutiny in public service delivery was the establishment of the Audit Commission (AC) at the end of the 1970s to provide an independent review of efficacy and efficiency in council services. The emergence of fragmented policy networks has required the AC to develop more specialized guidance and inspection. In the housing field, their brief covers wide-ranging activities from community care planning to housing benefit fraud. The dominant view that public management was less efficient than the quasi-private models transformed the role of the AC in the late 1990s. Levels of inspection were increased and new specialist inspection teams were created. The New Labour government took the inspection agenda a step further with the introduction of 'Best Value', which aimed to inform the public about local authority performance. It replaced the overt hostility of the Conservative government to public services (through, for example, Compulsory Competitive Tendering (CCT)) with a series of tests of competence and performance that must be passed at least every five years. Not unexpectedly, these tests lean towards measurable indicators such as 'use of money', efficiency and effectiveness and the users' experience. After some years of preparation the Best Value framework was embodied in the Local Government Act 1999 and local authorities in England were placed under a duty of Best Value from April 2000.

The Housing Inspectorate has been established as a branch of the AC, headed by the Chief Inspector of Housing (but does not operate in Scotland where there is a parallel body, Audit Scotland). The Housing Inspectorate has a regional structure with offices in the South (Bristol), London, Central region (Birmingham) and the North (Leeds). The principal aim is said to be to help housing authorities improve, but it seems clear that this implies driving forward the agenda towards commercial and private sector 'solutions'. A successful outcome of Best Value performance, for example, is the gateway to authorities qualifying for funding to establish arm's-length companies instead of embarking on stock transfer. The intention is to enhance the competition for central funding. The Best Value regime covers all aspects of an authority's work so that the Housing Inspectorate might well investigate areas of delivery outside the 'housing department' (finance, environmental health, social services, etc.). There seems little doubt, although it is early days in the inspection system, that the Inspectorate will be used by the centre to steer policy towards central objectives. The idea that the inspection system is independent of government and carries out inspection 'without fear or favour' (DETR, 2001) is a very naïve interpretation of the now quite long history of NPM. It simply is not independent of the dominant ideology of managerialism and the quasi-market policy agenda.

The Housing Profession

As we have noted, the housing profession emerged relatively recently, and provided some of the horizontal linkages in the development and implementation of government policy. The housing profession has been relatively weak compared to other professions because of its late start and origins in two different traditions of management. The Institute of Housing was formed by the merger of two organizations. The Society of Women Housing Estate Managers, formed in 1932, had its roots in the nineteenth-century philanthropy associated in housing with Octavia Hill. The Institute of Housing established in 1931, had developed among (mostly male) municipal housing managers. The two bodies merged to form a 'new' Institute of Housing in 1965, by which time the pattern of housing management was well established. The fear of the women's organization, that their concern with the welfare of tenants and their high standards of practice and training, would be compromised was generally justified. The Institute nevertheless won chartered status in the mid-1990s to become the Chartered Institute of Housing (CIH).

The Institute of Housing struggled to define its professional identity. What was the specific body of knowledge, services, experience and disciplines that constituted housing management? The definition was never fully defined nor the problems of the profession resolved. The CIH concentrated on raising the profile of the professionally qualified managers and the Institute itself. The pursuit of the royal charter, the development of graduate and post-graduate courses, the attempts to develop other professional qualifications – such as for workers in sheltered housing – and the development of lobbying and policy formulation, are all aspects of this. However, the CIH has remained unable to recruit more than approximately 10,000 qualified members out of the 100,000 plus people employed in the market as a whole.

During the first years of New Labour government the future of the CIH was called into question. This resulted from three main factors. First, the remodelling of local councils and the creation of an entrepreneurial style of governance, referred to above, also entailed remodelling housing services themselves. Housing functions – such as rent collection, arrears recovery, maintenance and renewal strategies are increasingly being removed from traditional housing departments and relocated in other agencies.

Secondly, New Labour has emphasized regeneration policies that are based on multi-layered strategies. The 'New Deal for Communities' (NDC) initiative is an example of this approach – the government is facilitating local planning and co-ordination of resources in small areas. The NDC allows limited transfer of funds between agencies, and new approaches to ownership and managing all aspects of the local environment – housing is a part of the picture alongside shops, schools, amenities, etc. The distinctness of professional categories is therefore valued less – and the difficulty in defining precisely what 'housing management' actually means – always a problem as we have seen above – potentially further erodes the importance of the CIH.

Third, there is a long-term trend in the wider economy, including the public sector, to replace many traditional approaches to management qualifications with work-based competency training. The net effect of this approach is to reduce emphasis on experience and knowledge, and increase the importance given to a more tightly defined series of assessed tasks and skills. The competency-based approach assumes that management skills are completely transportable, and can be applied in other professions and circumstances wherever appropriate. The CIH qualification is therefore reduced in importance because it does not necessarily add up to anything more than the sum of its parts. Anyone with a relevant set of competencies may be considered eligible for roles the CIH has previously considered suitable for CIH qualification. Perhaps more important, the CIH qualification does not carry special advantages for work in the new regeneration programmes.

From the late 1990s the government increasingly turned to external, quasi-governmental agencies to provide regulation. The development of the regulation of housing has become part of a range of public policy initiatives linked to themes of reduced central government management, revised and devolved local government and the need to find and legitimate new regulatory instruments in line with the wider 'hollowing out' of the state.

The Governance of Owner Occupation

The issues concerning home ownership are much less directly ones of governance but more concerned with its impact on changes to the broader welfare state, on wealth distribution and the cultural patterning of society. The main changes to the governance structures were the deregulation of the banking system in the 1980s and the incorporation of building societies into the wider financial services industry. Mergers – for example, between the Halifax Building Society and the Bank of Scotland – were essentially a rationalization and adjustment of two large commercial enterprises to a market that had become national and increasingly international in character. The tradition of regional and even local building societies has been destroyed by deregulation and on-line banking. Millions of account holders, both investors and borrowers, discovered that they had become shareholders in a company and offered a windfall allocation of shares, from the proceeds of the sale of the society, in exchange for the tradition of mutuality.

Another important feature of this new landscape in the mortgage industry has been the entry of new players into the market, often offering new or re-structured products. For example, the deregulation of the banking industry in the 1980s encouraged new 'private' banks to establish, often underwritten by large international financial houses. These banks target particular income groups and offer bespoke packages of financial services to these households. Using the internet and call centres they have dispensed with the conventional high street branches. By incorporating mortgages into the overall borrowing and savings profile of households and by using savings from dispensing with the branch structure, mortgages have become cheaper and a range of financial products bound into the clients' needs. This more competitive and diverse market has also become subject to greater regulation following the mis-selling of inappropriate products (endowment mortgages) and irresponsible lending practices of some building societies in the 1980s following deregulation. It is quite mistaken to believe that markets need to be devoid of control to be effective and this is one of the reasons why there is only now beginning to be an interest in Britain in the securitization of the mortgage market, which is a common practice in the USA. Securitization increases competition because it breaks up the mortgage process into its component parts, allowing mortgage providers to outsource functions that can be more cheaply provided by others. Lenders sell on mortgages by issuing bonds that are very secure because they are backed by the equity held in the properties. If successfully introduced in Britain, securitization will further increase competition in this market.

The structure of the mortgage industry has thus undergone considerable change since the 1980s mainly though mergers, the downsizing of high street branches and the emergence of new players and new products. Mergers have been inevitable owing to the decline in numbers of advances and the over-manned high street branches, which are a legacy of the housing boom in the 1980s. Rationalization cannot be achieved through internal measures only (Kearns and Stevens, 1997). The shift towards large hybrid companies and the demutualization of traditional, regionally based building societies is part of a wider restructuring of the financial services industry. The core relationship between borrowers and investors and the new bank/building societies, however, is essentially unchanged.

The mergers between banks and building societies and the creation of new companies and bureaux for the ownership and management of social housing are not unrelated events, for they are both symptoms of the impact of globalization pressures on the British economy. They are part of a reformulated governance of housing arising from adaptations to new national and international realities.

Conclusion

Changes to the governance of housing since 1975 could hardly be more dramatic. By 2010 the historic core of council housing may have been dispersed to a variety of new owners, continuing the progress of tenure re-structuring that has been at the centre of British housing for a hundred years. Only time will tell how many council houses will remain in the direct control of local authorities but it seems likely to be a small fraction of the historic stock of dwellings. English local councils continue to have a significant role as 'enablers' and a major role in land use planning, co-ordination of regeneration strategies and overcoming social exclusion by spearheading 'joined-up' local governance. In Scotland, the reality of devolution has been limited by the continuing influence of the Treasury's preferred policy options, but the rather more centralized orientation of housing administration with a wider scope for consultation suggests an element of divergence from the English system. Building societies have retreated from mutuality, representing the end of a tradition stretching back over 200 years. Housing associations have been driven into a new era of mergers and expansion through LSVT, the ending of the flexible HAG system which brought with it new commercial imperatives and the creation of 'social businesses'.

This period of dynamic change is not, however, special to 'housing', but is only one part of the complete overhaul and restructuring of the post-1945 unitary state and its replacement with a more differentiated and fragmented polity as the British economic and political systems respond to the pressures of globalization. The creation of the competition state through economic liberalization and Blair's constitutional reform agenda is the stimulus for the new governance of housing, which now consists of a series of inter-related policy networks rather than a vertically structured central–local system. The idea that fragmentation has led to 'an increase in the power exercised by central government' (Malpass, 1997: 10) appears to be a contradiction (except in the case of Scotland, where landlords are more dependent on state funding than in England), but is explicable if the nature of state is accurately characterized. We are no longer dealing with a modified version of the unitary state but a completely different form of governance. The centre overtly loosens its hold over the implementation agenda. The paradox of the globalization agenda is that it both unifies and fragments, leaving the state in a position to steer a course in the very rough seas of the global economy. The centre, via the Treasury, retains a major role, mostly regarding finance and shaping the new polity. The new social housing businesses have been the competition state's creation, designed to have autonomy and freedom in the marketplace. Centralizing while loosening is a paradox of post-modernism. As a result, unitary housing governance has been thoroughly 'hollowed out', to a degree that even a few years ago would have seemed inconceivable.

FURTHER READING

Hutton, W. (1995) *The State We're In*, London, Jonathan Cape.

Malpass, P. (2000) *Housing Associations and Housing Policy*, Basingstoke, Macmillan.

Perry, J. (2000) 'The end of council housing?', in S. Wilcox (ed.), *Housing Finance Review 1999–2000*, York, Joseph Rowntree Foundation.

Rhodes, R. A. W. (1997) *Understanding Governance: Policy Networks, Governance, Reflexivity and Accountability*, Buckingham, Open University Press.

Wilcox, S. (1997) 'Local housing companies', in P. Malpass (ed.), *Ownership, Control and Accountability: The New Governance of Housing*, Coventry, Chartered Institute of Housing.

3
Housing, Home and Society

CHAPTER AIMS

- To describe the concept of 'home' and evaluate its significance for housing studies
- To identify the origins of modern domestic culture in the Victorian era
- To show that the convergence of housing standards in the twentieth century was built around new perceptions of the home
- To show the 1930s origins of a divergence between middle class home ownership and working class council housing
- To describe how home life evolved during the course of the twentieth century.

Introduction

The idea of 'home' is universally and instinctively understood. Home is the place where we are most able to be ourselves, where we accumulate the clutter of daily life, tend to and protect our most treasured possessions and where we invariably experience, for better or worse, our most intimate and deeply felt relationships. As the well-known aphorism has it, 'Home is where the heart is', implying that it may not be a fixed place and not necessarily relating to a dwelling place. People who have lived abroad, for decades, may refer to the idea of 'coming home', a return to an intuitively understood haven in a hostile world. This, then, is the first lesson about the concept of home; that it is defined not only on its own terms but also in relation to a wider society 'out there'. 'Home' and 'not home' are the opposite sides of a single social entity.

As we saw in Chapter 2, globalization has significant repercussions at the level of the individual; as Giddens puts it: 'Alongside globalisation is the impact of individualisation. Individualisation is the personal pole' (Giddens, 1999: 7). The focus of this chapter is therefore precisely on the question of *self-identity*, which is partly given by cultural background and traditions but increasingly has to be a creation for each generation rather than a 'given'. The concept of 'home' is closely bound up with the creation and sustaining of self-identity. Home is a *source* of selfhood, a visible demonstration of chosen identities and the place where people (normally) find security from the risks and challenges of the world beyond the front door, a place where they can 'be themselves'.

Knowledge about the concept of 'home' is important to the study of housing policy because policy is partly shaped and evolved through changing perceptions of the home and home life. Changing ideas about the home interact with domestic architecture, impacts on the internal use of dwellings and changes in patterns of household formation. Despite this, the concept of 'home' has been relatively neglected in the housing studies literature. This may be due to the dominance of economists in housing research – whose interest is mainly in the supply and demand for housing – but is perhaps best explained by Kemeny, who suggests that the idea of 'home' is so embedded in the social structure that it has been taken for granted (Kemeny, 1992). In fact, there is a literature about the concept of the home, but it is an eclectic literature found in the work of anthropologists, architects, sociologists, historians, phenomenologists and psychoanalysts. A small sample of this work is discussed here.

The aim of the chapter is to show how knowledge of the ideas and concepts involved in the analysis of the home are central both to orthodox 'housing studies' and to thinking about how housing shapes the development of society. The key point is that at a very micro level home is the place where social formation is day-to-day created and recreated, stabilized and patterned. Home is a social glue that sticks society together. In the language of policy analysis, it is a key meso-level concept that links the realm of the individual to that of society.

Home and Self-Identity

The creation of the feeling of 'home' is of major significance for individuals and their relationships to the world and to other people.

As soon as we are born from the safety of our mother's womb as a human 'being' we enter an inescapable environment of air and light. We are at once in a relationship with our natural environment. This is what the sociologist G. H. Mead – one of the founding fathers of symbolic interactionism – called 'our social relationship with the world' (Mead, 1934: 110). Through sight we determine the form of objects and through touch we mould and shape them and learn our own 'boundaries' in the human form. Through this knowledge, so Mead argues, we learn to know ourselves. The environment we inhabit is potentially hostile, and this compels us to seek shelter not only from the elements but from encounters with unknown other people. As the French poet Birot puts it: 'Le monde bat de l'autre côté de porte' ('The world pulse beats beyond my door').

Housing is thus more than a shelter but is very fundamentally bound up with our psychic shell, the place where we attach ourselves to the landscape, both physically and socially. The French phenomenologist Gaston Bachelard writes about the house not only as a sanctuary from external danger but as a place of dreams: 'the house shelters day-dreaming, the house protects the dreamer, the house allows one to dream in peace' (Bachelard, 1964: 29).

Bachelard believed that the house is the harbinger and the locus in which the deepest memories, even those remembered in the womb, find their most poignant expression. He finds in this process a sense of reverie, which can be shared in even the most humble dwelling. Our house is our corner of the world, 'it is our first universe, a real cosmos in every sense of the word' (Bachelard, 1964: 28). For Bachelard, it is this sense of half-remembered memories, of encounters with the unconscious mind, which are the crucial knowledge about housing; the memory of places known, their smells, their echoes, their secret corners. The rooms, the nooks and crannies, the cupboards all have psychological meaning. It is commonplace in the literatures dealing with the concept of the home and the creation of cultural values to identify a 'back region' in the house where we are most able to be ourselves and where the business end of the house – food preparation, washing clothes, storage – take place, and a more public domain adjacent to the front of the dwelling.

These patterns of interaction and daily etiquettes are explained in Goffman's study of the sociology of space, and is highly relevant to discussions of the home. Goffman (1959) distinguishes between what he calls 'unfocused' and 'focused' interactions. The presence of strangers may generate non-verbal behaviour in which our body language – what

Goffman calls 'body idiom' – is expressive and shaped by patterns of expectations. The way we dress and move about in public in expectation of encounters is culturally patterned. Focused interaction with people we know produces very different signals and 'stage presence'. Crucially, it is the type of space that provides the stage set that shapes the nature of inter-personal encounters. Public open space, gardens, back yards, bedrooms, indeed the whole urban landscape, are resonant of our inter-actions and come to be defined by our use of them. Being 'at home' is as much an example of a 'situated' location as a prison or hospital for the mentally ill. Visitors to our homes cross a threshold full of symbolic and behavioural meaning.

Developing Goffman's sociology of place, Giddens suggests that the crucial role of the home is as a 'locale' in which social life is sustained and above all *reproduced*. Thus the home is not just the shell of social and cultural transmission but is also the means of its creation. There is nothing mysterious about this process. As Giddens points out, it arises from the day-to-day routine of life, what he calls 'time–space paths', when we can predict with some certainty how people will behave and how we are expected to respond. When men cut the lawns and check the anti-freeze in their cars and women attend to the household's clothes and organize the cleaning routine in the house with barely a thought, gender stereotypes, social roles and social relationships are, as Saunders and Williams put it, 'composed and contextualized' (Saunders and Williams, 1988: 83). More generally it has been shown that men, women and children experience the sense of home differently and to a large extent it is a negotiated concept (Munro and Madigan, 1993). It is precisely because domestic life is so embedded in this way that the home is the kernel, the vital centre where social reproduction takes place. Witold Rybczynski's book, *Home: A Short History of an Idea*, shows how the need for domestic well-being is deeply rooted through-out history and across the world. He shows how social and cultural changes, decorative fashions, the need for warmth and different types of space influence the meaning of home over time (Rybczynski, 1986). Home is a powerful focus of emotional life. As Gurney and Means show, it is frequently the wish of terminally ill people to return home to die (Gurney and Means, 1993: 123). Lewin shows how important the idea of home is for elderly immigrants, having lost their former residence, in finding settled acceptance in their new country. Personal autobiogra-phies are crucial to this settlement and by re-creating some of the physical features of the previous home environment loneliness may be to an extent overcome (Lewin, 2001).

Home and Ontological Security

The idea of the home as a focal point in the development of selfhood is found also in R. D. Laing's notion of 'ontological security' (Laing, 1966). The idea was the centre of a debate in the 1980s, when a number of sociologists associated the concept particularly with home ownership. The essence of the concept is that human beings need to feel that the basic parameters of the natural world are secure and that our day-to-day place in the world has reasonably predictable boundaries, that we can have confidence, as Giddens puts it, 'in the basic existential parameters of self and social identity' (Giddens, 1984: 375). Giddens argues that modern cultures have created a more abstract, socially 'disembedded' world compared to pre-Enlightenment society when social relations were bounded by localized patterns of life. Ontological security has thus been eroded by modernity and globalization, because natural patterns of time and place have been disturbed.

Saunders (1990) and others have argued that this sought-after sense of security is most particularly found in the modern world in home ownership and that tenants are unlikely to feel such a strong attachment to their home because of restrictions imposed by their tenancies. Saunders was writing at a time when English home ownership was in the ascendant during the 1980s and it is doubtful whether such a view could be generally applicable. As will be shown later in the chapter, Victorian domestic culture was built on the idea of the 'home' as a bastion against a threatening world beyond the front door. These homes were almost entirely privately rented. In contemporary Europe a high proportion of households live in rental accommodation, including over 80 per cent in Switzerland, and it can hardly be claimed that there is a lesser experience of 'home' in such a wealthy and highly cultured society. In short, the sense of ontological security is historically and culturally specific.

Reading through fictional literature is an interesting way to explore the settings for social relationships. E. M. Forster's novel *Howards End* (1910) is in effect a celebration of the idea of the 'the power of Home' (as described by Margaret Schlegel, the key character in the book). The idea of ontological security, of houses as a locus in which people find security and create the settings for their most intimate relationships, pervades the book. Charles Dickens, perhaps the greatest English novelist, writes time and again and in detail about particular places, stage sets, in which his characters act out their dramatic tales.

Anyone who wishes to experience the stench and squalor of what it was like in the slums of Victorian England can do no better than read his novels. Home is not always a haven of comfort but can be a hellish entrapment. So powerful was Dickens' impact on our way of thinking about housing that even today we speak of 'Dickensian slums'. Elizabeth Gaskell also gave graphic portrayals in her novels *North and South* (1855) and *Mary Barton* (1848) of housing conditions and home life in the north of England in the early nineteenth century. George Orwell's account of the experience of homelessness in Paris and London, *Down and Out in Paris and London* (1933), is not really a novel but is partly written in a fictional style, and is undoubtedly the most graphic and powerful portrayal of homelessness in the English language. His semi-autobiographical book, *The Road to Wigan Pier* (1937), gives detailed accounts of housing conditions in northern coalfields in the 1930s. In these fictional accounts, through our imaginations, we can experience quite vividly what it was like to live in other times and places.

One of the few social scientific studies empirically to test people's psychological attachment to the home was conducted by Cooper-Marcus using qualitative research methodology inspired by Jung's ideas about the sub-conscious mind. She encouraged people to conduct a role-play with their house and from her results constructed a series of biographical accounts of how the participants interacted with the dwelling. In childhood she showed that the growth of self-identity often involved seeking autonomy from parents in the area surrounding the dwelling, especially in gardens – a finding, she argues, that could be one reason for the popularity of gardening in later life, as a throwback to this early experience. In the process of growing up claims to personal space inside the house become more significant as does attachment to possessions. Thus the house interior and how it is decorated and arranged is bound into how people develop. She found that her respondents came to have specially close ties to particular objects. Domestic artefacts are a 'stage set onto which a self-image can be projected via moveable objects'. These objects might be particularly treasured during periods of change or transition but were disposed if they harboured unwanted memories from the past. Thus the house interior and possessions seems to track the changing patterns of life more significantly than the external appearance of the property. As Cooper-Marcus observes, 'Like the explanation of the self, the arrangements of the domestic interior is often in the process of becoming' (Cooper-Marcus, 1995: 59).

Home as a Nightmare

The results of the emotional and spiritual bonding with the home, irrespective of housing tenure, are clearly seen in the traumatic experiences
of women who are forced to leave home because of domestic violence.
Recent research has shown that people who lose their home due to
mortgage repossession suffer high incidence of illness and clinical
depression. Even the process of moving house has been associated with
feelings of grief and loss. The home, therefore, harbours within it a
series of dichotomies, of opposites, which reflect, for example, the
conscious and sub-conscious parts of human nature, security and
insecurity, familiarity and strangeness, sacred and profane.

Hockey illustrates this theme by juxtaposing Bachelard's 'dream
space' with the grotesque and mythical House of Doom – the house of
demons and horrors familiar at fairgrounds and in gothic novels, but all
too tragically present in the house of the mass murderers Fred and
Rosemary West at 25 Cromwell Street, Gloucester, which was eventually demolished. Hockey writes about the English home as the place
where self-identity is 'conceptualised' and where relationships to others
are forged. Her point is that the privacy of the home is constructed in
response to the horror of contact with the outside world where the
integrity of our social identities is threatened. The Victorian idea of
three classes of rail travel responded precisely to the need for bodily
separation from other people who whose cleanliness, status and personal characteristics were threatening. As George Orwell observes in
the autobiographical section of his social commentary about England in
the 1930s, *The Road to Wigan Pier*, upper and middle class children
were inculcated with the idea of the physical repugnance of working
class people:

> Very early in life you acquired the idea that there was something subtly repul-
> sive about a working class body; you would not get nearer to it than you could
> help . . . It is summed up in four frightful words which nowadays people are
> chary of uttering. The words were: *The lower classes smell*. (Orwell, 1937: 112)

This physical and olfactory sense of bodily proximity is, according to
Hockey, implicit in the sub-conscious and can be observed in people's
behaviour when they move house. In this case residential mobility
opens the movers to the risk of being tainted by those who inhabited the
dwelling before. Hence the deeply felt need to refurbish and decorate
so that every trace, every spot of dirt, every hair, any sign of the physical

presence of the previous inhabitants are cleansed. The House of Doom represents more than a 'fun fantasy' according to Hockey and 'represents and articulates that which is powerfully culturally repressed, the horror of unwanted proximity to the hidden selves of others' (Hockey, 1999: 160).

Home and Domestic Culture

The home environment is not only the focal point of personal self-identity but is also the *source* of specific types of domestic cultures. In England, with its unique heritage of early and rapid industrialization – forging new social classes and encompassing the globe with its powerful economic interests – a new form of domestic culture was invented. It arose from the moral codes and social mores that developed during the Victorian era (1837–1903) and, significantly, endowed the other major English-speaking nations with cultural values and behaviour associated with the life of the domestic interior. This domestic culture was imbued with the sense of home as a retreat from an alien and corrupting world beyond the front door or the garden gate. A deeply felt moral panic resulted in a general retreat into domestic fortresses, producing a spectacularly rich and distinctive architecture and, above all, interior design. Throughout the twentieth century interest in the domestic interior persisted and has found a contemporary expression in the obsession with home decoration and 'make-over' of rooms and gardens, as seen in numerous TV programmes. The BBC's 'Changing Rooms' acquired cult status in the 1990s with a weekly following averaging over 11 million. The sense of re-making, of being acceptably fashionable to the outside world, is not a new theme but a contemporary expression of conformity through home-making, which is the essence of Victorian domestic values.

What was particularly significant in the nineteenth-century experience was that the new middle class, especially entrepreneurial venture capitalists, very quickly looked away from the growing squalor and over-crowding of town life and towards the suburbs and countryside. Here they hoped to emulate the domestic life of the landed classes, who continued to dominate the rural social and physical landscape. The flight of the middle class from the town may thus be read both as a response to the increasingly squalid urban environment but also as a social aspiration. To own rural property, or to ape it in the suburbs, was to associate with the landed aristocracy at least symbolically if not socially. The suburban detached villas and gothic mansions were both a physical and symbolic response to a political and social culture forged in the uneasy alliance between the landed aristocracy and the new bourgeois class that was the legacy of the seventeenth-century English Civil Wars. It was their mutual unease at the other great social force unleashed by the eighteenth- and nineteenth-century Industrial Revolution, the working classes, that lead to the search for new securities in the suburbs and villages.

The garden walls, hedges and fences that surrounded the villas and country mansions were both a symbolic barrier against the urban working class, an attempt to create social distance, and simultaneously an attempt to civilize, to bring shape and order. Victorian gardens were an integral part of this moral crusade. Until the return to vernacular 'cottage gardening', inspired by William Robinson and developed in the twentieth century by Robinson's follower Gertude Jekyll, Victorian gardens took their inspiration from the formal landscapes of the great estates of the aristocracy. Gardening became a middle class fashion and depending on the availability of resources no expense was spared to cultivate new and exotic plants. In their conservatories and gardens the respectable classes sought to tame and cultivate the plant order just as they hoped to tame and improve the moral life of the working classes. As with so much else associated with English domestic culture, gardening was an elevating pastime redolent with moral improvement.

Better Housing, Better Lives – for Some

The creation of conditions in which families were able to live respectable lives was greatly assisted by the improvement of housing standards arising from the creation of powers for local authorities to pass byelaws (following the Local Government Act 1858). Municipal authorities were able to regulate the width and layout of streets, air spaces above houses, areas of windows, etc. In particular, housing byelaws enable authorities, where they wanted, to control the building of 'back-to-back' housing. This was a form of dwelling, common in the areas of heavy industry in England, put up by speculative builders in which two terraces of houses shared a back wall, each dwelling facing in the opposite direction and therefore having windows (and access) only at the front of the property. Although not mandatory 'byelaw housing' gradually took the place of back-to-backs; as Burnett suggests byelaws:

acted as a useful guide to the more progressive towns and, at the same time, created an important precedent for national involvement in housing matters. (Burnett, 1986: 158)

Further development of these powers in public health legislation in the 1870s enabled authorities to scrutinize developers' plans and to inspect and demolish work that contravened regulations. This all meant that in the second half of the nineteenth century new property was built in streets with backyards – private space – and to a higher standard in which both middle class and working class families were able to live much more fully private lives than at any time before. With somewhere to do their washing, hang it to dry, go to the privy, even grow plants in small plots (a particular tradition in the Midlands), families were no longer under the constant scrutiny of their neighbours. Before, these had been semi-public functions but in byelaw housing it was possible to lead 'respectable' lives (Thompson, 1988). Although these new streets were subtly differentiated by social class and status, it was undoubtedly the case that lower middle class and working class housing standards converged. As Ravetz suggests, 'a peculiarly English atmosphere of residential repose was created' (Ravetz with Turkington, 1995: 5). Indeed this convergence towards a more or less universal standard of domesticity is a key part of the unfolding history of housing in the twentieth century.

It should not be forgotten, however, that at the extremes were vast differences between the middle class and working class experience of housing and home in the nineteenth and twentieth centuries. Even within the working classes there were major divisions between the better and worse off strata. Better-quality and more expensive byelaw housing was of little benefit to the poorest for whom it was no longer economic to build. Households in which income was low or where there was persistent unemployment lived in squalor and frequently shared with another household. The number of children in the household was a key factor between poverty and relative affluence. The appalling conditions of life for working class households in the industrial heartlands were graphically described by Orwell during his travels in the Yorkshire and Lancashire coal fields during the mid-1930s. He commented that it was possible to walk for literally hundreds of miles in streets inhabited by miners, 'black from head to foot every day', and never pass a house with a bath (Orwell, 1937: 48).

Further up the social scale the main difference between better-off working class families and the middle class was the boundary drawn between those who could afford servants – even one or two made a difference – and those who could not. Having some form of live-in domestic help permeated surprisingly far down the social spectrum. The problem of attracting and retaining domestic staff was already a major difficulty before the First World War, largely because the number of households able to afford servants was declining. But even so being 'in service' was easily the most important occupation for single women until the outbreak of the Second World War (Ravetz, 1995: 209). The point is that the care of the home was the almost exclusive duty of women – with or without servants. For those able to afford servants much of the daily drudgery of domestic life – of producing a warm and cosy home environment, keeping clothes clean and meals on the table – was lifted from their shoulders. Victorian families were generally much bigger than their twenty-first-century counterparts and the sheer hard graft of the daily round, with no electricity, often no internal water supply, certainly no inside WC, should not be underestimated.

For working class women life offered an exhausting routine built around long years of pregnancy and child-rearing – it was common in the nineteenth century to have ten or more children – keeping fires going, cooking, washing and mending clothes. These were exacting and physically demanding tasks. She was expected to provide a comfortable home for her husband and family and was judged according to her skill and success in performing this role. The visible signs of respectability – a frequently cleaned and polished front door and window ledge and immaculate lace curtains screening the interior – were essential in all layers of society. Working class housewives rarely left the home for purposes other than to collect water, go shopping, arrange delivery of coal or to clean her door steps (and quite often the pavement in front of it).

Home as a Cultural and Moral Stage Set

Middle class home life was a much easier proposition for the 'woman of the house' although it too was fraught with the daily round of preparation and cleaning. These homes were hierarchical and gendered. They were not necessarily very private places because of the constant presence of servants. However, the main preoccupation of middle class women was with the presentation of the home as a bastion of moral virtue and an accompanying display of material comfort. Relationships were not always or even routinely harmonious and there was scope for deviancy inside as well as outside. In this sense, it was not merely a place of display and privacy but was a complex social system involving the different use of rooms (the male study, the parlour, the bedroom, the servants' quarters, the functional 'back region' and the garden) and structures of interaction between the inhabitants.

For these housewives the parlour had a special significance because it was there that she was expected to create a cultural 'stage set', which expressed the core values of comfort and security. The parlour was a ubiquitous feature of housing in all social classes except the very poorest whose dwellings had too few rooms or were so overcrowded as to need it for other purposes, quite probably, as Orwell observed, as a bedroom. But in 'polite society' parlours were a major social statement. Positioned at the front of the house it was strategically placed between the inner realms of the home and public domain beyond the front door. The parlour was the best-decorated, cleanest room and was specifically designed to be expressive of the housewife's tastes in interior decoration and display – her ability to arrange flowers, keep potted plants, arrange and display 'best' china, cut glass, pictures and prints (conventionally on the theme of idealized rural landscapes) – and where her choice of velour curtains and matching furniture and décor would be judged. These rooms were the apex of Victorian domestic culture. Here the female virtues of good taste and moral virtue were to be ranged against the public persona of the male, potentially tainted by contact with the world of work and his natural brutishness. Religious pictures were commonly hung on parlour walls. As Hepworth observes, the parlour was the symbol of polite society, of security and respectability in the face of the threatening and inhospitable world outside. Life expectancy was short and disease and death were commonplace:

> the ideal Victorian home is therefore more accurately defined as a kind of battleground: a place of constant struggle to maintain privacy, security and respectability in a dangerous world. (Hepworth, 1999: 19)

Victorian homes and gardens were designed as moral bastions against the corrupting influence of poverty and deviancy as much as they were built to provide bodily comfort. The castellated architecture of these dwellings, their fences, walled gardens, and generally solid construction were the physical form of a much more significant moral and spiritual purpose. Victorian hymn books are replete with references to the home as a bastion against evil. The idea of the 'heavenly home' was the culmination of this association and had a poignancy that it is difficult to imagine in secularized and sanitized twenty-first century society.

The English-Speaking 'Family of Nations'

Finally, it should be emphasized that Victorian domestic culture was emulated throughout the English-speaking world and became embedded into the 'home owning' Anglo-Saxon societies, closely linked to England through the legacy of Empire. As Hepworth points out, the influence of Victorian values, 'goes well beyond the shores of Britain and the boundaries of the nineteenth century' (Hepworth, 1999:17). He cites a study by Grier, of North American domestic culture, which points to the significance of the 'parlour' (or drawing room) as the epitome of Victorian domestic values, 'an Anglo-American, transatlantic, bourgeois culture of industrialising, western civilization' (Grier, 1988: 2). Housing and domestic culture can thus be seen to be at the very heart of the English-speaking family of nations (see Chapter 1) (Esping-Andersen, 1995; Castles, 1998). Despite national variations Victorian domestic culture harboured a fundamental and highly socially embedded value system, which has a profound significance for the cultural identity of the English-speaking nations (Britain, Australia, New Zealand, the USA and Canada). In the 'new world' countries, housing was provided through owner occupation and this housing tenure was closely associated from the very beginning with private ownership, literally 'home ownership'. In New Zealand, for example, owning was linked to social respectability and home-making:

> Home for most New Zealanders has been constituted through ownership; owning one's house has been seen as a secure base for the development of a household and family. (Perkins and Thorns, 1999: 128)

Land in these countries was cheap and plentiful. The situation in Britain was rather different because Victorian housing was almost entirely a product of speculative investment by private landlords. However, once this system of provision ran into crisis, at the end of the nineteenth century, home ownership asserted itself as the principal housing tenure with council housing filling the gap left by the declining privately rented sector (see Chapter 6). It was a paradoxical case of British catch-up.

The key point that unites this, aptly termed, 'family of nations' is not housing tenure or even the linguistic and historical heritage but that these nations are suffused with common, core values concerning personal and social self-identity, the way we think about the world and our place in it. Ideas about the home were the shell within which these values were transmitted between countries. The intrusion of Victorian domestic values into the sub-cultures of these societies is thus of enormous contemporary significance.

The Twentieth-Century Experience of Home

The Convergence of Housing Standards

The most fundamental change in the experience of home-making in Britain in the twentieth century was the dramatic and substantial improvement in housing conditions across all strata of society, but particularly for working class families. The convergence in standards between middle class and working class housing, begun with the advent of 'byelaw housing', was continued, but for rather different reasons in the twentieth century. The two key elements here were the general increase in incomes and large-scale state intervention through the provision of high-quality local authority housing. The rise of home ownership and the advent of state housing provision created, however, rather different experiences of home-making which to begin with enriched British domestic culture but later in the century became the basis for a major social cleavage.

During the course of the twentieth century something in the order of 15 million dwellings were built in Britain, achieving the long-stated objective of housing policy, to provide 'a home for every family', even though it was not until the end of the 1960s that the crude shortage of dwellings to households was finally overcome. (More detail on this is given in Chapter 6.)

Here it should be noted that the rising real incomes of a very large proportion of the population across the twentieth century (assisted by massive state support through reliefs on their tax burden) allowed millions of families to become homeowners. For those households who could not afford to buy on the market, the provision by local authorities of subsidized rental accommodation, at its zenith in the mid-1970s catering for nearly a third of the population, enabled access to decent and often high-quality accommodation. Together owner occupation and council housing, albeit very belatedly, achieved the aim of 'a separate house for every family that wishes to have one'. How, then, was the experience of home-making and the concept of the home developed as a result of this achievement? Gradually every household came to have their own private space, but what did they do with it? The answer to these questions was influenced by changes in the demographic structure, new technology and the more flexible workforce required in the service economy. The globalization of the economic order thus became closely entwined in the legacy of Victorian domestic culture and it was through these interactions – global, social and historical – that twentieth-century British people set about creating their vision of home.

The house building programme throughout the course of the twentieth century revolved around two very distinct forms of provision, home ownership and council housing, albeit that they began with a common cultural and architectural heritage. Nevertheless the division between estates of homeowners and council tenants became the battleground for some of the most vicious social conflict witnessed during the century.

Utopianism and Council Housing

The social, geographical and symbolic distance between the two sectors were subtly different from the outset, and to begin with this did not particularly matter. Council housing was an attractive proposition for lower middle class households as well as the upper strata of the working class (skilled manual workers, foremen, etc.), those who could afford the rents. Addison Act housing built between 1920 and 1922 was, of course, brand new, of high quality and relatively affordable. It was much sought after. But there was a paradox in the situation even at this early stage. It concerned the architectural styling and design features of council housing compared to the speculative housing built by private developers for the owner-occupier market. It was an issue of little significance and barely recognized at the time but was to assume monumental significance in later years. Note also that the architectural founding fathers of these styles of domestic architecture, Raymond Unwin, Norman Shaw and Edwin Lutyens, all drew their inspiration from the Victorian Arts and Crafts movement, so that the common origin of these architectures adds to the paradox. The Arts and Crafts movement was based on an anti-urban critique of industrial society. It combined aesthetic and social ideas, the latter drawn from writers such as William Cobbett and Blatchford. The key influence on the emergence of Arts and Crafts as a movement was William Morris (1834–96). He had a utopian and highly romantic vision of medieval rural society and worked closely with the Pre-Raphaelite poets and painters. His main influence was as a designer with a strong social philosophy.

The design of 'council housing' was closely connected with Morris' idealistic, utopian vision and came down through the Garden City movement, the most notable advocate of which was Ebenezer Howard

(Ravetz, 2001). More specifically this utopianism was converted into an architectural tradition of vernacular, 'cottage' housing associated with the work of Unwin. Unwin, with his partner Parker, were chosen as the designers of the first of Howard's social experiments, the new town of Letchworth and were also the architects of Joseph Rowntree's garden suburb estate at New Earswick in York (and, later, Hampstead Garden Suburb). The connection between these ideas and council housing resulted from Unwin's appointment as the architectural and planning consultant on the Tudor Walters Committee, which met during the First World War to plan the development of post-war local authority housing. The style of housing proposed and its standard of space and amenities were a revolution in social policy (Burnett, 1986: 222). As has been said, Unwin drew his inspiration from the Arts and Crafts movement associated with William Morris, a movement looking back to pre-industrial notions of simple, rural ideals. The key principle of the movement was 'the Morrisonian belief that functionality should coincide with beauty' (Ravetz, 2001: 59). This simple idea was crucial in the history of council housing. By making the design of houses and the wider environment better, so people would improve. Unwin's housing, therefore, was designed around a set of principles aimed to enhance the quality of people's life and health. His facades were broad and open and faced towards the sunniest aspect, and paid rather scant attention to the conventional parlour room (in this, his designs were unpopular with tenants). 'Back regions' were sometimes at the front of the house with fewer and smaller windows facing the street. Gardens were essentially thought of as a source of fresh, home-grown vegetables and fruit. The gardens of the New Earswick houses, built over a number of year beginning in 1902, were all planted with three fruit trees. This purist view, however, was very different to the architecture of the private sector, speculative semi-detached property which engulfed the country during the inter-war period. As Ravetz notes:

> [The] gulf between the suburban vernacular and architectural purism proved to be of crucial importance for the suburban council house. The earliest examples of this followed the model village and garden city tradition: a tradition where ideal standards for working class homes rather than any consideration of market appeal were the main consideration. (Ravetz, 1995: 23)

Unwin's drawings, based on New Earswick in York, were incorporated into the Design Manual that was sent to local authorities in 1919. The answer to the question of what 'council housing' should be like was in essence Unwin's designs for New Earswick, which he had drawn nearly twenty years earlier. There were two problems for this housing model; the purity of the design concept set against the highly marketed, middle class, suburban semi-detached villas and, secondly, the implementation of the council house programme, which fell very short of Unwin's vision.

His ideals very quickly ran up against the need for economy and although the generous subsidy given in 1919 by the Addison Act for the first wave of mass council housing enabled most authorities to build to a high standard, later legislation imposed much more stringent cost limits. As a result council estates grew in size, houses were laid out in straight lines and fronted the road, terraces lengthened, internal layouts changed and much of the subtle brick decoration and detailing of Unwin's original designs were lost. Different legislation allowed different opportunities (see Chapter 6) and although council housing was identifiably linked to its origins in the garden suburb cottage vernacular, in its mass production it fell far short of Unwin's architectural standards and ideals. The simple truth was that 'council housing' was visibly different from the speculative housing built in the private sector, despite its more principled architectural heritage. The difference between owning and renting a house was there for all to see. Indeed the sociological studies conducted at the time contain evidence of considerable hostility to the construction of council housing estates from neighbouring private residents. It was common for tenants' associations to be set up to combat the sense of isolation and hostility experienced by the newcomers. As Durant observed in her study of the Watling estate in north London, 'antagonism from without breeds association from within' (Durant, 1939: 21). It is clear that by the 1930s middle class owners and working class tenants were physically and socially separate communities, even when geographically adjacent (Lowe, 1986).

But it should not be forgotten that for working class housewives their new council house marked a dramatic improvement in housing standard, and this was their priority. Less well-off households could not furnish them or even afford curtains, and sheer poverty continued insidiously to demarcate between the respectable working class and the less respectable, especially with the lower-quality properties that were built in the 1930s to replace slums. These working class homes were more austere, with few of the new goods and gadgets which were so much a part of owner occupied semi-detached suburbia. Nevertheless, many visions of home were constructed in council housing and for millions of households they offered a real material and social advance. Ravetz notes that a significant change associated with the move to council housing was the gradual engagement of men with the life and maintenance of the home, with a greater willingness to join in decoration projects and child-rearing duties (Ravetz, 1995: 219).

In the private sector there was more choice of housing types, but the speculative building industry imposed its view of the 'ideal home', assuming rather than proving they were in accorded with public taste. The most popular type was the half-timbered mock Tudor semi-detached house and these were avidly marketed to capture the imagination with symbols of independence and social ambition. The sources of this style of building were the renowned architects Norman Shaw (most well known for designing Bedford Park, Chiswick) and Edwin Lutyens, who built a series of mock Tudor/Renaissance 'manor' houses for wealthy clients in the early years of the twentieth century. The architects of the middle class suburbs that sprang up in the 1920s and 1930s used a pastiche of Shaw and Lutyens' designs. Given the social gulf that opened between council tenants and owner occupiers, it is interesting to note that Shaw, Lutyens and Unwin were all inspired by the Arts and Crafts movement, so that the models for the inter-war working class 'council' estates and middle class suburbia had a common heritage inspired by William Morris and his followers. The fact that conflicts, little short of class warfare, broke out in some areas between middle classes home owners and council tenants should not blind us to the common source of these architectural forms, nor to the fact of the convergence of housing standards that took place at this time.

The middle class 'semi', more than Unwin's workers' cottages, were criticized by intellectuals as mere kitsch and revealing of the shallow intelligence of the middle classes. But despite scathing criticism semi-detached suburbia became, and remains, a popular place for home-building. Victorian domestic culture was re-born in the inter-war semi. 'The Bendix automatic home laundry makes a house an ideal home', (Sherman, 1946, cited in Chapman and Hockey, 1999: 9) trumpeted the adverts in the *Daily Mail Ideal Home* book. These were the new objects of display and became important features in establishing the family's status in the neighbourhood and its sense of self-esteem. Home ownership became synonymous with ownership of consumer goods, and the marketing companies frequently connected the two with a heavy emphasis on the gendered nature of life in these new, ideal homes.

Just as in the Victorian era so in the 1920 and 1930s the archetypal family consisted of father out at work, mother tending the home and providing for her husband's comforts while the (now only two) children – ideally one of each sex – were asleep in their cots or out at school. Declining family sizes and the acquisition of labour-saving devices certainly benefited middle class women and reduced the burden of the heaviest chores, especially washing. But the social surveys showed that time spent on housework did not markedly decline at first (although it did after the Second World War), instead new functions were created – time spent on child care increased, more time was spent stocking the house with the new 'necessities' and meal-time preparation also increased.

Whether on the middle class or working class estates a first observation about the nature of the home in the twentieth century is that for many people access to their own property where they could bring up their children and create their own vision of home was a new experience. Especially for women, whose role as 'housewives' was a ubiquitous feature of society at all levels, the opportunity for new housing and vastly improved standards of accommodation and facility changed very considerably the experience of the home after 1914. Being able to live on their own without sharing with others was a liberating experience for millions of households. It is, of course, not an even pattern, as we have seen already, but as housing conditions improved and incomes rose so household sizes began to decline and a great deal of the weight of day-to-day graft for women was eased. For working class women in particular the fact of having their own home and smaller families was a crucial turning point. Middle class women were rather more affected by the decline in the availability of servants, assuming crisis proportions during the First World War, and never really recovering despite the fact that domestic service remained easily the most important occupational choice for single women until 1939, finding employment in the homes of the upper middle classes.

As servants became unaffordable during the inter-war period so lower middle class housewives were persuaded to acquire the new forms of labour-saving devices, notably the vacuum cleaner, the refrigerator and the sewing machine, all of which had lengthy histories dating back into the nineteenth century (and meant to be used by servants). None of these could be more than of passing interest in middle England until electrification during the inter-war period saw the first wave of heavily marketed 'labour-saving' devices. The growth of home ownership, electrification and the early spread of domestic gadgetry were synonymous, and through marketing in newspapers and women's magazines a new model of the ideal home was created. Self-identity became associated with the personal acquisition of 'white goods', which were linked to glamorous and idealized images of family life.

At the other end of the spectrum, it should not be forgotten that many working class households did not share this new prosperity and standard of domestic comfort, either in semi-detached suburbia or on council housing estates. Until the slum clearance programme began in the 1930s most of the worst-housed families had no option but to stay where they were. They could afford neither home ownership nor council housing, indeed could barely scrape together rent for their private landlords. As we have seen, Orwell and other social commentators were shocked at the scale and depth of poverty in the northern coal-fields and mill towns, and even though the worst slums began to be cleared their legacy of morbidity and squalor remained a national disgrace. As Holmans reminds us, as late as 1947 over 2 million households did not have either electricity or gas, relying on open fires and/or ranges for cooking and heating and candles for lighting (Holmans, 2000:16).

The Second Half of the Twentieth Century

In many ways the inter-war years were the seminal period in the story of twentieth-century housing. By 1939 home ownership was established as the most rapidly growing housing tenure (already over a third of households) and council housing catered for 10 per cent of households. After the war both these forms picked up the momentum of the 1930s, the Labour government directing the initial effort to overcome the large scale of shortages through a campaign to build council houses. However, it was widely recognized that the war years had changed forever many of the presumptions about the social life of the nation. As early as 1944 the Dudley Report suggested that domestic life was bound to change in the post-war period and in this it was truly prophetic. The activities of the new National Health Service (NHS) quickly took home-births and, for that matter, deaths out of the home. For generations the home had been the place for these seminal rites of passage.

Patterns of home life gradually evolved. Burnett noted that a majority of men (and children) came home for lunch at midday until the end of the 1950s. This was the main meal of the day and it took a considerable part of the morning to prepare, being complemented by 'high tea' in the late afternoon (Burnett, 1986). Sunday lunch also held a pivotal place in the weekly round and for poorer households was the only time fresh meat was eaten during the week and provided a 'cold' meat for several days. Apart from the obvious need to eat, the main function of these meals was, 'to reinforce solidarity, hierarchy and discipline' (Ravetz, 1995: 212). However, the relative improvement of incomes across the social spectrum in the 1950s supported a greatly expanded range of takeaway meals – Italian, Indian, Chinese – complementing traditional fish and chip shops. 'McDonaldization' was not far behind. McDonald's rapidly became a household word and through its intensive marketing strategy and 'fast-food' service, from the 1970s onwards penetrated every corner of the country. Eating out became commonplace and by the end of the century it has become unusual for families to sit round a table for a formal meal at any stage of the week. The penetration of deep freezers and microwave ovens enabled meals to be pre-cooked and served quickly as household members returned to the home-base. Concern has been expressed about the nutritional value of fast-food and food 'grazing' – of continuous eating of snacks throughout the day – especially on the well-being and fitness of children.

Changes due to new patterns of household formation were already under way in the 1950s, notably the trend towards single-person households, resulting initially from an increasing number of widows in the population. During the 1970s, due to increasing levels of divorce, a growth in the numbers of single men and women living alone together with the rising incidence of single parenthood led to a massive increase in smaller types of household. Between the 1971 and 1991 censuses two-thirds of the net increase in households was due to the formation of one-person households (Holmans, 2000b. 14).

There were also inter-generational issues, concerning wealth transfers, disputes over the use of rooms in the house and an increasing pattern of relationship breakdown, all of which implied greater diversity in the use of housing. Mid- and late twentieth-century homes also underwent considerable functional changes arising from economic restructuring and the rapid deployment of new technologies. There is here an important connection between the globalization of the economic order and changing notions of what the domestic sphere encompasses. For example, a quarter of households in Britain have a 'home' computer and many of these are connected to the internet. The growth of home working relates closely to the more flexible working practices required by many companies. The internet also spawned a new form of commercial activity, 'e-commerce', with trading conducted on-line or in virtual markets. It is a feature of these internet companies that they often originated in the home.

As a result of these activities the meaning of 'home' began yet again to be reinvented and underpins the lesson that the notion of the home is perpetually changing in accord with inherited domestic cultures and its interaction with the world outside the front door. In this case, the evolution of the home is a response to globalization processes and the fundamental restructuring of the British economy, which is now essentially a service economy. The collapse of traditional manufacturing industry and the rise of suburban and more dispersed service occupations is at the core of these changing perceptions and uses of the home. Particularly from the 1980s onwards a very high proportion of new service industry employment engaged part-time women, making up almost half the total workforce. For the first time in the industrial history of Britain as many women as men are in paid employment.

There is a sense in which this economic era recaptures elements of the pre-manufacturing period when home and work were closely connected. It clearly is less necessary to 'go out to work'. Such activity enables two-earner households to operate more efficiently through shared patterns of child-care and more flexible working times. Rooms have been redesignated and redesigned to meet these new functions, notably the creation of office space and studies. While there is evidence that men take more part in home life as a result of these new patterns, the traditional division of labour between men and women has remained rather stable. For example, it is still women who take most of the burden of washing and ironing – 79 per cent always or usually doing this – look after sick family members and decide what to have for meals. Men very rarely figure in these categories, although share responsibility for shopping about equally and are mainly responsible for small repairs around the house (*OPCS*, 1996). Although the amount of time spent by women on housework has declined steadily since 1945, mainly due to mechanization, the drop has not been dramatic. In 1975 middle class women spent 45 hours per week and working class women 40 hours on housework (Gershuny, 1983). The problem is that women take the primary responsibility for housework while also being in paid employment, often away from the house. It is commonly the case, however, that dual-earner households employ some form of child-care or help with washing and cleaning, gardening or property maintenance. In recent decades there has been a rapid expansion in domestic labour of this type, often paid for in cash outside the formal economy (Gregson and Lowe, 1994). This practice has more than an echo of very old social relationships between the well-off middle classes and their armies of servants.

Privatism and Self-Provisioning

Finally, changing patterns of leisure have impacted on the home. DIY decoration and house maintenance was common in working class homes in the inter-war era due to lack of resources. Since the 1970s, with increasing leisure time and the rapid growth of home ownership, DIY came to assume huge proportions with superstores, cathedrals of consumerism, selling cheap tools and materials and spawning a new era of what Pahl called 'self-provisioning' (Pahl, 1984). As in the 1920s and 1930s, when the growth of home ownership was closely connected by marketing strategists to consumption of goods and services, so from the 1970s onwards a huge industry has been constructed around DIY. Social values of independence and self-reliance are deeply embedded in product advertising and are clearly associated with property ownership and privatism. As demonstrated on the countless 'make-over' programmes on television, in which rooms and gardens are transformed by neighbours and friends assisted by celebrity interior designers, this is a pastime shared by men and women. Working class 'Handy Andy' steps in when needed to deal with latest fancy of his flamboyant but impractical middle class 'designer'. It should be clear, however, that this obsession with appearance is a replay in modern guise of the core Victorian value of presenting a respectable but fashionable decorative order to the world. It is an expression of domestic values, which in essence are those of conformity and respectability.

Leisure activities based around the availability of digital and satellite television have made an impact on patterns of domestic life. Access to endless entertainment opportunities via the internet and home shopping and internet banking facilities were widely available by 2001. To what extent such activities displace conventional facilities remains to be seen but telephone and internet banking had caused a considerable reduction in the number of over-the-counter bank branches, especially in rural areas. The problem with these developments is, of course, that access to the virtual world of the internet depends on having a computer and being 'wired up'. Already there is a sharp division between the 'information-rich' and 'information-poor' households. This new social cleavage is not necessarily related to conventional divisions of class, gender or age and in theory digital television opens most households to the information revolution. But the true impact of these developments has yet to be seen. One thing is certain, in due course the twenty-first century will define more clearly its own sense of 'home'.

Conclusion

The concept of 'home' is of monumental significance as a source of self-hood and core social values. It has been written about by sociologists,

architects, social psychologists, and others, and is perhaps most percep-
tively understood and described in fiction, especially novels. Novels
have the advantage of being able to span time and place so that we can
intuitively comprehend the experience of home in other cultures and in
history. Related non-fiction can also be a useful source. For example,
Jenny Diski's autobiography (*Skating to Antarctica*) gives a graphic
account from a child's eye-view of growing up in a block of flats at the
beginning of the twentieth century (Diski, 1997).

It is rather a mystery why such an important concept has been
relatively unexplored in the 'housing studies' literature until recently,
and even now remains a neglected field of study. Kemeny perhaps best
explains this neglect when he suggested that the idea of 'home' is so
socially embedded that is has been taken for granted. It should be added
that in *some* of the social sciences, and particularly in the architectural
literature, there has been a significant level of discussion, albeit bound
into specialist discourses. But it remains true that such a seminal concept
as 'home' is marginal set against the great sociological pillars of 'class'
and 'community'.

The chapter sought to draw out from a very diverse and far-flung
literature something of the significance of the concept of home to the
social and cultural foundation of Britain. Attention was drawn to the
changing pattern of domestic culture and meanings of 'home' during
the course of the nineteenth and twentieth centuries. Early industrialization in England was shown to have instigated a distinctive break with
pre-industrial experience of domestic arrangements, especially the
divorce between 'home' and 'work', initially also implying distinctive
female and male domains. It also endowed the country with a powerful
domestic culture, which spread across the globe to the other English-
speaking nations and became the basis of a distinct 'family of nations'
(Castles, 1998). The values associated with the Victorian sense of home
were disseminated through literature, hymns, art and poetry. Through
gardening the wilderness was tamed and inside their conservatories and
parlours an elaborate stage set was constructed as a harbour against the
(the very real) dangers of the world beyond the front door. Middle class
and working class versions of core values, both centred on respectability, were encapsulated in the very fabric and even structures of these
homes, with their garden gates, castellated brickwork, iron railings and
chinz or lace curtains. Suburban vernacular architecture, following Unwin
and Lutyens, evolved into two distinct built forms – working class
council housing estates and middle class owner occupied suburbs –
which changed the face of the country's built environment and forced

council housing into an inevitably subordinate position. The fortune of
council housing was shaped by the social divisions of twentieth century
Britain.

The rest, as they say, is history. As the twenty-first century dawned
patterns of home-building continued to evolve, reflecting economic
restructuring, new patterns of work and leisure and a new demography
built around longer lives and smaller households. How to cater for these
new needs is the subject of Chapter 4.

FURTHER READING

Chapman, T. and Hockey, J. (eds) (1999)
*Ideal Homes? Social Change and Domestic
Life*, London, Routledge.

Forster, E. M. (1910) *Howards End*,
London, Edward Arnold; various edns,
Harmondsworth, Penguin.

Ravetz, A. with Turkington, R. (1995) *The
Place of Home: English Domestic Environments,
1914–2000*, London, E. & F. N. Spon.

Rybczynski, W. (1986) *Home: A Short History
of an Idea*, New York, Viking Penguin,
paperback edn, Pocket Books, 2001.

4
Housing Need

<table>
<tr><td>

CHAPTER AIMS

- To provide an overview of the principles that lie behind defining housing needs
- To describe how housing need should be measured and the main models used for this purpose
- To describe the main components of and recent developments in patterns of household formation in Britain
- To list the factors which influence the delivery of the house building programme.

</td></tr>
</table>

Introduction

By the year 2000, the UK's housing stock had risen from a mere 6.8 million in 1900 to over 24.8 million dwellings. Virtually all the Dickensian slums had been cleared in two waves of slum clearance (in the late 1930s and between the mid-1950s and 1960s). The massive growth in the housing stock was largely a consequence of the rise in household numbers and was produced by a combination of rising real incomes – for higher-income groups could buy their new space – and for those unable to afford market access, of council housing, in its heyday as desirable as any other form of provision for a wide variety of social groups, as we saw in Chapter 3. Together, home ownership and council housing brought a separate 'decent home', the frequently cited objective of twentieth-century housing policy, within reach of the overwhelming majority of the population, by about the end of the 1960s.

Housing needs have not, however, been completely consigned to the dustbins of history and there remain major inequalities in housing, particularly, although by no means exclusively, between the two main housing tenures, home ownership and social housing, which have changed dramatically in the quality of life each offers in recent decades. There are also major inequalities *within* tenures – for example, half the poorest households living in the worst housing conditions are owner-occupiers. There is a perpetual agenda of population growth and new household formation. How many new properties are required from this point in time to house decently all existing and new households? How many of these should be supplied in the market and how many by the providers of 'social' housing?

This chapter aims to provide a brief overview of the principles and practice of housing needs analysis. It draws heavily on the palette of concepts in the policy analysis literature. There is a strong emphasis on decision analysis and implementation issues. The result of this is to show how a definition of housing need should be arrived at, what the core indices of need are, how they should be measured and finally how they equate with the reality of house building, which is largely privately supplied. Governments in Britain are able to give a steer to the process, but not much more than that. Inherent in a system that is predominantly demand-led is the issue of where housing fits in the macroeconomic planning process. Recent controversy over the proposal to build a high proportion of new housing in the south of the country and on Green Belt land indicates that this is not merely an academic exercise.

Drawing on the division of the policy analysis literature outlined in Chapter 1, consideration is initially given to translating these policy analysis concepts into the range of questions addressed in the chapter. Without such conceptual foundations, it is difficult to make sense of the complicated issues involved in housing needs analysis.

Policy Analysis and Housing Needs

Using the approach outlined in Chapter 1, the issues and questions relating to housing needs fall under three headings – those to do with meso-level analysis, decision analysis and implementation. Meso-level analysis is concerned with the spectrum of processes involved in policy-making, starting from the broadest contexts (globalization) and ending with the evaluation of policy. In essence, this is the pathway that traces the policy cycle through its various stages.

A central focus of meso-level analysis revolves around agenda setting, and in the case of housing needs is concerned with the key issue which dominated twentieth-century housing policy, the balance between the public and private sectors in the delivery of the housing programme. The private market has been dominant but there were key moments, notably after the two world wars, when the state needed to step in to deliver the housing building programme. Should the market be allowed to lead when issues of inadequate supply cause hardship? By extension, this leads to consideration of the role the state should take in influencing where and how much housing should be built and the proportion allocated to the public and private sectors. A key issue here concerns how public policy should deal with the high demand and consequent high house prices in the south of England. What should be done if nurses and teachers cannot afford to live there? The 'non-decision' literature is also a central feature of agenda setting with its focus on the extent to which these issues are amenable to influence from public opinion generally and groups that have a direct interest (residents in areas earmarked for new building, young people unable to afford even the cheapest house, consumers in general). These issues relate to analysis of who the main players are in the policy community that determines and drives the housing programme – the builders, land owners, social landlords, local authority land use planners, civil servants in the regional government offices and others. What kind of network is involved here?

The decision-making literature is located mostly in the area identified by Laswell as 'knowledge in' the policy-making process. Here, the questions are more technical in nature, although this should never detract from seeing that there are wider agendas that shape what can be achieved. For example, cost-benefit analysts pose questions about the relative gains and losses of policy decisions. In the housing context, this translates into a series of issues concerning the economic advantages or disadvantages of building more houses in the south of England when there are surpluses in parts of the north (see Chapter 5). To what extent should governments adjust policy to account for known problems caused by the house price cycle? Decision analysis also involves forecasting so that decisions can be made about the planning of resources and where priorities should be placed. Clearly it is important to know how many households there will be in five, ten or even fifty years time, and how many dwellings will be needed to house them.

There are inevitable resource constraints, so what share of public spending should housing attract, given that most people buy in the market using their own money? Should the state build more housing in the north where land and building costs are cheaper but demand lower?

Finally, at the delivery stage issues are raised about the influence that planners should exert over what is in effect, in Britain, a decision process lead by the private sector? How effective is the land-use planning system in directing the building industry to build where the government decides housing is most needed? The planning system can be used to compel house builders to provide 'affordable' social housing as a condition for receiving planning permission. A delicate balance has to be struck, however, between achieving the overall building targets for the different regions of the country and the planning system acting as a restraint on the market. Street-level bureaucrats such as planners can be influential for better or worse. Policy review and evaluation is also an important part of the implementation agenda because it is important in designing programmes for the future to know accurately whether and how previous policy has worked out. Was the right sort and quality of housing provided where and when it was needed, and if not, what should change?

These policy analysis concepts provide the basic steer through what is certainly the most difficult aspect of housing policy – how to provide housing where it is needed, at a standard that is adequate for the day and at prices that can be afforded. The rest of this chapter is a detailed consideration of these issues, beginning with the most fundamental of all the questions, the definition of housing need.

The Definition of Housing Need

The first stage in the analysis is to devise a working definition of 'housing need' before consideration of some of the principles that ought to inform how it is measured. Later, the chapter considers the problems and benefits arising from the implementation of the measurement of housing needs:

- How many new houses need to be built.
- Where and what type should they be in relation to current and forecast household numbers and types?

Such questions are at the heart of housing policy analysis.

Stock, Flow and Backlogs

At the most fundamental level, the concept of housing need has to cater for analysis of the housing stock as it currently exists and for the 'flow' of new needs which are constantly being created. 'Housing stock' refers to the total quantity of housing that is required to provide accommodation of at least the minimum acceptable standard. By contrast, the notion of a 'flow of needs' is the shortfall between the actual supply of housing and the quantity required. By convention, the flow is made up of households who move in (and out) of need over the period of a year. This assumption, however, does not cater for the 'churning' (rapid mobility) of an increasing number of households who move two or three times (or more) during a year, behaviour that is particularly prevalent in areas of low demand in the declining old industrial cities of northern Britain (see Chapter 5).

Although the distinction between stock and flow sounds somewhat artificial it is a fundamental of housing needs analysis. Generally it is the flow issues that are of greatest concern and have dominated the literature on this topic. It is perhaps best expressed as a *deficiency* concept, between what is required and what is supplied (Barnett and Lowe, 1988; Bramley, 1989). Bramley *et al.* helpfully liken this situation to the example of a bath: 'Newly arising need comes through the tap, new social housing provision is the plughole, and the backlog is the level of water in the bath' (Bramley *et al.*, 1998: 26). Social housing, at least in theory, makes up the gap between what the market provides and overall need, which incorporates households unable to afford access to the market.

Finally, recognition must be given to the fact that the housing market is not a single entity but consists in reality of a series of inter-related markets for different types of housing. Some households can afford to be in particular segments of the market and whether or not they can access housing in their price range depends in large part on the availability of that range in their area. Household types change over time, and the form housing policy takes at any one time is very likely to be based on the requirements for accommodation of particular household types.

The Influence of Holmans' Housing Needs Methodology

Some of the most influential work on housing needs measurement has been conducted in a series of studies by Alan Holmans (see, for example, Holmans, 1995; Holmans, Morrison and Whitehead, 1998). In his studies, Holmans brings together fundamental population data with housing supply and demand information, also using the notion of stock and flow. He suggests that housing needs is best understood by focusing on two main elements, need that is *new* – made up mostly from newly forming households – and what he calls 'the backlog of unmet need' (in effect the *deficiency concept*). The backlog consists of households who are homeless, living in over-crowded conditions, 'concealed households' living with another household and others who do not have access to independent accommodation of a decent standard. These people are already part of the housing system but are not housed satisfactorily. Newly forming needs are made up mostly from new household forma-tion, but also includes those whose circumstances change so generating a new need – for example, in the case a couple in a small flat who have started a family. If these households do not find accommodation then they, too, as we have seen, measured over one year, become part of the backlog. It is very important to realize that people in similar circum-stances will appear in both the backlog and the newly forming needs categories. The point is, from a needs assessment perspective, whether they are part of the tap water gushing into the 'bath' of housing needs or are already floating about in the pool of existing unmet need.

In Britain, it has been the aim of housing policy since the end of the First World War to provide every household with a separate 'decent home' and for those unable to access this through the market, this has largely been achieved by the provision of council housing. Thus one of the key issues in thinking about the flow of housing required to meet this need has been the estimate of how many new households (and by implication how many in the backlog) can afford to buy or rent in the housing market. The residual of households unable to buy or rent in the market are those for whom the 'non-market' sector of 'social' housing provides. Otherwise the basic assumption is that housing supply will meet demand, albeit with lags – because of the length of time it takes to build a house from scratch – or because of exogenous factors – for example, the severe impact of the two world wars during the twentieth century.

It should be clear, therefore, at the outset that the measurement of housing need has to be built on two or three fundamental concepts. The first of these, and the one which stands at the heart of all housing policy, is that there must be an agreement over what constitutes an acceptable standard of accommodation. This has generally been enshrined in phrases such as access to a 'decent home' or, in 1945, 'a separate house for every family'. The current formulation of this policy objective is 'to offer everyone the opportunity of a decent home and so promote social cohesion, well-being and self-dependence' (ODPM, 2003). The definition of 'decent housing' evolved in the course of the twentieth century, with a quantum leap after the First World War as the public and private sectors developed their housing types in tandem, as we saw in Chapter 3. Periodically, legislation and associated building regulations have defined minimum standards and increasing incomes have enabled higher standards. Data from 1947 showed that only 36 per cent of pre-1919 dwellings had what was then defined as the three basic amenities of a fixed bath, hot water and an inside WC. By 2000, the proportion of dwellings without these basic amenities was negligible. There are new standards for the numbers of bedrooms families should have and central heating has become a new standard, available to only 5 per cent of households in 1960 but in the late 1990s the English House Conditions Survey found that over three-quarters of pre-1960 property had central heating as did virtually all post-1960s homes (Holmans, 2000: 15).

Household Numbers, and How to Count Them

The second key element in the housing needs equation is that of the total number of households and the associated issue of the scale and speed of population growth and change. During the course of the twentieth century the stock of dwellings tripled although the population only grew by 62 per cent (England and Wales). The reason for this is that the number of households within the population grew very rapidly indeed, arising from a combination of economic, housing policy and demographic changes. The demography has two main components. First, during the course of the twentieth century there was an increasing number of adults relative to the overall size of the population (i.e. more people in the household formation age group; only 57 per cent of the population were over age 20 in 1901 but 75 per cent in 2001). Secondly, changes in the age structure and marital status of the population also accounts for a significant growth in households relative to population size.

Holmans (2000) shows that about 9 million of the 15 million increase in separate households during the twentieth century can be accounted for by the increase in the adult population and nearly 3 million by changes in age structure and marital status (Holmans, 2000: 13). Figure 4.1 shows the trend for households to grow more rapidly than the population across most of the century. The economic and policy elements underpinning the ability of separate households to form are directly associated with the increasing availability of dwellings to live in. This, as we have seen before, arose from the increasing ability of people to set up on their own in the housing market, and the very large state rental sector put in place

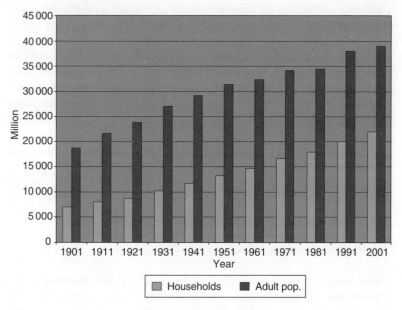

Figure 4.1   **Households grew faster than population during the twentieth century**

Source: Holmans (2000: 13).

across five decades of the twentieth century for those unable to enter the market. Household growth is thus a result of increasing numbers of adults in the population and other changes in the population (notably its age structure), increasing incomes and housing policy.

The difference between crude population figures and numbers of households in the population is thus of crucial significance. Population growth and change is relatively straightforward, in that the current population size is a known quantity and predicting how it will grow is, at least in the medium term, straightforward. Forecasts are, however, always subject to unforeseen developments. For example, between 1991 and 1996 official population estimates showed an increase of 539,000 in the population aged over 16, which was over 100,000 above the forecast. This was due mainly to migration into the UK being considerably more than expected, with a high proportion of this growth being in the south-east of England. The clear implication of this is of higher than expected demands for housing in the south of the country. But generally for housing purposes the basic demographic calculations have reasonable certainties. A current cohort of 50–60 year olds containing, say, 75 per cent of owner occupiers will translate into 60–70-year-old cohort with the same proportion of home owners in ten years time.

Translating this increased population into households is not easy, not only because of unforeseen factors but because some of the key measurements are quite subjective. Some people may be constrained from forming a household because of shortages of suitable/affordable accommodation. This includes so-called 'concealed' households, such as newly married couples living with their in-laws or lone parents staying with friends, as well as people in temporary accommodation such as hostels or in B and B arrangements. In this case, the forecast is of a *potential* number of households. These potential households form part of a backlog which, in theory, should be gradually eliminated. There is also here a value judgement about who is eligible to form an independent household. A far higher proportion of 18-year-olds expect to be independent of their parents than in the past when young adults typically left home to get married. This is important in relation to housing supply, because if supply is increased to meet new demand it is bound to stimulate the formation of households becoming independent sooner than in the past, and thus the new housing supply will reduce housing need by rather less than the quantity of housing supplied. Similarly if housing supply is increased in the south of the country to meet high demand there is bound to be a feedback effect which increases demand and reduces housing need by rather less than was planned for. As will be seen later, this principle is at the heart of a major dilemma in the implementation of the house building programme.

Finally, it should be noted that short-term economic factors play a significant part in household formation. People's decisions about whether they can leave home or form a new partnership are closely connected to patterns of economic change, the economic cycle and the changing balance of disparities between the regional economies of Britain. Forecasters need to be aware of these underlying and ever-shifting influences on household decision-making.

The 'Simple' Definition of Housing Need

Despite these feedback effects the two foundation concepts of a simple definition of housing needs are:

- an acceptable standard of accommodation and total number of households at a particular point in time
- an estimate of the potential numbers.

By putting these elements together and assuming that a deficiency concept is appropriate here, housing need at any particular point in time can be defined *as those households who do not have access to accommodation of at least the required standard*.

Measuring Housing Need

The focus for assessing both current and future housing need are built around the two components of the number of newly forming house-holds and those households already housed but whose circumstances change and so put them into need:

- How should these needs be assessed and measured?
- How many of newly forming households (or those whose circum-stances change) are unable to satisfy their housing needs in the marketplace, and so require access to 'social' housing?

Similarly there may be questions to be asked about what constitutes an 'adequate' standard of housing. Some of the main components of 'adequacy' have already been mentioned – the issues of physical com-fort, and/or over-crowding, or at what age young adults should expect to leave their family. What other indicators should be included in needs evaluation, and how should they be measured?

Top Down and Bottom Up Approaches

These questions are central to many aspects of decision analysis. They raise the key issue, introduced in Chapter 1, of the dichotomy, inherent in the policy approach, between the rational/hierarchical view – the top down approach – against what might broadly be called a 'consumer-preference' – or bottom up – approach. The bottom up approach also includes the influence that Lipsky's street-level bureau-crats have on the determination of needs indicators and, above all, on the implementation of policies based on needs assessment exercises. Their influence is felt at the most basic level of data collection on which the central government apparatus builds its needs indicators. The quality of the data collected by local authorities has been much criticised in recent years as inadequate or inaccurate. Street-level influence operates most especially in the policy implementation stage.

For example, the problem of low demand for housing in some areas of the country – explored in Chapter 5 – was partly the result of a policy failure involving the activity of local housing officers in the north of England. Policy failure due to lack of inter-organizational integration and problems faced by front-line staff was famously described by Pressman and Wildavsky's Oakland study (Pressman and Wildavsky, 1973). Early versions of policy network theory also characterized the political system in Britain as one based on fragmented sub-systems, causing lack of integration in policy formation and delivery (Richardson and Jordan, 1979).

Housing needs analysis has a strongly 'top down' emphasis, even though in recent years local needs assessment exercises have incorporated data collection from household surveys. Although the system has changed in recent years, housing subsidies are distributed to local authorities and to housing associations (RSLs) by using a *needs index*. They are quasi-objective measures but contain many of the difficulties inherent in implementing a financial distribution between different regions of the country. The indices of housing need, the General Needs Index (GNI) and Housing Needs Index (HNI) (used to distribute subsidy to the regions) are both centrally determined by officials in the ODPM and incorporate a range of indicators. They are used currently to allocate up to 60 per cent of central government subsidy. In this way, it is government officials who determine the flow of funds from the centre. Their needs indices are based on objective standards rather than on issues such as privacy or independence, which may be more important from a consumer's perspective. There is a clear danger in needs indices being set by professionals who are also responsible for the attainment of the policy outcomes. Needleman argues that this leads to excessive caution in defining standards; policy-makers have their own interests to secure in shaping housing programmes and how housing resources are allocated (Needleman, 1965).

A consumer preference (bottom up) approach, which is often used in cost-benefit analysis, attempts to find out what the (housing) consumer values. This can be done in a variety of ways such as looking at decisions that consumers have made in the past ('revealed preferences') or by using questionnaires to elicit their ideas and preferences. Until the mid-1990s the clear emphasis in housing needs modelling was firmly top down in character, but more recently surveys, for various reasons, have become an integral part of local needs assessment, although their use, validity and how they integrate with national estimates of housing need are all questionable.

Implementation

Implementation, as discussed in Chapter 1, is the key moment in the policy process. This section outlines key issues in housing needs analysis that impact on the delivery of policy. In short, the literature generally supports the view that it is unusual for a policy initiative to be delivered 'cleanly' and intentions and outcomes are frequently at variance. One of the principal reasons for this is that the needs modelling methodologies contain a range of assumptions which, unless made explicit, lead to distortions in subsidy distribution and/or policy that does not carry out its intended effects and may indeed have unforeseen consequences. This section outlines some of the issues which should inform the housing needs modelling process, and a number of issues of principle that are inherent in this process.

As we have seen above, whether a consumer preference view or housing professional view is adopted, in the end there must be indicators which pinpoint those households that do not have access to accommodation of the required standard. This list is almost certain to include those who have no access (the homeless), those in overcrowded households and those in sub-standard property, and there is likely to be an indicator for a sub-standard neighbourhood. In the current HNI and GNI system, the latter is catered for by a so called 'stress area enhancement'. This indicator is not really a direct indicator but is a *proxy* (or indirect) measure which uses unemployment, crime, poor services, etc. as indicators of poor neighbourhoods. This, of course, is a vital element in housing needs because access to a house of at least the required standard is partly determined by the type of area in which it is located. The problem of 'low demand' discussed in Chapter 5 is just such an example of a place where poor neighbourhood and housing demand (or, as in this case, lack of it) interact, with severe social consequences.

In theory, however, there should be, at the end of the day, a series of indices of need. The next stage, from a policy analysis perspective, is to consider how these measures of housing need can be operationalized. Where there is a list of indicators, such as the HNI and the GNI, it is quite likely that that each item on the list will not be considered of equal importance. In this case a weighting exercise will be needed, otherwise the assumption is that all the indices are of the same value. But before weighting, a number of other adjustments need to be made to avoid distortions in implementing the model.

Normalization of Indices

A model is not reality and it is rarely the case that policy analysts operate with a blank sheet. In housing needs modelling two sets of circumstances are particularly significant:

- Those arising from housing management and other locally determined housing policies and practices
- The need to account for the cyclical nature of some of the needs indicators.

Without some attempt at a 'normalization' exercise there will be anomalies in the implementation of the model. For example, in relation to housing management practice, it is reasonable to suppose that housing authorities with high management costs which are beyond their control – high numbers of old property, high numbers of elderly people in the local population – will be compensated in some way for these problems. But it is undesirable that inefficient management practices should be allowed for in the allocation of funds. Performance monitoring is an established procedure in local authority and RSL management as a means of measuring organizational inefficiencies. Local authorities (LAs) are currently committed to a discipline over ensuring 'Best Value' for their communities. Whatever method is chosen, it is clearly unacceptable that housing agencies which employ less than 'best practice' should be compensated via the housing needs index.

In similar vein, the policy stance of authorities is an important influence on the implementation of the housing needs model. For example, housing indicators, such as homelessness acceptances, are likely to be key indicators of housing 'stress' in a locality. The assumption is that all authorities operate with the same or a similar policy stance and the data is aggregated and used as though this is the case. However, in cases where the authority has a relatively liberal or 'open' policy stance on homelessness, the number of acceptances may be higher than authorities that operate a more conservative and hard-line policy. In short policy stance affects *how* the housing needs model is operationalized, and it is clearly unfair that more effective or more open-minded authorities should be penalized for dealing with problems before they show up in the statistics.

The House Price Cycle

Although this is more an issue of weighting than normalization it points to another key question in housing needs analysis: the well-known fact that the economy in general, and the housing market in particular, is subject to a *cyclical pattern*. In British housing there is also a particularly pronounced *geographical dimension* to this issue. This is illustrated in Figure 4.2. Due to a variety of factors (higher prosperity, shortage of building land, high economic activity, population density) house prices in the south are considerably higher on average than in the north of the country. This results in the cyclical pattern of boom and recession being not evenly spread across the country, with the strong tendency for the southern housing market to 'drive' the pattern of change. House prices in the south go up or sink into recession some months, even years, ahead of the north. There is a clear 'rippling out' effect, with the areas furthest away from the south-east being the last to experience the change in the cycle. Thus, as can be seen on Figure 4.2, the disparity in house prices between the north and the south varies according to the point in time on the cycle when the measurement is taken. Various repercussions follow from this for housing needs modelling, especially in the distribution of subsidies between the regions. It would seem to be best to take an average or trend over time than to rely on the picture at a particular point in time. Moreover, account should be taken of disparities which are not just 'north v. south' issues, for example the fact that increasingly there is a gap in prices and quality of experience between city and countryside or between inner city and suburbs.

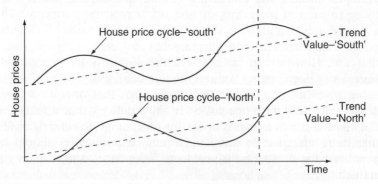

Figure 4.2   **Point of maximum disparity on the house price cycle**

So it is that a number of questions need to be considered in the implementation of housing needs models. The main issues concern housing management practices, local authority policy stances and the complex geography of the house price cycle. Without some attempt at the normalization of these factors housing needs modelling can be – indeed, has been – misleading and unreliable. As will be shown below, since the early 1990s, housing management performance indicators have become important in the allocation of funding under the reformed HIP system.

The National Housing Needs Models

Deciding on the scale of building programme required to meet new housing demand and need is a complex and technical modelling process. It requires detailed knowledge of past trends and the current balances in the supply and demand for housing. Some of the key issues of principle have been outlined above and this section describes briefly two of the most influential approaches to this modelling process. The aim of most models is to report on the likely areas of deficiency in past and present provision in the market, and in the need for social housing. Some models are devised specifically to provide forecasts, which are needed to inform macroeconomic planning. Many attempts have been made to model housing needs, ranging from a simple calculation of the number of dwellings relative to the number of households through to complex econometric models, such as that devised by the University of Cambridge (DETR, 1997). The basic methods are:

- A statement of the size of the national housing stock at any one point in time
- A net stock approach
- An ability to buy at a point in time.

Statement of the Size of the National Housing Stock

The simplest model is not actually an estimate but merely a statement of *national totals*, at a particular point in time, of the size of the housing stock and numbers of households. The main importance of this type of work has been in historical studies by showing the evolving balances of population change and housing provision at different stages of development (see Chapter 6).

Net Stock Approach

An extension of this form of analysis led to what became known as the 'net stock' approach and it is this type of model that is the basis of nearly all the modern estimates of need. It has been used by the AC (1992), Wilcox (1990), 'Shelter' (Holmans, Morrison and Whitehead, 1998) as well as by the DETR itself. More recently, a modified net stock model has been used by Holmans in a series of influential studies (Holmans, 1995; Holmans and Simpson, 1999). Holmans' 'modified' net stock model uses a method for further dividing owner-occupiers and tenants, by controlling for age and household types, and builds in adjustments to account for the effects of the right to buy (RTB) (households who buy and then move into mainstream home ownership). These are key adjustments, otherwise the model would be totally static, merely rolling forward past trends. Behaviour in relation to household formation can significantly influence the outcome of the forecasts. For example, married couples are more likely to be home owners than single-person households, so that any growth in single-person households relative to married couples, as was the case in the 1980s and 1990s, implies a need to reallocate households between the two tenures (Holmans, 1995).

The foundation of all these models is the population and household projections made by the Office of National Statistics (ONS), looking forward over a ten- or twenty-year period. Increases in new households are set against the size of the current housing stock and likely changes to the stock arising from demolitions and the number of unfit dwellings. The numbers of 'concealed' households are added to the total (lone parents/married couples living with in-laws/friends, etc.) and a variety of adjustments are made to cater for people in temporary accommodation and the quantity of vacancies in the housing stock. These are then off-set against new private sector output to arrive at a requirement for social housing which is the residual of the calculations, those unable to afford access to the market. As we saw above, this division into the two basic components of effective demand for houses in the private sector and the need for social housing is the central feature of the net stock approach. The models differ in the assumptions that they make, for example, about the definition of concealed households or what constitutes an 'unfit property'. For example, Wilcox's estimate (1990) of social housing need of 130,000 per annum differed significantly from the AC (1992) calculation of 75,000 per annum, although both used the 1989-based household projections. The disparity was due to their different interpretation of concealed households and degree of unfitness in the housing stock.

It should be added that there have been and remain some question marks over the reliability of the underlying demographic projections. For example, it was assumed in the 1992-based population projections that there would be no additional increase in cohabitation, but research suggested that there had been an increase in cohabitation by separated people entering new relationships and by 'never-married' men and women. As a result the 1996-based projections assumed an increase in cohabitation, which by default reduces the number of single-person households. This changed assumption on its own accounts for a reduction in the growth in the numbers of households between 1996 and 2011 of very nearly 1 million (Wilcox, 1999). Distinguishing between married couples, cohabiting couples and single-person households is an important development in the underlying data which, if it fails to reflect changing patterns of social behaviour, can lead to inaccurate and misleading base data which in turn feed into the needs modelling procedure.

Ability to Buy at a Point in Time

A second, very different, approach to housing needs assessment is Bramley's 'affordability' model (Bramley, 1989a, 1989b). Bramley's is not a forecasting model but makes a 'snapshot' of the position at a particular point in time, and so is different in intention to Holmans' work. The basis of the idea is that housing need is mainly generated year-on-year by newly forming households who cannot afford to buy a house in their local market. 'Ability to buy' is measured by reference to income data drawn from secondary sources, the Family Expenditure Survey (FES) and in the recent version of the model, the *Survey of English Housing* (SEH) (Bramley, 1998). Local house price information is taken from the data files of the Nationwide Anglia building society. This measure of affordability (who in an area is able to buy the cheapest house?) is applied to calculations of gross new household formation, giving a sum of those in each District Council area unable to buy in the local housing market. Next, the existing supply of new housing and re-lets in the council sector and RSL stock is then deducted to give a final figure of the need for additional social housing. Summing the District data then provides the national and regional pictures.

In the most recent round of estimates Bramley's bottom up affordability model and Holmans' top down, modified net stock method produced broadly similar national results. Bramley's total of new need for social housing provision in 1997 was 96,700 units, compared to Holmans, Morrison and Whitehead (1998) of 88,000. Thus in ballpark terms two radically different studies (although using some common demographic sources) have arrived at a consensus of opinion of new need *at national level*. Holmans' results are aimed mainly at forecasting over long periods the scale of public expenditure to sustain the broad aims of housing policy of a decent house for every household. It provides an on-going insight into the fundamentals of population and household growth and change nationally, and how these match the demand and need for housing.

Bramley's model is not a forecast but a point-in-time estimate of housing need. His direct evidence has the advantage that it gives a much more local perspective and can be aggregated into regional as well as national totals. Probably the main drawback with this method is that by using District Councils as the base unit the model does not account for the fact that housing markets are not confined to administrative boundaries. There is a significant problem that unmet need might spill over into neighbouring authorities.

As with much in the policy analysis approach it is important to be clear about the intentions and implications of modelling procedures. Bramley's and Holmans' analyses both aim to inform the same policy issue, the nation's housing demands and needs. They show how the same problem can be addressed from a very different perspective but provide complementary findings.

Population Growth, Households and Migration

The most recent estimates derived from the ONS 1998-based population forecast suggests that the population has grown faster than earlier projections suggested, due mainly to inward (international) net migration (62 per cent of the additional growth), higher levels of births and lower male death rates. The projection shows that the population will grow by an apparently modest 2.2 per cent in the early years of the twenty-first century, but even this is an annual growth rate of 184,000 people and means that there will be nearly 1 million *more* people in 2016 and 1.2 million by 2021 than the 1996-based estimates. In the context of the overall national population growth, this converts to an increase in households numbers between 1996 and 2021 of 4.3 million.

In regional terms, the greatest pressure is felt in the southern regions of England, especially the south east. Patterns of migration are a central part of an area's population change, which is made up, as we have seen, of changes in births and deaths and net migration (the balance between the number of people moving into and out of an area). Most households who move (currently about 5 million a year) move relatively short distances. Generally the drift is of people moving from the suburbs of the larger towns and cities to more rural locations, and for their place to be taken by people moving out of the inner cities and into the suburbs. Only about 15 per cent of moves are between regions (Bate, Best and Holmans, 2000). The greatest volume of these inter-regional moves is between the *southern* regions rather than from north–south migration; 48,000 people per annum have been leaving London since the early 1990s, moving mostly into the south east region. There was a net flow to the south of some 30,000 people per year during the 1990s from the North and West Midlands regions (Bate, Best and Holmans, 2000). In London, the outflow has been more than replaced by younger-aged immigrants, a high proportion of them international migrants, and by an unusually large excess of births over deaths (about 39,000 per annum). Elsewhere there are also many incomers to the cities, often younger people, but the *net* position is for a steady depletion of population in the metropolitan and other urban centres.

The forecast by Bate, Best and Holmans shows continued pressure on the southern regions, especially the south east and, exceptionally for a metropolitan city, London. The northern regions and the major cities, by contrast, will continue to lose population, a problem that filters down to the inner cities where surplus housing, low demand and an associated social malaise have become major problems (see Chapter 5). As we will see below, these regional and inter-regional imbalances are not necessarily aided by demand-led housing policies. Building more houses in the south of the country, with many attendant environmental and resource implications – with, as it were, housing chasing jobs – may serve only to exacerbate the problems of over-crowding in that part of the country, with economic and social decline elsewhere. Without policy moves to regenerate the northern economy it is inevitable that vast areas of the south will be built over with new housing. The establishment of the Regional Development Agencies (RDAs) appears to have done little in this direction.

Recent Changes in Household Types

A key feature of the current situation is the rapid increase in the number of single-person households. This raises questions about the type of housing as well as where it should be built. In the 1990s the number of single-person households increased very rapidly, partly due to the increasing propensity for divorce among people married during the 1970s–1990s. In the 1990s, 100,000 home-owner couples were divorced and of the resulting 200,000 divorcees, 80,000 stayed in the matrimonial home, 65,000 moved to another owner occupied house, 25,000 moved into rental housing, 35,000 moved in with someone else (often men to live with parents), while there were some 20,000 remarriages involving former owner-occupiers (Holmans, 2000). It is readily apparent, therefore, that one of the main factors contributing to the number of single-person households is increasing divorce. Holmans shows that 80 per cent of these divorcees occupy houses, not small flats. Having been owner-occupiers of houses it is unlikely that, as single people, they will be satisfied with flats. As Wilcox observes, 'Plans for inner city flats for single people as part of the strategies for urban renaissance have their place; but they will not respond to the aspirations or market choices for the majority of post-divorce single people' (Wilcox, 2000: 68). For those moving into rental housing there may be a need for subsidy through the Housing Benefit system to households unable to be in the market. The costs of sustaining low- and even average-income households in the south are substantial.

There many other important changes to household and family structures too numerous to mention in detail here. Those most likely to impact on housing provision and building plans, as we have seen, are the dramatic decline in marriage rates. In 1997 there were 309,000 marriages in total, which was the lowest since records began 160 years ago. The average age of first marriages has increased sharply since the 1970s, from 25 in 1971 to 29 for men in 1997, and from 23 to 28 for women. Increased female participation in the workforce has meant that women are less likely to want children and if they do the first-born is much later than in previous generations (for women born in 1943 only 10 per cent were childless at age 45; the figure for women born in 1973 is 25 per cent). As Jackson observes, 'Fertility is not an independent variable, unaffected by events, but is determined by the conditions of people's lives' (Jackson, 1998: 78). The mean age at which women have their first child is currently 28. The growth in cohabitation (rather than marriage) means that in 1992 31 per cent of children were born to unmarried couples (compared to only 6 per cent in 1972). Divorce is easily achieved and leads to the creation of many 'reconstituted' families – i.e. adult couples containing children from previous unions. Remarriages in which at least one partner is divorced account for over 36 per cent of marriages compared to 17 per cent in 1971. Stepfamilies with dependent children account for about 8 per cent of all families (Hantrais and Letablier, 1996). In 1971 lone-parent households made up 8 per cent of families with dependent children; in 1992 this figure had risen to 21 per cent (Utting, 1995).

Households have become much smaller, with widows and widowers living for long periods after the death of their spouse/partner, young people ('singles') and others choosing to live alone and increasing lone-parenthood all contributing to the reconstitution of contemporary household structure in Britain. These changes are closely related to the economic restructuring since the 1970s, especially the decline of male full-time employment in manufacturing and the rise of the service industries. In addition, major cultural changes have swept aside the old certainties and solidarities (for better or for worse). As Coote, Harman and Hewitt suggest, marriage has evolved into, 'a private relationship where couples place more emphasis upon the personal qualities of their partner, and focus upon the search for companionship, communication and sexual compatibility' (Coote, Harman and Hewitt, 1990: 24).

As Holmans' work has shown above in relation to marriage and divorce, all these patterns of change, and the speed with which they occur, have significant effects on household projections, and by implication on the housing programme. The most recent projected population growth produces an increase in household numbers in the order of 4.3 million between 1996 and 2021. To achieve the universal standard of a 'decent' home clearly requires a substantial building programme. Not to address this new demand and need implies increasing levels of over-crowding, unfitness in the stock and an inevitable increase in homelessness. The pressure will fall most severely on the south-east region and the southern market in general. How much sharing, living with in-laws and friends, squeezing into small rooms, children of different sexes sharing bedrooms, etc. can be sustained remains to be seen, but these are the sure outcome of a failure to deliver the house building programme. The question arises, therefore: will the forecast and reality eventually synchronize?

Evidence of House Building from the Past

One way of addressing this is to look back at the record of achievement in recent years in house building, and the evidence here is of a continuing shortfall in supply in the private market and in the provision of social housing. For example, in 1999 the English housing associations completed only 17,523 properties while the local authority sector built only

79 units. The average annual addition to the housing stock during the ten years between 1990 and 1999 by the social housing providers was 25,500. In 1999 the private sector completed 122,296 dwellings. Their average for the 1990s was rather less than 126,000 per annum. Even allowing for the recession in the housing market in the early 1990s the private sector additions to the stock arising from new building is considerably below the forecast demand and need. Holmans' forecast for the 1991–2001 supply of new building in the private sector was over 150,000 His estimate for the required provision of social housing was set at about 90,000, without any allowance for reducing the backlog. Holmans' estimate of an annual need in the region of 240,000 when set against what actually happened (an average annual total of a little over 150,000) implies that the backlog grew by 100,000 per annum in the 1990s. It is certain, however, that some of the need for social housing was taken up by the rapid growth of the PRS in the early 1990s (30,000–40,000 additions per annum), but it is readily apparent that there is a sustained and substantial deficit in what is actually supplied and the scale of need forecast. The New Labour government announced a series of major initiatives to stimulate the social housing providers, both RSLs and the authorities, reversing years of budget cuts to the housing programme. It nevertheless seems more than probable that need and supply will not match. The reason for this is discussed in the next section.

Delivery of the Housing Programme

Local Demand and Supply Factors

Whatever the outcome of the national estimates of housing need, what gets built where and when is largely outside of the direct control of the central state. It is not at the national but at the *local* level that the scale of new building is determined. It is this that accounts for the shortfall (increase in the backlog) of provision.

Indeed, local authority housing and planning departments have their own duties to measure local housing needs, for two very practical purposes: knowing their own levels of need, which is not possible to determine from disaggregated national data, and the statutory duties of planners to control local land use. One of the major paradoxes in housing needs analysis is the substantial discrepancy between locally assessed housing needs and national estimated forecasts of need. Needs studies conducted by private consultants often over-state the position because of ignorance or misunderstanding about the science of needs measurement. And in practice, it is quite often the case, for example, that in areas of growing population there is not sufficient land available to build on, or that planners, seeking to make increased housing compatible with environmental sustainability, will not grant planning permission. In this way the planning authorities – protecting 'green field' sites at the behest of local councillors – seek to reduce their required provision, according to the DETR national building plans. Either way, there is a problem at the heart of the house building programme. The number of new household formations determines the calculation of the number of houses to be built, but in reality it is the availability of land (with planning permission) that determines new supply and, therefore, the number of households at the end of the day who actually come to live in an area.

The next section of the chapter analyses some of these key delivery issues, especially those relating to local housing needs measurement and house building. The section begins by an assessment of the important issues of re-lets in the social housing sector.

Mobility and Re-Lets

Newly occurring housing need, as discussed above, is the *net annual addition to the existing flow of households* through and around the housing system. Lettings by local authorities and housing associations is made up of existing households in other housing tenures (those already in the system) and newly forming households who join the 'stock' of those unable to buy in the market. Figure 4.3 gives an indication of the type of flows that occur based on the social housing sector. It shows households who moved within the three years before the year 1998/9 and the tenure from which they came. Three years was chosen in order to increase the sample size. Almost 630,000 households entered social housing during those years and about one-third of them (220,000) were newly formed households. The Survey of English Housing (SEH) chart is not quite complete because more people move 'in' than 'out'. This is because they have not shown household dissolutions, notably deaths. But it is useful in showing the kind of flows that occur, even if incomplete.

As we have seen above, the annual additions to the social housing stock are relatively small and far below the requirement to meet new need, let alone the backlog. Indeed for households seeking to move into social housing new building accounts for only about 5 per cent of new lettings made. Meeting local housing needs has become increasingly

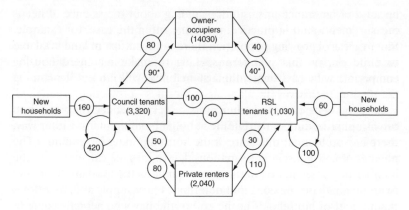

Figure 4.3   **Households moving into and out of social housing, 1997–9**
Source: DETR (1999b 59).

dependent on vacancies occurring in the existing stock rather than new building. Re-lets thus account for 95 per cent of lettings in the social housing stock, although there are significant variations to this pattern around the country. It means, of course, that there is a great deal more mobility of households moving into and out of the sector and that the historic image (and fact) of council housing as a stable housing solution for millions of working class families is much less applicable (Bramley and Pawson, 2000). The residualization and instabilities in council housing will be discussed at greater length in Chapter 10.

The point at stake in the housing needs modelling process is that this increased mobility needs to be taken into account. Most of the net stock models treat re-lets as a more or less fixed figure. But this is clearly not the case. Re-lets are subject to local and regional patterns of variation, which might reflect such factors as the type of stock available in an area, and there is much greater volatility in mobility that is not captured in 'trends' data. Even the use of annual data is suspect because there is evidence that in some 'low-demand' areas large numbers of households move two or three times a year (see Chapter 5).

Local Needs Assessment for Local Housing and Planning Strategies

At the heart of the housing programme is the fact that privately supplied housing is largely outside the scope of government control. House building operates through a poorly integrated policy community made up of builders, planners, housing officials, financiers, landowners, central government officials and their regionally based colleagues. Most new housing is built by private developers on privately owned land. Developers must seek planning permission, but whether they build and what they build is largely their own choice. This is a fundamental of the housing supply system.

Local authorities, on the other hand, have specific duties arising from the Housing Investment Programme (HIP) system and the local land use planning system to develop local housing strategies, and so far as possible within their budgetary constraints to fulfil their part of the housing programme. The authorities are not now, of course, the direct developers of the housing programme but function as 'enablers' of other agencies, notably RSLs. They have increasingly a strategic over-view role which encompasses the private sector, both home ownership provision and the PRS. A key part of this is their assessment of local housing needs which arises from a statutory requirement (Section 8, Housing Act 1985), although in practice the policy instrument which central government wields to force compliance is the increasingly com-petitive HIP system. The HIP system developed in the late 1970s and was, at that time a very top down system with great emphasis placed on statistical modelling through the use of the GNI. In the 1990s this gave way to a more competitive system, in which the DoE (and lates DETR) allocated 50–60 per cent of resources on a discretionary basis. In this new approach there is a strong emphasis on performance indicators. Guidelines issued by the DoE in 1992 (the basis of the current system) listed as indicators the quality of housing strategy statements, the author-ity's record on implementing its capital programme, management practices as landlords and tenant involvement in the overall process.

Of growing significance, especially in relation to the housing strategy statement (arising from the HIP bid process) has been that statements of local needs should be evidence-based, particularly including know-ledge of demand for housing in the different tenures. Although a multi-million pound industry (Bramley *et al.*, 1998 estimated that about £9 million had been spent up to 1998), there has been no standardization of research methodologies employed and the quality of results has been criticized. Bryan, for example, shows that the sum of local authority estimates of need considerably exceed the national estimates (Bryan, 1999). Problems of inadequate sampling and mistakes in calculating sample sizes are commonplace. 'what counts is only the conclusions of the consult-ants and the thickness of the report rather than the quality of analysis involved' (Bramley *et al.*, 1998: 18).

Resource Allocation

A key factor that underlies the delivery of the social housing programme arises from the all-too-apparent fact that funding is limited. It
is rarely the case, if ever, that sufficient resources are made available to
meet the total of new need, let alone wipe out existing backlogs. In
terms of the theory of housing needs modelling, resource allocation is
the final hurdle before programme implementation. Having arrived at
a normalized and properly weighted model, having decided that there is
a national need for some tens of thousands of new dwellings and knowing where they should be built, there still remains a question about the
basis on which the funding should be distributed. The scale of funding is
a public spending decision made by the government in its annual spending review. The point here concerns what economists describe as
'equity' versus 'efficiency'. Given the disparity in house prices and the
cost of building land between the regions, a decision has to be made
whether to spend the resources on producing a considerably smaller
number of houses in the high-priced south (which would be the most
'equitable' solution but would lead to there being a much-reduced
programme in the north) or to build for the same amount of money a
greater number of houses in the lower-priced northern regions. By implication, this could also apply to high-priced greenfield rural sites against
low-demand, low-cost inner city areas. As can be seen in Figure 4.4, in
practice the choice of where on the 'efficiency'/'equity' line the balance
should lie is an issue of the policy stance of the decision-makers. In
practice it is quite likely that neither point '*x*' or '*y*' will be chosen and
the likely outcome is to pick a point somewhere on the mid-point of the
trade-off frontier.

   The issue of cost compensation for the high-priced southern housing
markets raises one final crucial issue in the analysis of national housing
needs. This is the question of whether it is justified in the case of social
housing provision to use public money to 'chase the market'. The concentration of public subsidy for new social housing into the southern
regions inevitably leads to distortions in market adjustments. By encouraging such high levels of housing development in the south the government
intensifies the problem it purports to address with strong feedback
effects, notably encouraging migration to the most-populated area of
the country and in so doing meeting less of the overall housing need of the
country as a whole.

   The environmental impact of the plan to build 80 per cent of the
forecast housing programme in the southern regions has already caused

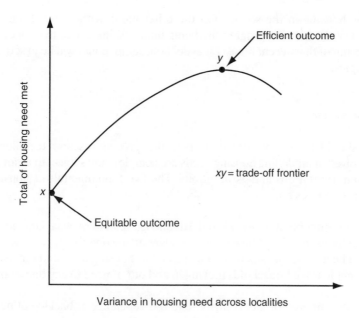

Figure 4.4 **Equity versus Efficiency trade-off**

furious opposition from local residents, and is strongly echoed through the planning system, with some local planning authorities seeking to downplay their national targets. It has been argued, following the floods of the winter of 2000–1, that such a large concentration of building further jeopardizes housing on flood plains because natural drainage systems cannot cope with increased run-off. On the other hand the government's advisors have vociferously supported the use of 'marginal' agricultural land, supporting the policy that up to 60 per cent of new housing should be built on 'greenfield' sites.

The adjustments and feedback effects of the housing programme are complex and wide-ranging. Beneath all these issues and complex calculations is a problem that is not fundamentally a 'housing' question, namely, the considerable disparities in the performance of the regional economies. It can be characterized as a shift from a northern industrial base in manufacturing to a services-based economy heavily concentrated in the south of England and the 'suburbs' (see Chapter 5 for a more detailed account of this process). It may well be that attempts to regenerate the northern economy are directly and adversely affected by a demand-led response to meeting 'national' housing needs (by building new housing in the south). On the other hand, without a substantial part of the housing programme being built it is inevitable that meeting the aim of the 'decent house for every household' policy will be in serious jeopardy.

Conclusion

It should be readily apparent that the procedures and techniques involved in modelling housing needs are complex, and subject to a variety of interpretations and assumptions. The two fundamentals of housing needs analysis are:

- A definition of housing standards and agreement on what constitutes a 'household' and how many there are at any one time
- The idea of the 'stock' of housing and of housing need and the 'flow' made up of households moving in and out of need in any one year.

Needs that are not met contribute to the deficiency or backlog of need to be met at some future time. The depth of water in the housing needs 'bath' inexorably increases.

At the implementation stage, needs models that do not proceed by adjusting for endogenous factors, such as local policy stances, poor management, etc. or exogenous factors, such as the house price cycle, are likely to cause serious inequities in the calculation of levels of need and the targeting of subsidies round the country. Needs indicators have to be carefully chosen within either a top down or bottom up paradigm, although in reality the process is strongly top down in character. Caution should be exercised with the use of affordability indicators. All of these are relatively technical points but they are fundamental to needs evaluation, whether in designing needs indicators or forecasting needs.

The policy analysis literature alerts us to the likelihood that policy design and implementation are rarely, if ever, harmonized. In the 'real world' forecasts of new need are rarely met because the planning system and the process through which house building actually occurs is not amenable to central control. At best, the centre can exert a reasonable steer. This is a consequence of the fact that the house building programme is largely demand-led. This leaves social housing in the position of chasing the market. Housing in general follows economic drift and tends therefore to intensify the over-heating of the southern economy and thus, paradoxically, demand-led housing policy interferes with market adjustments. Ultimately, it can be argued that this is not actually a 'housing' problem *per se* but is a reflection of deep imbalances and inequities in the regional economies of the country. The decline of the old manufacturing industries and mining, and the growth of the post-industrial, services-based economy has generated a new geography of inequalities and exclusion. Modelling procedures can reveal an overall picture of national housing demand and need, but it is readily apparent that what follows in terms of the implementation of a housing strategy is a highly political process.

FURTHER READING

Bramley, G. (1998) 'Housing surpluses and housing need', in S. Lowe, S. Spences and P. Neenan (eds), *Housing Abandonment in Britain: Studies in the Causes and Effects of Low Demand Housing*, York, Centre for Housing Policy, Conference papers.

Bramley, G., Pawson, H., Satsangi, M. and Third, H. (1998) *Local Housing Needs Assessment: A Review of Current Practice and the Need for Guidance*, London, DETR.

Holmans, A. (1995) *Housing Demand and Need 1991–2011*, York, Joseph Rowntree Foundation.

Holmans A.E., Morrison, N. and Whitehead, C. (1998) *How Many Houses Will We Need? The Need for Affordable Housing in England*, London, Shelter.

5
Housing and Social Exclusion

CHAPTER AIMS

- To define the concept of social exclusion and how housing contributes to and can create social exclusion
- To define and describe the causes of low demand for housing and the social problems created by it
- To discuss definitions of homelessness and how these relate to notions of housing need
- To describe the current scale of homelessness and the policy agenda designed to alleviate the problem.

Introduction

The idea of social exclusion is not a new one and has a provenance deeply embedded in the policy analysis literature. The recent use of the words has been contested but seems to have had its modern incarnation from within the EU. Rather than nations admitting to poverty the term 'social exclusion' became a surrogate concept (Room, 1995). As the great English prose writer and social commentator George Orwell said. 'When there is a gap between one's real world and one's declared aims, one turns instinctively to long words' (Orwell, 1954: 363). 'Social exclusion', in Orwell's sense, is a concept that has the potential to obfuscate and obscure reality as much as it does to clarify it. The term has, however, come to have an important place in the vocabulary of the New Labour 'Third Way' and almost the first initiative taken by the newly elected government in 1997 was to establish a Social Exclusion Unit (SEU) inside the Cabinet Office, the Prime Minister's personal domain. Two of the three initial topics of concern to the unit were housing issues – the problem of the so-called 'worst estates' and rough sleepers, the third being single parenthood.

After a brief introduction to the concept of social exclusion, the aim of the chapter is to examine the way in which housing contributes to, and can create, social exclusion, using two cases identified by the SEU. The 'worst estates' issue relates most closely to the problems of low demand for housing (not only council housing) in some parts of the country, especially the areas where deindustrialization has been most rapid since the 1970s. There is a close connection here to the discussion on housing needs in Chapter 4, especially concerning intra-and inter-regional demography. Low demand for housing has been the most salient housing issue during the term of the 1997 Labour government and solutions to this problem are at the heart of their urban regeneration programme. The evidence of the fundamental, structural issues suggests that 'urban renaissance' is not easily achieved.

The case of housing contributing to social exclusion focuses on homelessness. The issue of homelessness, of which 'rough sleepers' are but a small part, describes a form of social exclusion that also connects to underlying social and economic changes discussed in the low-demand study. Homelessness strips its victims of the very essence of life in society. As we saw in Chapter 3, 'home' is the core of every person's psychic and physical well-being. To be without a home is the most destructive form of social exclusion imaginable.

Agenda Control and Social Exclusion

There are at least three books graced with the title of 'Housing and Social Exclusion' (Spicker, 1998; Spiers, 1999; Anderson and Sims, 2000) and there are several influential research studies, notably Lee and Murie (1997). Readers are referred particularly to Anderson and Sims and to Lee and Murie for the most comprehensive discussion of the link between housing and social exclusion. The purpose of this section is not to repeat their ground but to show, from a policy analysis perspective, how the notion of 'social exclusion' should be evaluated and then related to housing. It is a case of needing clarity concerning definitions and meaning, in the quite literal sense. Laswell writes a great deal, especially in his later work, about how social ideas and language connect and the need to be aware of different 'levels' of analysis (Laswell, 1959). The connection between ideas and language in the policy analysis literature is also very influenced by the Italian Marxist Gramsci, who showed how the ruling class created a 'hegemony' of ideas which became orthodoxies. The way in which people see, indeed think about, social reality is patterned by concepts and language that are uncritically absorbed. The aim of the hegemonic class is to control society by a subtle process of 'social inclusion'.

These ideas had a significant impact on the authors of the agenda setting literature, for example, in the work of Bachrach and Baratz (1970), Crenson (1971) and Lukes (1974), especially in the development of the idea of 'non-decision'. These writers were part of a radical critique of orthodox pluralism. They argued that analyses which did not take into account the unequal distribution of power in society were not realistic. As Schattscheider said, 'whosoever decides what the game is about will also decide who gets in the game' (Schattscheider, 1960: 105). Bachrach and Baratz's 'mobilization of bias' thesis showed how some sections of society were systematically excluded from political influence or that certain issues were marginalized because they threatened established interests. In short, it became a central contention of the agenda setting literature that policy-makers had the capacity to create areas of 'non-decision'. Probably the best case-study of this was Crenson's analysis of air pollution in US cities, in which he showed that high pollution was directly related to the strength of industrial lobbies. He showed that where there was pressure for jobs and new employment opportunities, environmental issue were frequently sidelined.

The idea of social exclusion came from within this long line of discourse about social control and the structuring of social and political power. The idea that the words themselves were crucial to this is an important lesson. Edelman showed how the policy process is intimately connected to the type of language used. How a social problem is constructed in words and concepts is closely bound up with defining which solutions are available and which are not (Edelman, 1988). The language of social exclusion has been taken up by existing schools of thought and used in some cases uncritically. One case of this is the version, promulgated by new right theorists, that society is divided into the socially included and excluded, the latter taking the form of a state-dependent underclass unwilling or unable to engage in society (Murray, 1990). When the 1997 Labour government established the SEU it was not at all clear what meaning they attached to the concept, although it was clear that reductions in crime, juvenile delinquency and truancy were seen as positive steps towards a more inclusive society. Later it was apparent that such symptoms of social distress were closely linked in the government's mind to lack of paid employment, leading to the 'workfare' idea. The other main concept which under-pinned the SEU's work was the idea of 'joined-up government' – that it was the inability of previous social policies to cut across departmental boundaries that inhibited solutions to social malaise and breakdown. New Labour's idea of 'social exclusion' was thus to tackle by targeted programmes of action particular manifestations of social breakdown. Awareness of the deeper structural cause of these problems was also on the agenda but immediate, targeted actions aimed at 'cleaning up' society were at the forefront of policy. A puritan ethic of kindness tempered by discipline was a feature of the government's method for tackling social exclusion.

More generally, especially among the applied social science research community, the consensus of opinion has been that the phrase is useful in demonstrating how social problems *cause* division. As Anderson suggests, social exclusion should emphasize 'separateness from the life experiences common to the majority within society, rather than the notion of being outside of society' (Anderson and Sims, 2000: 21). In particular, the concept draws attention to the relationships which inhibit participation in society; people's lack of integration into decision-making processes and lack of power (Room, 1995). The focus is not on poverty *per se* (who is poor and by how much compared to social norms) but on the *processes that cause poverty*. As Lee and Murie suggest, the concept is a useful way of showing that poverty is not only a distribu-tional issue but fundamentally bound up with a wider delivery of social rights through access to jobs, education, decent housing and services: 'Social exclusion is not something that you measure in the way of poverty but is concerned with processes and dynamics which generate poverty' (Lee and Murie, 1997: 4). In relation to housing, they show how living in areas of multiple deprivation can be a *cause* of social exclusion. It is not just that individual dwellings may be damp or over-crowded but that living in a 'poor neighbourhood' can create the experience of social exclusion. It is this aspect of social exclusion that is graphically illustrated in the case of low demand for housing in some parts of the country.

Case Study 1: Low Demand

The Declining Inner City

Housing entered the social exclusion debate in the 1980s through the process of the residualization of council housing. The housing market and the role of social housing within it changed dramatically in the following decades. Council housing was reduced to a welfare tenure catering for the poorest social strata. Later it was apparent that the low-income home owners (see Chapter 7) and a high proportion of households in the PRS were also implicated in the seismic transformation of the housing system. These shocks were creating fragmentation and differentiation, especially among home owners (Forrest, Murie and Williams, 1990) although what was happening to the local authority stock was clearly the epicentre of the residualization process.

As we saw in Chapter 4, the amount of mobility into and out of the sector dramatically changed the whole character – indeed, purpose – of council housing. It was also shown that there were nevertheless signifi-cant regional and local variations in this pattern. More detail on the particular position of council housing and its changing role and purpose in the wider housing system is found in Chapter 8. The aim here is to focus on one of the fundamentals of this situation, the changing levels of demand for social housing and the consequences of this in creating inner city areas devoid of social and economic life, whole communities which have become marginal to the mainstream of society. Moreover, there is evidence that household behaviour inside these traumatized neighbourhoods changes so that these socially excluded areas are not only the residual of wider social and economic processes but *generate* from within peculiar forms of social malaise which threaten social cohesion.

The problem of low demand for housing, particularly social housing, came rather belatedly on to the political agenda and was for some time a hidden phenomenon, partly because the focus of attention in the economic recession of the early 1990s was on the problems of London and the south of England. Housing officers had been grappling with its first manifestation in the form of 'difficult-to-let' estates, mainly in the north of the country, since the 1970s. More recently it became apparent in the scale of housing abandonment that local authorities eventually disclosed in their HIP returns and the level of demolitions of council housing that began to be widely reported in the late 1990s. Research commissioned by the DETR, for example, discovered that between 1991 and 1997 about 40,000 units of council housing were demolished in England and Wales, representing 1 per cent of the stock. These were not slums or in particularly bad condition but were undertaken as 'selective demolition' as part of wider attempts to regenerate housing estates or where rehabilitation had failed (DETR, 2000). Webster reported that about 10 per cent of Glasgow's council housing was demolished between 1981 and 1999, some 20,000 units. Abandonment of housing in all tenures in the north of England was reported in a variety of studies (Lowe, Keenan and Spencer, 1999; Power and Mumford, 1999). The cause of demolition of fit property and the appearance of abandonment were clearly symptoms of low demand for housing in those areas (CIH, 1998) and the SEU report on its 'worst estates' research concluded that 'Surplus housing is a growing problem and in some areas leads to near abandonment... and yet in other areas, particularly in parts of London, demand remains high' (SEU, 1998: 27).

Compelling evidence of the regional picture of low demand was presented by Bramley in the revised version of his affordability model (see Chapter 4). As we saw, his figure for new social/affordable building in England and Wales was close in absolute terms to the estimates made by Holmans but was strikingly different when the figures were broken down at local authority level. Bramley showed that in 1997 ninety local authorities had a social housing surpluses, with the top twenty-two on his list (see Table 5.1) containing surpluses equivalent to half the total national need for new provision of social housing. What

Table 5.1 **Bramley's list of twenty-two local authorities with surplus housing, 1998**

LA name	Surplus flow p./1,000 hhd[a]	Surplus flow p./number	Net social re-lets number	Social housing % of stock
Newcastle – u – T	27.9	3,269	5,828	38.7
Rochdale	22.1	1,850	2,925	30.6
Oldham	21.0	1,843	2,925	27.5
Manchester	19.5	3,548	8,298	45.2
Blackburn	18.8	1,037	1,665	25.0
Gateshead	18.7	1,573	2,604	38.4
Salford	18.6	1,740	3,242	40.0
Easington	17.1	677	1,177	37.9
Sunderland	16.6	1,897	3,339	38.6
Leicester	16.3	1,789	3,655	33.8
Knowsley	15.3	883	1,753	40.8
Hull	13.8	1,485	3,270	40.3
Rossendale	13.3	365	663	21.0
Wansbeck	13.0	342	654	30.5
Sandwell	11.7	1,368	2,828	39.6
Derby	11.5	1,069	2,366	23.2
Sedgefield	11.3	418	801	34.1
Wolverhampton	11.2	1,104	2,706	37.0
Bradford	10.9	2,069	4,700	19.7
Walsall	10.7	1,074	2,338	34.1
Kirklees	10.6	1,636	3,571	21.4
Birmingham	10.5	3,975	11,060	33.5

Note: *a* hhd = household.
Source: Bramley (1998: 22).

was very striking about his analysis was that 80 per cent of the need for additional provision was in three regions in the south of England (including London). He argued that this re-asserted the position in the 1980s of the north/south divide in the housing market.

The corollary of shortages in the south was the existence of areas of considerable surplus in the north. The twenty-two local authorities (6 per cent of the total) with the highest surpluses between them they had total annual surpluses of 35,000 units per annum, 60 per cent of the national total (Bramley, 1998).

Bramley's analysis clearly showed that most of the low-demand localities coincided with areas where traditional manufacturing industry had declined. His complete list of authorities with surplus stock included not only Tyne and Wear, Teeside, the Yorkshire conurbations, most of Merseyside and Greater Manchester, but also cities in the East Midlands and three East London boroughs. In a revision of his earlier studies Holmans also accepted that there was a 'strong regional divergence' in the demand for social housing, although the overall figure for new housing provision remained largely unchanged (Holmans and Simpson, 1999). As we discussed in Chapter 4, during the 1990s about 40,000 people annually migrated out of the northern and Midlands conurbations. It was further noted, *inter alia*, that much of this movement was to other parts of the same or adjacent regions, rather than the south. A large share of out-migration from the inner cities was by people seeking more pleasant living environments, and thus involved suburbanization. This, of course, makes no difference to the residual problem of areas of low demand in the inner cities of the great conurbations and larger towns of the north. But it does suggest that the emphasis on a purely 'north/south' explanation is only part of the story.

A further large-scale study by Bramley and his colleagues measured the quantity of housing in areas affected by low demand and unpopular housing (mainly in the south, not necessarily in low-demand areas). They showed that in England the social housing agencies (councils and RSLs) managed nearly 500,000 houses in these areas and that some 375,000 private sector properties were also affected (much of it pre-1919 terraced housing) (Bramley *et al.*, 2000).

Explanations for Low Demand

Explanations for low demand in some vicinities include the unpopularity of certain estates or neighbourhoods, particularly associated with the residualization of council housing. It is also likely that in some areas the supply of housing in the current stock over-represents dwellings built for certain types of households – for example, where there is too much 'family' housing and insufficient property for single-person households, creating a surplus of larger dwellings compared to demand. It is possible, depending on the structure of house prices in an area, for there to be a surplus of more expensive properties which local residents cannot afford, especially if the income distribution is below average for the area. In other areas a larger amount of 'cheap' housing, particularly in the north of the country, often represents a very poor investment, potentially creating liabilities for the house-hold. In these cases attention needs to be given to the structure of local housing markets.

But the evidence suggests that the principal explanation for the widespread pattern of low demand in some parts of the country is closely bound into patterns of employment change due to economic re-structuring since the 1960s and 1970s (Bramley *et al.*, 2000). This has involved the collapse of manufacturing industry and mining in the north of England and the Scottish industrial heartland. Economically active households moved away from these areas in search of work or simply to escape the decline of their neighbourhoods (Figure 5.1). Moreover, the new white-collar and service industries, with fewer locational constraints, have gravitated towards the suburbs, further depleting the inner cities. According to Webster: 'Most big cities have lost two-thirds of their manufacturing employment since 1979, compared to a national loss of around a third' (Webster, 1998).

Figure 5.1 correlates areas of high 'real' unemployment and low demand for social housing. 'Real' unemployment is a more accurate measure of unemployment because it includes people on Incapacity Benefit and others who were moved off the unemployment register in the 1980s. The figure shows the close link between job losses in the northern cities, the centres of the 'old', heavy manufacturing industries, and low demand for social housing. The only areas where high unemployment and low demand do not correlate are coastal towns and London boroughs, both receiving in-migration which counteracts the high unemployment levels. London lost 75 per cent of its manufacturing jobs between 1960 and 1991, but in its role as a global city there is intense competition for housing space. Coastal areas receive in-migration by retiring people, commuters *et al.* (Webster, 1998).

Loss of work was composed to a very high degree of full-time male manufacturing employment. By contrast, the growth of the service sector has been very dependent on part-time female work and the expansion of self-employment. The analysis of employment change made by Turok and Edge (1999) reveals the geographical impact of

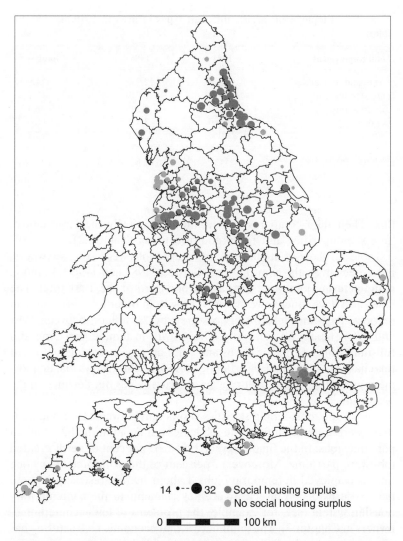

14 •--● 32 ● Social housing surplus
● No social housing surplus

0 ▄▄▄▄▄ 100 km

Figure 5.1 **English local authorities with real unemployment, and the incidence of social housing surpluses, January 1997**

Note: The size of the circle is proportional to the real rate of unemployment, on a scale from 14 to
32 percent.
Source: Webster (1998: 52).

Table 5.2   **Employment across different types of area in Britain, 1981–96 (000)**

Total employment	1981	1996	Change (%)
Towns and rural areas	11,278	12,953	+14.9
Free-standing cities	1,730	1,749	+1.1
Conurbations	4,497	4,208	−6.4
London	3,560	3,348	−6.0
Britain	21,064	22,258	+5.7

Source: Turok and Edge (1999: 3).

this. Their data compares 'conurbations' (basically the large cities), 'free-standing cities' and 'towns and rural areas' (Table 5.2).

Table 5.2 shows that male manufacturing jobs were lost everywhere, but especially in the conurbations. Between 1981 and 1996 1.4 million manufacturing jobs were lost, about one-third of the 1981 total. The cities also have much lower rates of growth in other jobs, especially in services. Part-time jobs in services grew by 2.2 million between 1981 and 1996 (nearly 60 per cent). The growth in female part-time and full-time work in smaller towns and rural areas is a striking feature of this change (Turok and Edge, 1999). Table 5.2 clearly shows that employment grew sharply in smaller towns and rural areas but declined in the bigger cities.

One of the most telling statistics shows that between 1981 and 2001 there were 2.1 million full-time job losses but an additional 2.8 million part-time jobs. In the financial year 1995/6 65 per cent of newly created jobs were part-time. Moreover, 7 per cent of the workforce at any one time is employed in temporary jobs. Labour market restructuring and new patterns of job insecurity are key elements in the contemporary housing system (see, for example, the problems of low-income homeowners in Chapter 7). The point here is that economic restructuring has been geographically uneven in its impact, with the major conurbations, the Pennine industrial towns and mining communities in the north very adversely affected. The new private service industries, by contrast, have grown more slowly in those areas and tended to concentrate in small towns and suburbs especially, but by no means entirely, in the south of

England. As Turok and Edge conclude from their analysis of employment change: 'The decline of manufacturing is responsible for the bulk
of job losses in most cities . . . and they have also suffered from urban–
rural drift, or net decentralisation of economic activity' (Turok and
Edge, 1999: 50).

It is thus readily apparent that population decline is a general context
for the existence of surplus housing. Old industries have been replaced
by new ones but in different places, creating low demand in some areas
of the country but under-supply in other areas. This analysis does not
explain why, in the context of the low-demand scenario, some neighbourhoods become epicentres of social malaise and decline where
others nearby do not. A closer inspection of more localized factors
needs, therefore, to be made because not all areas in the low-demand
vicinities are affected equally.

Micro-Level Analysis

It is very striking in Lee and Murie's (1997) study of local communities
that deprivation operates at almost a micro level within individual
streets, even clusters of houses. Streets, literally round the corner, seem
to be much less problematic. Other studies have made the same observation – that the spiral of decline in some inner city neighbourhoods is
highly localised (Lowe, Keenan and Spencer, 1999). Given the underlying
loss of population, for the reasons discussed above, what accounts for
the spiral of decline in some inner city neighbourhoods and not others?
Is there a post-code lottery or is there an explanation at the micro
level for the breakdown of the social and economic vitality of some
communities?

One of the explanations concerns the appearance in particular
streets of abandoned housing which, if not boarded up in time, will be
vandalized. Once this happens, neighbouring houses come under
pressure and house prices plummet. Sometimes a whole street becomes
infected by a range of problems – corner shops close, people able to
leave move out while the going is good, drug abusers colonize the area
and petty criminals move in, unscrupulous private landlords desperate for income from their property manipulate the Housing Benefit
system. Economic and social life ebbs away with remarkable speed.

It is noticeable that neighbouring streets, quite literally round the corner, do not necessarily suffer these symptoms, at least to begin with, so that there is an element of *contagion*, which is partly geographically random.

Serial Movers and the Collapse of Stable Community

Where low demand is endemic in the structure of a local housing market there is often a large amount of vacant property, in both the public and private sectors, and it is relatively easy for households to move both within and between housing tenures. The existence of one or two abandoned houses create a kind of contagion, spreading out from the empty properties until clusters of dwellings or a whole street are affected. Keenan (1998) tracked over 700 moving households in Newcastle's West End, and found that they mostly moved very short distances and nearly half moved at least twice within a year. Very few (only 15 per cent) improved their housing situation as a result of the moves. Subsequent interviews discovered that the 'serial movers' were subject to multiple pressures, reporting high stress levels due to crime and vandalism. Often this was combined with mounting personal debt. For almost half the group there were disputes with neighbours or a perception that their neighbours were a problem in some way. Rather than being resigned to this situation these households – single parents, young childless couple, one-person households – tried by moving and drawing on support from relatives and friends to stay in the area but in the end were often forced to move out (Keenan, 1998).

These types of social process are probably at work in other stressed communities. Pawson concluded from his analysis of the increasing frequency of re-lets in council housing that this implied growing residential instability and a weakening of social cohesion (Pawson, 1999). He also found evidence that rapid movers were switching between housing tenures because it was relatively easy to find lets in either the public or privately rented sectors with contrary movements in due course (Pawson, 1998). 'Churning' was identified in the social rented sector by Burrows who also spoke of the increasing difficulties of sustaining stable communities (Burrows, 1997b).

Under the weight of these problems personal relationships can be affected perversely by the choices available to move, or even to occupy more than one house, possibly with different partners or possibly none. If people become unable to conduct stable, long-term relationships then the glue that sticks society together starts to weaken. This is a source and not a consequence of social exclusion because the lack of social cohesion and the withering away of the foundations of stable social life, often in the shell of poverty, in effect, detaches people and communities from the mainstream of society. Social exclusion is structured by this sort of social process and mechanics. It is important to hold together both the underlying or macro-level processes and the more localized, micro-level context.

Economic restructuring and demographic change are the main macro-level context. But why some neighbourhoods rather than others enter the spiral of decline is more intimately connected to local factors. As we have seen, the abandonment of even one or two houses in an area can trigger the chain of events which eventually, and with alarming speed, drains communities of their economic and social viability. The sociology of these neighbourhoods is complex and not yet fully understood. These streets contain a very large number of the most socially excluded of all our citizens and where the brunt of economic decline and restructuring, and of housing policy and housing market failure, are most acutely felt.

One of the most extreme forms of social exclusion which arises from similar sources as these is homelessness. Once again, structural causes are at work but in the end manifest themselves in the experience of individuals. The purpose of the rest of the chapter is to explain how structural and the individual connect in the homelessness issue. In this case there is a long conceptual underpinning to the treatment and characterization of homeless people. This takes us back to the agenda setting literature mentioned in the introduction to the chapter where, it will be recalled, words and language play a crucial role in shaping the nature of the problem and the policies that are designed to deal with it. So deeply embedded is the conceptualization of homelessness in English political and social culture that the first stage is to describe briefly this provenance and then to show how these political ideas helped construct the policy agenda.

Case Study 2: Homelessness

The concepts that surround the experience of homelessness and, to an extent, define it are some of the most deeply socially embedded ideas in the vocabulary of English social thought. This language has permeated beyond the specific issue of destitution and lack of stable and decent housing to inform a wide range of social attitudes and prejudices and so, in this case, such a legacy is more than usually important for interpreting current social policies, including housing but also shows that the idea of social exclusion is an age-old concept rooted in the national political culture. The section begins, therefore with a brief history of this conceptual heritage and then considers how best to define the notion of homelessness and, in the light of this, how it should be measured. Finally, there is a consideration of its contemporary scale (which builds on the methodology for measuring housing needs discussed in Chapter 4) and the policies used to address this issue. There are important connections to Chapter 4, because homelessness is the most extreme case of housing need. In addition, the material should be read in the light of the discussion of the concept of 'home' in Chapter 3. There it was shown that 'being at home', although not necessarily attached to a specific dwelling, is crucial to an individual's sense of well-being and is the basis on which the world beyond the front door can be faced with confidence. Being 'homeless' is a severe and extreme form of social exclusion.

The Long History of the Marginalization of Homeless People

What is most startling about the long history of the homelessness issue is the continuity of treatment afforded to the destitute, the most consistent feature of which has been the attempt to marginalize them from mainstream society. In practice, homelessness and the policies to deal with it operated originally through the Poor Laws. The Elizabethan Poor Law began in 1563 when church parishes were allowed to impose a tax, overseen by JPs and church vestry officials, to cater for the needs of their destitute and homeless families. Aid was in the form of domiciliary support, known as 'outdoor relief'. Nineteenth-century values permeated the Victorian Poor Laws (Poor Law Amendment Act 1834).

This legislation is one of the great moments of English social policy. It marks a fundamental turning point from the old, misguided system of half-hearted benevolence to a determination by the national state to rid society of the moral scourge of poverty by its ruthless subjugation. Its central purpose was to end outdoor relief and concentrate assistance through centrally organized workhouses. The idea of 'less eligibility' was designed to ensure that workhouse occupants were 'in no case so eligible as the conditions of persons of the lowest class subsisting on the fruits of their own labour'. Such conditions were bound to be deplorably poor and degrading because urban and rural wages were already very low. Indeed, as Chadwick, the first Secretary to the new Poor Law Commission acknowledged, 'The diet of the workhouse almost always exceeds that of the cottage' (quoted in Finer, 1952: 83). The power this system exerted over generations of the poor working class cannot be under-estimated. The ideas of 'deserving' and 'undeserving', of 'local connection', of 'less eligibility' created a specific parlance about homeless people, the destitute and unemployed, the frail elderly and the disabled. A special language of concepts evolved and became ingrained into the social discipline of English life. Indeed, it was not until the National Assistance Act 1948 that the Poor Law system was abolished, but even then many of the practices of social exclusion, stigmatization and outright punishment were not consigned to history. Under the 1948 system (Section 2(1)) National Assistance Boards were created with duties to provide reception centres for the unsettled. But other forms of homelessness fell to the responsibility of local welfare departments. Local *housing* authorities had no duties in relation to homelessness.

It was not until the Housing (Homeless Persons) Act 1977 that homelessness was officially recognized as a housing problem. For the first time homeless families, albeit narrowly defined categories and only under strictly defined circumstances, were given the right to permanent, secure accommodation provided by local authorities. Many Poor Law attitudes, endemic to the way in which homelessness was conceived were, however, not so easily eradicated. In essence, the system established a series of hurdles which applicants had to jump before the authorities would accept that they were owed a duty of provision. Over subsequent years, precise meanings were hammered out in the courts. What does it mean to be eligible as a homeless applicant? Is the applicant in 'priority need' and 'intentionally' homeless? Do they have a 'local connection'? Such concepts are very redolent of the Poor Law echoing down the centuries.

This system remained the essence of the treatment of homeless people despite the fact that the statutory duty to provide permanent accommodation was abolished by the Housing Act 1996 and was not fully restored by New Labour until the Homelessness Act 2002 created a significant change in the treatment of statutory homelessness. The homeless legislation was one of the very few housing policies (indeed, social policies of any sort) to remain unscathed through the course of the Thatcher and Major governments between 1979 and 1992. Several reviews of the legislation were made and at that time it was decided to leave it more or less untouched. The local authority duties were incorporated as Part III of the Housing Act 1985. Furthermore, the Children Act 1989 aimed to give protection to the young homeless under the age of 18. This duty was given to local authority social services departments and was not properly resourced, so that many authorities failed to deliver an adequate service (McClusky, 1994).

Part VII of the Housing Act 1996

The Major government targeted this legislation for reform, arguing that homelessness applicants were abusing the system by treating it as a 'fast track' into secure accommodation and was a way of jumping housing waiting lists. Evidence that single young women were deliberately becoming pregnant to 'queue jump' was refuted by Butler *et al.*, who also found that 60 per cent of statutorily homeless households were *already* registered on council waiting lists. It was simply that their situation worsened as they waited (Butler *et al.*, 1994). It was also claimed that many of those accepted as homeless were not literally without a roof over their heads. Actual 'rooflessness', so it was argued, was relatively uncommon and that the focus of attention should be on solving the problem of rough sleepers.

In Part VII of the Housing Act 1996 the duty to provide permanent accommodation was abolished and definitions changed. A new test of 'eligibility', to be defined by the Secretary of State, was introduced and it was deemed that if a local authority thought there was 'suitable alternative accommodation' available in the area they had no duty to provide. Even when the full duty was owed to the applicant, authorities had to provide only temporary accommodation (maximum of two years), in either hostels or specifically leased accommodation in the PRS. All social housing tenancies were to be allocated through a combined 'single housing register' so that there would be no separate access into this accommodation by homeless applicants. Homeless households, indeed, were to be specifically excluded from council housing, except by becoming eligible through the waiting list. The idea was to help the homeless temporarily while they found their feet, but not to owe them any duty to provide permanent secure accommodation.

Part VII of the 1996 Act was in essence a throwback to the Poor Law workhouse mentality, rekindled in the guise of hostels and temporary accommodation. It treated homelessness as a consequence of individual actions and set out to create a punitive system of deterrence. In practice, many local authorities circumvented Part VII by redefining their waiting lists so that high priority or a high number of points were allocated to homeless households who then, by default, went to the top of this list for housing. This is a classic case of the way in which policy delivery systems, through the influence of street-level bureaucrats (most of who supported the long-standing '1977 system'), can defeat the intentions of policy-makers. What happened under the New Labour government is discussed below.

The next section discusses the definition of 'homelessness', as it is apparent that the new policy direction has responded to the accumulated evidence about the nature and causes of homelessness in the 1980s and 1990s. There is in the first instance some dispute over what actually constitutes 'homelessness', and which types of households are eligible for help.

Definitions of 'Homelessness'

As seen above, only certain categories of people in 'priority need' were accepted as homeless, notwithstanding that other types of people, notably single people, were in equal need. This division clearly echoed the punitive Poor Law tradition of deserving and undeserving with its emphasis on individual causality. People fell into homelessness owing to their feckless character, drunkenness or whatever. The idea that the underlying structural causes – that this was in large measure, although not exclusively so, a housing problem – was only reluctantly conceded and even now is not wholeheartedly accepted despite the plethora of evidence (see Fitzpatrick, Kemp and Klinker, 2000, for an overview of research on single homelessness).

The statutory definition is a useful starting point because it tells us as much about who is not (officially) homeless as about who is homeless. The non-statutory homeless, as we will see, is potentially a very large group of households.

The Homelessness Continuum

One of the most useful ways of understanding homelessness is to consider it as a continuum from outright literal 'rooflessness' to those arguably in 'housing need' rather than actually homeless. Robson and Poustie built on an earlier categorization (Watchman and Robson, 1983) and identified five main categories (Robson and Poustie, 1996):

- First, at the most extreme end of the spectrum are the *rough sleepers* and people such as asylum seekers who are quite literally roofless.
- Second, people *without access to a home* (so called 'houselessness') because they are living temporarily in hostels, night shelters/ refuges. Also included here are families or couples who are living in B&B accommodation awaiting transfer to suitable permanent housing.
- Third, are people *living insecurely* with friends and relatives, and including tenants with notices to quit.
- Fourth, households living in *'intolerable' housing conditions*, which might be over-crowded or property in need of repair and unsuitable for habitation. This category also includes people living with violent partners or in other unsafe situations.
- Finally, are all those households who are *sharing accommodation on a long-term basis*, made up mostly of 'concealed' households many of whom cannot afford to buy separate accommodation of their own. This group incorporates all those in the housing backlog, discussed in the Chapter 4.

Whether households sharing accommodation really are homeless is perhaps questionable, as Pleace has argued: 'Quite simply, being poorly housed is one thing, having nowhere at all to live is something else' (Pleace, 1997: 8). There clearly is a grey area between those described in Chapter 4 as in 'housing need' and people who are literally roofless or living involuntarily in abusive relationships, etc. The distinction is not always clear. Recent studies in which young people were interviewed found that they tended to emphasize security and permanence more than the physical condition of the property (Fitzpatrick, 2001).

Single Homelessness

Among the non-statutory homeless easily the largest group are the single homeless who fall outside the terms of all the legislation if they are not 'vulnerable' in some way. This group of people has been the focus of considerable concern because on the face of it their circumstances are often as problematic and diverse as those of the statutory homeless groups. The single homeless are mainly men and have been catered for through a variety of voluntary and local authority provision – hostels and day centres. Organizations like CHAR (the Campaign for the Homeless and Roofless) have shown that the single homeless frequently need care and support services. The commonly held notion that the single homeless were a homogeneous group has been shown to be very wide of the mark. The study by Kemp and his colleagues (1997), for example, conducted in 1990, showed significant differences between those sleeping in hostels and night shelters on a long-term basis and those who slept rough. This study also showed that the single homeless suffered from a variety of disadvantages; most were long-term unemployed, had very poor health, had often experienced life in children's homes, borstals and prisons, and suffered from a high incidence of drug and alcohol abuse. The study concluded that tackling single homelessness was not just a housing question but required outreach and resettlement support such as the Rough Sleepers Initiative (RSI) began to supply (Kemp, 1997).

One classification makes a specific recognition of the significance of single homelessness by dividing the homeless into three categories: statutorily homeless, single homeless and rough sleepers. They go on to warn of the danger of including 'hidden homelessness' in the classification, 'since seemingly *any* form of housing need such as a teenager wanting a place of their own can fall within its definitions' (Pleace, Burrows and Quilgars, 1997: 8).

Homelessness can thus be thought of in a number of different ways – as a subjective experience through to a tightly defined statutory definition, quite often adjudicated in case law. Is a pregnant woman living in a beach hut homeless? She was found to be so but only after her local authority tested her circumstances in the courts. As Pleace argued, it is important to clarify definitions in order not to detract attention from those who are 'narrowly' homeless, particularly rough sleepers (Pleace, 1997). Concealed households and others not satisfactorily housed in independent accommodation should more properly be thought of as part of the backlog arising from the continued deficiency of dwellings to households. The former is a more micro-level issue of locally targeted resources – night shelters, resettlement units and move-on accommodation – and the operation of the statutory system. The latter are part of the wider issues concerning housing supply and its affordability. Both of them must be read in the light of wider analyses about economic restructuring and the fragmentation of the unitary state. The danger in making this distinction is that structural causes of homelessness become subsumed in individualistic explanations. The need, however, for some form of classification which incorporates a large element of 'bottom up' experience is important to inform the policy process. There are no discrete categories and a considerable degree of overlap between them. Following the 'garbage can' explanations for the agenda setting process (see Chapter 1) homelessness may be thought of as a case in which available or politically and socially acceptable *solutions* have to a large extent defined the nature of the problem.

The Measurement of Homelessness

Concealed Households

It follows from the discussion of definitions that the measurement of homelessness is necessarily imprecise. However, some reasonable measures are important for informing policy-makers of the current scale of the problem, changes over time and the impact of past policies (evaluation).

The numbers concerned with concealed and potential households was discussed in Chapter 4. Arguably most such households are not homeless but are part of the population most vulnerable to it and who have not yet achieved a 'decent' home. It will be recalled that this deficiency or backlog of dwellings to households represent a problem of supply in the market – or, more likely, unmet need from those unable to afford market solutions. The figure was put very roughly at some 500,000 households but grows every year to the extent that new building, especially in the social housing sector, falls short of demand. As we saw, this is also partly an issue of socially determined standards – for example, at what point are young people entitled to accommodation separate from the parental home? The idea of *potential households* is important in housing needs evaluation.

The Prevalence of Homelessness in Society

One of the most useful ways of looking at the prevalence of homelessness is by taking a 'bottom up' approach and asking a sample of the population whether they have been homeless. A Scottish and an English survey provided the opportunity for just such an open-ended expression of need. The Scottish Survey of Consumer Preference showed that 5 per cent of respondents said that they had been homeless at some time during the previous ten years (Pieda, 1996), although less than 1 per cent had ever experienced rough sleeping. The survey found that 70 per cent of those saying they had been homeless had stayed with friends or relatives while trying to find a solution, suggesting a high degree of concealment. Only 30 per cent had been involved in more visible homelessness, such as rough sleeping or staying in a night shelter. The study also found that 97 per cent had been homeless for less than twelve months. This is an important finding, because it shows that the vast majority had not experienced long-term homelessness.

The 1994/5 *Survey of English Housing* (SEH) asked a sample of 20,000 people in England whether they had been homeless in the previous ten years, and whether they had approached and been accepted by a local council as homeless. In the English study, the result was that 4.3 per cent said they had been homeless, 75 per cent said they had approached their local council for help and just over 50 per cent said they had been accepted as homeless by a local authority under the statutory system (DoE, 1995). This is also an important finding because it shows that a large proportion of those who described themselves as homeless were not helped by the statutory bodies (Burrows, 1997a). Both the Scottish and the English studies showed that, spread over a ten-year period, *long-term* homelessness was experienced by a tiny minority of people. Nevertheless, an experience of homelessness, albeit for a matter of months in most cases, was quite widespread in the population and that to rely on the figures of the statutory homeless as a measure of the problem is seriously to under-count it. This accords with a research review conducted by Greve in the late 1980s that, 'large numbers of people – especially single homeless persons – are excluded from the statistics' (Greve, 1991: 12). It is further evidence that a large part of the problem of homelessness is hidden, a similar number to those households statutorily re-housed.

Official Homelessness Numbers

The official statistics on homelessness exist in two sets: the returns made by local authorities in fulfilment of their duties under the legislation and counts of rough sleeper made by voluntary agencies (and a highly inaccurate measure made by enumerators during the 1991 Census). Homelessness is the most extreme end of the housing needs spectrum and it will be recalled from Chapter 4 that, as with any form of housing need, it should be considered both as a 'stock' and a 'flow'. Stock figures provide an important fix on how many homeless households were accepted by the local authorities at a particular point in time, typically measured over a year but more important is to estimate the *flow* of those moving into and out of homelessness over the period. The SEH's 4.3 per cent saying they were homeless were not homeless all at the same time but at various times during the ten years before 1994 and, as we saw, typically for less than twelve months. The idea of the flow of needs is critical to designing policy responses.

Clearly the passage of the 1977 legislation brought the problem of homeless families to the surface, and acceptances grew rapidly. Figure 5.2 shows the annual stock of acceptances from 1977 through to 1999. After 1977 acceptances grew rapidly, not only in London but elsewhere in the country, so that by the 1990s over 80 per cent of homelessness acceptances recorded by local authorities were outside London and grew at a faster rate in the north than the south. Acceptances in England grew rapidly to 145,800 in 1990, and peaked in 1991 at 151,720.

The vast majority of these households were families with children, and although the data was not published the number of people affected would be, on a conservative estimate, three times as many. It can be estimated, for example, in 1991 statutory homelessness in England involved over 400,000 individuals (and in the UK as a whole in excess of 500,000). Furthermore, not all applicants were housed. Many more who were driven to seek local authority assistance were deemed ineligible. For example, in the financial year 1997/8 102,580 households were accepted as unintentionally homeless and in priority need

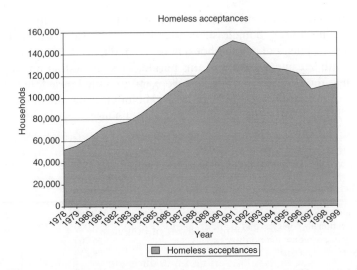

Figure 5.2 **Number of statutorily homeless households, 1978–99**
Sources: National Audit Office (1978–86) and DTLR (1986–1999)

(and re-housed) but a further 56,700 were classified as homeless but not in priority need, and 78,850 applicants were deemed not homeless (Table 5.3).

Thus of 244,130 households that presented themselves for consideration as homeless only 42 per cent were entitled to be re-housed. The total number of people involved in this process whether re-housed or not is equivalent to the whole population of a city the size of Leeds! This data accords with the SEH finding of a widespread prevalence of homelessness with the majority applying for help from local authorities.

It should be recalled that despite the large numbers involved the annual flow of homeless households through the statutory system was in most cases fairly rapid. Relatively few fell into long-term homelessness. But the numbers of people touched by an experience of homelessness, as can be seen, is very considerable indeed and excludes those living in concealed situations and many hundreds of thousands who live on the margins of acceptable housing standards in over-crowded and unsatisfactory conditions.

Allocations to homeless households fell to only 14 per cent of local authority lettings in 1998/9 from a peak of 35 per cent in 1992/3. Regional variations in this pattern hold important clues to the explanation of the decline in statutory homelessness after 1992. As we saw earlier, in the chapter surpluses of council housing in the midlands and especially in the north became a feature of this period. This meant that applicants through the ordinary waiting lists were more easily housed, enabling families in housing stress to be re-housed before they became homeless. Equally important is the fact of the much lower house prices in the owner

Table 5.3   **Decisions taken on homeless applications, 1997–8**

Households found to be	Number	(%)
Unintentionally homeless and in priority need	103,580	42
Intentionally homeless and in priority need	5,000	2
Homeless but not in priority need	56,700	23
Not homeless	78,850	32
Total decisions	**244,130**	**100**

Source: DETR (1998).

occupied market in these areas compared to the south of England, making home ownership more affordable at lower income levels (see Chapter 7). The recovery of the housing market from the long period of slump also had the effect of reducing the number of people presenting to local authorities due to mortgage arrears and repossession. This cause of homelessness more than halved from 12 per cent of reasons for homelessness in 1991 to 5 per cent in 1999.

Counting Rough Sleepers

The RSI was launched in London in 1990 during the Major government. The aim was to fund street-level projects, new hostel places and resettlement services, and to reduce the numbers of people sleeping outdoors. After the election of the first Blair government in 1997 and building on research conducted by the SEU, a further development, in July 1998, was the creation of the Rough Sleepers Unit (RSU) within the DETR to assume control at national level of the programme to tackling rough sleeping. Contact and Assessment Teams (CATs) were established in London and then in other cities to count, monitor and work intensively with rough sleepers. Rough sleeping in central London has been monitored regularly by the Homeless Network.

It is impossible to make an accurate count of rough sleepers because there is bound to be a large flow of people newly arriving in London or other cities and others moving on into hostels or night shelters. Rough sleepers and the occupants of night shelters are quite likely to be the same people, so that counts of the stock of rough sleepers are inevitably inaccurate. However, the visibility of it and the extremity of the problem necessitate some attempt at quantification. Enumerators of the 1991 Census counted 2,703 rough sleepers on Census day, including 1,275 (47 per cent of the total) in Greater London. However, this is certainly an under-count because of the poor methodology employed. For example, no rough sleepers were found in Britain's second biggest city, Birmingham, despite local knowledge of a considerable problem (Fitzpatrick, Kemp and Klinker, 2000: 15). The Homeless Network found 367 cases in May 1997 in the London CAT areas, 272 in 1998 and 302 in 1999 (Homeless Network, 1997). These figures are considerably lower than in the early 1990s and suggest that the RSI has had a significant impact in reducing the incidence of street sleeping in the capital city.

The DETR also started a regular count of rough sleepers and suggested that the main problem area was still central London, based around the three central London CATs. Their measure of the flow of new rough sleepers in central London showed that there were 1,900 new cases during the 1996/7, an average flow of five new arrivals each day (DETR, 1999c). This means that in total at some stage during 1996/7 about 2,600 people slept rough in inner London, of whom the 1,900 were new to street homelessness. A national (England) figure for a single night in June 1998 was 1,850, 34 per cent in Greater London, mostly counted in the inner London boroughs (DETR, 1999c). Table 5.4 shows the list of authorities who counted twenty or more rough sleepers during June 1998.

Counts of rough sleepers and single people staying in night shelters, direct access hostels, women's refuges, and other forms of provision are not compatible with each other because it cannot be known for sure which are stock and which are flow figures or the extent to which the data might double count a rough sleeper who opts to stay for a few

Table 5.4   **Local authorities in England counting twenty or more rough sleepers, 2000**

London boroughs	Street count	Other areas	Street count
Westminster	237	Birmingham	56
Camden	59	Brighton	44
City of London	41	Bournemouth	44
Tower Hamlets	31	Bristol	42
Brent	29	Oxford	39
Croydon	25	Manchester	31
Ealing	24	Cambridge	30
Kensington/Chelsea	23	Exeter	27
Lambeth	20	Southampton	22
Hounslow	20	Portsmouth	21
		Leicester	20
		Worcester	20
		Stoke on Trent	20

Source: Fitzpatrick, Kemp and Klinker (2000: 16).

nights in a winter shelter. Pleace and Quilgars estimate that in the last quarter of 1995 there were 15,000 people living in hostels and 11,000 in squats in London (Pleace and Quilgars, 1996). On this basis, it is reasonable to assume that the scale of single homelessness in the county as a whole, 'can probably be counted in the tens of thousands' (Pleace, Burrows and Quilgars, 1997: 11). A more recent count of bed spaces in hostels in London found over 450 hostels providing some 19,600 bed spaces (DETR, 2000b).

The research data show that it is very difficult to generalize about who these people are or why they have become homeless. Anderson, Kemp and Quilgars showed that compared to a 1972 study of common lodging houses and hostels 91 per cent were men compared with their 1991 study of hostels and B&B accommodation, when the figure was 77 per cent. In almost all homelessness settings it was apparent that women and young people were a much higher proportion in the 1990s than previously. The women staying in the hostels and B&Bs tended to be much younger on average than their male counterparts. Anderson, Kemp and Quilgars found that the majority of homeless single people were middle aged: 75 per cent of rough sleepers and 54 per cent of hostel dwellers were aged 25–59. Overall, the most striking change from the earlier studies was the increase in the number of young single homeless people and the increasing proportion of women (Anderson, Kemp and Quilgars, 1993). A study by Warnes and Crane of the profile of single homeless people in London confirmed the evidence of the 1991 study (Warnes and Crane, 2000). They found that about 20 per cent of the sample of rough sleepers and people in hostels were women, although rather strikingly it was found that women were more numerous than men among *teenage* rough sleepers and hostel dwellers.

These studies showed that there are significant differences between people living on the streets compared to those in hostels. Some hostels dwellers were long-term residents and had never slept rough and vica versa, some people sleep outside in the summer and inside in the winter, some in both settings are experiencing homelessness for the first time, some are 'old hands'. Warnes and Crane showed that the difference found in the 1991 study between the profiles of rough sleepers and hostel and B&B dwellers persisted through the 1990s, suggesting that the demographic characteristics of the single homeless has remained more or less unchanged. All these studies indicated that there is no stereotypical homeless person, as sometimes represented in the mass media (Kemp, 1997: 85), and this was confirmed by the evidence on the causes of homelessness which now is much better understood as a result of the recent research effort.

Causes of Homelessness

It will be apparent that there are several different ways of looking at the nature of homelessness and it is equally the case that the causes of homelessness cannot easily be ascribed to one single factor. It is clear that shortages of affordable housing and the growing backlog of social housing provision remains fertile ground in which homelessness occurs. The incidence, at least of 'official' homelessness, does appear to be sensitive to some degree to the house price cycle and north–south disparities in prices (affordability in the market) and the availability of social housing re-lets, which are also subject to considerable regional variations. The idea that, as Greve asserts, 'The principal cause of homelessness is a critical shortage of affordable rental housing' (Greve, 1991: 18) requires two significant qualifications. First, it cannot be only an issue of shortages of rental housing, but its quality and location. Homelessness remains a problem even in the northern cities where there is evidence of low demand and surplus housing in both the public and private sectors. Secondly, the interaction between structural causes and individual risk factors is more complex than simply providing more housing and is much more clearly understood as a result of the huge research effort made during the last decade. It is now possible to see more clearly the relationship between the structural context and the immediate individual causes of homelessness.

The main structural factors identified in the research studies are labour market changes – especially the loss of manufacturing and the growth of part-time working – rising levels of poverty in the 1980s, and increasing quantity of less stable forms of household structure. The way in which these broad factors create a propensity towards homelessness among particular individuals is less clear but the events and circumstances that are the immediate context of homelessness is now well documented. These include unemployment, sexual or physical abuse, relationship breakdown, people with a background in local authority care, ex-offenders, an experience of army life, substance abuse, school exclusion and a record of physical and/or mental ill-health. What Greve called the 'immediate reasons' (Greve, 1991: 21) and more recently Fitzpatrick and Klinker called the 'individual risk factors' (Fitzpatrick and Klinker, 2000), which trigger the actual incident can be quite accurately portrayed as: 'leaving the parental home after arguments; marital or relationship breakdown; eviction; widowhood; discharge from the armed forces; leaving care; leaving prison; and a sharp deterioration in mental health or an increase in alcohol or drug abuse' (Fitzpatrick and Klinker, 2000: 2). It is known that rough sleeping often starts at an early age. DETR research found that almost half those interviewed had slept rough after leaving their parent's home or care (DETR, 1999c: 7).

The immediate causes of homelessness are implicit in many of the definitions above. Local authority returns to the DETR provide quite detailed knowledge of the immediate cause of homelessness. These have changed considerably over the post-war decades. In the 1960s a high proportion of reported homelessness arose from the loss of privately rented accommodation, largely accounted for by the easing of security in the Rent Act 1957 (Greve, 1964). Indeed as the rental sectors have declined so rent arrears has given way to problems with mortgage payments. By far the largest change in the LA figures during the 1990s was the increasing incidence of domestic disputes and relationship breakdown, reflecting the social trend of increasing rates of divorce and cohabitation.

New Labour and Homelessness

'Rough sleepers are at the sharp end of social exclusion ... It is time to solve it' declared the Prime Minister in his foreword to the SEU report on street homelessness (SEU, 1998). The establishment of the SEU was, as we have seen, one of the Blair government's first initiatives, with tackling the problem of rough sleepers as a high priority and the aim of reducing it by two-thirds by 2002. The CATs established in central London in 1990 were multi-disciplinary teams runs by the voluntary sector but with statutory support and involvement (for example, with the assistance of mental health specialists). New CATs were established in four other London boroughs based around day-care centres and similar multi-disciplinary teams have been set up in the other major cities, a total of thirty-six areas across the country. A RSU was established in April 1999, to assume overall national control of the rough sleeping projects and funding. The aim was to target specialist help to the most vulnerable people, many of whom are extremely ill or addicted to drugs or alcohol. In addition to the original three central London CATs new CATs were established in four other London boroughs and similar projects elsewhere round the country. In addition to the new hostel spaces the RSU is working towards providing 4,500 permanent move-on homes in London, linked to teams of support workers. New facilities for particularly vulnerable care leavers (Safe Stop) and for long-term, elderly rough sleepers (Nightcentre) have also been set up (DETR, 2000b). There can be little doubt that these initiatives have reduced the scale of rough sleeping, although not nearly to Prime Minister Tony Blair's aim of zero. Even the more realistic target of reducing its visibility by two-thirds by 2002 was not achieved despite the large scale of resources targeted at the problem.

Statutory Homelessness under the Homelessness Act 2002

The Homelessness Act 2002 marks a major change of direction in the treatment of homeless households by abolishing and heavily amending various sections of the Housing Act 1996 and the addition of a number of new provisions. The idea is that statutorily homeless households are to be provided with a guarantee of suitable accommodation in the short term until they are able to find a 'settled' position in any part of the rental sector, public or private, with no time limit on the support they will be given by the local housing authority. Local authorities have a new duty to review homelessness in their area and at least every five years publish a homelessness strategy based on the results of the review.

Although not part of new legislation the government announced its intention to add to the list of groups considered to be in priority need. Groups being added are homeless 16- and 17-years-olds, care leavers aged 18–21, people considered vulnerable as a result of fleeing domestic violence or harassment, and people vulnerable as a result of leaving an institutional background (such as those leaving care, the armed forces or prison). The Secretary of State will make an Order under the 1996 Act (and, it should be added, could do so at any time under existing law), extending the groups considered to be in priority need. This is a clear response to the research community's findings on those most vulnerable to homelessness, as shown earlier in the chapter.

The duties which local authorities have under the Homelessness Act are to ensure that all unintentionally homeless people who fall in the priority need categories have somewhere suitable to live while they look for a long-term, 'settled' solution. This is not quite the same as the 'old' duty under the 1977 (1985) system to provide 'permanent' accommodation in council housing, but means in effect that the duty on the housing authority remains until a solution that is 'not precarious' is found. Thus the duty would come to an end if the applicant accepted an assured shorthold tenancy (for a fixed term) with a private landlord or a housing association (RSL) which was approved by the authority. A new power is introduced to give authorities a flexible option to assist non-priority homeless households, principally by offering them secure accommodation from their own stock if they have scope to do so. Various features of Part VII of the 1996 Act are as a result abolished in the Homelessness Act, notably the removal of the two-year time limit (Clause 21) on the main duty towards homeless households, and the abolition of an authority's powers not to assist directly if they consider 'other suitable accommodation' is available in their area. The idea that an authority's duty could be as little as advice and assistance only is scrapped.

In carrying out these duties the Homelessness Act establishes a more inter-agency approach to the prevention of homelessness and re-housing when needed. The Secretary of State established a new Homelessness Directorate comprising the Bed and Breakfast Unit (then under the auspices of the Government Office for London), the RSU and a new unit to assist local authorities in tackling homelessness. Housing and social services departments are required to work together and to work closely with the voluntary sector. The DTLR published a lengthy document *Homelessness Strategies – A Good Practice Handbook* to provide a framework for inter-agency working and a ministerial committee, initially chaired by Lord Falconer, was also set up to oversee the implementation of the new system.

Lettings Policy

The new approach needs to be read, however, in the context of the government's intention to develop a more choice-based system of allocating social housing because the homeless are incorporated into a system giving them 'reasonable preference', alongside a range of other vulnerable groups of people. A key aim of the Homelessness Act, following the plans outlined in the Green Paper, is to provide greater choice for applicants, including the statutorily homeless, in the type of property they are able to access. The Green Paper spoke of a more customer centred lettings system giving applicants and existing tenants who want to move greater flexibility in choosing a house that suits them, including being able to move outside the local authority area and to move more easily between council housing and RSL property.

Thus the Homelessness Act allows authorities not to have a housing register ('waiting list') but instead to have a clear and integrated mechanism for allocation depending on their circumstances. People with particular needs to move to an area will be given 'reasonable preference' although 'local connections' will be taken into account. Reasonable preference must also be given to the homeless, those living in unsatisfactory housing conditions, people with a need to move on medical grounds and people who need to move 'to avoid hardship'. The idea of 'reasonable preference' thus moves to the centre of the allocation system and local authorities are asked to design allocation systems that offer greater choice to those in greatest need.

There is, however, a sting in the tail because Section 167 of the 1996 Act has been heavily amended by the Homelessness Act so that certain people do not necessarily have any preference when an authority considers they have been guilty of unacceptable behaviour, even in the past, if it makes them unsuitable to be a tenant of *their* authority. The behaviour in question is that which if the person had been a secure tenant would have entitled the Authority to seek a possession order, for example, non-payment of rent, anti-social nuisance behaviour, obtaining a tenancy by fraud, or maltreating a property. This means that in

deciding whether a person is considered to have 'reasonable preference' there is a highly judgemental investigation into the current
circumstances and the *past* behaviour of the applicant *or* a member of
their household.

Local authorities will have a considerable influence over the type and
quality of housing made available to homeless people, and so the new
system offers choice, but *within a strong regulatory system*. New Labour's
somewhat puritanical, judgemental attitude is very near the surface of
the Homelessness Act and without doubt opens up a fertile seam of
new case law. The heavily amended Section 167 of the 1996 Act is
a potential stumbling block. Nevertheless, the new duties and provisions in the Homelessness Act 2002 and the amended Housing Act
1996 combined with the regulations and the promise of bringing in
vulnerable single people and others (by ministerial Order) adds up to a
significant advance on the 'Poor Law' treatment of homeless people,
although there is still a strong whiff of 'deserving' and 'undeserving' at
the heart of the new legislation.

Conclusion

The first part of the chapter outlined ideas about the origins of the
notion of 'social exclusion' and a note of caution was introduced both in
imagining that 'social exclusion' is somehow a new concept (which it is
not) and the danger that its uncritical use can obscure more than it
illuminates. As Marsh and Mullins suggested: 'Arguably it is used
rather indiscriminately to stand in place of a range of existing social
scientific concepts...such that it has brought less precision to debates'
(Marsh and Mullins, 1998: 755). The point is that while the concept has
undoubtedly refreshed some stale debates about the causes of social
problems, in itself it does not necessarily advance thinking or contribute
anything new. Its main focus is on structural issues which underlie
poverty but, as the case of homelessness shows, the relationship between
structures, agents and individuals is not easily expressed in a phrase
such as 'social exclusion'.

In more general terms, the case of 'housing' demonstrates how
exclusionary processes operate against people in particular places
and types of community. The low-demand Case-Study 1 shows

precisely how structural and local issues interact. Lack of employment and the associated decline in population in areas of long-established erstwhile core manufacturing, with deeply rooted cultural traditions, have created communities devoid and drained of economic and social vitality.

Three points summarize the relationship between housing and social exclusion:

- First, lack of income simply excludes sections of the society from the range of housing choices enjoyed by the majority of the population. People dependent on social housing provision also suffer uncertainties and additional risks caused by landlords and housing managers who 'gatekeep' their access.
- Second, a particular property (and/or where it is located) can be a source of social exclusion. It is well known that damp and insufficiently heated housing causes ill-health, children living in over-crowded houses do less well at school, those living in poor neighbourhoods suffer many anxieties, living in fear of crime, abuse or simply a deterioration in services. As Lee and Murie argue, social exclusion happens not just as a result of being deprived of housing (homelessness) but also *through* living in particular dwellings or particular neighbourhoods (Lee and Murie, 1997).
- Third, and perhaps the main lesson drawn from the low-demand Case-Study 1, is the way in which under certain circumstances normal housing market behaviour breaks down, rental property becomes unlettable and inside these communities unorthodox moving behaviour becomes endemic. Under the weight of these problems normal social relationships break down, and the paradoxical ability to move quite freely round a low-demand area leads to a range of unconventional and highly unstable relationships, so that partnerships form and break easily, relationships between family members and friends become strained and the social bonds that bind stable communities together begin to melt. The ability to conduct long-term, stable relationships becomes much more difficult under these circumstances. Social and personal trauma goes hand in hand. Case Study 2 shows how the structural and the personal are closely connected.

FURTHER READING

Anderson, I. and Sims, D. (2000) *Social Exclusion and Housing: Contexts and Challenges*, Coventry, Chartered Institute of Housing.

Burrows, R., Pleace, N and Quilgars, D. (eds) (1997) *Homelessness and Social Policy*, London, Routledge.

DETR (2000c) *Coming in from the Cold: Progress Report on the Government's Strategy on Rough Sleeping (Summer 2000)*, London, Stationery Office.

Fitzpatrick, S., Kemp, P. and Klinker, S. (2000) *Single Homelessness: An Overview of Research in Britain*, Bristol, Policy Press.

For government statistics and links to organizations dealing with homeless people, including the RSI visit: www.odpm.gov.uk

See also the papers by Bramley, Keenan, Lowe, Pawson, Spencer and Webster, in S. Lowe, P. Keenan and S. Spencer (eds) (1998) *Housing Abandonment in Britain: Studies in the Causes and Effects of Low Demand Housing*, York, Centre for Housing Policy, University of York.

6

Tenure Re-Structuring

CHAPTER AIMS

- To explain how Britain became a home owning society during the twentieth century
- To use an historical institutionalist approach to understanding the progress of policy change
- To point to the critical moments in the development of housing policy
- To account for the impact of the two world wars on the provision of housing
- To explain the reasoning behind the deep residualization of rental housing in the last few decades of the twentieth century.

Introduction

Britain underwent a dramatic restructuring of its housing tenure pattern during the course of the twentieth century. Why this should be the case requires explanation. Its significance is not only in the transformation of property rights and financial gains and losses in the housing stock but also to wider society. As Kemeny has shown, different configurations of housing tenure impact on urban form and welfare state development. 'Home owning societies', for example, are more likely to have private insurance-based, workfare forms of welfare provision (Kemeny, 1981). The scale of tenure restructuring in Britain over the twentieth century should make us vigilant for evidence of these wider issues. Looked at in this way 'housing' is not simply an accumulated stock of dwellings but is also a source, or at least a catalyst, to social change. It is something of a paradox that such an immovable entity as a stock of dwellings could be the focal point of dynamic social change. The explanation and development of this issue is discussed in detail in Chapter 10.

Here we are concerned with why Britain transformed during the course of the twentieth century from a nation of private renters to a nation of homeowners. It was a quiet revolution not experienced to the same extent by other European nations or any of the comparable industrial-ized countries and which had its antecedents, as we saw in Chapter 3, in the invention of a distinctive domestic culture in the Victorian era. It was noted that this model of respectability and female centred domes-ticity was transferred to the English-speaking 'New World(s)' and became one of the foundations of the home owning family of nations. The para-dox in this was that Britain itself was left in a catch-up situation as it progressively converted to owner occupation during the twentieth century.

The core questions concerning the process of tenure re-structuring are:

- Why did the country become by the end of the twentieth century a nation of owner-occupiers?
- Why did Britain, unlike the other nations in the home owning cluster, develop such a large state rental sector that was largely owned and managed by local councils?
- What, therefore, happened to classical nineteenth-century private landlordism that it ended the twentieth century at barely 10 per cent of households and playing a very different social role?

The chapter is not, and could not be a detailed 'history' but is intended to point to key moments and underlying causes of change. As has been argued at several points in the book the explanation is based on a meso-level or middle-range of social theory (Merton, 1957). The aim is to dis-cern the pattern of events and social forces that combined to shape what happened. To this end, the chapter draws on a range of ideas in the policy analysis literature, notably the distinctive body of literature within the institutionalist approach referred to as 'historical institution-alism' (Table 6.1).

Table 6.1   **Key reading on the history of housing**

There is no shortage of excellent reading material dealing with 'the history of housing' in Britain, especially the earlier years of the century. Students wishing to dig deeper into this fascinating story are referred to the following texts:

- **Bowley (1945)** *Housing and the State 1919–1944* The eye-witness account of a leading left-wing economist written in the aftermath of the Second World War, an invaluable source.
- **Gauldie** *Cruel Habitations (1974)* A beautifully written and sensitive account of housing during and after the Industrial Revolution, including an authoritative view of the 1890 legislation and the events surrounding it.
- **Merrett (1979)** *State Housing in Britain* A classic account of the development of council housing written by a left-wing academic and coloured by this perspective. But a scholarly account and the source of some key interpretations, some now disputed.
- **Burnett (1986)** *A Social History of Housing* A classic account of the relationship between housing and society, focusing on architecture, the evolution of housing standards and the social impact of housing change.
- **Holmans (1987)** *Housing Policy in Britain* An awesomely detailed account of British housing in the twentieth century, containing many key statistics, its focus is on the unfolding balance between households and dwellings. Not for the faint-hearted but above all others the book that rewards those prepared to grapple both with its attention to detail and the big picture.
- **Lowe and Hughes (1991)** *A New Century of Social Housing* A collection of accessible, short chapters by many of the leading scholars, written as a retrospect to the century of housing policy that followed the 1890 Housing of the Working Classes Act. A good book from which to get a 'quick fix' on the key topics of twentieth-century housing.
- **Ravetz (2001)** *Council Housing and Culture: The History of a Social Experiment* A marvellous, plainly written account focusing on the influence of the garden suburb ideals on the pattern of council housing over the course of the twentieth century. It deals with topics not usually discussed in such detail such as housing management, the influence of council housing on patterning working class life and the utopian roots of council housing. Written with a delightful sense of personal commitment to the subject by one of the most authoritative historians and writers from an architectural/planning perspective.

Historical Institutionalism

The policy analysis literature is replete with ideas about how policy change occurs. It was shown earlier in the book there is a fundamental division between those analysts who focus on rationality and those who emphasize the incremental, and 'muddling through' nature of the policy process. The most useful conceptual basis for understanding tenure restructuring in Britain can be found in the new institutional literature.

As we saw in Chapter 1 it is possible to discern a number of quite distinct institutionalist positions, although they all begin from the assumption that the structure of a society's political institutions matter greatly in how the decision-making process operates (see also Chapter 10). The nature of the electoral process, the relations between different tiers of government, how interest groups are accounted for, as well as wider social influences such as the class structure of a society and its core norms and values, are all components of the manner in which social change occurs.

The use of historical institutionalism is in linking between approaches to change that emphasize the state and those that emphasize social forces. It draws from both classical pluralist ideas – on the role of interest groups and coalitions but also from the more critical influence of neo-marxism, which shows that class conflict can occur around issues that are *not* centred on the workplace (such as urban politics, environmental issues, etc.). One of the aims of historical institutionalism is to discern what causes differences between nations, families of nations or welfare state 'regimes'. Hall and Taylor pay particular attention to the unintended consequences of strategic action, the uneven distribution of power between social groups and interests and on the 'path dependency' of institutional change (Hall and Taylor, 1996).

Path dependency is a useful conceptual tool in the context of an account of change in British housing policy because it shows how differences between societies become ingrained in the political culture. It would be logical to suppose that all comparable societies would broadly behave in the same way, which patently they do not. It is by examining key moments and junctures in the historical narrative that 'paths' are established that point to and limit future choices. The decision, for example, to provide subsidies to British local authorities to build 'council houses' was a very different solution to the similar problem faced in most industrialized European nations early in the twentieth century, of how to provide housing for workers. It was a decision built from within an existing set of constraints and alignments of social forces.

Historical institutionalism is well suited to an analysis of change over time, as here in the explanation of the restructuring of British housing tenure during the course of the twentieth century. What follows is a narrative account intended to portray only the main lines of development and the key moments and junctures when new forms of tenure structure were laid down. The idea of 'critical junctures' is an important development inside this approach, broadly dividing history into normal periods and critical junctures, or turning-point moments when significant institutional change occurs. These moments are often found in periods of crisis – or, as in this case, arise from marginal advantages enjoyed by one solution or policy direction over another such that a path dependency is set up (Hall and Taylor, 1996). Crises offer new opportunities for change and the possibility of new ideas being embedded in the institutional structure. The idea of 'punctuated equilibrium' usefully suggests that periods of rapid change and crisis are then followed by a time of consolidation (Steinmo, Thelen and Longstreth (eds.), 1992).

The story of the evolution of British housing has a number of critical moments following long gestation periods. The narrative begins with an explanation of how 'housing' came to be a distinct strand of public policy towards the end of the nineteenth century and follows through until the period of governments lead by Margaret Thatcher, a time when housing policy reached a major juncture. The narrative is divided into nine sections:

- The origins of housing 'policy' from within Victorian public health legislation
- The reasons surrounding the first stage of the demise of classical private landlordism
- The origins of the idea of housing subsidies
- The decision to support local authorities to build housing to rent for the 'working classes'
- The impact of the First World War and the policy direction taken in its immediate aftermath
- The seminal inter-war period and the rise of home ownership
- The impact of the Second World War and the policy direction taken in its aftermath
- The era of the 'numbers game' when policy was focused on shortages (1950–65)
- The era of the 'maturation' of council housing and the critical juncture of late twentieth-century housing policy.

The two major leitmotifs of twentieth-century housing in Britain were the restructuring of the tenure system and the challenge of providing a suitable quantity of housing (adequate to the standards of the day) for the number of households, a challenge set back considerably by the world wars and not finally met in broad terms until Man had walked on the moon (and arguably still not met – see Chapter 5).

The first key moment arose from the question of why 'housing' became an issue of national policy at all when it had never before been considered as such, despite nearly a century of rapid urbanization. This narrative is very bound up with Victorian public health legislation and the character of nineteenth-century private landlordism and these are the themes of the next section.

The Origins of Housing Policy

The first stage in answering this question is to consider the relationship between public health and housing and the point at which *housing policy per se* became distinct from the former. Two key features of this concern how housing was financed and paid for and, secondly the structure of ownership of the private rented sector itself. The analysis at the outset confronts one of the fundamentals of the tenure change narrative, namely the character of British private landlords. Theirs is an unusual and insufficiently researched interest group but perfectly illustrates the political institutionalist position that key actors and social groups should be a central focus of policy analysis.

The story begins for our purpose in the nineteenth century. The issue of how housing was built and accessed at this time was closely tied up with the Industrial Revolution. The nineteenth century was a period of dynamic change with rapid urbanization taking place in the wake of industrialization. The population of England doubled between 1801 and 1850 from 9 million to over 18 million, and the rate of growth never fell below 10 per cent per annum until the 1930s. The abolition in 1834 of the 'Speenhamland system' of poor relief, by which the wages of destitute agricultural labourers were subsidized from local rates, swelled the ranks of rural households who turned in droves towards the industrializing towns and cities in the hope of work and a new life. Housing standards for many of these families was poor and the morbidity and poverty of the Victorian slums are well documented. Over-crowding was rife and rents were high in relation to average industrial earnings. At the heart of the 'housing question', as it became known as the century wore on, was the contradiction between the relatively high cost of building compared to the return available to developers and landlords. As Gauldie suggests, the unquestioned assumption of a return on investment meant that even employer-provided housing had to make a profit and to avoid pressure on wages rent levels had to be low. The consequence inevitably was the provision of low-standard housing and over-crowding (Gauldie, 1974). Low wages, and the simple inability to afford what was on the market, were the root cause of most housing problems, then as now.

Measures to address this problem were very slow to develop because intervention in the logic of the market was not a politically acceptable solution or particularly in the mind-set of a social order constructed on *laissez faire*. As Holmans points out it is not readily apparent why poor housing standards that had endured for centuries should, towards the end of the nineteenth century, have become the subject of debate and concern (Holmans, 1987). The fact that standards did improve, especially for the 'better class of poor', in the second half of the century can be traced to two sources. First, real incomes grew by about 50 per cent between 1850 and 1900, so that for large sections of the working class, despite periodic recessions, there was a marked improvement in housing and consumer standards. Secondly, attempts to deal with the public health problems endemic in slum areas, and prone to spill over to better areas, gradually led to a recognition that insanitary housing *per se* was the source of a social problem rather than the result of individual fecklessness.

In an obvious sense, therefore, one source of 'housing policy' can be traced to public health concerns. Indeed, some historians have read into this the notion that the origin of state intervention, leading to the development of council housing itself, is to be found in Victorian public health legislation (Wohl, 1977). The key factors in the awakening 'housing' dimension of the problem were the impact of public health legislation on the profitability of private landlords and beneath that, the composition of the landlord 'class' itself.

The majority of private landlords in the nineteenth century were individual middle class people, and some better-off artisan workers, most of whom harboured their savings in housing or had inherited property. It had been a generally safe investment. Slum clearances and stricter building standards (byelaws regulated the width and layout of streets, window sizes, air spaces in roofs, etc.) both impacted on land-lords' profitability and many of them began to look for alternative investment opportunities. These were not difficult to find especially as overseas investment was becoming more available and financially attract-ive. The extension of the franchise during the 1880s also served to damage the interests of private landlords because property taxes, especially local rates, increased as new demands were placed on authorities to provide better and more services to satisfy public demand. So it was that in the decades before the First World War landlords' profits were being squeezed from a variety of sources while new investment opportunities were opening up.

Thus the origins of state intervention in housing do have a 'public health' dimension but it should not be read as a logical progression guided by enlightened reform. Rather it is a combination of an investment crisis caused by local taxation and public health controls, and new opportunities to buy stocks and shares. It was these factors that signalled the beginning of the long decline of private landlordism in Britain. It was a significant historical juncture that had an extended gestation over many decades and was only very belatedly recognized as a 'crisis'. It lead to the revolutionary idea that there might need to be intervention into the market, albeit only as a temporary measure and, to the even more startling notion, of housing subsidies – a completely new and radical departure.

Housing Subsidies

The problems faced by private landlords suggested that what was happening in the latter decades of the nineteenth century was a 'housing' problem. For the first time serious consideration was given to the new question of the supply of affordable housing. With it in due course came the revolutionary idea that it might be necessary for the state to provide subsidies, until the market 'recovered', so that housing could be let to working class families at rents below cost. A variety of alternatives were discussed or were implicit in the situation – stronger enforcement of public health measures, or lowering land prices – but as Holmans suggests:

> It is hard to avoid the conclusion that the only feasible way in which housing that was adequate by the standard of the day could be brought within reach of the very large numbers of households that could not afford it unaided was by building for letting at subsidised rents. (Holmans, 1987: 46)

Recognition that there was a housing problem, at least in London, was given force through the establishment in 1882 of the Royal Commission on the Housing of the Working Classes and in their report published in 1884. The commission, whose members included the Prince of Wales no less, collected evidence of a measurable decline in housing conditions. Dockers and costermongers, among other occupational groups, were found to have incomes considerably below Booth's poverty line and, moreover, were paying a high proportion of their wages in rent. The conclusion was inescapable. These people were not feckless and undeserving but were the victims of a *housing* problem *not of their own making*. It was a startling and salutary realization, although attributed in the report to the temporary circumstances of a slump in the housing cycle. Their analysis is summed up by Morton:

The inner urban poor were being driven outwards by a conversion of city centres to public and commercial uses but were being halted in their tracks by lack of access to newer, cheaper housing further out, of a kind which had eased similar congestion and high charges in the middle years of the century. (Morton, 1991: 14)

Recognition of the problem did not immediately lead to a solution, not least because the Royal Commissioners understated the reality and were hopeful that the market would adjust in due course. But the logic was inescapable. The state had an obligation to ease the situation in the meantime and especially for families affected by clearances arising from municipal activity and also where conditions were very poor.

It was not until Salisbury returned to power in 1886 with a programme to reform local government that the housing crisis was addressed. The Local Government Act 1888 put in place a unified system of local government by the creation of county and county borough authorities across the whole country. The previous framework for the ad hoc provision of urban services was gradually incorporated into a system of local administration which lasted more or less intact until the major local government reforms of the mid-1970s. With housing supply tightening and some local authorities already experimenting with building projects, the Housing of the Working Classes Act was passed by Parliament in July 1890. This was key legislation because it provided the context in which local authorities could intervene positively to address the housing crisis (Gauldie, 1974). In this sense it can be understood as the first statement of the need for a national 'housing policy'. The Act was very largely consolidating legislation and Parts I and II brought together the Torrens and Cross Acts (legislation that made provision for clearance of slum houses), but in Part III local authorities were empowered to build and also to renovate and improve 'working class lodging houses', defined (from the 1885 Act) to mean individual dwellings.

The assumption remained that housing schemes would be self-financing and at first a rate of return was stipulated for authority projects. It was still generally assumed that the model dwelling companies were the main source of 'social' housing. Local authorities had to obtain the permission of the Local Government Board (LGB) to build and in the absence of any financial support were reluctant to get involved. A few progressive authorities did begin experiments, notably the newly established London County Council (LCC) and in the north Glasgow, Leeds and Sheffield built small schemes under the terms of the 1890 Act. Liverpool City Council made perhaps the greatest effort to reach down to some of its most badly housed citizens in its dockland neighbourhoods. Finance was still a major stumbling block. The use of local rate funds was constrained by local political opinion wary of any new centrally imposed plans and demonstrates the significance of the way coalitions and interest groups fought to impede progress. The need for a nationally supported subsidy system began to be debated openly but various attempts to introduce parliamentary Bills for this purpose were thwarted. Nevertheless, it is clear that by the time of a further slump in the housing cycle, beginning in 1910, the issue was not whether subsidy was needed, but who should provide it.

The Position of the Rental Market before the First World War

As we have seen, some local authorities were active before the 1890 Act but the new legislation and the example set by the vanguard authorities encouraged others to follow. By the outbreak of war in 1914, 316 councils had built using Part III permissions and between 1910 and 1914 over 11,000 council houses were built. Compared to the scale of the problem it was small fry. By 1914 the sum total of local authority provision was a meagre 28,000 new dwellings nationally, about 90 per cent of which had been built since the 1890 Act. This was a much smaller contribution than the model dwelling companies and the charitable trusts, which had a combined total of about 50,000 dwellings. The importance of what these figures mean lies in the facts of the wider context of what was happening even before the war. 1913–14 witnessed a strong recovery in the housing market and Holmans calculates that 4 per cent of the housing stock was vacant. Despite this, about 15 per cent of households were sharing with another household, unable to afford even the lowest standard of housing of the day. It is apparent, therefore, that the main reason for over 1 million households (out of 8 million) not having separate accommodation of their own was one of affordability rather than lack of supply (Holmans, 2000a). Over-crowding was a common experience and, despite their powers under the 1890 legislation authorities were powerless to do much about it.

It was against these circumstances that the need for central government intervention was debated in the decade before war broke. Local authorities were reluctant to do more than tinker with the problem in the absence of central funding and the Liberal government was already engaged in an expensive programme of social reform – old age pensions, national insurance, etc. – and, belatedly, in an arms race with the Germans. Nevertheless, it is clear that at the time of the fateful assassination of Archduke Ferdinand in Sarajevo on the morning of 28 June 1914, the event which triggered the outbreak of war, the government was planning a large-scale housing programme of some 120,000 houses, albeit thought of as a one-off intervention. It was a scale of intervention far in excess of anything previously attempted or achieved. As Morton suggests: 'The notion predates the war, predates any decision on subsidy and had the support of both main political parties' (Morton, 1991: 30). Moreover, it was unequivocally the decision that this programme of building was to be carried out by local authorities.

Why 'Council' Housing?

The reasons why local authorities picked up the mantle of provision of rental housing are not difficult to see in the context of the preceding history:

- In the first place the model dwelling companies and trusts were mainly *private enterprises*, mainly based in London. Their interest was in provision for the 'better class of poor' at cost rents. Building a national programme of housing for the working classes generally was beyond their competence.
- Second, the *quality* of local authority housing, albeit of limited numbers, was superior to the model dwelling companies. The significance of this should not be under-estimated. The most progressive authorities had already demonstrated what could be achieved using limited finance.
- Third, most urban local authorities already had a body of professional *public health inspectors* who had hands-on knowledge of the technical standards and design principles of housing. This network of officers arose from the widespread use of byelaws to control speculative house building in the second half of the nineteenth century.
- Fourth, there was by 1914 an established, nationwide structure of *local government administration*, the only bodies really capable of implementing a national programme.

Thus it was that before the outbreak of hostilities in 1914, reluctant as they were, the local authorities were waiting in the wings. In the private rented sector wartime rent restrictions (imposed following the famous rent strike in Glasgow) remained for fear of provoking social unrest and the increases in rents that were permitted still left returns to landlords by the mid-1920s 25–30 per cent lower than in 1914.

Why it was not possible to subsidize private landlords? Apart from the poor reputation of landlords, especially following the events leading to the wartime rent strikes, the question must be traced back to the social composition of British private landlords, the majority of whom were individual owners of only one or two properties. Then as now private landlordism was a cottage industry run by amateurs. On the Continent – in Germany, France and Hungary – private landlords did receive subsidy to build housing for workers. These cases all have their own story to tell but in the main the municipal route was not the preferred option and subsidized private landlords were part of a much more plural system involving provision by trade unions, non-profit housing co-ops, housing associations, as well as municipal authorities and central government. Apart from the fact that the reputation of private landlords was seriously tarnished during the war, it is clear that, unlike these other countries, British landlords were a politically disorganized class and did not have the powerful position at the centre of government enjoyed, for example, by German landlords (Daunton, 1990: 23). At the time when the housing question was being debated and decisions about subsidy made private landlords were political outsiders.

The Inter-War Years

The inter-war years are seminal in the narrative of tenure restructuring. By 1939 the trajectory of change and the institutional context were clear and what happened after the Second World War was in many ways simply an extension of the pre-war pattern. It will be shown, however, that the response to post-war circumstances was very different after 1945. Taken together these two wars lasted over ten years and set back the achievement of a balance of dwellings to households by a quarter of a century. The severity of their impact should not be under-estimated.

'Homes Fit for Heroes'

The election of November 1919 resulted in a coalition of Liberals and Conservatives led by Lloyd George. They won the campaign principally on the famous slogan of 'Homes Fit for Heroes' and gave legislative force to this intention in the Housing and Town Planning Act 1919. If the issue of the funding of the building programme was unresolved in 1914, by 1918 it was unequivocally established. In order to mount the national programme of 'council house' building the local authorities would have to be given a large and generous subsidy. This would be the only way their reluctance to become involved, so readily apparent before the war, could be overcome. This legislation was enthusiastically advocated by Christopher Addison, the Minister of Reconstruction and a confidante of Lloyd George. Indeed, his advocacy of a new structure for the delivery of this plan, by breaking up the housing role of the LGB, created a new governance of housing. A Ministry of Health was set up embracing the housing function (a situation that remained in place until the 1950s). Addison became the first Minister of Health and the Housing and Town Planning Act 1919 was nicknamed the 'Addison Act' (Ravetz, 2001: 75).

The war, as we have seen, created an absolute and sizeable shortage of property as the number of new households grew, new building ceased and pre-war vacancies were quickly taken up because rental housing was in real terms much cheaper after the war than before. What had been before the war a problem caused by an inability to afford available property had in the early 1920s become a serious and substantial absolute shortage of some 1,300,000 dwellings. The huge scale of housing shortages was, as Holmans observes: 'the background to all the housing policies in the inter-war years' (Holmans, 1987: 56).

The scale of the Addison Act programme was in a completely different league to pre-war council housing. It was designed as a temporary measure, albeit with a programme stretching to 1927 when it was assumed that normal market conditions would have resumed. The assumption was that investors would return to the private rental market when the high building costs of the immediate post-war period had abated. In the meantime rental housing was to be provided by local authorities. A second 1919 Housing Act (the Housing (Additional Powers) Act) was designed to encourage the private sector to build for rent to working class households, although the specific requirement that it should provide only for the working classes was overturned in committee. When construction was aborted by the government in July 1921 only 170,000 council houses had been built or contracted. This was far short of Addison's target of 200,000 houses per annum for the first three years, a target he regarded as the brute minimum to tackle the overall housing crisis. He resorted to lowering standards by introducing a new 'C'-type house (which had no parlour) and using prefabrication. His efforts to get the programme moving foundered in the face of skills shortages, contractors and unions unwilling to commit themselves to this new and risky venture and spiralling building costs. By the end of

1919 not a single house had been built and as late as March 1921 only 16,000 houses had been completed (Homans, 1987: 299). Indeed, in the first five years after the war only 340,000 houses were built, which was insufficient to keep up with new household formation let alone make any impact on the existing shortages. As will be shown later there is an important contrast here with the Second World War.

The Addison Act subsidies were terminated because the Conservative members of the coalition opposed the escalating costs. Well before the shortages had abated, indeed in the early years of the 1920s, the deficiency of dwellings to households worsened quite considerable. In these circumstances it was imperative for the government to continue with an interventionist strategy, although the policy direction changed very considerably under the new Conservative governments of Bonar Law and Baldwin. They did not terminate the role of local authorities but shifted the emphasis for provision towards housing for sale in the private market with council housing making up deficiencies in supply for those who were unable to access home ownership. Here is to be found the emergence of a *residualist* attitude to council housing. Thus the theme of the next phase concerns the *raison d'être* for continuing council house building and how this related to the owner occupied market.

Table 6.2 provides a detailed breakdown year by year of the building programme. The main features to be noted are the very slow start made after the war due, as we have seen, to high building costs and the badly disrupted building industry. During the 1920s the story is of the very uneven growth of council housing and from 1923–4 a large and consistent contribution made by the private sector, roughly half of which was built using government subsidies. Taken together the public and private programmes in the middle and late 1920s is a significant advance on the late nineteenth-century building booms. As Holmans observes: 'When the number of dwellings completed passed 200,000 in 1926/27 this was for the first time ever' (Holmans, 1987: 67). But the scale of this achievement was about to be overshadowed by the huge implant of new properties built during the house building boom years of the 1930s.

Over 2 million houses were built by the unsubsidized private building industry during the ten years before the outbreak of the Second World War. This quantity of output has never been reached before or since. Indeed, it was not until the mid-1960s that the total of housing output at the height of the boom years (1934–8) from all sources was exceeded. The 1930s house building boom is a key moment in the narrative of British housing policy, indeed, as we saw in Chapter 3, was the basis of a new culture of consumption and contributed to a significant advance

Table 6.2   **Housing completions in England and Wales, 1919–39 (000)**

Year	Local authorities	Private sector with state finance	Private sector without state finance	Total
1919/20	0.6			
1920/1	15.6	12.9		
1921/2	80.8	20.3	53.8	251.8
1922/3	57.5	10.3		
1923/4	14.4	4.3	67.5	86.2
1924/5	20.3	47.0	69.2	136.9
1925/6	44.2	62.8	66.4	173.4
1926/7	74.1	79.7	63.9	217.6
1927/8	104.0	74.5	60.3	238.9
1928/9	55.7	49.1	64.7	169.5
1929/30	60.2	50.1	91.7	202.1
1930/1	55.9	2.6	125.4	183.8
1931/2	70.9	2.3	128.4	200.8
1932/3	56.0	2.5	142.0	200.5
1933/4	55.8	2.9	207.9	266.6
1934/5	41.6	1.1	286.4	329.1
1935/6	52.4	0.2	272.3	324.9
1936/7	71.7	0.8	273.5	346.1
1937/8	78.0	2.6	257.1	337.6
1938/9	101.7	4.2	226.4	332.4
Totals	1,111.4	430.2	2,456.9	3,998.2

Source: Holmans (1987: 66).

in living standards, reaching down through the new middle classes to the 'respectable' working classes. The numbers in Table 6.2 tell a highly significant story.

The private sector columns include houses built for sale and for letting by private landlords. They also include a relatively small output by 'public utility housing societies' that now would be counted as registered social landlords. Housing built by the private sector with and without subsidy is distinguished. The balance between the public and private sectors is a key analytical question, and there are various explanations for it. But it is clear that there was, throughout the inter-war period, a general, all-party, consensus that state housing was a necessary part of the equation. The 'Chamberlain' Housing Act of 1923 provided building subsidies to *both* the public and the private sectors. The Treasury offered local authorities only £6 per dwelling over twenty years with no requirement for rate fund contributions. The aim was to limit the scope and scale of local authority housing programmes and encourage private builders to supply housing for sale to the working classes. Central controls were more stringent than under the Addison legislation and local authorities had to demonstrate to the Ministry that the private sector was not supplying the housing needs of the area before they were given permission to build.

Emphasis swung back to the public sector with the election of the first Labour government which came to power for only nine months in 1924. Equally as pragmatic as Chamberlain, and also with roots in local government, was John Wheatley, the Minister of Health. Wheatley was a 'Red-Clydesider', a Glaswegian, Catholic socialist hardened by years of campaigning in Clydeside local politics; quite how he came to be a leading Cabinet member in this government is not entirely clear. His ideal was to use municipal construction to replace the private rented sector and had written about the nationalization of private landlords in several pamphlets. In government he stopped short of pushing his radical agenda, so that once again pragmatic solutions came to the fore. The Housing Act 1924 was in essence a financial measure and so its parliamentary passage was easy and largely uncontested. Wheatley's intention was to establish a long-term investment programme in high-quality council houses. His vision was that council housing would be a socially and geographically ubiquitous housing tenure. Authorities no longer had to demonstrate 'housing need' to get building permission. The subsidy was significantly increased to £9 per dwelling payable over forty years, instead of £6 over twenty years under the 1923 legislation, and the rate fund contribution to council house building was restored. The private sector was also able to benefit from this subsidy so long as it could be shown they were building for working class households.

Although the Labour Government was quickly replaced by a new Conservative administration, under Prime Minister Baldwin, the Wheatley Act subsidies continued in place until 1933 by which time over 500,000 houses had been built under its terms, nearly half the production of inter-war council housing. For several years both the Chamberlain and the Wheatley subsidies operated in tandem. An intriguing and not entirely clearly answered question concerns the reasons why a right-wing Conservative government did not immediately abolish Wheatley's generous subsidy. As with most questions of this type, there are a series of contributory factors. There appear to be at least three issues to consider:

- First, was that investment in the *private rented sector* remained at a low ebb until the 1930s and when the surge of building by private landlords occurred it was not in the part of the market which met the needs of low-income households. There was no other source of large-scale building for rent and the subsidy needed to be generous to persuade the more reluctant authorities, of whom there were many, to build.

- Second, the attitude of *Baldwin* is also a key factor. According to Holmans' reading of this the Prime Minister approved of the Wheatley subsidy for its role in tackling the shortages, and so, somewhat para-doxically, it is to Baldwin's 1924–9 Conservative administration that the establishment of council housing as a core element in the story of twentieth-century British housing can be attributed (Holmans, 1987: 307–8).

- Third, as we have seen there was *cross-party consensus* over housing, arising from the fact that building costs had until recently been extremely high and that the Chamberlain legislation had given the building industry confidence in state sponsored housing, whether public or private.

It was this combination of factors that led to the continuation of building under the Wheatley terms. It was not so much an issue of ideo-logical choices but of pragmatism. Shortages at the bottom end of the market needed to be tackled and the generous Wheatley system worked.

Output figures fluctuated from year to year in response to cuts in subsidies, building costs, labour shortages and also uncertainties about the relationship between subsidy levels and rents. The growing number of Labour controlled local authorities during the 1920s, especially in the cities of the north of England and in the industrial heartland of Scotland, ensured more progress than would otherwise have been the case. Wheatley Act housing was strongly focused in urban areas, whereas Addison Act housing had been both rural and urban. And, in the main, the standard of building was superior to any previous working class housing. The best Addison and Wheatley dwellings were better even than any comparable housing in the private sector. For millions of people, as we saw in Chapter 3, this was the beginning of a new life on 'council estates'. Although based on Unwin's Design Manual, mass provision lost a great deal of his subtle vision when constructed on large estates with the houses laid out in straight lines. Nevertheless, what was happening, as Burnett describes it, was 'a minor revolution in the standards of working-class housing and living' (Burnett, 1986: 234).

The Private Sector Building Boom

The shortfall of potential households to actual numbers of dwellings reached a peak of about 1,500,000 in 1925 (Holmans, 1987: 73). That this figure had been reduced to about 500,000 in 1939 when the catastrophe of the Second World War broke is very largely due to the huge and unprecedented scale of building for sale in the private sector. House building output rose from 100,000 per annum in the mid-1920s to peak at over 250,000 in the five years before 1939. Private construction for home ownership overshadowed the municipal building programme. As Table 6.2 shows, the vast majority of the private sector contribution to the inter-war housing stock was made without the help of direct subsidy.

Ubiquitous semi-detached suburbia was encouraged by several factors at work in the wider economy of the 1920s and 1930s. Despite mass unemployment during the Depression years the number of people in secure, mainly white-collar salaried posts increased very sharply – jobs in banking, insurance, teaching. Personal disposable income per head rose from £305 in 1920 to £391 in 1938 (at 1970 prices) and those in regular employment were able to meet mortgage repayments relatively easily (Merrett, 1982: 8). Not all sections of society, of course, shared in the rise in real incomes, especially workers in the northern mining and manufacturing centres. Very important in the housing case was the *decline* in wage rates in the building industry due to unemployment. This had a significant impact on house prices because house building is very labour-intensive (Bowley, 1945: 277). Thus the world economic slump, which affected major sections of the British economy at this time, was very instrumental in producing conditions favourable to the growth of the speculative building industry.

These same conditions kept house prices stable. The 1930s was unique both before, going back throughout the Victorian era, and up to present, for house prices to remain in line with or, as through most of the twentieth century, above the growth of average incomes. In fact house prices *fell* in the early 1930s and were then stable. This period witnessed the most phenomenal, never again repeated, expansion of the housing stock.

This massive addition to the housing stock was made possible not only by the wider economic conditions but because it coincided with, as Holmans puts it, the 'hey-day of public transport' (Holmans, 1987: 70). This was before car ownership was very widespread and public transport enabled people to travel to work easily from homes some distance away. 'Suburban sprawl' was further assisted by the very weak land use planning system, so that there was very little restraint on the use of greenfield sites. Farming had become more intensive and the price of agricultural land was low. Not until the establishment of the Green Belt around London in 1938 was the spread of suburbia finally checked.

The key to the home owning boom was the rapid expansion of building societies. In the nineteenth century building societies were a small-scale bodies based on a tradition of activity of working class self-build co-operation. Private landlords bought their properties directly from the builders, using rental income from tenants to pay for any loans they might require. Building society investment was literally 'as safe as houses' and they sailed through the inter-war economic crisis unscathed. The inflow of funds, which grew from £120 million in 1924 to £636 million in 1937, was advanced to borrowers and thus became the seed-corn for the home ownership boom. House prices were relatively low, average incomes for those in work was growing and the new white-collar 'professions' were generally thought of as jobs for life. 240,000 new loans were made in 1936 alone, and this large scale of lending was typical of the 1930s (Holmans, 1987: 221). Even though about a third of this money was loaned to purchase second-hand houses, often sitting tenants in the private sector buying from their landlord, the impact of this financial activity in facilitating the house building boom was very considerable.

The Situation in 1939

The overall picture of change in the inter-war years is dramatic. Between 1918 and 1939 the housing stock had increased by nearly one-third. Shortages were still a significant problem but the deficit of households to dwellings had been reduced to about half a million. The local authority contribution to this was substantial and since 1919 councils had built 1,112,000 houses and flats, representing one-quarter of new construction, accommodating by 1939 one in ten households. But this achievement is highly qualified by the ambivalence of most government towards it and, by the fact that relatively few poorer working class families could afford to live in council housing. As Bowley suggested, there was a contradiction at the heart of the council house programme. The high building standards reflecting the visionary, indeed utopian, ideals of the founding fathers of council housing contributed very considerably to the high cost of rents and therefore the failure of this major programme of social engineering to reach down to those in greatest need (Bowley, 1945). In the years leading up to the Second World War, the crucial issue of the

Table 6.3 **Summary of net change in tenure structure, 1918–38**

	Owner-occupied	Local authority	Private landlords	Total
Dwelling stock 1918				
Units	0.8	negligible	7.1	7.9
%	10	–	90	100
1914–38				
New building Purchases (+)	+1.8	+1.1	+0.9	+3.8
Sales (–)	+1.1	negligible	–1.1	0
Demolitions, etc.	negligible	negligible	–0.3	–0.3
Dwelling stock 1938				
Units	3.7	1.1	6.6	11.4
%	32	10	58	100

Source: Merrett (1982: 16).

balance of households to dwellings deteriorated, leaving a backlog in the order of 500,000 dwellings to be taken forward into the war when, once again, building ceased.

In the big picture of the restructuring of the tenure system, the balance in 1939 was that in the twenty years before the new war private sector builders had constructed nearly 3 million dwellings, 430,000 of which were built with state aid. Over 1 million private rented dwellings were sold by landlords, commonly to sitting tenants, although at the upper end of the PRS 900,000 houses and flats were built in the 1930s, taking advantage of the more favourable investment conditions. Owner occupation grew by 2.9 million dwellings by the combination of new building (60 per cent) and sales from private renting (40 per cent) and was clearly in the ascendant. By 1939 homeowners accounted for 32 per cent of total households. Council tenants accounted for 10 per cent. The net effect, including losses through slum clearance, was that the privately rented sector lost about half a million dwellings, although at 58 per cent was still the majority housing tenure at the time the Second World War broke out (Table 6.3).

The Consequences of the Second World War

The housing consequences of the Second World War were even more severe than between 1914 and 1918. During the conflict 218,000 properties were destroyed, mostly in the Blitz in 1940 and later in the unmanned rocket 'doodle bug' attacks in 1944. In addition, 250,000 dwellings were so severely damaged as to be rendered uninhabitable. But the main problem from the point of view of the housing stock was the loss of housing *production* for the duration of the conflict. Even allowing for a slowing of the pre-war boom this loss was about 1,750,000 properties (Holmans, 1987: 91). Together with those destroyed or made unusable by aerial attack, the impact of the war on a housing stock of just over 11 million at the outbreak of hostilities in 1939 is readily apparent. More-over, as many as 2 million households did not have gas or electricity and would therefore have no lighting except candles or oil lamps (Holmans, 1987: 138). Nearly 60 per cent of households lived in dwellings with no hot water.

The deficit of about half a million dwellings was carried forward from before the war and large number of city slums still awaited demolition. In addition, during the war years the birth rate grew very sharply and by 1946 the population of Britain, despite war casualties, had grown by over a million. More important than this was the dra-matic increase in the number of new household formations arising from early marriages (2 million during the six war years) and also from an increase in family dissolutions. Millions of households were forced to share, and it was common for newly married couples to live with their in-laws. One expression of this after the armistice was the mass invasion of hundreds of disused military camps, involving some 40,000 people. This form of self-help was not discouraged by the authorities although the squatting campaign in disused flats and hotels in London and some other major cities had eventually to be broken up.

The Balance between Households and Dwellings

As we saw in Chapter 4, the number of households grew much more rapidly than the population across most of the twentieth century. A fun-damental part of the equation was whether the number of dwellings kept could pace with new household formation. Basically this was on track apart from the devastating impact of the two world wars which set the aim of a 'decent home' for every household back by decades. It was not so much the destruction as the combination of virtually no building or renovation of the stock for a combination of nearly ten years and the injection of large numbers of new household formations created in the turmoil of war – hasty marriages, families breaking up, increased

Table 6.4 **Dwellings and households, 1901–91**

Region/ Year	Dwelling stock (000)	Potential households (000)	Vacants (%)	Sharing households (000)	Households/ dwellings balance (000)
England and Wales					
1901	6,710	7,007	Na	na	−300
1911	7,691	8,143	(4.4)	(1,200)	−450
1921	7,979	9,289	(1.5)	1,732	−1,310
1931	9,400	10,583	1.7	1,948	−1,180
1939	11,500	12,000	Na	na	−500
1951	12,530	14,194	1.1	1,872	−1,660
1961	14,646	15,426	2.1	886	−780
1971	17,024	17,144	3.8	780	−120
England					
1971	16,065	16,183	3.8	750	−120
1981	17,912	17,472	4.1	440	+440
1991	19,780	19,377	3.3	340	+400

Source: Holmans (2000: 14).

birth-rates – causing a surge in the numbers of households. Holmans, once again provides the key data by which to assess the key balance of households to dwellings (Table 6.4).

As can be seen in the final column, after each of the wars the gap between households and dwellings widened considerably. As Holman suggests: 'For half the century the housing scene and the pressures on policy were governed by the legacy of war' (Holmans, 2000: 15).

Taking into account the large number of concealed and sharing households, Holmans estimated a shortfall of 2 million dwellings to potential households by 1945. It was this huge, absolute deficit of housing that was the context in which housing policy in the post-war decades was formulated. The Second World War had set back the nation's housing progress on a scale it is difficult to conceive. It took two decades after 1945 to recover the position regarding the balance of dwellings to households achieved by 1939. It was not until the mid-1970s with the early evidence of difficult-to-let council housing, particularly in the north of England, that the new problems associated with low demand in some areas of the country began to emerge, as was shown in Chapter 5. For nearly a quarter of a century after the Second World War, housing policy was dominated by the effects of the war.

The Cultural and Demographic Underpinnings of Post-War Housing Policy

Within this broad context other historical and social forces (particularly patterns of demographic change) were at work in providing the particular character of British housing and domestic life in the second half of the twentieth century.

The two factors where 'policy' and 'culture' most closely overlapped were in the continuing convergence in housing standards and domestic life between the middle and working classes, noted as a feature of inter-war society in Chapter 3, and the dramatic changes that took place in the pattern of household structure and formation after the war. The war was a very egalitarian experience. People learned to 'pull together' and the social classes mixed and met in a way hitherto unthinkable. Domestic servants quickly disappeared from the homes of the middle classes and were retained only by the most wealthy. Thus, although it was common for ordinary households to have 'lodgers' well into the 1960s, the requirement for servants' quarters somewhere in the dwelling ceased. This was one reason why new building tended to converge towards a common size and pattern of layout. Meanwhile, inside the existing housing stock, the 'back regions' assumed a new prominence as utility rooms began to fill with 'white goods' – refrigerators, electric cookers, washing machines – and kitchens, rather than being the dark and dingy preserve of cooks and housemaids, and became a focal point of family life. In working class households the front door which, especially with terraced housing, often opened from a living room straight onto the street and was routinely locked, bolted and barricaded with furniture, was opened up, expressing a new confidence, and breaking down the 'kitchen mentality' (Zweig, cited in Burnett, 1986: 284). At the bottom end of the housing system, slum clearance took out hundreds of thousands of the worst nineteenth-century dwellings and this also made a considerable contribution to the levelling up of housing standards.

The second key factor which was gradually to assume greater significance in housing needs evaluation and the housing projections was the changing pattern of household structure towards more and smaller households. There is here something of a paradox but which shows the significance of the distinction between housing stock and households, for as the new post-war house building programme put in place a generally larger and more homogeneous type of housing so household sizes began to fall – indeed, plummeted in the 1970s and the decades that followed. In the decades between 1971 and 1991 over two-thirds of the increase in net households was accounted for by the formation of single-person households. By the time of the millennium celebrations in 2000, over 60 per cent of the demand for new housing was from this type of household.

A significant part of the explanation for the increase in the number of households relative to the size of population is in its *age structure*. As people live very considerably longer in 2000 than they did in 1900 there is simply a larger proportion of the population in the age groups which form households, basically the over-20s. This is bound to be the case if the population grows and life expectancy improves. About three-quarters of the population in 2000 are 'adults' but in 1900 this figure was much lower, less than 60 per cent. A large part of the rise in the number of households in the twentieth century is accounted for by this factor. But the expansion in the number of households in the post-1945 period was increasingly accounted for by the growth of small and particularly single-person households. It was apparent that this trend was already appearing as early as the 1930s and 1940s and was for the decades up to 1970 principally associated with the very large number of elderly widows (and to a much lesser extent widowers) who were able, by choice, to live alone (Holmans, 1987).

It was this blend of economic, social, demographic, historical and cultural factors that set the parameters for post-war housing policy. The political system and the choices made by politicians provided the particular direction that was taken at any one time although what they wanted to do and what they could deliver was a perennial problem. It is the interplay between the impact of these contextual issues and political choice that the policy agenda was shaped. The first major decision in the immediate aftermath of the war was to determine the balance of new provision and reconstruction between the public and private sectors.

Public or Private Reconstruction?

Given the momentum of the private sector building boom in the 1930s it might have been assumed that this would be the route to follow after the war. In their 1945 election manifesto the Conservatives promised to provide housing subsidies to both the public and private sectors. Labour politicians had mixed views about what to do and it was by no means clear whether the local authorities or the owner-occupier market would spearhead the post-war housing drive right up to the election.

However, Labour won a landslide victory at the election on a popular belief that the sacrifices of the war years should lead to a renewal in

Britain's economic, social and cultural life. The issue of the balance between public and private provision of housing was very quickly resolved with the appointment of the Welsh socialist politician Aneurin Bevan as Minister of Health. Bevan was vociferously opposed to the role of the private sector saying that he refused to let the private developers, 'suck at the teats of the state'. His vision was similar to John Wheatley, which was that housing policy should not be socially divisive and that local authority housing should provide for all social classes. Accordingly the speculative building industry continued the war-time practice of supplying under a system of licences, to complement wider policy objectives. 80 per cent of new house building was allocated to local authorities and 20 per cent to private house builders. In the event the Labour Government oversaw the building of 1,017,000 dwellings before it was defeated in the election of 1951. 146,000 of these were 'pre-fabs,' small factory made bungalows built in 1946–7 as an emergency measure, but nevertheless this scale of programme was impressive and was the first large-scale positive investment in public housing since the Wheatley legislation. It should be noted that the high quality of both 'Wheatley' and 'Bevan' housing reflects the vision of two socialist politicians who held ministerial office at a time of national political crisis following wars. On both occasions much of the groundwork for this improvement in standards was put in place during the wars by government committees. During the Second World War the housing programme was considered by the Dudley Committee. In its report, published in 1944, the committee proposed a significant improvement in housing standards, perhaps not so dramatic as the Tudor-Walters Committee during the First World War, but of great significance nevertheless. The design manual sent to local authorities described properties which were much better equipped and significantly bigger and with more rooms than ever before.

The emphasis on public sector housing in tackling the shortages after the Second World War, compared to the mixed public/private strategy after the First World War, was impressive. It seems unlikely on available evidence that the private sector could have achieved more. Indeed, when the Conservatives were returned to power in 1951 pledged to build a programme of 300,000 houses per annum it was on the basis of a mixture of public and private provision that this pledge was to be redeemed. Table 6.5 shows the record of the balance of public and private provision.

Building starts in the private sector broke the 100,000 barrier in 1954 and accelerated year on year to peak at 247,000 in 1964 and was never far short of 200,000 up to the mid-1970s. Advances by building societies grew in conjunction with this second boom era in home ownership. The

Table 6.5 **New house building completions, England and Wales, 1946–79 (000)**

	Public Sector	Private owners	Total built in both sectors
1946–50	693	153	846
1951–5	940	312	1252
1956–60	622	675	1297
1961–5	579	917	1496
1966–70	777	940	1817
1971–5	573	678	1251
1976–9	499	520	1019

Source: *Housing and Construction Statistics* (London, HMSO).

influx of funds into building societies was crucial to the speed with which the boom accelerated. Personal disposable income grew from £377 per annum in 1948 to £581 in 1965 (Merrett, 1982: 41). Inflation was modest and unemployment by the standards of the 1930s and the 1980–1990s was very low. Macmillan was not far short of the truth when he told the nation that 'they had never had it so good', and the seeds of the home owning society, planted among the middle classes in the inter-war period, now began to grow to fruition as it filtered down the social class structure. A key feature of this second home ownership boom was the incorporation of skilled manual worker households into the 'property owning democracy'.

Thus the pattern of post-Second World War housing was established. Council housing at first provided an implant of new properties followed by the switch of policy towards building for sale. The failure of the private rented sector to revive even following the deregulation of a significant part of the market under the terms of the Rent Act 1957 meant that under both Conservative and Labour governments council housing continued to be built as the main form of rental accommodation for families unable to afford home ownership. Accommodating nearly one-third of households by the mid-1970s, a new crisis emerged caused by the sheer weight of numbers of council housing stock and the subsidies that had underpinned their creation.

The late 1960s and 1970s were a seminal time in the next stage of policy development. Up to then the main effort of policy in the post-war decades had been to overcome the crisis of shortages. By the early 1970s this, at least in numerical terms, had been achieved. There was a rough balance of households to dwellings for the first time in the twentieth century. The solution had, as we have seen, entailed two massive home ownership booms and the construction of a substantial stock of local authority houses and flats. Indeed it was the very scale of this stock of public housing that was to be key to the new direction taken by British housing. A new stage of tenure restructuring was about to commence which would see council housing decline from 32 per cent of households to less than half that number by the early years of the new millennium and, as we saw in Chapter 2 the likelihood that council housing would become a small remnant in a more plural social housing sector. Why did this happen when the record of achievement over six decades had been so outstanding? Far more council houses were built under Conservative than Labour governments, albeit that the former were the more 'reluctant collectivists'. What happened to cause the rapid reversal of fortunes of council housing? As we have seen, its place was firmly rooted only at certain points (under Wheatley and Bevan) but it is a record of achievement and a vision of social reform that spans over half a century. Council housing brought very real improvements and provided a solution to the housing needs of millions of ordinary working households.

Explaining the Residualization of State Housing Provision

Such a major turning point in the fortunes of council housing is unlikely to be accounted for by a single overarching factor, and the purpose of policy analysis is to discern key underlying issues and tendencies in both the policy arena and the wider economy and society which, taken together, explain what happened. The residualization of state housing in this 'middle-range' approach hinged on five main issues:

- The end of the era of shortages (as discussed above)
- The financial 'maturation' of the council housing stock
- The impact of globalization pressures, forcing the re-structuring of the economy away from its historic manufacturing base and towards services
- The impact of community action groups, mainly of homeowners
- The 'New Right' welfare agenda of the Thatcher governments.

Unprofitability versus Maturation

The reversal of fortunes of council housing has been explained in a number of different ways. The most detailed conceptual assessments have been made by Harloe (1995) and Kemeny (1995). Harloe argues that government intervention into rental housing is a function of the profitability of housing to private capital. State intervention thus fluctuates according to profitability and the long-run global economic cycle, with all countries passing through the same stages of commodification (private market supply), decommodification (state provision) and recommodification (privatization) in a cyclical manner. In periods of relative unprofitability the state intervenes to create a social housing sector as a means of boosting capital and in more profitable periods the state withdraws from this activity. Harloe discerns according to this thesis three distinct periods in rental housing in the post-war era with the current period being one of the re-marketization of state rental housing (Harloe, 1995).

There are a number of problems with this thesis, not least of which is that it is very unnuanced. It does not usefully explain, for example, why very little state housing was built in the USA, which suffered a catastrophic collapse of profitability in the 1930s. In essence Harloe's argument is that the USA is an exceptional case, but this too is difficult to sustain because it is the strongest and most powerful capitalist economy. Universalistic social theory in general suffers from a danger of trying to force or predetermine evidence to fit theory and tends to lead to convergence explanations. As Kemeny and Lowe argue, more culturally rooted approaches, which use middle-range theory and do not attempt to generalize out of a few specific cases, especially that of the UK, come to very different conclusions with an emphasis on policy divergence (Kemeny and Lowe, 1998).

Kemeny explains the changes that took place in British housing in the 1970s and 1980s as a response to what he calls a 'maturation crisis' in the state housing sector. It is a form of crisis faced by any country that supported state housing using historic cost subsidies. In the British case council housing grew for over fifty years, becoming a major housing tenure. In time, large parts of this housing stock became debt-free as subsidies and rents gradually paid off outstanding capital. As a result, the main costs associated with this older stock were relatively small (current management and maintenance). This was somewhat counteracted by the fact that the properties were ageing. But the implication of this 'maturation' process, as Kemeny described it, was that council house rents would be reduced, the 'mortgage', as it were, having been paid off (Kemeny, 1995). Research on this thesis is still rather inconclusive and may well reveal the high cost of renovation and the high cost of newer stock, especially high rise housing. In the private rental sector, according to Kemeny, landlords of necessity have to charge a market rent in order to obtain a return on their investment. This means that they have to charge a rent based on the current capital value of their properties. The alternative would be to sell the house or flat at its market value and invest the money. Without a real return there is no sense in being in the rental market.

The implication of the maturation idea is that the public sector would come to be more popular than the private sector because rents, in theory, could be lower. In the long story of housing in Britain the 'maturation of council housing' thesis might well prove to be a key factor because, as Kemeny pointed out, in some forms of market economy it would be untenable simply to let the public sector become more popular than the private sector. As a result a policy intervention was bound to 'correct' the imbalance. At any rate, the only option *not* available was to do nothing. In due course, as will be seen, the choice was to increase council rents (unsuccessfully attempted as early as the Housing Finance Act 1972) and ultimately to break up the council stock, first through the Right To Buy (RTB) policy and latterly through stock transfer – in other words, to privatize it. As will be shown in Chapter 9 most of the 'social market' economies in Europe used historic subsidies in their state housing programmes in a different way to Britain, opting for a policy direction which supported the state sector rather than undermining it. In a market economy, with a strong home owning 'catch-up' imperative it is not very difficult to see that state renting, with its long and rather parlous history, would need to be restructured in some way.

It is against this background that housing policy in the latter decades of the twentieth century has been played out. Shortages having been overcome, the issue moved to one of reasserting the market 'norm', and the well-known RTB policy enacted by the Thatcher government through the Housing Act 1980 and the more recent break-up of the remaining council housing stock by the Blair government are different elements of how the old-fashioned British state has been restructured in the face of globalization imperatives. As was discussed in Chapter 2, the new governance of housing has to be read in this wider context. The maturation crisis created the need for an early strategic withdrawal of state activity in housing production and the initial attempt to re-engineer the subsidy system so that council housing would be captured by the logic of the private market for housing, through market-level rents and eventually by the wholesale shedding of the public sector housing stock. This is the second great 'critical juncture' of British housing in the twentieth century, following the circumstances leading to the collapse of classical nineteenth-century private landlordism described earlier in the chapter.

The impact of the two world wars together provide us with the third critical 'moment'.

Conclusion

The chapter has identified critical junctures and the alignment of social forces, mediated largely through the party political system, which created the quiet revolution in housing tenure that overtook British housing in the twentieth century. The narrative account has been argued from within an historical institutionalist approach which argues that institutions shape strategies and ultimately policy direction. Preferences are not simply determined by the self-interest of any one of the actors. In this case the very origin of the notion of 'housing policy' can be seen to have emerged against the fundamental logic of Victorian *laissez faire*. The outcome of this early stage of development was the recognition of the need for an albeit limited view of state intervention. This hinged on the investment crisis of private landlordism and the structure of the landlord class, a class of small-scale, amateur investors with little or no political organization outside their own interest. The uneven distribution of power between the various actors engaged in this area of policy and the point in time (set against the circumstances of the late Victorian economy) are key features of the narrative and exemplify the historical dimension of this approach.

The emergence of council housing to fill the gap left by the private sector was achieved with very little conflict and a considerable degree of political consensus. Even though council housing was not a preferred option, especially for Conservative politicians, it came to be a distinctive feature of the achievement of 'decent housing' during the course of most of the twentieth century. As Hall and Taylor (1996) point out historical institutionalists pay particular attention to *contingency*, to the unintended outcomes of the policy process – as witnessed in this case-study by far more council houses having been built under Conservative governments than Labour. It is most clearly demonstrated in the maturation crisis of the 1960s and 1970s when the state housing sector threatened to become the cheaper and more popular part of the rental housing stock, indeed of the whole housing system. Such disequilibrium at the heart of a society with a strong cultural predilection to property ownership created the need for decisive policy intervention and is the backdrop to much of the housing policy of the 1980s and 1990s.

Historical institutionalists by and large view 'change' as the consequence of strategic action in an institutional context that favours certain options over others. According to this approach, institutions are not the only causal force in making a change. The approach identifies path dependency and policy feedback, particularly in the context of the 'long-view' of history. Policy transfer and policy learning are also central ideas and attention has been drawn to key decision-making moments and junctures when paradigm shifts occurred, not usually quickly but always with a decisive outcome. The path of British housing policy took a clear turn after the First World War compared to most of comparable European nations faced with the same issue of what to do about the provision of working class housing. It was a decisive moment that lead British housing down a quite different path of development. Sensitivity to path dependency of this kind is a key feature of historical institutionalism. As Hay and Wincott argue:

> The order in which things happen affects how they happen; the trajectory of change up to a certain point itself constrains the trajectory after that point; and the strategic choices made at a particular moment eliminate whole ranges of possibilities from later choices while serving as the very condition of existence of others. (Hay and Wincott 1998: 955)

In short, the same forces and issues will not always generate the same results everywhere. The 'effect of such forces will be mediated by the contextual features of a given situation often inherited from the past' (Hall and Taylor, 1996: 941). Historical institutionalism therefore attempts to go beyond purely state centred approaches and attempts to link the analysis of institutions with a long historical view and the structure of wider social forces and interests in order to determine and evaluate the logic behind such changes. In its widest sense the tenure restructuring of British housing during the twentieth century is a case of just such a socially and politically constituted process of change.

FURTHER READING

Daunton, M. J. (1987) *A Property-Owning Democracy – Housing in Britain*, London, Faber & Faber.

Holmans, A. E. (1987) *Housing Policy in Britain*, London, Croom Helm.

Kemeny, J. (1995) *From Public Housing to the Social Market*, London, Routledge.

Merrett, S. (1979) *State Housing in Britain*, London, Routledge & Kegan Paul

7

The Sustainability of Home Ownership

CHAPTER AIMS

- To descibe the factors leading to the maturation of British home ownership
- To discuss the question whether the current position is sustainable, and if so why
- To discuss the new insecurities in the home owning market, especially for low-income owners
- To consider the evidence of home ownership as a source and generator of wealth
- To discuss the impact of home ownership on the macroeconomy and the development of the modern welfare state.

Introduction

Over the course of seven decades in the twentieth century home ownership replaced private renting as the predominant housing tenure. By the dawn of the twenty-first century Britain had caught up with the other English-speaking nations in the OECD group and indeed, with nearly 70 per cent of households living in owner occupied property, was at the upper end of the English-speaking cluster. The major reason for this transition was the underlying improvement in incomes as the twentieth century progressed, but policy choices also played a significant role. Home ownership became more diffused across the social spectrum, drawing into it the vast majority of heads of households with non-manual and skilled manual occupational backgrounds. Home ownership is, however, still not an option for millions of households, about a third of the total, many of whom cannot afford its cost and, with the aid of housing benefit, live in rental accommodation. Is this, then, the more or less stable state of British housing? The aim of this chapter is to answer this question and to examine the consequences of the conversion of Britain into a home owning society. The three main issues here concern the impact of the growth of home ownership on the macroeconomy, its influence in reshaping the structure of the British social system and, finally, the impact of Britain's conversion to home ownership on the welfare state. The central point is that it is almost inconceivable that such a major reshaping of the housing system spread, as we saw in Chapter 6, over nearly a whole century of change, would not impact on other aspects of the political, economic and social systems.

The Sustainability of Home Ownership

The foundation of the analysis revolves around what has come to be called the 'sustainability' of home owning. This issue has two parts. The first, concerns the extent to which home owning can continue to expand and/or is sustainable at its current level. Key issues here concern the process by which home ownership grew and how this relates to the rest of the housing system. The second issue arises from the process by which home ownership has filtered down the social classes. The more home ownership grew the more its future expansion came to depend on households at the lower end of the income spectrum. The 'affordability' of owner occupation for low-income households is thus an important focus of the extent to which home ownership is sustainable. The fact of its expansion also had profound repercussions on the distribution of wealth in society, leading indeed to a levelling-up of inequalities. The redistributive consequence of the expansion of home ownership is a rather neglected corner of the literature and housing research agenda.

The first stage, therefore, is to document and explain the current position of the tenure in the early years of the twenty-first century. In doing this, it should be recalled that the 1990s witnessed a prolonged and deep slump in the housing market, the worst since the origins of the property owning democracy in the 1920s. This complicates the interpretation of the housing data during the 1990s, making it less clear whether what happened was part of underlying structural change or a short-term consequence of the slump.

The Size of the Owner Occupied Sector

The current size of the home ownership market varies slightly between the constituent nations of the UK. The figures in the 2001 Census were 71 per cent of households in Wales, 63 per cent in Scotland, 69 per cent in Northern Ireland and 68 per cent in England, giving an overall UK average in 2001 of nearly 68 per cent. The biggest change was in Scotland, which increased from 52 per cent in 1991. The overall pattern in the UK is one of very little change in the ten years between 1991 and 2001. What is the explanation for this, given that the trajectory was one of sharp and rapid increase almost continuously over the previous fifty years? The answer is crucial to how we view the sustainability of the sector and its long-term future. The assessment requires a return to some of the fundamental elements of the housing system:

- An analysis of the sources of home ownership
- Key demographic components which influence demand
- Changing patterns of household formation, especially emerging trends in 'youth transitions'
- The occupational class composition of the current generation of home owners.
- The recent experience of lower-income owners.

Low-income home ownership is an important element in the analysis because any future expansion of the sector must by default result from its filtering down into unskilled manual worker households. Whether home owning in Britain has reached a stable state after its many decades of 'catch-up' to the comparable English-speaking nations is largely a consequence of the balance sheet made up of these factors. Other than these the size of the owner occupied sector will be dependent on the balance of new provision supplied by the public and private sectors, but because annual additions through new building are relative small compared to the overall size of the stock the impact of this in the future will be quite slow. Finally, an assessment must also be made of the extent to which the recession in the early 1990s was a cause of the slow-down in the rate at which home owning had grown previously. Was it a coincidence that home ownership ended its 'catch-up' phase at a time when the market was in a deep and prolonged recession or was there something 'different' about the 1990s down-swing in the housing market compared to the previous cycles as some commentators claimed (Forrest, Kennett and Leather, 1999; Hamnett, 1999)?

The Sources of the Growth of Home Ownership: Sales to Sitting Tenants

The first part of the analysis of the expansion of owner occupation concerns sales to sitting tenants. There are two sources here:

(1)   sales by private landlords
(2)   sales by public landlords.

Sales by private landlords

It will be recalled that a significant proportion of the long-term expansion of home ownership arose due to transfers from both the private and public rental sectors. As we saw in Chapter 6, 40 per cent of the net increase in owner occupation in the inter-war period was due to sales by private landlords to sitting tenants, and this trend continued – indeed, accelerated – in the late 1950s and 1960s. These sales finally bottomed-out during the 1980s, by which time the PRS had been reduced to only 10 per cent of households through a combination of expansion in the other tenures, sales and slum clearance, and had become a fragmented and residual housing tenure.

In total during the period when tenure restructuring was at its most intense, between the 1920s and the 1980s, some 4.5 million dwellings were added to the owner occupied stock from sales by private landlords to sitting tenants, representing 40 per cent of the net increase during that period. It should be noted that these were mainly old, urban terraced properties at the bottom end of the market. In due course these houses became an important source of first-time-buyer properties. Furthermore these transfers were a key explanation in the slowing of the slum clearance programme. Owner-occupiers were much more difficult to compensate than private landlords, who were often thought of as supplying a sub-standard service. Homeowners were resistant to clearance – and, indeed, very largely at their own expense, stabilized and then improved this older part of the dwelling stock.

Sales by public landlords

In the 1980s and to a lesser extent the 1990s a significant part of the growth in home ownership was due to sales to sitting tenants in the *public* rental stock, carrying on the net additions to owner occupation when sales of private rental housing subsided. Through the terms of the Housing Act 1980 tenants were offered discounts on the market value of the property and access to low-interest mortgages. 'Right to Buy' (RTB) sales are thus rather different from normal housing market transactions and need to be treated somewhat differently in the overall analysis. Nevertheless, the simple point is that between 1980 and 1999 nearly 1.9 million council tenants bought their home from local authority landlords, representing a shade over 7 per cent of all households. Mainstream owner-occupiers were 61.6 per cent of households in 1999, producing a combined total of 68.7 per cent. The RTB stock is heavily concentrated in the south of England and in the 'leafy suburbs', property that is of high value (thus inflating the value of the discount) and in good condition. As will be shown in Chapter 8, the residual council housing stock is now disproportionately composed of flats and inner-city estates. Social housing has become much more identified with 'big cities' than at any stage in its long history.

RTB sales, however, have slowed considerably from their peak in the 1980s. There were some 330,000 sales between 1991 and 1999 but the net contribution to the expansion of owner occupation was relatively small owing to about 200,000 existing RTB owners moving into the mainstream market during this period. In 1991 there were 1,349,000 RTB owners remaining in the house they originally bought under the 1980 Act, and this number had increased to only 1,452,000 by 1998/9. Thus the rate of exiting RTB owners roughly balances the new inflow. As the pace of sales declines because those who can afford or want to transfer have already done so, and if the pattern of moves out of RTB properties persists, so sitting tenant purchasers in the public sector will also wither away as a source of expansion of home ownership. This is increasingly likely to be the case because of the planned scale of stock transfers described in Chapter 2. Whatever endgame is eventually played out, stock transfer agencies are usually outside the terms of the RTB legislation and so by default reduces the quantity of housing available as a source for future growth in home ownership.

Thus private and public sector sales to sitting tenants can no longer be a major source of tenure transformation as they were through many decades of the twentieth century. Including RTB sales the current stock of some 16.5 million owner occupied properties contain nearly 6.5 million houses and flats that were originally occupied by tenants and sold on by landlords. The balance of some 10 million dwellings is made up of the relatively small number of remaining pre-1914 owner occupied properties, added to the huge output of new building – a large proportion of which dates from the great house building booms of the 1930s and the mid-1950s and 1960s – less older owner occupied properties that were destroyed in the Second World War or demolished, mainly in the post-1945 slum clearances. It is clear, therefore, that the well-spring of rental housing which fed the rising tide of home ownership has all but dried up.

The Impact of Demographic Change on Home Ownership

Several changes in the basic demography of Britain, particularly arising from new patterns of household formation, began to influence the home owning market during the 1990s. Their impact was on balance to dampen, at least in the short term, the further expansion of owner occupation. The most important development was evidence that the proportion of younger people, especially those under age 24 who became owner-occupiers during the 1990s fell considerably (see Table 7.1). In 1991 35.3 per cent of the under-24 cohort were owner-occupiers but by the end of the decade this proportion had fallen to 23.7 per cent (Holmans, 2000b). The effect of this was to dent the long-term growth of the sector. This is simply because there will be fewer owner-occupiers working their way into the system as this cohort ages, unless they catch up at some future stage. Part of this decline may be a response to the

Table 7.1   **Owner-occupier households, by age, selected years**

Age of head of household	1991	1994/5–1995/6	1997/98–1998/9
Under 25	35.3	26.9	23.7
25–34	63.5	60.0	58.9
35–44	70.5	67.1	67.8
45–54	68.7	69.3	69.4
55–64	61.6	65.3	65.5
65–74	53.0	56.4	59.3
75 and over	49.6	54.0	53.1
Total	**60.6**	**60.6**	**61.6**

Source: *Survey of English Housing, 1998/9* (45 DETR).

house price slump, leading to more cautious attitudes to a first-house purchase. As there was a considerable expansion in the PRS at this time, some 30,000–40,000 additional units per annum until the mid-1990s, young people leaving home for the first time will have found an easy alternative to house purchase in the rental market (see Chapter 8). There is also evidence that young, recent entrants to home ownership were caught up in the repossessions crisis of the early-1990s, and this will certainly have depressed the number of under-25 year olds in the sector (Holmans, 2000b).

These changes and problems are part of what has broadly become known as 'youth transitions', the timing, pattern of choices and behaviour when young people leave the parental home for the first time. This may be accelerated by increasing incidence of divorce among parents and, in turn, early partnership formation and dissolutions among young people themselves (Burrows, 1997b). These less stable relationships tend to prompt the search for separate housing, often in the absence of adequate resources. Early relationship formation and breakdown tend, therefore, to make the transition to settled adulthood less easy and more pro-longed, and depresses interest in house purchase. In a similar way the expansion of higher education clearly impacts on the timing, motivation and financial ability to enter the home ownership market. Currently about 45 per cent of school leavers go on to some form of higher education. The sheer numbers of the student population and the amount of debt and expense involved in funding higher education almost certainly delays decisions on house purchase.

The impact of changing household structures generally during the 1990s had a significant effect on the home owning market. This is partly an effect of the 'youth transitions' issue, but by no means exclusively so. For example, Holmans (2000b) estimated that the number of married couple households fell by over half a million between 1991 and 1998, whereas the number of lone parents increased by over 300,000. Because married couples are much more likely to be home owners than single parents it follows that these changes in household structure depressed the growth of home ownership by several hundred thousand during this period.

The Diffusion of Home Ownership down the Social Class Spectrum

Demographic change and the decline of sales to sitting tenants have dampened the previous rate of expansion of the home owning market. One further key to the slowdown in the expansion of owner occupation

Table 7.2   **Spread of owner occupation, by socio-economic group, 1961–91**

	1961	1971	1981	1991	1961–91
	(%)	(%)	(%)	(%)	(%)
Professionals and managers	67.3	75.8	82.7	90.3	+23.0
Intermediate and junior non-manual	53.4	59.3	70.5	78.4	+25.0
Skilled manual	40.0	47.8	58.4	73.0	+33.0
Semi-skilled	28.7	35.6	41.6	49.0	+20.0
Unskilled	21.9	27.0	30.9	38.0	+16.1

Source: Hamnett (1999: 58).

in recent decades, and how it is likely to evolve in the future, is its gradual diffusion through the social classes and into the lower income group (Table 7.2).

Before the Second World War, homeownership was mainly confined to middle class households, although some parts of the country have a tradition of working class owner occupation which dates back to eighteenth-century self-build, co-operative, organizations in areas such as the South Wales coalfields and the mill towns of Lancashire. As Daunton observes, it was a tradition, 'associated with independence from the state and from middle-class philanthropy and patronage' (Daunton, 1987: 73). But the great private sector housing boom in the 1930s was quintessentially a middle class phenomenon (see Chapter 3). After the Second World War, skilled manual worker households increasingly took the opportunity to become owner-occupiers as incomes rose. As Table 7.2 shows, over 90 per cent of professionals and managers were owner-occupiers by the 1990s but the greatest percentage growth between the 1960s and the 1990s was among the skilled manual worker strata. The working classes divided very sharply between skilled workers, nearly three-quarters of whom were owners by 1990, and unskilled households, the majority of whom remained renters, mainly from local authorities. Long before the 1980 'Right to Buy' (RTB) legislation a majority of skilled workers were home owners, although RTB sales were heavily concentrated in that social group and this is what accounts for the considerable boost between 1981 and 1991 in skilled manual home ownership that shows up in Table 7.2. Indeed by the landmark year 2000, nearly 80 per cent of them were owner-occupiers. Forrest and Murie's (1988) classic study of council housing in the 1980s showed precisely that in every income decile there were fewer council tenants than in the

1960s with the exception of the *lowest* decile, in which the proportion of tenants had increased significantly.

The Emergence of Consumption Sectors

The corollary of this was, of course, that home ownership became much more socially diverse and as it accelerated through the 60 per cent level so it came to reflect all social strata, *except* the poorest 10 per cent of households. Indeed, only 18 per cent of RTB purchasers were by tenants with incomes in the lowest income quintile (Burrows, Ford and Wilcox, 2000: 17). The consequence of the RTB legislation was not, therefore, to spread home ownership further down the social class structure but to underpin and sharpen the division *within* the manual worker strata between predominantly skilled manual owner-occupier households and predominantly unskilled manual tenanted households. Some sociologists have argued that these divisions in society have become more important than social class as determinants of people's living standards (Saunders, 1981) and created distinct 'consumption cleavages' which were analytically distinct from social class (Dunleavy, 1979). In other words, society had become divided not by horizontally stratified social classes but by a vertical division between those who lived in a predominantly privately ordered consumption sector of which home ownership was the most important element, alongside car ownership, access to private health care, dentists, etc. – and those whose living standards were determined by reliance on the public sector – council tenants, public transport users and dependent on NHS provision of health. The idea that consumption sectors could outweigh social class in importance was a radical view and at its most persuasive in the 1980s when house prices were booming and the 'New Right' agenda dominated government. Saunders argued that, 'Consumption locations may generate effects which far outweigh those associated with class locations ... An analysis which insists on asserting the primacy of class is likely to achieve less and less understanding of patterns of power, privilege and inequality' (Saunders, 1986: 158).

Moreover, the capital accumulation potential of home ownership had created an autonomous source of wealth that was of increasing, if not greater, significance than people's occupational incomes. Thus belonging to one or other of these sectoral cleavages shaped people's life chances and living standards, implying much higher standards in the private (and more popular) sector than those dependent on the residual public sector. There is considerable merit in this case as the data on the effects of home ownership on wealth redistribution suggest. But the evidence also shows that owners in higher social classes made the largest gains over time compared to manual worker owners, although in the short term this calculation was dependent on the point in time when the purchase was made (Hamnett, 1999: 100). Equally, the influence of social class remains significant in shaping inter-generational wealth transfers. One of the claims of the consumption sector theorists was that the spread of home ownership would lead to a wider distribution of inherited wealth as owner occupation filtered down the social class spectrum. The evidence (see below) is that this has not (yet) happened so that middle class owners tend to consolidate their wealth rather than it being spread more widely. Thus the more extreme versions of consumption sector theory need to be modified to account for longer-term patterns of accumulation and the cultural transmission of wealth. But there can be little doubt that consumption location – that is to say, people whose access is to predominantly privately provided services and consumption against those who rely principally on the public sector – has become a major structural rift in early twenty-first century society.

There is, however, one major exception to this general pattern. Many tens of thousands of homeowners on low incomes have chosen unwisely or been forced through lack of alternatives to become owner-occupiers and find it difficult to sustain their place in the sector because of the financial costs they incur. This is a case in which being in a private consumption sector is not advantageous and these owners do not share the financial benefits of their more affluent counterparts.

Low-Income Homeowners

Low-income owners are an important element to the sustainability of home ownership because the expansion (or contraction) of the tenure in the short and medium term is increasingly dependent on low-income households moving in or out of it. Low-income owners are different from mainstream owner-occupiers because their access to the tenure and their ability to sustain their position in it has often been the product of policies that do not apply to better-off households. Governments of all political complexions have promoted schemes of low-cost home ownership (see Booth and Crook, 1986), its maintenance and renovation, and for those in receipt of Income Support, assistance with mortgage payments. RTB clearly drew a large number of lower-income households into owner occupation, although as we have seen, few of the very lowest income group.

Among households whose gross income fell in the bottom income decile in 1998/9 only 6.5 percent were owner-occupiers with mortgages while a further 17.1 per cent were outright owners of the property, the vast majority of whom were elderly pensioners. (This compares with 76.2 per cent who are purchasing property and 16.3 per cent outright owners in the top income decile.) However, because home owners comprise nearly 70 per cent of all households, the apparently modest proportion of low-income owner-occupiers represents 57 per cent of households in the bottom income decile, as shown in Table 7.3.

Thus the first key point is that half the poor, indeed a clear majority of low-income households, are owner-occupiers (Burrows, Ford and Wilcox, 2000). Data from the 1997/8 *Survey of English Housing* (SEH) further shows that nearly half the households with incomes below £5,000 were pensioners and 28 per cent of heads of households were unemployed. Only a quarter of low-income homeowners were in paid employment at the time of the most recent SEH (Burrows and Wilcox, 2000). About half of these low-income owners live in properties that are in poor condition and at the bottom end of the house price scale.

Most owner-occupiers currently living on low incomes were better off when they bought their house but due to changed circumstances, such as unemployment or simply moving into retirement, have become much worse off. These changes, especially for households with out-standing mortgage debt, can lead to them being forced to move out of homeownership. A recent analysis of the *Survey of English Housing* showed that there had been a net *loss* of the most marginal homeowners from the sector. Between 1995/6 and 1997/8 only 33,000 people with incomes in the bottom income quintile (the lowest 20 per cent) moved into owner occupation while some 82,000 households moved out, producing a net outflow of some 49,000 households (Burrows and Wilcox, 2000).

Table 7.3   **Tenure of lowest income decile, 1979–98**

Tenure	1979	1990/1	1997/8
	(%)s	(%)	(%)
Owned with mortgage	11	27	29
Owned outright	28	24	28
All owned	40	51	57
Rented	60	49	43

Source: Burrows, Ford and Wilcox (2000: 12).

In the context of the sustainability of home ownership – whether it is growing, falling or stable – the preceding analysis shows that home ownership has filtered down the social class spectrum but inevitably reaches a threshold below which it is simply unaffordable, even with the support and encouragement of government schemes. There is a point at which filtering down touches an impenetrable barrier of low income. This would suggests that there is little scope for further diffusion of home owning into the low-income strata, despite evidence that many, if not most, of these people would rather be owners than tenants.

Lack of Support for Low-Income Homeowners

One of the factors which currently underpins the likelihood of this situation continuing is that, despite the plethora of policies over many decades that have encouraged entry into owner occupation by households with modest incomes, the social security system offers very little support to low-income owners compared to low-income tenants. Low-income homeowners in employment are offered no subsidy to sustain their housing costs. Burrows, Ford and Wilcox (2000) point out that means-tested support with the housing costs of homeowners amounts to less than 10 per cent of the equivalent help, principally in the form of housing benefit, given to tenants. There appears to be only marginal change in this position in the Labour government's Green Paper and subsequent policy initiatives (DETR, 2000b). While it is the case that most, but by no means all, low-income owners possess a capital asset once the mortgage is paid off there are considerable insurance and maintenance bills to face, and greater vulnerability to being unable to make repayments. Their properties tend to be at the bottom end of the market where it is much more difficult to unlock housing equity to support income.

Summary of Analysis on Sustainability

To summarize, owner occupation in Britain has been though a long period of catch-up but is now relatively stable at approaching 70 per cent of households. There is little prospect of further growth by sales to sitting tenants. The issues connected to 'youth transitions' indicate a slowdown in the rate of entry by the 18–35-year-old cohorts which will depress the size of the sector in due course (unless they catch up later on) – whereas home owning is currently growing among the over-60s as the cohorts who were mainly tenants die out and are replaced by middle-aged owners. New patterns of household formation, especially the more fractured experience of relationship formation and dissolution that grew strongly in the 1980s and 1990s, suggests delayed entry to home owning, struggles to hold on to the property during relationship breakdowns and more than usual vulnerability of such people to the peaks and troughs of the house price cycle. Among the lowest-income households we have seen evidence that showed a substantial net loss to owner occupation in recent years. The filtering down of owner occupation through the social strata has hit the bedrock of affordability.

New Patterns of Insecurity

As we saw in Chapter 2, one of the consequences of globalization – or, more broadly, of 'modernity' – has been to increase choice. But the paradox is that by extending choice so radically, rapidly and extensively people are confronted by new layers of risk, not always of their own making. The case of low-income home owners should be read in the light of this wider comment because the housing market is not a settled system and is, as we have seen, subject to cyclical patterns of boom and slump. For most owners this is not a problem, but those on the threshold of affordability, or who bought at the peak of the boom phase in an expensive area, or who become ill or unemployed while paying off an expensive mortgage, the promises of a secure future can turn rapidly to dust.

The sustainability of home ownership is not divorced, therefore, from wider economic and political changes and, as the case of low-income owners indicates, for some people it brings as many problems as it solves. In a market that is so differentiated and fragmented (Forrest, Murie and Williams, 1990) there are bound to be, in Hamnett's words, 'winners and losers' (Hamnett, 1999). Whether you win or lose, however, is very much a result of where you live and in particular *when* you entered the market, see Chapter 4).

One of the fundamentals of home ownership is its high dependency on long-term secure incomes in order to sustain mortgage payments. It is, however, striking that Britain has matured as a nation of owner-occupiers at a time when the employment structure has changed radically and become much less secure. As we saw in Chapter 4, there has been a massive growth in part-time, female jobs (although fewer women employed in full-time jobs) and a decline in full-time male work, especially in the traditional manufacturing and mining sectors. Reference was made to the growth of self-employment during the 1980s. The data showed an increase of 1.6 million self-employed jobs since 1981, reaching a total of 3.7 million in 2001. What is striking about these jobs is both the high proportion of them that are part-time and their high rate of failure. Moreover, 7 per cent of the workforce at any one time is employed in temporary jobs. The implications of this fundamental restructuring of the British economy for the sustainability of owner occupation are very significant. For example, the SEH showed that many self-employed people had borrowed against their housing equity to expand or shore up their businesses, especially during the 1980s. This strategy entailed a significant risk of 'losing everything' if the business failed or if the housing market moved into recession. At the nadir of the 1990s housing slump one-third of repossessions consisted of households affected by small-business/self-employment failures (Ford *et al.*, 1995).

Some of the consequences of this new insecurity were graphically illustrated during the 1990s recession in the housing market, notably in the scale of negative equity incurred by millions of owners and worse still a large increase in the rate of repossessions of property due to mortgage defaulting.

Negative Equity and Repossessions

Negative equity, mortgage arrears and repossessions are all problems associated with instability in the housing market, especially the 'boom – bust' house price cycle. In each case, the severity of the problem faced by owners was very closely associated with people who bought a house towards the peak of the cycle, in the most recent case in the mid-1980s. The slump in house prices in the late 1980s and early 1990s followed five years of unprecedented growth, which peaked in 1988. Property transactions were at record levels, approaching 2 million in 1988, representing nearly 15 per cent of owner occupied properties. The recession, when it hit, was steep and prolonged. By 1993 transactions were less than half the level of 1988 and real house prices fell every year between 1989 and 1996 with the exception of 1993–4. Although these changes of fortune were dramatic they are not significantly different from previous recessions in the housing market. In the 1973–7 slump, for example, real house prices fell by 35 per cent. The difference was that in the 1970s inflation generally was much higher so that during the recession *actual* house prices increased by slightly over 20 per cent. In a low-inflation period, as was the case in the 1990s, average house prices – the actual price of the property at the time – also fell. It is this factor more than the fact of the recession that was at the root of the huge increase in negative equity, and exacerbated the repossessions' crisis and the losses incurred by the lenders. At the time of writing – winter 2002 – property prices were peaking in London and the classic 'rippling out' effect was well under way in the new cycle. In benign economic conditions, especially with interest rates sustained at a low level, the danger of a catastrophic collapse in the market is much less likely than in the 1980s. A general slowdown seems a much more likely scenario.

The problem of negative equity grew rapidly in the late 1980s and early 1990s as the country entered the long house price slump. Various estimates were made of the scale of the problem. The Bank of England estimated that 876,000 households were in negative equity in 1992 with the deficit between outstanding loans and the value of the property amounting to an astonishing £5.9 billion (Bank of England, 1992). The following year was even worse, and with the addition of hundreds of thousands more cases the Council of Mortgage Lenders calculated that at its peak the figure was 1.7 million households owing £10.8 billion.

A study by Holmans and Frosztega showed that a very large part of this problem arose from the point in time when the house purchase was made, affecting buyers who bought at or just after the peak of the boom in 1988. The study also showed that three-quarters of the households affected by negative equity lived in the south of England. By far the worst affected area was the south-east region which accounted for 53 per cent of cases, including households that had re-mortgaged or had second mortgages (Holmans and Frosztega, 1996). In this respect, the slump in house prices in the 1990s was different from the previous down-turn in the early 1980s which mainly impacted on owners in the areas of manufacturing decline in the north of the country. Figure 7.1 shows the rise and fall of negative equity in the UK and the regional components in the South East and in the Yorkshire and Humberside regions.

Several studies were made of the characteristics of households in negative equity in the 1990s. Dorling and Cornford claimed that those suffering from negative equity were mostly low-income first-time buyers, under age 25, and living in the poorer areas of the south of the country (Dorling and Cornford, 1995). These findings were contradicted by Forrest *et al.* who found that 80 per cent were aged 25–44. Forrest *et al.* concluded that negative equity 'is not a problem of "marginal" home-owners' (Forrest *et al.*, 1997: 2). This is the same conclusion as Holmans who showed that it was a problem affecting all social groups (Holmans and Frosztega, 1996: 18). In a later summing up of evidence Forrest *et al.* conclude, 'In most respects those with negative equity can be characterised simply as having been in the wrong place in the housing market at the

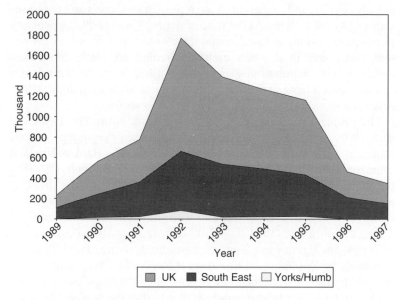

Figure 7.1   **The rise and fall of negative equity, 1989–97**
Source: Wilcox (1998: 137).

wrong time' (Forrest, Kennett and Leather, 1999: 50). The vast majority of those in negative equity suffered little more than short-term anxiety, and in some cases inability to move house for a number of years.

The dramatic increase in repossessions in 1989 was a qualitatively much worse experience and only partly a consequence of the slump in house prices. The problem would not have been so catastrophic for those caught up in it had the slump been less severe because some people would have been able to trade down to cheaper properties. As it was, prices fell sharply and transaction levels plummeted making it impossible for owners in arrears with their payments to move on. There were three other factors at work. First, financial deregulation had led during the 1980s to a situation in which new entrants to the market and movers were highly geared – mortgages were high in relation to the value of the property. Second, interest rates grew rapidly from 9.5 per cent in 1988 to 15.4 per cent in the early months of 1990 before deceasing, but in small amounts. This caused mortgage payments to increase sharply. Third, the economic recession of the early 1990s created very high levels of unemployment and a surge in small business failures (Ford *et al.*, 1995). It was the combined impact of these factors that produced the massive

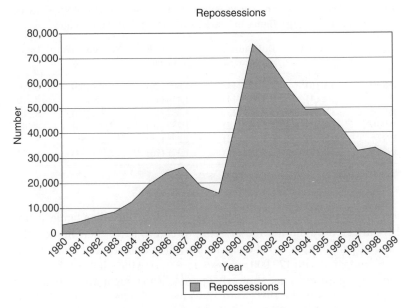

Figure 7.2 **Mortgage repossessions, England and Wales, 1980–99**
Source: Wilcox (1998, 2000).

increase in households in arrears with their payments and for those hit by unemployment, illness and other catastrophic problems, the surge in repossessions (Figure 7.2).

Mortgage arrears peaked in 1991 when 850,000 mortgagors were estimated to be in two months' arrears with their payments, nearly 9 per cent of all households with a mortgage. This fell to half that number within a few years and was less than 3 per cent of mortgagors by 1996 (see Table 7.4). Arrears are an important measure, because it suggests a pool of people with an increasing vulnerability to repossession. Households that tipped over into repossessions grew from only 16,000 in 1989 to 44,000 in 1990 and peaked in 1991 at 75,000. As conditions in the housing market improved in the later 1990s the problem eased very considerably. By the year 2000 fewer than 23,000 properties were taken back by the lenders, a fall of 25 per cent over the previous year as interest rates stabilized at lower levels and the property market moved steadily upwards.

In relative terms repossessions, even at their worst, were a small proportion of households with mortgages, in the peak year (1991) 0.77 per cent of mortgagors. Nevertheless some 350,000 homeowners

Table 7.4   **Problems with mortgage payments, England, 1993/4–1998/9, Owners buying with a mortgage; figure in brackets = % of total with mortgages**

Year	In arrears	Difficulties, not in arrears	Total with problems	No problems	Total
1993/4	480 (6)	1,129 (14)	1,609 (20)	6,581 (80)	8,190
1994/5	355 (4)	1,115 (14)	1,470 (18)	6,750 (82)	8,220
1995/6	326 (4)	1,061 (13)	1,387 (17)	6,932 (83)	8,319
1996/7	268 (3)	1,013 (12)	1,282 (16)	7,001 (84)	8,283
1997/8	252 (3)	1,047 (12)	1,298 (15)	7,219 (85)	8,518
1998/9	236 (3)	1,135 (13)	1,371 (16)	7,134 (84)	8,504

Source: *Survey of English Housing, 1998/9* (38) DETR.

lost their property during the 1990s recession, and including family members affected by the trauma of being forced to leave their homes, the total of people involved is equivalent to the population of a large city. This compared with 129,000 repossessions during the whole of the 1980s. Once again the evidence shows that people who bought property during the boom years in the 1980s were most badly affected but the profile of those repossessed differs considerably from households suffering from negative equity. Burrows, concluded from his study of households with serious mortgage indebtedness and other related research that, 'In particular, the results highlight the continued vulnerability of increasingly large numbers of owner occupiers with low and/or discontinuous incomes streams, who unlike tenants, have no entitlement to "in work" benefits' (Burrows, 1998: 20).

Repossessions arose from a crisis of affordability caused by extreme increases in interest rates coinciding with high levels of unemployment and small business failures due to the wider economic recession. The economic cycle and the house price cycle produced a conjunction of events that lead to major disruption of some parts of the housing market and, for some people, disaster. Those affected by repossessions were in the main, although not exclusively, low-income households vulnerable to shocks in the employment system. The slump in house prices was the last straw.

Home Ownership as a Source of Wealth

The problems of negative equity, mortgage arrears and repossessions impacted on a very large number of people but, even at its very worst, in relative terms, only a small minority of owners suffered any lasting harm. In the long run, however, despite the boom and slump house price cycle, almost all owner-occupiers who stay in the market for any length of time benefit from the accruing value of their property. Accumulation potential provides opportunities to increase personal wealth and access housing equity.

For the vast majority of homeowners their house, over the years, serves as a store of gradually accumulating wealth. Indeed during the course of the twentieth century homeownership has been the most important single factor in levelling wealth inequalities (Lowe, 1988). Atkinson and his colleagues showed that in the pre-Second World War era the vast majority of wealth, measured by property, stocks and shares, etc., was owned by a tiny fraction of the population. But the share of wealth among the top 5 per cent of wealth holders fell from 82 per cent in 1923 to less than 60 per cent in 1960, a significant part of this change being attributed to the expansion of home ownership and house price inflation. The role of housing as a source of personal disposable wealth has increased during the last three or four decades, and has grown more rapidly than the other main forms of wealth accumulation (financial assets and pensions). In the early 1970s private pensions and net housing accounted for about 30 per cent of personal sector wealth and grew to about double that proportion by the late 1980s (Lowe, 1988). By the mid-1990s housing had grown to 40 per cent of net personal wealth and, as shown in Table 7.5 far outstripped any other form of asset in magnitude.

A study, comparing financial assets, net housing and pension wealth found that in 1995/6 private pensions and housing accounted for three-quarters of personal wealth, indeed, housing on its own (excluding *state* pension wealth) accounted for 47 per cent of personal disposable assets (Whyley and Warren, 1999). The Family Resources Survey, which was conducted towards the end of the house price recession in the mid-1990s, showed that mean housing wealth was £31,700 and for pensioners (most of whom had paid off their mortgages) £56,900. As home owning has spread throughout society it was bound to change the relative distribution and the absolute quantity of wealth.

A key feature of this situation is the long historical tendency for house prices to inflate at a faster rate than other prices. Holmans estimated that house prices increased in real terms by 200 per cent in the two decades between 1969 and 1989. This was an exceptional period of growth but the trend can be traced back to the nineteenth century

Table 7.5   **Scale of different assets in personal wealth, 1994**

(% total assets)	Gross	Net
UK residential buildings	45.2	40.0
Insurance policies	19.4	17.1
Cash, including bank, etc. accounts	17.1	15.1
Stocks and shares	12.7	11.2
Loans and mortgages	3.7	3.2
Other personal savings	3.2	2.8
Household goods	3.7	3.3
UK land and buildings	2.9	2.6
Government securities	2.4	2.1
Trade assets and partnerships	2.2	2.0
Foreign immovables	0.6	0.6
Total	**113.1**	**100.0**
Less: Mortgage	–8.6	
Other debts	–4.5	

Source: Inland Revenue Statistics (1997: table 13.1).

and is well documented in the twentieth, with the only exception being the 1930s.

Figure 7.3 shows the trend for house prices to accelerate away from average earnings during most of the second half of the twentieth century. It is this feature of housing in Britain that has provided the basis of significant gains for millions of owner-occupier households, despite the relatively high costs of ownership and their reliance on the availability of mortgage funding. This is not to say that wealth inequalities between the top wealth holders and the rest are no longer significant, or that capital accumulation through housing is a windfall for owner-occupiers everywhere and in all social classes (Saunders, 1986). Wealth inequalities still remain very extreme, with the top 10 per cent of the population owning 50 per cent of disposable wealth. The point is that home ownership has brought possession of a sizeable asset to the majority of the British population for the first time in history. As Hamnett observed: 'Housing wealth is not just widely owned, it is the most equally distributed of all assets' (Hamnett, 1999: 105). Indeed, the redistributive impact of home owning is an important part of the social history of the twentieth century, a fact that is insufficiently debated in the social policy and 'housing' literatures.

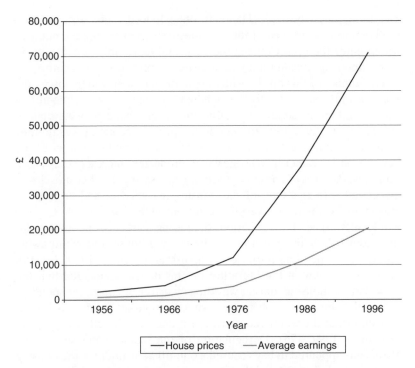

Figure 7.3 **House price inflation against average earnings, 1956–91**
Source: Council for Mortgage Lenders, 'Housing Finance', 31 (August 1996).

The Impact of Housing Capital on the Macroeconomy

The assets and debts associated with home ownership have become central to the budgets of a majority of households in Britain. Home ownership grew from 55 per cent to 67 per cent between 1980 and 1990, and has now stabilized at nearly 70 per cent. During this period of growth the value of physical assets, mostly held in the form of housing, doubled from £553 billion to £1,137 billion. Personal sector debt also rose from £178 billion to £343 billion, but this was more than outweighed by the value of assets and growing real incomes. Moreover, owners are very well aware of the accumulation potential of their property. In the south east of England, where house prices are at premium levels, a high pro-portion of owner-occupiers design housing careers with the intention of 'trading up' to larger, more expensive property well aware of the long-term gains to be made (Hamnett, 1999). Indeed, capital accumulation is a common experience of the vast mass of owner-occupiers, many of whom enter the sector during their 20s and leave only at death or, in increasingly significant numbers of cases, to enter residential care.

The impact of this on the wider economy has been widely discussed. Some economists point to the damaging effects of huge volumes of capital and credit circulating round the second-hand housing market (Muellbauer, 1990). Investment into the primary economy was thereby damaged and interest rate policy was influenced by the politics of the housing market rather than by the wider, productive interest of the macro-economy. Patterns of consumer spending and saving thus became closely associated with the state of the housing market and had an adverse impact on the ability of governments to control the economy. As Carruth and Henley argue: 'During periods of housing market boom, households may adjust their income upwards by moving house and withdrawing equity...for spending purposes' (Carruth and Henley, 1990: 30). But Hamnett's review of the literature on this debate concluded that the view that the housing market was the key driver of consumer spending overstated the case: 'The home ownership market reinforces booms and slumps in the wider economy, but it does not directly cause them' (Hamnett, 1999: 176). Deregulation of the financial markets in the 1980s thus appeared to have caused a one-off adjustment in the housing market, which destabilized the economy.

Equity Withdrawal

Equity withdrawal is the process by which some – and, on occasion, all – the equity stored in a property can be taken out or used to secure new lending. It is this possibility that makes capital accumulation of more than theoretical importance in housing policy analysis, providing access to new resources for consumption on goods or services.

The definition of 'net equity withdrawal' is the balance of new lending set against capital injection – for example, through home improvements or simply from new house building. The fundamental principle is that equity withdrawal is balanced by new borrowing somewhere in the system. It should be made clear, therefore, that equity extraction from the housing market is, in accounting terms, not a 'free lunch' for homeowners. When the beneficiaries of a housing legacy receive money from the sale of a property the buyers typically will have borrowed from a bank or building society to finance the purchase. Equity extracted is replaced by other people's debt. The significance of it, however, is that it allows a flow of huge quantities of money out of the housing sector into the wider economy. Holmans identified three main sources of equity withdrawal. First, and initially the most common form, arose from '*last-time sales*' when an elderly owner-occupier died or moved into residential care. Sales by people permanently leaving the country also fall into this category. The scale of this type of withdrawal depends both on demographic patterns – particularly the increasing number of elderly owners – and the point in time in the house price cycle when the final sale of the property was made. Beneficiaries of a will may decide not to sell the property until house prices appear to have reached a premium level. Part of the growth in the PRS in the early 1990s almost certainly arose from beneficiaries 'parking' such property until the housing market revived (Table 7.6).

Table 7.6 shows that the number of estates with UK dwellings as part of them has remained relatively stable from the mid-1960s to the mid-1990s although the *value* of housing within estates has grown considerably, from 24 per cent in 1968 to 49 per cent in 1988. It should be noted that nearly 40 per cent of estates pass to the surviving spouses and so do not pass into the wider family network. For example, in 1992/3 this factor reduced the number of estates passing to non-spouse beneficiaries from 142,000 estates (with dwellings) to about 87,000 (Holmans and Frosztega, 1994). Nevertheless in that year alone over £8 billion of housing assets were passed at death to beneficiaries. This phenomenon has become an increasingly common experience for hundreds of thousands of people and, it should be added, from all social classes.

The second type of equity withdrawal arises from *moving house*. A mover may opt to 'trade down' to a cheaper property and having redeemed their mortgage keep any remaining proceeds from the sale of

Table 7.6 **Number and value of estates passing at death, 1968–95**

Year	No. of estates with UK houses	Total number of estates	% of total with dwellings	Value of housing (£m)	Total value (£m)	Housing as % of total
1968/9	125,085	271,238	46.1	465	1,923	24.2
1971/2	149,052	288,796	51.6	638	2,275	28.0
1984/5	147,717	273,762	53.9	4,163	10,372	40.1
1989/0	154,225	276,412	55.8	9,460	20,121	47.0
1992/3	142,446	254,450	56.0	8,016	19,511	41.1
1994/5	150,807	270,868	55.7	8,567	21,758	39.4

Source: Hamnett (1999: 128).

the original house. Up-market movers can also take on a sufficiently large mortgage to release some of the capital accumulated in the previous house. Finally, equity can be extracted from a property without moving or selling it. *Re-mortgaging* involves existing owners borrowing against the accumulated equity by taking on a 'further advance' of mortgage funds – or, as has become common in the recent years in the more competitive marketplace for mortgage finance – homeowners switch lenders frequently in order to obtain the best finance package. Internet banking has lead to new products in which owners re-mortgage and at the same time open savings and current accounts with the same bank so that interest from these accounts can be offset against the mortgage debt. Any of these changes, which allow mortgagors to reschedule their payments or rebalance their equity and debt, offer opportunities for equity 'leakage'.

Net equity withdrawal through these different means began to be significant in the national accounts in the early 1980s, partly arising from the deregulation of the money markets. Net withdrawals leapt from £407 million in 1980 to £1,586 million in 1981 and peaked at £16,169 million in 1988 at the height of the housing boom (Holmans, 1991). During the 1990s recession net withdrawals fell sharply although, as Hamnett points out in his review of equity withdrawal, there was in the 1990s a shift in the composition of equity extraction. As the value of withdrawals by movers fell, arising from the decline in house prices and number of moves, so over-mortgaging and re-mortgaging grew in importance. Holmans suggests that these types of equity withdrawal are counter-cyclical because banks and building societies encourage new business through re-mortgaging and re-structuring of debt during troughs in the housing cycle.

Figure 7.4 shows a calculation of equity withdrawal as a percentage of consumer spending. As can be seen, this rose to a massive 7 per cent at the peak of the boom period in the mid-1980s and has risen steadily during the current benign market conditions. The chart shows that despite the worst and most prolonged housing recession on record there were only three years when equity withdrawal was not positive. So long as there is sufficient mortgage funding to replace 'lost' equity there is no reason why equity withdrawal should not remain an endemic feature of the housing market, albeit responding to the boom – slump cycle. It is significant because it is a source of spending power relatively difficult for governments to control and, as will be shown in the next section, is arguably one of the factors that underpins welfare state re-structuring.

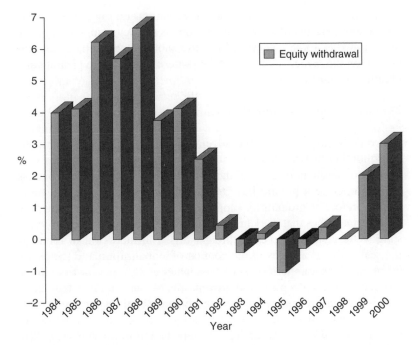

Figure 7.4 **Net equity withdrawal as a percentage of consumer spending, 1984–2000**
Source: Wilcox (2000: 50).

Home Owning and Welfare State Re-Structuring

One of the major leitmotifs of the book is the extent and speed with which the British state has had to adjust to globalization pressures. This process reflects the precipitate collapse of the old industrial heartland based on a manufacturing economy and switch to a predominantly 'post-industrial' economy based on services. As will be shown in Chapter 9, those countries which have shared this experience are also those which have experienced the biggest growth in home ownership. It is not very difficult to see why this should be the case. The new service economy has been based on a huge expansion of part-time female employment at the expense of full-time male jobs. Two-earner households are now a norm and average incomes have risen accordingly. Moreover, there has been, as we saw in Chapter 5, a strong locational readjustment away from the inner-city and mining towns of the old economy and towards suburban and small-town locations. This geography is the key component of the move towards home ownership because suburbanization is essentially built upon the owner occupied market, where locations are pleasant and greenfield land relatively cheap.

The Macroeconomy, Welfare Restructuring and Owner Occupation

The relationship between the advent of the 'workfare state' and the consolidation of Britain as essentially a home owning society is a vital connection in the narrative. All the other English-speaking home owning nations operate a private insurance, residual welfare state and there must therefore be grounds for supposing that Britain would be influenced by the same forces that work in those societies. The attempt to restructure state welfare spending (even though largely unsuccessful in reducing the scale of it) is a reflex in the context of globalization and the establishment of the competition state (see Chapter 2). The growth of home ownership, with a deep cultural provenance, became an important factor in this reform process because of the high costs of owner occupation. As Kemeny pointed out several decades ago, the cultural pressures for higher levels of home ownership would be bound to cause resistance to increasing taxation for welfare spending (Kemeny, 1981). The idea of a 'low-tax, low-spend' economy was undoubtedly underpinned by the existence of large-scale home ownership. Both Daunton and Castles suggested that owner occupation in the long term reduces the room for manoeuvre in tax policy because the relative high costs of home ownership depletes peoples' income (Daunton, 1990; Castles, 1998). By the same token, societies with long-term commitments to high public spending need the resources of a high-tax regime to function but, in the process, make it more difficult for even highly paid workers to afford the costs of buying their homes. 'New Right' incumbency during this period, followed by what have been in effect neo-liberal Labour governments, have accelerated the emergence of the workfare state. Home ownership, with its long-established cultural imperative, has been the perfect instrument around which this new policy system has been shaped.

The Microeconomy of Home Ownership

At a more micro-level, referred to in policy analysis as the *implementation* or *delivery* level, there is a further set of questions about the mechanics of how the conversion from the Beveridge welfare state to the modern workfare state has happened in tandem with the expansion of owner occupation. The broad parameters were outlined above, notably the low-tax/low-spend fiscal regime. A subsidiary process involves the possibility of using finances resources generated inside the home ownership market itself. This takes us back to the evidence presented in the previous sections about the significance of the assets owned by owner-occupiers and the related issue of equity withdrawal, including housing inheritance. It was shown that, at its peak in the late 1980s, equity withdrawn from the housing market was equivalent to nearly 7 per cent of consumer spending and allowing for the boom and slump cycle, billions of pounds have leaked from the housing market into consumption or savings. The question is the extent to which these massive resources find their way into the private and insurance-based workfare state

One of the more obvious direct uses of home equity has been to sponsor access to residential care during the 1980s. This market grew rapidly between 1975 and 1984 from about 20,000 to over 60,000 places (DHSS, 1985). As it further expanded, evidence emerged that a very large part of it was sponsored by the 'last-time' sales of the elderly residents' property. Lowe and Watson (1990) estimated that there may have been as many as 51,000 owner-occupier movers into residential care in 1984, using housing equity in excess of £1.3 billion. Holmans and Frosztega (1994) estimated 30,000 older owner-occupier households dissolved through moves to residential care or to live with relatives representing equity withdrawal in the order of £1.8 billion. Hamnett argued for a somewhat higher figure of between 40,000 and 56,000 elderly owners entering care in the mid-1990s using the sale of their home to finance the move (Hamnett, 1999: 133). Whatever the outcome figures it is clear that equity leakage played a very significant role in the burgeoning expansion of residential care in the 1980s and 1990s. The scale of this development is also one of the explanations for a lower than expected growth in housing inheritances, which as we saw above is a major form of equity leakage.

It remains unknown, however, to what extent the care needs of the elderly will use up the potential of inheritance to trickle into the economy. For this purpose, the point is that home equity, whether used directly to sponsor residential care or the growing market for private sheltered housing, or whether it circulates through the household budgets of the inheritors, is a multi-billion-pound addition to consumption and spending. Over-mortgaging and re-mortgaging having increased considerably in recent years, further extending the use of housing equity to influence consumption patterns and by implication choices on services and welfare.

The scale and potential for equity withdrawal to sponsor other welfare needs is not documented, but it seems very likely that owners trading down in the market, families in receipt of housing inheritances and those with an ability to re-mortgage increase the scope for decisions to be made about how the household budget can be geared to support non-state services, such as opticians, the increasing proportion of non-NHS dentists or private medical care. It would not be surprising to find evidence of some of the finance to pay for these being sourced in the housing market. Other examples might be the funding or part-funding of private school fees, or the sponsorship of higher education. Care should be taken in the absence of direct evidence, but the connection between the maturation of Britain as a nation of homeowners and the advent of the stakeholder, agency-based welfare system with a broad range of services delivered through private companies seems quite predictable because it is the mirror image of the other home owning societies in the English-speaking tradition.

Equity withdrawal in its various guises seems, therefore, almost inevitably to oil the wheels of family budgets in the era of privatized care services. Lending and gifts within the family enables inter-generational transfer of these assets. The case of the sponsorship of the care needs of the elderly through residential care and private sector sheltered housing are the major documented example of this process. Equity accumulation and leakage have helped in the process of welfare re-structuring that has been an inevitable complement to the emergence and then maturation of Britain as a home owning society. Low-income owners and tenants remain, of course, excluded from this potential to self-provision using housing-sourced finance and, as a result, a considerable gulf has opened in society not fundamentally arising from social divisions by class, but from housing tenure. The relationship between Britain's maturation as a nation of homeowners and the re-treading of the welfare state is not yet properly documented. It is, however, at the very least, inconceivable that such a major social revolution as the creation of home owning society would not impact on the wider shape of the welfare state as it has done in the comparable English-speaking nations.

Conclusion

This analysis has shown that as home ownership grew during the course of the twentieth century it had profound effects on the political, economic and social systems of Britain. The chapter has pointed to several key issues. First, that there is evidence that home owning has been and remains rather damaging to the macroeconomy and yet became an irresistible force, popular with politicians and people alike and bedded into a receptive social fabric, patterned by powerful echoes of Victorian domestic culture. British society trades its love affair with home owning for underlying economic instability.

The second macro-level finding, which will be examined more in Chapter 9, is that housing does seem to be closely elided with welfare state development. In the British case there seems little doubt that the emergence of the workfare state with its accompanying residual, private insurance-based approaches to welfare has been significantly influenced by the maturing of British homeownership in the latter decades of the twentieth century. Residual insurance-based welfare systems are characteristic of the English-speaking home owning family of nations. Home ownership, and by implication 'housing' generally, is a key element in patterning welfare states.

Thirdly, is the fact that Britain completed its 'catch-up' phase as a home owning society at a time when new agents of insecurity entered the equation, creating problems of sustainability and risk at the moment of its fullest maturity. The evidence of less secure work and contracts, more part-time work and the high rate of small-business failures all create problems of vulnerability to house price recessions. Issues of 'youth transitions' are also prominent in the analysis and are strongly evidenced by the declining rate of entry into the tenure by 20-year-olds. These generational and other household formation issues will help pattern the future level and sustainability of home ownership. Despite these insecurities all the survey evidence shows that home owning is a popular and enduring form of housing. This point leads to the fourth key issue, namely that home owning has been a major contributor to the very large realignments of wealth that have figured prominently in the social and economic history of the twentieth century. Home ownership has been the single most important factor in levelling-up wealth inequalities during that century. Moreover, it has contributed enormously to the radical improvements in housing standards enjoyed by the vast majority of households.

There can be little doubt that for these millions owner occupation has been the ideal housing solution and to the extent that the real level of incomes has grown during the twentieth century this ideal has been realized. The painful lessons of the 1980s and 1990s, especially the 1990s recession, are that it is irresponsible for governments and policy-makers to extol the virtues of home owning as a blanket solution for everyone, especially in the absence of social security assistance to low-income owners. People at the margin of affordability should be supported, on a basis of equality with tenants, or should simply not enter the sector.

Home ownership has stabilized at what seems a sustainable level of about 70 per cent of households. Britain has finally caught up with her English-speaking daughters and the mother of their powerful domestic cultures has finally, quite literally, come home. However, by becoming a home owning society Britain has become *less* like its partners in the European Union, especially the major powerhouse economies of the organization. Rather paradoxically, as we saw in Chapter 2 and will revisit in Chapter 8, British social housing, on the other hand, is in the process of becoming rather *more* European.

FURTHER READING

Burrows, R., Ford, J. and Wilcox, S. (2000) 'Half the poor? Policy responses to the growth of low-income home-ownership', in S. Wilcox (ed.), *Housing Finance Review 2000–2001*, York, Joseph Rowntree Foundation.

DETR (Department of the Environment, Transport and the Regions) (2000b) *Quality and Choice: A Decent Home for All. The Housing Green Paper*, London, HMSO, Chapter 4, at www.odpm.gov.uk, click on 'Housing'.

Forrest, R., Kennett, P. and Leather, P. (1999) *Home Ownership in Crisis?*, Aldershot, Ashgate.

Hamnett, C. (1999) *Winners and Losers – Home Ownership in Modern Britain*, London, UCL Press.

Saunders, P. (1990) *A Nation of Home Owners*, London, Unwin Hyman.

8
The Residualization of Rental Housing

CHAPTER AIMS

- To describe and evaluate the changing roles and purpose of rental housing in the contemporary housing system
- To profile the modern private rented sector and to evaluate the introduction of Assured Shorthold tenancies
- To describe the characteristics of landlords and tenants
- To describe tenant – landlord relations
- To evaluate housing conditions in the PRS
- To describe the changing role of social housing and to profile social housing tenants
- To discuss the future of the rental sectors and how their futures are connected.

Introduction

It will be recalled that the division of rental housing into two unconnected systems is a core of the explanation about Britain as a 'home owning society'. On the one hand stands the experience of the private rented sector (PRS) with its century-long history of decline and on the other hand is the legacy of council housing which grew to accommodate nearly one-third of households at its zenith in the early 1970s but then it too declined to about half that level currently. The story of the last

217

decades of the twentieth century is of these two residual rental housing tenures unable to compete against home ownership, the preferred option of almost everyone, including most tenants should they ever have the opportunity to buy.

The analysis in Chapter 7 showed that home ownership had reached a mature position at about 70 per cent of households by the early 1990s, and under present circumstances is unlikely to grow much further. The consequence of this is that for the foreseeable future 30 per cent of the population will continue to be tenants of landlords. This chapter discusses these residual rental sectors of British housing. 'Residualizion' refers to two processes. First is the point that public and private renting, both in the not too distant past major housing tenures (indeed, the source of accommodation for a majority of the population until as recently as the early 1970s), were conflated into smaller, marginal sectors of the housing system. In a second sense the term 'residualization' also refers to the changing social composition of these sectors, which have come to house a disproportionately large number of the nation's poorest, most socially and economically deprived households. The process of boiling down the rental housing stock also resulted in the social distillation of households, leaving behind only those unable to move out from the declining, under-funded rental sectors. The long decline of private renting and the break-up of the historic stock of council housing are thus closely related processes in the face of the powerful cultural and political ascendancy of home ownership.

As we saw in Chapter 2, a large part of traditional council housing has been dispersed to new non-local authority owners most of whom fall under the umbrella label of Registered Social Landlords (RSLs). At this point in time RSLs and council housing make up about half each of the social housing stock, although transfers out of council housing are continuing. Whatever the eventual outcome in terms of ownership and management, roughly one in five households will remain inside the 'social' housing sector. The private rented sector, for its part, bottomed out of its long historic decline in the late 1980s at just under 9 per cent of households but grew considerably in the early 1990s and has stabilized at about 10 per cent of households, thus containing about a third of all tenants in rental housing.

The purpose of this chapter is to provide a parallel discussion of rental housing to that of home ownership in Chapter 7. What types of people live in the rental sectors, public and private? What roles do these housing sectors play in the wider housing system? How should they be characterized in these early years of the twenty-first century, and what is their future? Despite the common elements in the rental housing system – funding via housing benefit, residualization processes, evidence of considerable mobility between them – public and private renting in Britain are separate systems, operating with different rules of access, different types of housing stock, different legal foundations and latterly have come to have distinctive functions in the market (albeit it that there are important areas of overlap). However, there are enough common elements that private and public rental housing need to be discussed in the same chapter. For clarity, the discussion is separated into two sections, one for each of the sectors.

The Changing Face of the Private Rented Sector

One of the major features of tenure restructuring during the course of the twentieth century was the long process of decline of the PRS. The reasons for this were outlined in Chapter 6. The story was one of the gradual undermining of the logic of the sector as an investment vehicle, lack of subsidies and the inability of the landlord 'class' (in truth, no such thing) to make a coherent and organized stand to defend the sector. From being the form of housing provision which accommodated 90 per cent of the population before the First World War, this housing tenure had become a minor, fragmented part of the housing system by 2000, consisting primarily of a series of niche markets and overwhelmingly occupied by young people. A small, rapidly dwindling number of elderly tenants living in the regulated tenancies are all that is left of the 'traditional' PRS. There is, however, an important nuance in the long-term pattern of decline in recent decades. Having slumped to under 9 per cent of households in the late 1980s the PRS underwent a mini-revival during the course of the 1990s owing to a combination of factors – changes to tenancy arrangements in the 1988 and 1996 Housing Acts, the availability of housing benefit, the state of the home owning market (in recession) and the coincidence of the working through of a number of demographic factors, notably the growth in single-person households.

The key point is that the PRS has also in a sense 'matured' into its new role since the 1970s in parallel with the maturation of home ownership, and closely related to that development. In addition, there is now a significant body of evidence that shows a more fluid relationship with the other forms of rental housing. Changing perceptions about the role and function of social housing – particularly that it is much less regarded, especially by younger people, as a permanent housing solution – have a symbiotic relationship with the PRS. Aided by housing benefit it has been possible to move between and around the rental housing market more freely than in the past, most especially in those parts of the country (mainly in the north) where housing demand has been low. The PRS has been usefully characterized as the bottom rung of a housing ladder – where new entrants to the housing market begin their climb to home ownership, with social housing representing a stopping-off point in some cases. The metaphor does not, of course, include the shrinking number of elderly tenants in regulated tenancies many of whom have lived in the same house for decades. It should also be remembered that some households have gone down the ladder, from social housing (often by choice) and from owner occupation (often by necessity).

The aim of this part of the chapter is to document and evaluate the shifting picture and role of the PRS in the contemporary housing system. The section begins by outlining the changing size and nature of the PRS, the dramatic ascendancy of Assured Shorthold Tenancies and the collapse of regulated lettings during a period of less than five years. Patterns of mobility into and out of the sector, which largely arise from these developments, are then outlined. Finally, the characteristics of tenants and landlords and the changing nature of the tenant–landlord relationship, including a short section on the state of repair of the PRS housing stock, are evaluated.

The Size of the Private Rented Sector

The first stage is to describe the size of the sector, its recent re-structuring and trends in its pattern of growth in recent years. As can be seen from Figure 1.1 (p. 3), the PRS declined to a small fraction of its previously dominant position early in the twentieth century. The long-term decline finally bottomed-out at a low point of 8.6 per cent of households in 1989 (1.6 million households). The nadir of the sector was closely connected to the final maturation of owner occupation, as described in Chapter 7, because there was virtually no further scope for home ownership to expand by transfers to home owning of sitting tenants in the PRS. By the late 1980s the PRS had become a fragmented, residual tenure serving specialist niche markets. A small number of regulated tenancies remained as the only evidence of 'traditional' private renting (less than 20 per cent of the PRS as a whole by 1999/2000). Having slumped to its lowest level historically at the end of the 1980s the PRS underwent a significant growth in the 1990s which was revealing not so much of the long-sought-after 'revival' of private renting but a confirmation of its new role and purpose in the contemporary housing system. This spurt of activity in the early 1990s, followed the near full-scale deregulation of the market and the injection of housing benefit (subsequently controlled) so that numbers increased by between 35,000–40,000 new lets per annum through to 1995/6. The sector grew to 10.2 per cent of households in 2000, an increase of 15 per cent on the 1989 level (Figure 8.1).

To a considerable extent this growth was made up from tenants, often supported by housing benefit, who would otherwise have been seeking accommodation in the social housing sector. The symbiosis between the rental sectors is apparent here because, of course, demand for social housing was reduced by about that amount (see Chapter 4). The mini-revival resulted from a combination of factors:

- Deregulation of the market
- House price recession
- Injection of housing benefit
- Impact of the economic recession on youth transitions
- Growth in student numbers.

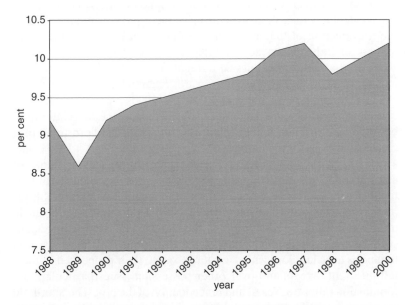

Figure 8.1 **The size of the private rented sector, 1988–2000 (percentage of households resident)**

Sources: *Survey of English Housing 1998/99; Housing Finance Review 2000/2001.*

Deregulation of Tenancies and New Types of Lettings

It is very important to the analysis of the newly deregulated market to be reminded of the fundamentals of the PRS, the core of which is the balance of advantage between landlord and tenant. It should not be forgotten that from 1915, when rent control was first introduced, up to 1988 the Rent Acts constituted a significant interference with the property rights of landlords, arising in essence because of shortage of supply in the market. For most of the twentieth century the pattern of legislation, despite attempts at changing it (notably in the Rent Act 1957), favoured security of tenure for private tenants. People's homes were considered sacrosanct against the commercial interest of landlords.

As was pointed out in Chapter 6, the key point of the failed 1957 attempt to deregulate was that decontrolled tenancies were virtually devoid of security of tenure against the full security that was enjoyed by controlled tenants, including rights of succession. Tenants' rights were in effect all or nothing. Tenants of decontrolled lettings had only one week's notice to quit (lengthened to four weeks in the 1957 Act). In response to the Rachman scandal, the Eviction Act 1964 attempted to address the problems caused by scurrilous landlords. The Housing Act 1965 sought a wholesale restructuring of the rapidly dwindling PRS by the introduction of 'fair rents' and extended security of tenure to all tenants of unfurnished accommodation. Thus it was that after the short-lived attempt at wholesale deregulation under the 1957 Act the balance of advantage swung back towards tenants.

The deregulation of the market in the 1990s was the result of a conscious effort by government to shift the balance of the relationship between landlord and tenant to once again favour landlords, and thus create conditions for increased investment. The Housing Act 1980 began a process of re-engineering this relationship through the creation of assured tenancies for licensed landlords and was extended to all new tenancies in the Housing Act 1988 with the creation of Assured Shorthold Tenancies, and finally confirmed in the Housing Act 1996 which, in effect, made assured shortholds the standard tenancy arrangement (with assured tenancies mainly limited to tenants of RSLs). Assured tenancies gave landlords much easier access to their property if tenants fell into rent arrears and over other possession issues particularly on termination (after two years) and renegotiation of the rent. The Shorthold version simply reduced the minimum period of the tenancy to six months, giving very limited security to tenants. Possession is automatic provided that the landlord has followed the correct procedure in serving the notice to quit. From March 1997 all new tenancies were assured shortholds unless there was a specific agreement that the tenancy was of some other type. Such was the advantage to landlords of the new tenancy types that as early as 1996 nearly three-quarters of tenancies were, or had converted to, assured tenancies (see Figure 8.2).

These new tenancy types could hardly be more beneficial to landlords. Because of the high turnover in this market already over 90 per cent of new lettings in the PRS are of the assured type. Shortholds accounted for 54 per cent of all lettings in 1998/9 compared to only 8 per cent in 1990, the first full year after the 1988 reform. By contrast, *before* 1989 most tenancies in the PRS were regulated under previous legislation. Assured shortholds are very easy to establish, indeed since the 1996 Act such tenancies can be created verbally, without any written terms unless expressly requested by the tenant. In 1988 nearly 60 per cent of tenancies were regulated but by 1998 this figure had fallen to only 8 per cent (a decrease from 1.1 million to only 190,000). Regulated tenancies mostly fell under the 'old' system of 'fair rents' by which landlords or tenants could appeal to local authority Rent Officers for registration of

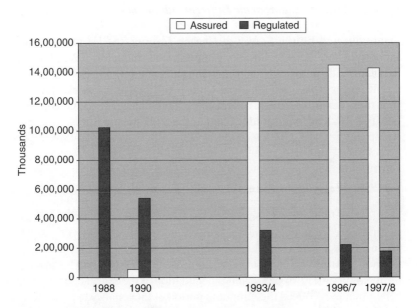

Figure 8.2 **Change in main letting types, 1988 and 1998/9**
Source: *Survey of English Housing, 2000.*

a fair rent – determined mainly on the size and amenities of the let and much less on its local market value.

Figure 8.2 shows the dramatic change to the structure of the tenancy types over a ten-year period after the deregulation of the sector in 1988. The long, historic pattern of the relationship between landlord and tenant was fundamentally altered.

Other Forms of Letting

As Table 8.1 shows, other forms of lettings make up a small proportion of the sector, notably tied accommodation, owned by employers and available only to their employees and their families. Health authorities, some universities, land owners/farmers and police authorities are typical landlords in this small sub-sector of the PRS. Together these 'closed lettings' accounted for 17 per cent of all lettings in 1998/9, nearly two-thirds of which were rent-free arrangements. This was a much lower proportion than in the past. The only other significant sub-sector consists of resident landlords and some lettings with no security, together accounting for 9 per cent of lettings in 1998/9.

Characteristics of Tenants in the Different Sub-Sectors

Data collected by the *Survey of English Housing* (SEH) showed that there were considerable variations between the characteristics of tenants living in the different sub-sectors of the PRS market. The dominance of the two types of Assured tenancies (over two-thirds of the market) means that these tenants strongly reflect the overall character of the contemporary PRS. Key features identified in the SEH were:

Table 8.1   **Structure of letting types in the PRS, 2000**

Type of tenancy	(%)
Assured	12
Shorthold Assured	54
Tied to employment	17 (10% rent-free)
Resident landlord	9
Regulated	8
Total	**100**

Source: Survey of English Housing, 2000.

- In the Assured tenancies 80 per cent of tenants were under age 45, including 20 per cent under 25. Tenants in the regulated sector and other small fragments of the PRS had an older age structure, but taken together still over 70 per cent of the whole PRS tenants were under 45. Only 13 per cent of PRS tenants were over age 65.
- 45 per cent of Assured tenants were single, 19 per cent married and 16 per cent cohabiting

Table 8.2 shows the pattern of household types in the two main types of tenancy. Single adults show up as the main type of household in the Assured categories, with a variety of other types, notably 11 per cent of Assured tenant households are headed by a single parent. By contrast, nearly a quarter of tenants in the regulated sector are over age 60.

The SEH data also shows that well over half the PRS tenants are in full-time work, compared to social housing tenants where the figure is only a quarter. Including part-time work 65 per cent of PRS tenants are in employment, with a mean gross weekly income (for the year 1999/2000) of £338 (compared to social housing tenants' mean weekly income of only £168). Other features of the circumstances of tenants in the PRS were that:

- 43 per cent lived in older property, built before 1919 (less than 25 per cent of the housing stock was built before 1919)
- Nearly 60 per cent of properties were small, either terraced houses (33 per cent) or converted flats (26 per cent).

In summary, the SEH data revealed a typical profile of tenants who were young, recent entrants to the assured lettings market and mainly lived in older, small properties. By contrast the smaller, rapidly dwindling, regulated sector contained tenants who by definition were of long-standing

Table 8.2 **PRS tenants, household types, 1998**

Household type	All Assured types	Other lettings	All
Couple, no dependent child(ren)	23	28	24
Couple with dependent child(ren)	12	16	13
Lone parent with dependent child(ren)	11	2	9
Other multi-person household	18	10	16
One adult aged under 60	30	21	28
One adult aged over 60	5	24	10

Source: *Survey of English Housing 1998/99*, table A4.1.

because no new regulated tenancies were started after January 1989. Typically these tenants were older (two-thirds over age 60), often living alone in unfurnished accommodation (and continuing to be protected by the Rent Acts with a form of rent control and security of tenure). Over 60 per cent of regulated tenants had lived in the property for more than twenty years, dating back to the time when private renting was a mainstream tenure. Indeed, taking the PRS as a whole, by 1998/9 only 16 per cent of tenants were aged over 60, a very large decease from earlier years (tenants 60 and above were over a third of all tenants only ten years previously). The PRS is very largely a tenure of mobile young people, incorporating both the upwardly mobile but also a large number of severely disadvantaged, unemployed and otherwise vulnerable young people living in unsatisfactory conditions in bed-sits in Houses in Multiple Occupation (HMOs). It contains a disproportionately large number of single parents. About 750,000 (out of about 2 million) tenants in the PRS rely on housing benefit to pay all or part of their rent (although this figure has been falling). Restrictions on housing benefit payments since the mid-1990s have caused new strains between land-lords and tenants in the deregulated market (see below).

Mobility and Turnover

During the period from the mid-1980s to the mid-1990s there was a large increase in the turnover of tenants in the PRS. The proportion that had been resident at their current address for less than one year increased from 25 per cent in 1984 to 40 per cent in 1993/4 and has stabilized at about that level. It is noticeable, however, that in the under-30 age group this fig-ure is 65 per cent and measured by those who have been at their current address under three years the figure increases to 93 per cent. The fact that this pattern of mobility was apparent *before* the deregulation of the market suggests that, at least initially, it was not the tenancy structure that caused this pattern. Almost certainly increasing mobility into, out of, and moves within, the PRS must largely be explained by the increasingly youthful character of this sector of the housing market. As the residual group of elderly tenants in the regulated sector die or otherwise move out of their homes so the function of the PRS has changed very rapidly to become a more transitional and flexible housing form accommodating a highly transient population of younger people. As Wilcox observed:

> the combination of PRS deregulation and the structure of the housing benefit scheme was such that in the early 1990s it became much easier for

lower-income households, and newly forming low-income households, to access the private rented sector. (Wilcox, 2002: 35)

Data in the most recent *Survey of English Housing* showed that of all tenants living in the PRS in 1998/9, 44 per cent had rented privately for less than a year and just over three-quarters for less than five years (SEH, 1998/9: 76–7). This data include the small number of long-standing tenants continuing to occupy regulated tenancies. In this case, 70 per cent had been private tenants for twenty years or more, mostly living at the same address. Mobility is thus very much associated with the large, youthful, Assured Shorthold sector of the market.

However, reasons for movements into and out of the PRS vary considerably, as might be expected depending on people's circumstances. Kemp and Keoghan's interrogation of SEH data (Table 8.3) showed that there was a 'reverse flow' of households out of social housing and owner occupation, as well as large numbers of newly forming households. Taking very recent movers (who had moved into the PRS in the previous twelve months) they found that less than half the entrants were new households (Kemp and Keoghan, 2001).

The data showed that while there were 356,000 new entrants to the PRS in the twelve months before the SEH interviews, there were also 327,000 leavers (127,000 moving into social housing and 200,000 into owner occupation). Of the entrants to the sector most of the new householders were young, leaving the parental home for the first time (Rugg and Burrows, 1999). Mostly they moved into furnished accommodation and had low transaction costs. Typically this group were single and either lived alone or shared with other single people; 20 per cent of new householders were students, reflecting the expansion of higher education in recent years. The revival of private renting in university towns and cities has to a considerable degree been stimulated by the growth in

Table 8.3 **The origins of households entering the PRS within the previous twelve months, 2001**

	(000)	**(%)**
Ex-owner occupiers	127	36
Ex-social housing tenants	57	16
Newly formed households	172	48
All households	**356**	**100**

Source: Kemp and Keoghan (2001: 24).

student numbers. What happens in any particular place is, however, subject to variation depending whether there is an adequate supply of PRS lettings and the economic strength of other tenant groups in local markets (Rugg, Rhodes and Jones, 2000; Davis and Hughes, 2002).

Tenants leaving social housing for the PRS were found to have very distinct social characteristics: a high percentage were unemployed or long-term sick or disabled and there was a high proportion of single parents. Especially in areas of low demand in northern cities it is easy to move between the rental sectors, especially for housing benefit claimants. As the quality of life deteriorated, especially in inner city and peripheral estates, single parents and others with children hoped to improve their situation by moving into the PRS, away from the council estate. As we saw in Chapter 5 this often proved not to be the long-term solution and serial movers might return quite quickly either to council housing or to RSL accommodation. As Keenan pointed out, such very rapid mobility – households moving two or three times a year – would not necessarily be picked up in annual data (Keenan, 1998). But the SEH data does show that a quarter of households leaving the PRS for social housing were single parents.

By contrast, households leaving owner occupation to enter the PRS were mainly in work (86 per cent in full-time work compared to only 30 per cent of social housing leavers) and nearly a quarter of them had moved to take up a new job, treating the PRS as temporary accommodation until they could buy a house. The other main factor associated with owner-occupier entrants to the PRS was relationship breakdown, with nearly 40 per cent of entrants saying this was why they left home ownership. Once again finding easy-access, temporary accommodation that was affordable in the short term were key reasons for the move. Not surprisingly the great majority of tenants leaving the PRS to move into owner occupation were in full-time employment and likely to be couples or couples with children. People leaving the PRS to enter social housing were a much more diverse group. By contrast to the movers into home ownership this group were mainly unemployed, retired, sick or disabled and otherwise economically inactive (notably a high proportion of single parents). As Kemp and Keoghan pointed out the median income of leavers for owner occupation was over four times that of leavers for social housing (Kemp and Keoghan, 2001: 27–8).

There were thus considerable contrasts between the new households entering the PRS, existing households moving in from another tenure, and between the leavers moving either into social housing or owner occupation. The story underpins the idea of the role of the contemporary PRS as a highly diverse and fluid tenure catering for transient populations moving up and down the housing ladder and in very different financial and social condition.

Profile of Landlords

Historically, the PRS in Britain has been owned by small-scale landlords, and this remains the case today. Ownership is dominated by private individuals and there are relatively few commercial companies involved in this sector of the housing system. Research conducted in the mid-1990s found that over 60 per cent of landlords were private individuals or couples. Only 15 per cent of landlords were private companies. Neither did this mean that there were a small number of very large business landlords owning a disproportionately large number of properties. The companies themselves were not large, indeed the total of lettings by the business sector accounted for 20 per cent of addresses (Table 8.4).

Of the so called 'corporate landlords' 57 per cent owned a portfolio of less than 100 properties. Only 16 per cent of addresses were owned by businesses with over 1,000 properties, a scale of activity which would be considered relatively small-scale by comparison with RSLs, some of which own tens of thousands of properties all over the country (see Chapter 2).

Crook and Kemp (1996) showed that 43 per cent of individual landlords owned only one property, two-thirds owned four or lower and 82 per cent owned nine properties or fewes. Only 9 per cent of individual landlords owned a stock of more than twenty-five properties. Further investigation of landlord characteristics found that only one in seven individual landlords said that being a landlord was their full-time job. In

Table 8.4 **Type of landlord, 1996**

Private individual/couple	61
Partnership	5
Private company	15
Public company	5
Charity or charitable trust	4
Church or Crown Commissioners	1
Government department	3
Educational establishment	1
Other	5
Total	**100**

Source: Crook and Kemp (1996).

effect, all the rest were amateur, part-time landlords. Thomas *et al.* referred to these types of landlords as 'sideline' landlords (Thomas *et al.*, 1995). This type is overwhelmingly the most significant type of landlord in Britain, owning just under three-quarters of privately rented addresses. Neither was the return to these landlords a major part of their income; 70 per cent of sideline landlords received a quarter or less of their income from their propert(y)ies. It should also be noted that since Crook and Kemp's benchmark study in the mid-1990s the sector grew and then stabilized at about 10 per cent of households. Most of the recent growth arose from investment by sideline landlords. The number of tenancies let by individual landlords increased from just over 1 million in 1990/1 (53 per cent of all lettings) to nearly 1.7 million lets in 1998/9 (75 per cent of all lets) (MacConaghy *et al.*, 2000 : 228).

The growth in the number of sideline landlords in the 1990s is due to a combination of reasons, the main one of which is that Assured Shorthold tenancies gave landlords much greater flexibility and access to properties without recourse to court orders. Studies of the opinions of private landlords have not surprisingly found high levels of support for the new forms of tenancy. Thus the attitudes common in the 'old' days of the regulated tenancy, that being a private landlord was uneconomic and property rights were weighted far too much towards the interests of tenants, have very rapidly changed. The expansion of the 'buy-to-let' scheme is witness to this new impetus. Under the scheme loans are more attractive than normal and management of properties is normally handled by letting agents. A development of this is the increasing number of parents who buy a property for their children when they leave home to go into higher education (famously, UK Prime Minister Blair and his wife). Their hope is to help fund the increasing costs of high education by letting rooms not occupied by their child. By mid-2000, 80,000 buy-to-let mortgages involving about £6 billion of loans had been taken out (Crook, 2002a: 24) and at the time of writing in the spring of 2003 the figures had soared to over 275,000 loans worth £24.2 billion (Council of Mortgage Lenders, 2003).

PRS growth was also encouraged by the availability of housing benefit, which allowed tenants to move more freely between social housing and the PRS in the early part of the 1990s. However this became less significant after 1996 owing to the introduction of local reference rents on eligible rents and also the single-room rent limit in the PRS. Both these factors caused a significant decline in the numbers of households receiving housing benefit in the PRS since 1996. Wilcox estimates a decline of about 30 per cent (to 783,000 claimants), resulting in a saving to the Exchequer of some £6.5 billion in the four years after 1996 (Wilcox, 2001). Recent SEH data suggest that this has fallen even further to only 540,000 (only 28 per cent of all PRS tenancies). Wilcox concludes that, 'changes in the housing benefit system particularly to the private rented sector ... have been the major factor in the decline in the numbers of housing benefit claimants able to secure accommodation in that sector' (Wilcox, 2001: 2). Another dampening factor from the mid-1990s was the increase in house prices, which probably encouraged owners to sell on in the owner occupier market rather than 'park' property in the PRS while house prices were low in the early 1990s.

Despite these downward pressures, however, other factors have continued to sustain the PRS at or slightly above 10 per cent of households after the mid-1990s. As we have seen the increasing ease with which landlords, especially sideline landlords, can claim possession through Shorthold Assured tenancies is a major and historic incentive to private landlords. As we saw above, landlords can purchase off-the-shelf tenancy agreements and begin to let property with a minimum of legal knowledge (Lister, 2002). Indeed, it is not only lack of knowledge of legal procedure that typifies individual landlords but also generally low levels of management expertise and skills. There may well be a new range of problems in the tenant–landlord relationship arising from this now highly deregulated market in which neither side has a strong grasp of the legal foundations of the let. Given the overwhelmingly youthful character of the PRS, young people, with little or no experience and entering the housing market independently for the first time, are particularly vulnerable to unscrupulous or ignorant landlords.

Unlawful Evictions and Harassment

One of the features of the PRS historically has been the problem of unlawful and illegal evictions, most notoriously in the Rachman scandal following the 1957 Act (see p. 00). The dramatically different role, legal status and social composition of the contemporary PRS would appear, at least in theory, to raise questions about the scope for illegal harassment in the now almost totally deregulated market. This is an important policy and legal issue given that as, Morgan notes, rental accommodation 'is increasingly the preserve of vulnerable households with complex social or behavioural problems who are in receipt of housing benefit' (Morgan, 2002: 113). As we have seen, in the order of three-quarters of a million tenants in the PRS rely on the housing benefit system for part or all of their rent. However, a series of reforms and tightening surrounding the system have significantly changed the balance and created new areas of tension between landlord and tenant. The main developments have been:

- the introduction of local reference rents, which create a ceiling for housing benefit payment
- payments to the under-25s have been restricted
- Pre-Tenancy Determinations aim to help tenants to find out how much housing benefit is payable on the property – although the aim of strengthening the tenant's ability to bargain with landlords is highly optimistic
- benefit is paid four weeks in arrears, meaning that new tenants have to fund the first month from their own resources.

Most recently attempts to defeat housing benefit fraud have led to a requirement that claimants verify their identity (with original documents).

The result of this more complex regime for claiming housing benefit is that the *average* delay in making payments has risen to five months (approaching 25 per cent of the length of a Shorthold tenancy). Given that most landlords, as we have seen above, are small-scale amateurs, these changes to benefits procedures and the resultant delays in payments, create a climate in which illegal evictions are likely to grow (Marsh *et al.*, 2000). For small-scale landlords many with only one or two properties on which they rely for part of their income, delays in payment can be serious financial problem.

These difficulties are magnified by the generally low level of knowledge by landlords and tenants about legal entitlements and duties. As Nelken pointed out, in the classic study of tenant–landlord relations, this whole area of housing is surrounded by ignorance of the law on both sides (Nelken, 1983). With individual rather then company landlords, vetting of prospective tenants is likely to be low and arrangements commonly made on an informal basis. Many tenants do not receive a rent book or even a written statement of the conditions of the tenancy. In cases where rent is not paid promptly, or is not paid at all, landlords may well seek equally informal methods of redress, particularly through harassment and pressure on tenants to vacate the property.

Harassment can take many forms and is not normally the heavy-handed intimidation associated with Rachman. In fact, most harassment is not associated at all with commercial companies but is very much the province of small landlordism (Morgan, 2002). Proving and defining 'harassment' is not easy because a succession of small events – late-night visits from the landlord, opening mail, delays in repairs, persistent phone calls, etc. – may not in themselves amount to much, but taken together can be calculated to disturb the tenant. This form of intimidation is not only difficult to detect but also to bring to court. Moreover, tenants of *resident* landlords enjoy no protection from harassment offered by the Rent Acts or the Protection from Eviction Act 1977 and they have no rights under the Housing Act 1988. The numbers of tenants involved may be very considerable indeed given that it is estimated that about 1 per cent of households have a lodger (DoE, 1995: 204).

Thus the position of tenants in the new climate of deregulated tenancies is much more precarious than at any stage since 1915. Research suggests that tenants often do not have any knowledge of the kind of tenancy they are under or the circumstances in which they can be evicted or asked to leave. It seems that tenants have a very low threshold of knowledge about what constitutes harassment and so seem to tolerate situations that are not in fact acceptable in law (Cowans, 2001; Lister, 2002). As was suggested above, harassment is not always easy to prove if it consists of persistent small intrusions and the legal remedies are generally weak even when it is possible to prove. Nothing appears to have changed since Nelken's observation that, 'the low level of fines generally imposed may discourage authorities from instituting criminal proceedings' (Nelken, 1983: 9).

The Labour Government's 2000 Green Paper made it very clear that there would be no changes to the system of Assured tenancies for fear of discouraging investment in the sector. Given that the PRS contains many young people setting up independently for the first time and a range of other people in disadvantaged positions informal and unrecorded harassment is likely to be considerable. Landlords no longer need to evade the Rent Act constraints because the new tenancy system effectively overturns the historic position giving landlords easy access to their properties. There is no doubt that this newly deregulated market is flourishing, but there may come a time when the rights of tenants will need to be more clearly protected. The history of the PRS sector in the twentieth century suggests that there is no easy way to balance the needs of investors with the needs of those who, of necessity or choice, make their homes in private rented accommodation.

Housing Conditions in the Private Rented Sector

The PRS contains, relative to its size, the worst housing conditions of any of the main housing tenures, although the situation has improved considerably in recent years. The most recently published English House Conditions Survey (DETR, 1998) showed that it was not only households and people that were very mobile but that the properties themselves were relatively transient, coming into and going out of the market quite quickly (Ellison, 2002). For example, at the time of the most recent EHCS in 1996 only 65 per cent of properties that were then privately rented had been so at the time of the previous survey in 1991. Studies of landlords' attitudes have shown that addresses were acquired for a variety of reasons, and initially not concerned with letting out. Indeed, only half the landlords, reported by one study, said they first let the address to make a capital gain or for income (Crook, Hughes and Kemp, 1995). Whatever the causes that underpinned the fluidity of the stock of properties in the PRS, it was this turnover in the PRS stock that accounted for the improvement in conditions in the sector during this period. In other words, the properties moving into the PRS in the early 1990s were in a better state of repair then those already in it. This may well have been due to the fact that at this period a large element of new lets were made by owner-occupiers or builders unwilling or unable to sell their property(ies) during the house price slump. The question, therefore, is whether in the long run housing conditions in the newly deregulated PRS will improve. Will the ability, at least in theory, of landlords to charge market-level rents enable them to invest more into the upkeep and renovation of the sector (Crook, 2002b)?

The position currently is that the PRS housing stock is quite varied, although there is a concentration of smaller properties at the bottom end of the Council Tax bands (suggesting low value). According to the 1998/9 SEH, only 24 per cent of Assured tenancy properties were detached or semi-detached houses, all the rest were either terraced houses or flats. However, 96 per cent of these properties were at or above the bedroom standard (including 44 per cent that were at least one bedroom above standard). 77 per cent of assured tenancy properties were in Council Tax bands A–C, the lowest level. These properties were worth less than £68,000, including nearly 40 per cent worth something less than £44,000 (roughly half *average* prices at the time). These valuations reflect not only the size of these properties but also their age. Half of housing in the PRS is at least seventy-five years old and it is in this older stock where there are significant problems of repair and housing standards. Despite the improvement in recent years people living in the PRS are more likely than any other form of housing to suffer poor conditions.

The EHCS estimated that about 30 per cent of tenants in the PRS live in poor housing conditions by modern standards and compared with the other tenures (14 per cent for of all households). For example, nearly 30 per cent of properties do not have full central heating (22 per cent have none) compared to owner occupation where virtually everyone who wants central heating has a full system. Only 17 per cent of PRS properties have double-glazing, compared to 30 per cent in all the tenures. The EHCS found that two-thirds of PRS properties had an urgent external repair likely to cause a significant problem for its occupants if not dealt with soon, indeed 18 per cent were considered to be in such a poor state of repair as to be unfit for human habitation. These problems are mainly associated with poor pre-1919 terraced houses than with converted flats and more modern houses. They are also particularly associated with Houses in Multiple Occupation (HMOs) – bedsits, shared flats, hostels and B&B hotels – which represent the bottom end of the PRS market, although are among the most lucrative owing to overcrowding and poor levels of services provided. Recent attempts have been made to control conditions in this niche of the PRS through a system of licensing. It is compulsory in Scotland for HMOs to be registered with the local authority, and plans are in hand to extend this to England and Wales (Currie, 2002; Hughes and Lowe, 2002).

There are several reasons why the state of repair in this sector has been so poor. Firstly, rent controls imposed during 1915 deprived landlords of the ability to make returns on investment, indeed so low were the returns at the lower end of the market that the *only* way to avoid losses was to restrict investment on repair and maintenance. Second, the PRS has increasingly catered for households with low incomes so that even in a deregulated market (supported by housing benefit) profit margins were low. Moreover, the tax system for much of the twentieth century disadvantaged private landlords against the other housing tenures. Indeed, it was famously observed by Nevitt that there was a negative return on properties that had been improved (Nevitt, 1966). The ownership structure is such that the majority of landlords, who own only one or two properties, are unlikely to be able to make economies of scale in their repair and maintenance work, although as Crook and Hughes point out financial return is not always what motivates landlords (Crook and Hughes, 2001). However, the underlying logic of these factors is that there has been historically a serious level of under-investment in the PRS, especially at the lower end of the market.

The poorest condition stock is invariably occupied by those with the least resources and unable to access the other housing tenures. It may be recalled that this was precisely the point made by Gauldie (1974) about the PRS in its heyday at the end of the nineteenth century (see Chapter 6). Low income equated with low housing standards, over-crowding and squalor. Although without comparison to the 'cruel habitations' of the Victorian slum, the contemporary PRS contains the highest proportion of poorly housed occupants than any of the other tenures. The 1996 EHCS found that nearly 40 per cent of younger households (aged 16–24) lived in poor conditions, while over half the long-standing (over thirty years), ageing tenants in regulated tenancies lived in poor-quality housing.

It must be stressed, however, that these figures are a significant improvement on levels of unfitness found in previous EHCSs, due mainly to the higher quality of the more recently let property. The problem is that there continue to be significant niches in the PRS sector where poor management, ageing stock, lack of investment and exploitative landlords create unacceptably sub-standard housing. Nearly a third of PRS tenants live in properties that are in poor condition by modern standards, lack central heating, have significant repair problems, lacking fire alarms and secure locks, etc. These problems are mainly confined to the body of older terraced houses (often occupied by ageing tenants on regulated (low) rents) and HMOs more generally (where financial yields are often high). Unemployed young men, other social security claimants and the elderly are the most likely to suffer these sub-standard conditions. As Crook and Hughes argue, despite deregulation it does not follow that a smoothly function and efficient market has been instantly produced. Both tenants and landlords still do not have sufficient knowledge of market conditions in their area. Prospective tenants do not shop around sufficiently to find the best deal and small-scale landlords do not necessarily operate in a commercial framework. If a property is in poor condition there is no easily available way of finding out what is its true value. Moreover a prospective tenant is more likely to be concerned about whether the property has functioning utilities and adequate heating than, say, the state of repair of the roof. The rapid turnover of young, inexperienced tenants in this market is also likely to increase pressure for better repair and maintenance. From a landlord's perspective there is little incentive to spend money on improvements if demand in the area is low or rental income is limited by the market (and housing benefit levels). Crook and Hughes conclude their analysis, 'The evidence ... that the belief that market forces will result in an improvement in the condition of the privately rented housing stock is not wholly well founded (Crook and Hughes, 2001: 44).

Future Prospects

In the landmark Housing Green Paper of April 2000 the first Blair government outlined their view of the housing system as a whole with a strong emphasis on home ownership and large sections of the paper devoted to the reform of social housing (DETR, 2000b). Only one chapter was devoted to the private rented sector, significantly headed 'promoting a healthy private rented sector', signifying that the government regards the continuation and development of the sector as a central part of its housing strategy. Of particular importance is the role of the PRS in providing easy-access accommodation to young people who as yet are unable or unwilling to purchase their own home. Its role in enabling labour mobility was also flagged as important, so that people can change jobs and more easily move to a different area, or while owner-occupiers, away from home for extended periods, can more easily let out their property. The Green Paper therefore declared its aim of supporting the PRS, seeing it prosper and grow, and expressing no major legislative changes. The main ambition for the sector was to see significant improvement in its organization and management, particularly because of the recognition of the largely amateur tradition of British landlordism.

How far this objective of policy will be met in the future is open to considerable question. About one-third of the PRS consists of poor-quality accommodation mainly occupied by young and vulnerable young people entering the housing market independently for the first time. We saw that in the early 1990s the PRS supplied a large amount of new lettings, mainly as a result of financial support through the housing benefit system. Since 1996 this support has been sharply curtailed, and expansion has slowed largely as a result of the increase in house prices, which encourages owners to sell on in the owner occupied market rather than hold property in the rental sector.

The only additional factor which seems to be shaping up is the growing interest in 'buy-to-let' mortgages. Following the terrorist attacks on 11 September 2001, and the Enron scandal, which called into question the moral veracity of multinational corporations, the global stock markets have struggled and values fell sharply in the early years of the new millennium. Some investors have diversified their holdings from stocks and share into property, using the buy-to-let vehicle. The growth of the student market is also a factor here. The scale of this market is not great in the overall amounts of mortgage lending (about 4 per cent of mortgage advances in 2001–2). But by 2002 the total of new supply through buy-to-let was probably in the order of 250,000 lettings, although it remained to be seen how stable this niche market would be in the long-term.

Law Commission proposals to re-define and simplify the legal nature tenancy arrangements may have little impact on the reality of tenant – landlord relationships, although it will help in strengthening the government's aim of improving the governance of the PRS (Law Commission, 2001). The role of local authorities in regulating landlords possibly through a system of licensing is further grist to the mill of improving the management of this housing sector, the problem being that landlords who feel threatened for whatever reason by licensing are likely to quit the market.

The wider implications of the decline in private sector supply needs also to be read in the context of the reduced supply of social housing re-lets. We saw that the expansion of the PRS in the early 1990s supported by housing benefit reduced demand for social housing. Indeed, it was a stated aim of government policy that one reason for not building more social housing was the increased role of the private rented sector in meeting demand at the bottom end of the market. However, with the restrictions on housing benefit after 1996 such an argument is not sustainable. As Wilcox observes, 'Together with the low level of supply of new social rented housing this has resulted in a resurgence in the numbers of households needing to be placed in bed and breakfast and other forms of unsatisfactory accommodation' (Wilcox, 2002a: 41). Moreover, people leaving council and housing association housing to become home-owners has declined sharply as house prices increased in the latter years of the 1990s and the early part of the new century. The implication all of this for meeting housing need is an increased demand for social housing. The next part of the chapter looks in more detail at the social housing sector which, together with the PRS, supplies a high proportion of low-income households with their housing.

The Social Housing Sector

The origins and development of council housing were described in Chapters 3 and 6, and the processes of residualization that have been at work during the last three decades of the twentieth century were outlined in Chapter 5 in the context of the discussion of low demand. The issues surrounding the governance of social housing which have followed in the wake of these social and economic processes were described in Chapter 2.

Drawing all the evidence together it is apparent that the social composition and the function of council housing have changed beyond recognition compared to its peak in the late 1970s when it housed nearly a third of the population. It has become a much smaller housing tenure, with a much less varied housing stock and much less diverse household types. As we saw this process of residualization had a long gestation period, spanning the decades from the 1960s onwards, princi-pally associated with economic re-structuring due to the need for the British economy to respond to globalization pressures. Council housing was very largely built to accommodate households headed by men working in full-time employment in manufacturing industry. The collapse of this sector of the economy (and the coal mining industry) under-mined the logic and social purpose of this housing sector. Other factors, of course, contributed to the weakening of council housing's traditional role. The most significant of these were the decision taken in the mid-1970s to destroy the historic cost basis of council house finance, followed by the logical outcome of this policy, which was the decision to allow sales to sitting tenants without replacement building (through the Right to Buy (RTB) in the Housing Act 1980).

These policy developments were, however, responsible only for the speeding up of existing social and economic processes in which housing tenure was becoming more aligned with social and employment status. Home ownership became the preferred option for all households who could afford access to it – becoming more socially diverse in the process – while council housing began to have a much narrower social base composed increasingly of the unemployed, households in low-income employment, those outside the labour market and, following the Housing Act 1980, a demographic structure focused on long-standing, elderly tenants and on younger, new entrants. Alongside this process of social residualization went a significant geographical re-orientation of social housing – as it declined numerically – away from the suburbs and towards inner city and peripheral estates, including a high proportion of flats and fewer family houses. This process was documented in Forrest and Murie's classic book *Selling the Welfare State* and a series of subsequent updates and related research programmes (Forrest and Murie, 1988).

The Changing Social Composition of Social Housing

Local authority tenants and those of other types of social landlords (principally tenants of housing associations) share very similar social characteristics and essentially draw from the same pool of housing need.

Given that an increasingly large share of local authority built housing has been transferred to RSLs, to all intents and purposes council and RSL tenants have a common identity for analytical purposes. Hence the term 'social housing' refers to these two sets of tenants.

The increasing concentration of low-income households into council and RSL housing is readily apparent from the *Survey of English Housing*, and before the first SEH was published in the early 1990s other government surveys, such as the Family Expenditure Survey (FES) and the housing trailer of the Labour Force Survey (LFS). As council housing began to decline in size through the RTB and other disposals or stock transfers, so it came to represent a disproportionately high percentage of poor households. In 1963 only 26 per cent of council tenants were in the bottom three income deciles (the lowest 30 per cent) but by 1979, *before* the RTB, this figure had increased to 47 per cent (Murie, 1983: 187–8). During the period of the three Thatcher/Major governments (1979–1992) this trend accelerated as unemployment increased and council housing became the only housing option for single parents, long-term sick and disabled people and, of course statutorily homeless families. By 1994/5 more than two-thirds of social housing tenants (still predominantly tenants of local councils) were in the bottom three income deciles. Research conducted by the Social Exclusion Unit (SEU) (see Chapter 5) on England showed also the geographical concentration of deprivation into some forty local authorities, mainly in the north of England and containing 85 per cent of the 'most deprived' wards, most of which contained high concentrations of council housing. The conclusion of this work was not only of a concentration of the poorest households into social housing but that as the stock was 'boiled down' through the RTB so these households were increasingly geographically contained in the so called 'worst estates' (Social Exclusion Unit, 1999).

It should also be noted at this point that the population of social housing tenants fell sharply in the 1980s, due mainly to the RTB, but this process has slowed considerably. In 1981 there were 5.1 million council tenants, but this levelled off at about 3.3 million social housing tenants in 1998/9, about 16 per cent of households in total. It seems unlikely that this figure will change very substantially and certainly not as rapidly in future owing to the affordability ceiling for access to home ownership discussed in Chapter 7. These will be the tenants of the new stock transfer companies, local councils and other forms of 'social businesses' that emerge in the next few years. At any rate they are likely to remain in the broad category of 'social housing' tenants. Taken together something under a third of households will remain in the public and private rental sectors if home ownership has indeed settled at about 70 per cent of households.

A considerable body of evidence about the social composition of social housing tenants was collected in the SEH. Table 8.5 summarizes key data from the most recent survey (1998/9). Table 8.5 shows that there was a much higher proportion of elderly households in social housing than in other tenures. Over a third of these tenants were over age 65, including a large number of widows (21 per cent of council tenant heads of households were widows). These elderly widows contributed to the high proportion of single-person households in social housing, 41 per cent compared to 28 per cent overall. Lone parents are significantly

Table 8.5   **Characteristics of social housing tenants, 1998**

	Council	RSL	All
Age of head of household			
16–24	5	7	6
25–44	36	42	37
45–64	24	20	23
65–74	15	13	14
75 or over	20	18	20
Marital status of head of household			
Married	30	25	29
Cohabiting	7	8	7
Single	20	29	23
Widowed	22	19	21
Divorced	21	20	20
Household type			
Couple, no dependent child(ren)	20	17	19
Couple with dependent child(ren)	17	16	17
Lone parent with dependent child(ren)	15	18	16
Other multi-person household	8	5	7
One adult aged under 60	14	19	16
One adult aged over 60	26	25	26
Economic activity of head of household			
Working full-time	25	26	25
Working part-time	7	9	7
Unemployed	7	8	7
Retired	37	32	36
Permanently sick or disabled	12	10	11
Other inactive	13	15	13
Total	**100**	**100**	**100**

Source: *Survey of English Housing* 1998/9, table A4.1.

over-represented with 1 in 6 social housing tenants in that household category (16 per cent compared to 7 per cent overall). Households with only one adult thus make up a majority of social housing tenants (58 per cent). Couples with no children at 19 per cent are significantly under-represented (36 per cent overall).

Perhaps the most startling figure in the SEH data was that only 25 per cent of social housing tenants were working in full-time employment. Over two-thirds of them were not economically active, about half of whom fell under the broad category of the 'real' unemployed (those without work, permanently sick or disabled and the large cluster of 'other' inactive people). It followed that gross weekly income was very low at only £168 at the time of the interviews, compared to £338 for tenants in the PRS and a third of the average weekly income of home owners, at £482.

Social housing can thus be seen to contain in relative terms a high concentration of the nation's poorest and most deprived households. In the region of half the poor live in social housing, a sector that accounts for about 15 per cent of households overall. (It will be recalled that most of the other half of the poor live in owner occupation although, of course, it is a much larger tenure at nearly 70 per cent of households.)

Residential Mobility in Social Housing

As we have seen at various points in the book, council housing in the past provided a long-term, settled solution to the housing needs of millions of people. It was a desirable, affordable and high-quality option. One of the consequences of its social and political residualization has been the accelerating rate of turnover in tenancies with households moving in for short periods of time with no perception of it as a long-term solution but a staging post for some other option, principally home ownership. Such high levels of mobility have wider social consequences for the stability of local communities and in some areas lead to a spiral of decline, especially where demand for housing is low (see Chapter 5). This increasing level of residential mobility is highly symptomatic of the changing role and purpose of social housing. It allows a rapid sifting of population which in turn contributes to the residualization processes at work in social housing (Burrows, 1997b). As Wilcox showed, in the absence of any sizeable programme of new building, 95 per cent of allocations rely on vacancies occurring in the existing stock (Wilcox, 1998). Housing managers confront problems of 'churning'.

The SEH provided important detail on the patterns of flows into and out of social housing and revealed quite different sets of motivations, depending on the trajectory of the move. There was a discussion of mobility and re-lets in social housing in Chapter 4 (see especially Figure 4.3, p. 114) and there is no need to repeat this ground. It is worth pointing out, however, that the increasing mobility arises from the significantly different perceptions of the role and purpose of social housing now compared to the past. The high number of young people in the sector certainly accounts for some of the more rapid turnover and, as Holmans and Simpson show increasing re-lets in council housing mainly arise from the growing number of local authority tenants moving into the private sector (Holmans and Simpson, 1999).

SEH data showed clearly the pattern of moves into and out of social housing. Its analysis considered a three-year period before 1998/9. It showed that there had been 660,000 moves within the social housing sector, mainly households looking for different-sized accommodation (34 per cent) or to move to a better area (12 per cent) although relationship breakdowns and other personal reasons were also a significant reason for the move. The data showed that 250,000 tenants left the sector to become owner-occupiers in the three years before 1998/9 (including 120,00 RTB purchases) and a further 80,000 left to move into the PRS. There were thus 330,000 movers into the private sector. These movers shared a number of characteristics:

- They were relatively young – 65 per cent were under the age of 45
- A third of them were couples with children (compared to only 16 per cent of all social housing renters), revealing the continuing drain of families with children out of social housing
- Movers were much more likely to be working full time than the average for the sector, 67 per cent against 24 per cent, and consequently had much high average weekly incomes (£340 against £160).

It should be noted, however, that there were significant differences between the three types of movers. Those going into the PRS included 21 per cent who were single parents. Sitting tenant purchasers were older on average than the other movers (53 per cent were over age 45) and contained a high proportion of childless couples than other owners. Households moving directly into mainstream owner occupation had the highest average weekly incomes of all the movers.

It is through this process of movement and sifting that the social composition of social housing has changed. As was discussed in Chapter 4, there are also significant differences of behaviour in areas of low demand – the north and midlands 'old' industrial cities – and areas of under-supply, particularly in the south east of England. The SEH data does not tell the story, for example, of the serial moving behaviour that is common in low-demand inner cities. Some vulnerable and disadvantaged households move two or three times a year (not therefore picked up in SEH survey work) escaping bad relationships, debts, drug abusers, etc. As we saw in Chapter 5, normal analysis of housing tenure becomes less meaningful in these circumstances as people can move quite easily because there are many vacancies and landlords compete with each other for tenants. These localized social processes can lead to communities spiralling into decline because they lack the normal stability created by people with long-term commitment to the area (Lowe, Keenan and Spencer, 1999). Particularly in areas of low demand rapid mobility is a symptom of dysfunctional neighbourhoods, leading to households fleeing the area after attempting to cling onto their home patch. This pattern of serial moving crosses all tenures but is associated with the poor image and low quality of neighbourhoods that were the consequence of the residualization process. The SEH supported this thesis by showing that the majority of people moving out of council housing had lived at their previous address for less than five years and 31 per cent moving after less than two years at the address. As Pawson and Bramley conclude from their study of re-lets in social housing, 'those entering council housing in the recent past are increasingly unlikely to anticipate a long-term future as local authority tenants' (Pawson and Bramley, 2000: 1257). This view challenges the traditional idea of council housing as an end point in a housing career, as a permanent solution to housing needs. On the contrary it is now regarded as a relatively short-term option, a stepping stone to something better, ideally home ownership. It has become, as Murie observes, a 'transitional tenure' (Murie, 1997: 457).

Conclusion

The PRS and social housing accommodate about one-third of households and it seems likely that this is a fairly stable position for the foreseeable future. Both sectors have been through periods of rapid change in recent years. The PRS, after nearly a century of decline, reached its lowest ebb in the late 1980s but following the deregulation of the sector, the availability of housing benefit and the house price slump, made a small but significant revival in the early 1990s. In its current configuration the regime of Assured Shorthold tenancies has made a created a dramatic re-orientation of interests to favour landlords. The evidence suggests that about a third of the sector continues to suffer from the very poorest housing conditions and it is not at all clear whether deregulation will lead to improvements at this level of the market. A very large number of young, unemployed, single men, and other disadvantaged people move around this sector with great frequency. Social housing, for its part, has also changed dramatically in recent decades and also suffers from lack of permanence and stability in its social composition, with mounting evidence that it too has lost its old image as a haven of permanent accommodation for a wide variety of household types. The rental sectors have thus assumed rather similar roles and the symbiosis between them is much closer now than in the past, both socially and in terms of meeting housing needs. As we have seen at various points in the book, the boundaries between them have in effect broken down as households move round in pursuit of an improvement in their situation, and in the areas of low demand landlords compete for tenants. With the continuing dispersal of council housing into private transfer companies the character of rental housing in Britain has changed almost beyond recognition, even compared to the early 1990s. It is a more fragmented, more socially residualized stock of property and increasingly integrated in its role as the sponge that soaks up all those unable to access, or to retain their position in, home ownership.

FURTHER READING

Crook, A. D. H. and Kemp, P. (1996) *Private Landlords in England*, London, HMSO.

Department of the Environment (1995) *Our Future Homes: Opportunity, Choice and Responsibility* (The Housing Green Paper), Cmnd 2901, London, HMSO.

Lowe, S and Hughes, D, (2002) *The Private Rented Sector in a New Century: Revival or False Dawn?*, Bristol, Policy Press.

Murie, A. (1997) 'Beyond state housing', in P. Williams (ed.), *Directions in Housing Policy*, London, Paul Chapman.

Pawson, H. and Bramley, G. (2000) 'Understanding recent trends in residential mobility in council housing in England', *Urban Studies*, 37(8): 1231–59.

9
Comparative Housing

CHAPTER AIMS

- To provide an introduction to the comparative housing literature
- To analyse the reasons for differences in European housing, particularly why the British case stands out as unusual
- To evaluate the development of housing in east and central Europe (ECE) during and after the communist period.

Introduction

Comparative themes are implicit in much of this text. For example, attention was drawn in Chapter 3 to the powerful influence that Victorian domestic culture had in fusing the historical links between a cluster of English-speaking, home owning societies. The consequences of globalization – with its themes of broadening, stretching and increased velocity – for the British state and the governance of British housing were discussed in Chapter 2. Finally, the idea that British housing is in some ways 'different' from most of its European neighbours can be sensibly argued only in a comparative context. In this chapter the emphasis is on the broad issues which fall under the heading of 'comparative housing', of how to analyse and conceptualize the relationship between different countries and so to evaluate Britain's position in the wider context of her European neighbours and those countries within the English-speaking domain. We have seen how, at the turn of the twenty-first century, Britain had matured as a nation of homeowners and simultaneously entered a period in which the break-up of council housing was being engineered. The structure of British housing – at least in terms of its tenure pattern – seems to be settling after nearly a century of change. In this broad-brush context, a key issue is to characterize British housing in this new post-modern condition. Has it become more 'Anglicized', through aligning more strongly with the English-speaking cluster and in a sense returned to its roots, or through the break-up of the monolithic state housing sector is it in the process of becoming more 'European'?

The first stage in answering this question is to address the broad issue of how to 'read' the comparative housing literature. It is a large and diverse literature and has grown rapidly in the last few decades. The first aim, therefore, is to provide a conceptual route, a 'map' with which to steer a pathway. Without such a map the chances are that students will find difficulty in positioning individual studies in the wider context – or, worse, imagine that parallel accounts of different countries constitutes 'comparison'. Such 'Cook's Tours' approaches are common in the literature. Not only do they suffer from not really being comparative but also from being ethnocentric (that is to say, written from the point of view of the author's own country). Many writers imagine home ownership is a normal paradigm and write of Britain as though home ownership had been this country's normal condition. As we have seen, it was only in the last quarter of the twentieth century that Britain could reasonably be described as a 'home owning society'. Without an attempt to be more conceptually aware Britain, and presumably every other country, might be thought of as unique such that comparisons between them would be meaningless. The point is to be able to account for similarities and difference between societies within a conceptual framework. How and why do housing systems differ?

Schools of Comparative Housing

During the 1990s there was a rapid growth in comparative housing studies, to such an extent that it is possible to identify several conceptually distinct approaches. The purpose of this section is to provide a 'conceptual map' for navigating this literature (and, by implication, the wider welfare state literature itself; see Chapter 10). Individual countries are not discussed in any depth because this is not the purpose of this chapter. It should already be apparent that there are limited returns from factual studies that align countries against each other (although there are some good country-by-country chapters in some books, notably Balchin (1996).

The first stage is to outline a 'map' by which it will be possible to make sense of this literature. Three dominant perspectives, or schools, can be identified (see Table 9.1 for summary): the many 'Cook's Tour' studies which take the form of parallel one-country, 'factual'/empirical accounts; at the other extreme, studies which take a very generalist approach, looking for similarities between countries to such an extent that differences are relegated to being 'variations' or 'exceptions' with the assumption that industrialized societies are all broadly moving in the same direction; and in between these two extremes is a meso-level of studies using theories 'of the middle-range' (Merton, 1957). The literature, at least initially, may thus be thought of as a continuum from very detailed empirical accounts of particular countries to highly generalized, universal studies (Kemeny and Lowe, 1998). Broadly speaking these equate with the macro, meso and micro levels of analysis introduced in Chapter 1, framing the policy analysis literature itself.

The 'Cook's Tour' Approach

The 'Cook's Tour' approach typically juxtaposes countries against each other using empirical data to link the countries together but without any real comparative analysis about the reasons for similarities or differences, the 'comparative' discussion usually confined to a concluding chapter. These 'series-of-country' studies were common in the past, although more analytically aware studies are still produced (McGuire, 1981; Emms, 1990; McCrone and Stephens, 1995). The Emms study, for example, focused on social housing provision and management in five countries – France, West Germany, The Netherlands, the (former) Soviet Union and the UK. It gave quite detailed descriptions of each country but made little attempt to think systematically across the countries or engage in overtly comparative analysis. The under-conceptualized nature of this work often leads to it being implicitly ethnocentric, in which the researcher's country is the default against which other nations are intuitively judged. On a wider scale, this is often the case with studies of 'housing indicators' (proportion of owners and tenants, percentage GDP spent on housing, etc.) conducted by international agencies such as the World Bank or the European Union (in social 'observatories'). These projects have a strong policy orientation, with the choice of countries related to a geo-political territory, in which the aim is to establish the basis for subsidy distribution or generally for the convergence of social policies through policy transfer. Such studies are comparative in the limited sense that they ask questions about how societies differ, but not

Table 9.1 **Schools of comparative housing research**

School	Trajectory of change	Key features	Conceptual base	Methodology	Examples
Juxtapositional/ 'Cook's Tour'	Convergence	Parallel accounts, no 'comparison'	None or implicit	Highly empirical	McGuire (1981)
		Policy centred		Quantitative data Large data sets	Emms (1990) McCrone and Stephens (1995)
		Ethnocentric			
Meso or 'Middle-range'	Divergence	Aims to discern typologies of housing systems	Middle-range theory	Cultural and historical emphasis	Kemeny (1981) Dickens *et al.* (1985) Kemeny (1992)
		Highlights differences		Qualitative and quantitative	Barlow and Duncan (1994)
Macro or universalist	Convergence	Industrialized countries all basically similar	General theory (e.g. Marxism, logic of industrialism)	Selective qualitative and quantitative	Donnison (1967) Harloe (1985, 1995) Ball *et al* (1988)
		Ethnocentric		Historical emphasis	

why. They very closely mirror the related comparative welfare state literature in following the *convergence tradition*, the idea that broadly speaking industrialized societies have been moving in the same direction, albeit at different rates of progress (Wilensky, 1975, famously spoke of 'leaders' and 'laggards'). There is thus in these studies some unspecified similarity between the countries causing convergence.

Universalist Approaches

At the other end of the spectrum, convergence is also a clearly distinguishing feature of the very general or universalist approaches. They attempt to account for why industrialized countries are more or less similar by basing their analysis on an explicit theoretical perspective, such as Marxism or most commonly the 'logic of industrialism' thesis – that industrialization inevitably draws societies in the same direction – or even, as with Wilensky, population structure (the 'ageing population' thesis) (Wilensky, 1975). At any rate in this approach there is some universal law that lurks behind, and therefore unites, the housing systems of all countries. One of the earliest of this type and perhaps the most famous comparative housing study, by Donnison (1967), identified three types of housing policies – 'haphazard', 'residual' and 'comprehensive' – and suggested that these represented a *continuum of development* (basically a 'leaders and laggards' idea). He cited countries such as Portugal and Turkey at the haphazard end of the spectrum and the Netherlands and Sweden at the comprehensive end. Donnison's was a path-breaking study not only for identifying a number of different housing 'regimes' but for showing (as he saw it) how countries progressed through various stages of development, driven-not by political ideology but by levels of economic development. This is an inherently convergence approach arguing a 'logic of industrialism' thesis.

The convergence of housing policies thesis is probably best represented more recently in the work of Harloe (1985, 1995), drawing on neo-Marxist inspiration found in the earlier writings of Castells (Castells, 1977). As was discussed in Chapter 6, Harloe argues that government intervention in the housing market is a function of the profitability of housing to the capitalist market. At times when capital is under pressure state intervention increases through the provision of public rental housing, although the normal condition is for the state not to intervene (different here from Castells), so that when conditions are favourable profit-making re-establishes itself. According to Harloe all countries pass through the same phases of *commodification* (dominance of private solutions), *decommodification* (state intervention into market processes) and *recommodification* in a cyclical manner. Harloe discerns three distinct phases of government intervention in the post-1945 period based around these developmental stages, with the current phase being one of the decline of social renting and the marketization of rental housing. Inside this thesis, which is clearly based on the idea of convergence of societies, is a subsidiary thesis, that in general there have been two models of social housing provision – mass housing and residual social housing, with the residual model being the dominant experience (Harloe, 1995).

Harloe's work made a significant impact on the comparative housing research agenda. There have been many studies which echo his basic thesis by demonstrating the residualization and marketization of social housing in a range of European countries (Elander, 1991, and Lundquist, Elander and Danermark, 1990, on Sweden; Priemus, 1995, on Holland).

Divergence Theory

More recently, a new stream of researchers has entered the debate, drawing their inspiration from the comparative welfare state literature, most famously the studies by Esping-Andersen (1990). Here, the emphasis is not on a 'Cook's Tour' of unique countries with little attempt to explain differences and similarities, or on the overarching, highly generalized studies in which, in essence, all societies are thought of as being the same. Instead, attempts have been made to discern patterns and types of housing system. Underlying these patterns there is often a thesis about how the type is generated and sustained. Unlike the convergence studies, which rely heavily on macro-statistical data, this approach is more sensitive to the cultural patterning of societies and the long historical view of the counties concerned. This approach is rather eclectic in the sense that different typologies may be developed to fit different theoretical perspectives. There is no attempt to try to fit some overarching theory to the data, but instead a wide range of different types of data is used to build 'families' of nations, although some countries may 'fit' imperfectly. This approach tends, therefore to draw attention to differences between nations not as 'exceptions' or 'variations' (which is common in convergence studies) but as a way to reveal *similarities and patterns between groups of countries*.

An early example of this approach was Kemeny's (1981) study of three countries – the UK, Australia and Sweden – all countries in which he had lived and worked. In this work, Kemeny showed how government policy, operated through the housing subsidy system, favoured either home owning, in the cases of the UK and Australia, and non-profit housing in the case of Sweden. Kemeny argued that these different strategies also underpinned, and to an extent created, societies that were more individualist in public policy and urban structure (low welfare state spending and suburbanized built form in 'home owning societies') or more collectivist with a more contained urban structure. This is an example of the idea of meso-analysis, introduced in Chapter 1, in which the research operates *between* broad macro analysis and a particularistic, micro focus. In this middle ground it is possible to discern similarities and differences between nations more clearly. The result of this approach often leads to a divergence conclusion, that industrialized societies are not converging towards some unspecified post-industrial norm, but quite distinct clusters of nations – albeit with differences and unique features – have emerged during the modernization process that swept the globe in the last half of the twentieth century.

For example, the English-speaking family (Britain, the USA, Canada, Australia, New Zealand) are a clear case of countries united by a strong emphasis on home owning with residual social housing sectors. An important distinguishing feature is that they all have a separate private rental sector (PRS), so that there are two unconnected rental sectors both playing a subsidiary role to owner occupation. It is also worth noting here that all these countries have residual welfare states with a strong emphasis on private insurance and weak public services. The main exception is the British case which, as we have seen earlier in the book, has been in a 'catch-up' position for most of the twentieth century. Another clearly identifiable cluster or family is the Scandinavian group, where the housing system is based on a much more pluralistic balance between renting and owning, underpinned by a strong welfare state. Barlow and Duncan (1994), following Esping-Andersen's 'three-worlds' classification of welfare states (1990), add a fourth 'regime' which brings together the south European nations – identified as a cluster by Donnison – Greece, Portugal, and Spain, with more rudimentary welfare states. These models or typologies of societies will be further explored in Chapter 10. The key point is that this approach is based on explanations that are historically and culturally rooted.

The British case, described and analysed in this book, should be read in the light of this meso-level/divergence approach. Britain has not been presented as an archetype towards which the rest of Europe, let alone the wider OECD nations, are converging, or as a unique, aberrant case standing quirkily on the European periphery. There certainly have been some common strands in recent decades reaching out across these countries – deregulation of financial markets, shift towards renovation, the idea of a holistic approach to urban regeneration, of which housing is but one part. But to imply, as some authors do, that this is the result of convergence under pressure from common economic imperatives is to misattend to the results of globalization which, as we saw earlier in the book, has the paradoxical effect of fragmenting while at the same time making nation states respond to its demands – for example, by re-patterning their welfare states generally towards a more 'workfare', entrepreneurial system. Britain should be read as part of the English-speaking cluster with a number of distinctive features, not least of which is its 'catch-up' history, a paradox given that it was the source of the cultural foundation in language and domestic social values which partly define this group. There is a sense in which there is a convergence thesis nested into Britain's 'catch up' history. But it should be clear that this is not the same as the universalist version of the convergence of all advanced societies, but a characteristic of the particular historical/cultural foundation of the British case.

Tenure Re-Structuring in the OECD Nations

Evidence does suggest some common trends in European housing – for example, the increasing role of markets in the production and financing of housing, reduced subsidies to social housing with an emphasis on income-supporting housing allowances rather than 'bricks and mortar subsidies and approaches to urban regeneration that emphasize 'joined-up' governance in which housing is part of a more holistic approach. One of the most commonly spoken of features of the convergence school in recent decades has been an assumption that home ownership has increased rapidly across the whole of Europe. British authors are particularly prone to the view that owner occupation has become dominant through rapid expansion, which is not surprising given that home owner-ship has grown more rapidly in Britain than in any other country, at least up to 1990. For example, Part III of Balchin's collection of one-country studies, called 'The Dominance of Owner Occupation', so it is claimed, 'reveals how owner-occupation has taken over from social housing as the dominant form of tenure and how this reflects a political and economic shift ... to neo-liberalism' (Balchin, 1996). What is the evidence for this claim, which clearly harbours a strong convergence thesis? And does it necessarily follow, if it was so, that this shift results from neo-liberal political influence?

The trend towards owner occupation amongst the European members of the OECD since the early 1960s – a growth on average of about 10 per cent (excluding Britain and Italy) – cannot be explained only by the influence of Thatcherism/Reaganism, which is a feature of the 1980s. As we will see, lower state spending on housing was not a contagion caught from the neo-liberal economic policies in the 1980s but has far deeper roots. It links to the story of how different nations found their way through post-war modernization. Right–left political incumbency is certainly *part* of the analysis, but must be read in a much longer time span and set against other important factors. How countries emerged from post-war reconstruction is highly relevant here. It is through consideration of this longer time scale and other related issues, notably the closely related pattern of economic restructuring, that the 'spread of home owning' thesis can be tested and put into perspective. Indeed, given the vast increase in personal disposable wealth in Europe since the end of the Second World War, the sub-text of the material is the question of why home ownership has grown *so little*.

Table 9.2 replicates Castles' (1998) data on housing tenure because it is the best available longitudinal material on this issue. It shows that since the early 1960s to the late 1990s the average growth in home ownership among the OECD countries (excluding Britain, Ireland and Italy) was only 6.5 per cent. In the European nations only, with the same exclusion, the average was just over 10 per cent, although the increase was significantly lower in the Nordic countries compared to central Europe (Germany, at 9 per cent being an exception here). The mean level of change for all the OECD countries between the early 1960s and the late 1990s was 9 per cent.

It can also be seen that some of the growth occurred in the decades before the 1980s, so that the contention that the increase in home ownership was a result of the Thatcher/Reagan 'New Right' is in part untrue and in most countries the trajectory of change was fairly even over the 1960s to the late 1990s. It is also clear from Table 9.2 that the growth of owner occupation among the European nations varied considerably from country to country and even among those that grew most the evidence of a 'dominance of owner occupation' thesis is questionable. Austrian home ownership, for example, grew more rapidly than any of the central European nations (17 per cent between 1960 and the late 1990s) but accounted for just over half of households (55 per cent) at the end of the period. France and the Netherlands grew strongly but reached only 54 per cent and 44 per cent of households, respectively.

Table 9.2 **Changing levels of home ownership, early 1960s–late 1990s**

Country	Early 1960s	1970s	Late 1990s	Change: 1960–late 1990s
Australia	63	67	70	7
Canada	66	60	64	–2
Ireland	60	71	81	21
New Zealand	69	68	71	2
UK	42	49	68	26
USA	64	65	64	0
Denmark	43	49	51	8
Finland	57	59	67	10
Norway	53	53	59	6
Sweden	36	35	42	6
Austria	38	41	55	17
Belgium	50	55	62	12
France	41	45	54	13
Germany	29	36	38	9
Italy	45	50	67	22
Netherlands	29	35	44	15
Greece	67	71	77	10
Portugal	45	57	58	13
Spain	–	64	76	–
Switzerland	34	28	30	–4
Japan	71	59	61	–10
Mean	50	53	60	9

Source: Castles (1998: 251).

Table 9.2 also shows that while North American levels of home ownership remained constant (falling slightly in Canada) there was an expansion among the European nations. A differential of about 20 per cent between America and Europe in the 1960s had narrowed considerably, suggesting a degree of convergence. By the early 1990s, 'the gap between the Old World and the New World had narrowed to 8.1 percentage points' (Castles, 1998: 252). It should also be noted from Table 9.2 that in three countries (Canada, Switzerland and Japan) home ownership rates *fell*.

Home owning is now the majority housing tenure in Europe's OECD nations, at about 60 per cent of households. There has been no rapid, ubiquitous growth in home ownership, and it is implausible that the growth can be explained only by the rise of neo-liberal economics in the 1980s. Moreover, 40 per cent of the population in these countries remain as tenants of landlords. The general pattern is not, therefore, one of general convergence, and a 'dominance of owner occupation' thesis is not sustained by these facts. Looked at through the long historical lens the pattern of re-structuring of housing tenure in the European members of the OECD suggests that difference is at least as important as similarity. The clue to this is buried, as ever, in the long history, which must be discussed, albeit briefly, as a preliminary step. As we have seen earlier in the chapter, the 'middle-range' approach to comparative housing analysis generally sustains a divergence outcome, and this is partly due to its sensitivity to the cultural and historical foundations of housing policy.

The Origins of Divergence in European Housing

Britain and then Western Europe were the 'engine rooms' of industrialization. Urbanization, which followed in its wake, impacted dramatically on people's changing social horizons. It created new opportunities and new pressures on relations between the sexes, impacted on fertility, divorce and the whole shape of domestic and family life. It also significantly re-divided society on the basis of social class. Housing for the newly urbanized working classes was very largely provided in the privately rented sector either by industrial employers or by rentier capitalists investing in housing as businesses. The idea of 'housing policy' was entirely absent for many decades but state intervention came onto the agenda in the mid-nineteenth century, especially around two issues: the public health consequences of insanitary housing (which was common in European cities) giving rise to the need to demolish so-called 'plague spots' and, secondly, the later but closely connected question of who would provide rental housing for the working classes at a standard and at a price they could afford if private landlords lost their incentive to invest. As we saw in Chapter 6, in Britain most private landlords belonged to a weak, dispersed *petit bourgeois* class and were never represented in the great housing debates before and after the First World War. But what happened when the same questions and issues arose on the European Continent?

The key to answering this was to be found in the configurations of classes and trade-offs between classes. Policy outcomes were very largely a product of these settlements, just as they were in Britain, but with very different results. For example, in Germany, as a result of the Prussian three-class voting system, property owners were able to resist the idea of large-scale municipal housing provision. There was to be no German equivalent of British 'council housing' built and managed by the municipal authorities. The two crucial factors which shaped what happened were:

- The *pattern of social and political structures* that supported private landlordism
- The character of *working class politics* in the decades before the turn of the nineteenth century and the run-up to the traumas of the First World War, an event destined to change European social and political life beyond recognition.

The political and social configurations built around the interactions of class politics were the key to the outcome and trajectory of housing policy in Britain compared to the Continent. Crucially, the experience of working class political movements in Europe in the latter part of the nineteenth century was very different to the British case, especially in the central European nations. The British working class, exhausted by a century of struggle, looked for their salvation to the political representation of trade unions through the establishment of the Labour Party. There was to be a parliamentary road to socialism, essentially and inherently reformist in character and with the expectation that the British state would deliver on their behalf social reform. Such a benign view of the state was not shared by the Continental working classes, nor by business interests who associated a strong state with socialism. In the case of housing, direct development by the state of working class accommodation was opposed by the landlord classes and their political representatives. As a result a tradition of direct provision, using their own organizations, grew strongly among the European working class movements. The state's response was to support working class housing indirectly through assisting in the provision of funding, most commonly in the form of cheap loans. In Belgium, France, the Netherlands, Germany and Austro-Hungary societies such as co-ops, trade unions, housing associations, etc. were permitted to borrow money from social insurance funds or savings banks to build housing schemes. With private landlords to some degree disinvesting in the market in response to the boom – slump economic cycle, cheap loans subsidized by the state became a significant source of funding for working class housing. In Vienna, for example, by 1913 20 per cent of residential building had been undertaken using cheap loans made available by the government. In Berlin, co-operative building societies were flourishing and had built 11,000 dwellings by 1914 (Daunton, 1990: 24). In the Netherlands, housing production for workers developed along religious, ethnic and regional lines through subsidized housing associations. Later on these 'bricks and mortar' subsidies were paid in return for local authority control over rent levels and allocation procedures, but the authorities themselves played little role in housing production and management (van Weesep and van Kempen, 1993). This was to be the main way in which non-profit housing was to be built on the Continent after the First World War.

Initially there were some parallels in Britain, where housing companies were allowed to borrow at cheap interest from the Public Works Loans Board (PWLB). But this form of provision made relatively little impact with the emerging Labour movement looking to municipalities to build 'council' housing. As a result the tradition of loans for housing societies, co-ops, trade unions, etc. died out in Britain. Divergence between Britain and a significant part of industrialized Europe was thus apparent at a very early stage. One of the keys to the 'peculiarity' of the British housing system – the almost total reliance on local authorities for the provision of working class rental housing and the demise of the private rented sector (PRS) – is found inside this early history. It is closely bound up with class configurations at the time, and the relationship between housing policy and the wider social insurance systems. Key features of this divergence were:

- Rental housing for the working class was provided in Britain by *local councils*, whereas in Europe there was a much greater diversity of providers
- Private landlordism in Britain was *weakly represented politically* because of its tradition of small-scale ownership and was unsubsidized, whereas in Europe private landlordism was often a powerful force, or at least not marginalized and retained the ability to attract subsidized loan funding
- In Britain, most affordable rental housing after 1918 was designated as *'working class' housing* (almost all the British housing legislation used this term in its titles until 1949) – whereas on the Continent rental housing, both public and private, continued to provide for a wide variety of social classes and strata of society.

After the Second World War

The initial reluctance of European governments to play a direct role in housing provision was shattered by the massive destruction caused during the Second World War, mainly in the conflict between Hitler's Nazi Party and Stalin's USSR. The British case was described in Chapter 6 – the decision to build council houses and the reassertion in the 1950s of the primacy of home ownership, although non-private construction continued into the early 1970s owing to the failure to revive the PRS and ran, on average through the 1945–70 period at about 40 per cent of housing construction.

What happened on the main European Continent falls into two geo-political zones, the 'Western' nations (all members of the OECD) and the 'Eastern bloc' dominated by communist governments inside an economic planning organization (COMECON) – although not a homogeneous group, at least no more so than the 'West'. All these countries, whether Western or Eastern bloc, followed a common road of post-war reconstruction. There were, however, significant differences between west and east in housing policy. In general the Eastern bloc nations were compelled to focus on rapid industrialization at the expense of housing so that it was not until the 1960s that new state-built flats, following the model of the USSR of prefabricated high-rise, 'mass' housing, began to be built on any scale. Countries such as Poland, Hungary and Bulgaria were predominantly rural economies and owner occupation continued to be the main form of housing as it had been before the war. Indeed, Hungary and Bulgaria have consistently had the highest levels of home owning of any of the European nations, east or west. Thus the popular idea of communist Europe as a ubiquitous, grey cluster of societies all more or less the same and dominated by state rental housing is very far from the reality. The most influential interpretation of what happened during the communist period in Europe presents it as a convergence based on a so-called 'East European model' of housing (Turner, Hegedüs and Tosics,1992), and so follows a similar generalist approach found in much of the literature on Western Europe.

For their part the 'Western bloc' literature found it difficult to incorporate east European housing into their approaches. It was argued, for example, by leading writers that the communist states were 'exceptions' and some of the literature even argued that it was not possible to account for the Eastern bloc. Writing about urban social movements – and by implication housing – the erstwhile neo-Marxist Castells argued that 'we have had to exclude analyses of the "state-planned societies" because of the absence of reliable data on urban movements in such a context' (Castells, 1983: xviii). Given the amount of space Castells devoted to discussing the role of Marx and Lenin in the historical process this exclusion (roughly one-third of the world's population!) seems somewhat incongruous. But, as we saw above, it was typical of generalist approaches to write off problem areas as 'exceptions'.

The next two sections consider the factors that shaped housing policy in the post-1945 period in the OECD countries and then the European communist states. In the latter case there is also the additional issue of what happened to housing after the fall of the Berlin Wall in 1990. The first part of the analysis focuses on Western Europe.

Factors Shaping West European Housing

In keeping with the active role played by the state during the war years the reconstruction of the devastation and havoc in central Europe was very largely accomplished by state intervention. Britain, as we saw in Chapter 6, reverted to an intense phase of council house building, with 80 per cent of new housing during the period of the 1945 Labour Government provided under the auspices of the municipal authorities. Following more closely their pre-war traditions the Continental nations also followed a strong state policy, but mainly operated through the form of subsidized co-ops, housing associations and small housing companies, with some local authority programmes, quite distinct from the exclusive focus in Britain on council housing. This divergence, built on long-term differences in history and political culture, continued to be important for the later period, after the post-war crisis. There was, nevertheless a clear convergence in the immediate post-war years towards large-scale state intervention. Once the unifying influence of the war crisis abated, more varied housing policies emerged following pre-war traditions. There was also clear evidence of a levelling-up during this reconstruction period, with some of the less developed nations, such as Spain, Portugal, Ireland and Italy catching-up to the more powerful and developed nations. Levelling-up of the post-war Europe economies reached a ceiling, strongly suggesting a convergence phase, but was then followed by decisions more related to long-term, cultural factors. Pathways through the modernization era were set to reassert themselves so that differences between countries became more apparent once again (Castles, 1998).

The most influential study that recognized this trend and challenged the 'convergence' orthodoxy in the welfare state literature was Esping-Andersen's *The Three Worlds of Welfare Capitalism*, which describes the development of three different types of welfare state (Esping-Andersen, 1990). The three welfare state models – social democratic, conservative and liberal – were defined around different constellations of class coalitions. Esping-Andersen's typology is thus not derived from empirical data, as is commonly assumed, but is imputed from an historical/cultural analysis of class. There are now many reinterpretations and variants of the Esping-Andersen model, for example, incorporating a 'Pacific Rim' type (Kwon, 1997) and a 'Latin Rim' (Leibfried, 1991). The thesis has been heavily criticised for ignoring issues of ethnicity (Cochrane and Clarke, 1993) and gender (Lewis, 1992) and both these criticisms point to the idea that class *alone* is not a determinant of different welfare systems. Other scholars have grouped nations on a different basis, notably Castles (1998), through his 'families of nations'. Castles English-speaking, Scandinavian, West European and Southern European families are clustered according to significant cultural and historical connections, such as language and ties to the British Empire (in the case of the English-speaking cluster).

The Changing Face of Housing in the OECD Nations

What were the key factors that shaped the new Europe? Table 9.2 shows that the period from about the 1970s onwards witnessed significant changes in tenure patterns in the OECD countries. How can these developments be accounted for? Three elements contributed to shaping the situation:

- The rapid progress of *economic restructuring* during and since the 1970s
- The scale and timing of *public policy intervention* to support particular housing tenures
- *Cultural foundations*, especially the influence of religion.

Economic Restructuring

A key component in the analysis of tenure change is the process of economic restructuring, particularly the transition of some countries towards a more 'post-industrial' society. In essence, as we saw above, the early post-war decades can be characterized as ones of catch-up, with the less-developed nations accelerating towards the more advanced societies (Castles, 1998). But after the 1970s, from a more equal economic position, questions resurfaced about the route nations would be likely to take through the next stage of modernization. The key here is the scale and pace of change away from economies based mainly on manufacturing to ones based on services. In Britain, the expansion of manufacturing supported and sustained the growth of council housing, especially in the northern industrial heartlands. The 'workshop of the world' was, however, especially vulnerable to expansion of the global economy and particularly the drift of manufacturing to areas of cheap labour costs (the Pacific Rim, parts of the African and South American continents).

The collapse of traditional manufacturing in the UK was precipitate. The appearance of difficult-to-let council estates and latterly the crisis of low demand in some parts of the country were the 'housing' manifestation of this fundamental restructuring process. As we saw in Chapter 5, the big cities in Britain lost on average two-thirds of their manufacturing employment between 1979 and 2000. This loss was mostly of full-time male manufacturing employment. By the year 2000 only about one-fifth of the workforce were directly involved in manufacturing.

The other side of the coin was the rapid expansion of the service economy, with the emphasis on peripheral and suburban locations, and the growth of two-earner households with the much greater engagement of women in the employment sector. The new white-collar and service industries had few locational constraints, and gravitated towards greenfield sites and the suburbs. The key point is that suburbanization and increasing real incomes, most commonly joint household incomes, strongly equated with the expansion of home ownership. It was Kemeny who first pointed out the association between home ownership and suburbanization (Kemeny, 1981) using the case of Australia. But the process is common in all the English-speaking nations where land is available for the outward expansion of population. There is thus a crucial link between economic restructuring and housing. As Castles observes,

> the story of post-war growth in home ownership is quite easy to tell. The decline in manufacturing from the mid-1970s onwards implied a lesser need for mass housing and fostered a shift to the suburbs. (Castles, 1998: 263)

The converse is also important to note – so that, for example, Germany retained a strong manufacturing base throughout the post-war period and continues to do so. As can be seen in Table 9.2, German's growth in home ownership was small in the post-war period, at only 9 per cent up to the early 1990s. But the key feature is that once the manufacturing base of Europe began to decline after the 1970s the need for state housing also abated and the construction of non-private housing halved in the three decades after 1970. As manufacturing declined so the rationale for state provided housing decreased. As we have seen, in most European countries the state was reluctant to intervene in housing markets and has withdrawn where possible without any great inducement.

Table 9.2 shows that a number of countries in the central European, 'corporate/conservative' cluster changed significantly between the 1970s and 1990s, with significantly higher levels of shift towards home owning than in Germany. It seems likely that this can be accounted for in the analysis by returning to the welfare state/housing interface. Germany's retention of a strong manufacturing base was not imitated to the same extent in countries such as Austria, Belgium and France.

Public Policy and Party Political Support

The immediate post-war decades were, in Europe, ones of reconstruction requiring a considerable scale of public intervention. Measured across the OECD as a whole public housing ranged from only a few per cent in the North American countries to a large scale of provision, Britain being the biggest provider of public housing. Some countries, notably Germany, France, the Netherlands and the Scandinavian group all had politically (and socially) embedded systems that favoured state-directed solutions. These are the countries which mostly operated in the context of a unitary rental market, with public policy favouring a harmonized rental system and new not-for-profit housing built and managed by housing associations and co-ops, etc. (see Chapter 10). There is thus an association between the societies with strong welfare spending programmes and high levels of public housing. The idea of the 'social market' had a provenance dating back to the 1930s, and this is also an important source of the division between the 'dualist' and 'unitary rental' systems (Kemeny, 1995). Previously these same nations had been referred to by Donnison as supporting 'comprehensive' housing policies against those with 'supplementary' strategies. These countries continued to build directly subsidized not-for-profit housing – about 40 per cent of new building – until the end of the 1970s, against an OECD average of 20 per cent (including the small public housing programmes of the English-speaking cluster). Kemeny's thesis that countries with a strong labour-movement and/or corporatist tradition would naturally look to the state rather than the market as the bulwark to its housing programme would appear to be vindicated, at least until the 1970s. There is evidence that this type of alignment is broadly associated with countries which have been over long periods of time influenced party politically by Left or Centre Left parties – most strongly observed in the Scandinavian cluster. By the same token, in countries where the long-term partisan tradition is to favour parties of the Right there is a strong association with policies supporting and sustaining home ownership (Castles, 1998: 254).

In the unusual case of Britain, the failure to revive the PRS following the Rent Act 1957 led to the continuation of a large-scale council house building programme (about 40 per cent of housing production) under both Conservative and Labour Governments up to the late 1960s. With a tax system favourable to home owning and a strong cultural impetus to consider home owning as the 'normal' housing form, Britain was significantly out of line with its cousins in the English-speaking family of nations. Post-industrial Britain, as we have seen, was thus left with a huge legacy of council housing in the old industrial heartlands. But other than the British case there seems to be a convincing case that the home ownership/state housing balance is to a considerable extent a matter of public policy, with home ownership, by default, being stronger in countries where direct public intervention has been weakest.

Cultural Heritage and Housing Systems

One of the key arguments of this book is that cultural patterning can play a central role in welfare state development and a nation's housing system. Through the concept of 'home' one of the mechanisms by which such patterning occurs was outlined. 'Home' is a powerful meso-level concept which links individuals to the wider society. It takes different forms in different traditions. The example discussed related to the Victorians' invention of a powerful female centred domestic culture, with a distinct decorative order and social purpose, related to 'respectability'. Through the literal export of this culture in the shape of parlour rooms, decoration and artefacts cultural values were spread to the four corners of the globe. Later this cultural export was the foundation of the English-speaking 'family of nations', strongly associated with home ownership and 'low-tax/low-spend' welfare. In the unusual circumstances of catch-up Britain, the embeddedness of the home owning culture has been of such compelling impetus that it has taken precedence over the macroeconomy, creating considerable long-term damage. Cultural heritage may thus impact as dramatically as class or other forms of socially constructed power. In this case there clearly is a social nexus – home ownership/welfare state type – built from the foundations of a specific cultural creation.

Another example related to this, and discussed in Chapter 5, was the powerful cultural discipline imposed by the creation of the Victorian Poor Law. Here once again values of conformity and respectability were threatened. The workhouse was in many ways an 'anti-home', the very negation of Victorian domestic comfort and culture, stripped even of social intercourse. Less eligibility was intended to thrash poverty out of the undeserving poor; its powerful symbolism and social practices continue to echo around society to this very day – for example, in the treatment of claimants and the homeless. Indeed, in very broad terms, a very large part of twentieth-century housing policy was designed to provide decent housing for the respectable working classes, so that the cultural framework built around 'deserving' and 'undeserving' might be thought of as deeply bedded in British housing policy. It was as late as 1949 that the term 'working class' ceased to be used in the statement of intent of most housing legislation.

The key lesson from these examples is that cultural foundations are by definition very long-standing once they take root and are often constructed around powerful social interests who control the development of the discourse and its 'practice'. A very good example of where historical contexts and culture create the foundations for modern societies is the impact of religion in patterning welfare provision, and by implication on the shaping of housing systems. Castles suggests this is not a question of degree of religious faith, but its type (Castles, 1998: 53). The mechanisms for this concern were the networks and alliances of groups which mobilized support for public spending programmes, particularly on issues connected with the family. In the European context the Reformation divided Christianity into two fundamental branches, Catholicism and the new Protestants. These seismic changes in social order impacted on every aspect of social and political life and have been contested by both sides more or less ever since. Broadly speaking, the Protestant tradition was based on the idea of personal salvation, fostering openness to individual self-sufficiency and support for social reform from outside the church. Catholicism has a confessional doctrine, strongly hierarchical in organization and opposed to the interference of civil society, especially on matters of family morality. European societies have evolved different social practices, party political configurations and distinctive welfare state forms under the influence of this cultural/religious foundation. Unlikely as it seems that the sixteenth-century division in European Christianity can be directly associated with modern housing policies: it is undoubtedly the case that this centuries-old cultural revolution has significant echoes in the pattern of contemporary social policies in European society. There is more than a plausible case linking Catholic-influenced societies with housing systems in which non-profit renting plays a significant role. Neither is it coincidental that all the

English-speaking 'home owning' societies, including Britain, are predominantly Protestant.

Cultural foundations may, in the end, be the most crucial element above all others in patterning contemporary societies, and comparativists, whether of welfare states, housing systems or whatever else neglect them at their peril.

Communist and Post-Communist European Housing

This section provides an introduction to the factors that shaped the pattern of housing development in the European countries (but not the USSR) that fell under communist government in the aftermath of the Second World War. It involves a parallel analysis with the West European nations, although the narrative is very different, particularly because of the implosion of the whole system at the end of the 1980s. The 1990s was one of so-called 'transition to the market', a phrase which alerts meso-level/divergence analysts that all is not well because of its patent convergence implication. The section, therefore, bases the discussion around the idea of *transition* – that there is in some sense a change from a 'known' before to a known after.

The 'Transition to the Market' Thesis

The so-called 'transition to the market' of the post-communist European cluster of nations involves claims of major social and economic change, often expressed in the form of a rapid expansion of home ownership through the privatization of state rental flats. 'Privatisation is at the heart of turning from a Communist to a market economy' (Strong, Reiner and Szyrmer, 1996: 1). There is indeed a considerable body of literature which asserts that through privatization and the introduction of 'Western' mortgage markets and other financial institutions the nations of Central and Eastern Europe (CEE) have gravitated towards a Western liberal democratic economic and political order (Hegedüs *et al.*, 1996; Muziol-Weclawowicz, 1996; Struyk, 1996). The idea of a transition is clearly based on a convergence thesis, which presupposes a common starting point (communism) and an end point ('Western liberal democracy'). This commonplace position is not, however, so easily defended in the face of the evidence of what happened either under the communist system or what has happened subsequently. Once again, the repertoire of historical, cultural and economic factors need to be harnessed to the analysis.

What happened to housing over the decade after the fall of the Berlin Wall and what role did 'housing' play in this so-called 'transitional phase'? As we have seen above, the cultural/historical perspective provides key insights into the relationship between housing and society, and housing and welfare state development in the west European context. We could expect to learn a great deal about 'housing' *per se* in this very traumatic and rapidly evolving decade, not least whether the 'special' features of housing also apply in post-communist Europe – do the sense of 'home', housing governance, the key relationship between housing and the patterning of welfare state development, etc. hold true in this situation? These issues might be thought of as particularly heightened in conditions in which societies were in the throes of a paradigm shift (Kuhn, 1962). For social scientists, the 1990s in post-communist Central Europe were tantamount to social laboratory conditions! Applying the middle-range or meso-level approach to this issue also suggests the need to avoid treating these nations as all the same. One problem with the 'transition to the market' thesis is that it is very unnuanced and tends, as we have seen with all universalist approaches, to treat countries as all the same. The explanation must begin with a short account of housing policy under the communist period before analysing the so-called 'transition period'. What happened in these European countries (excluding the former USSR)? Is there evidence that they were converging towards a common end game?

The Situation under Communist Rule

The most influential literature argues that under communism – that is, since the mid-to-late 1940s, when communist governments were established in the CEE nations – there was a ubiquitous 'East European housing model', the core of which was a centralized planning system. This is an orthodox, convergence position and is the mirror image of the west European convergence school:

> The general feature of East European housing was that resources spent on housing were controlled by the 'planning system', a power structure based on the dominance of one political party élite. Here a great variety of solutions can be found but the logic of the system was the same across all East European countries: key decisions were made by the centralized planning system. (Turner, Hegedüs and Tosics, 1992: 320)

The model ascribed the control of housing consumption to 'strictly regulated wage policies' and argued that differences between the countries should be thought of as 'insignificant model variations which did not alter the dominance of the state over all aspects of the housing system' Turner, Hegedüs and Tosics (1992). However, these 'variations' arguably amounted to much more than that. There is, moreover, a periodization problem with this thesis because it is not at all clear at what stage before the overthrow of communism in the late 1980s and early 1990s the 'East European model' became redundant or did it simply disappear with the Berlin Wall?

A comparison of only two countries suggests why an overarching explanation needs to be treated with some caution. Hungary was the most 'westernized' of the communist nations and Bulgaria was the furthest, both politically and geographically, from Western influence. How did housing policy evolve in these two contrasting countries? In Bulgaria, private sector building companies were active well into the 1960s and most housing was left in individual hands, including a PRS. But the decision to collectivize agriculture in the early 1970s caused such large-scale migration to urban areas that the Bulgarian leader Zivkov decided to adopt a Soviet-style high-rise construction system. This programme, which peaked in the 1980s, was designed to put in place large numbers of low-amenity flats for rural migrants. In keeping with the rural tradition, these flats were created for owner occupation. Quality was very low and the residents were sold only the bare shell, with water and electricity but little else. This system aimed to limit the state's financial liability not only by brute minimal standards but by making applicants for the flats pay large amounts of cash into the state bank at low interest with mortgages provided at higher interest.

In Hungary, by contrast, the 1956 revolution against the communists forced housing onto the agenda and led to the establishment of a 'deep-subsidy' system through which high-amenity flats were built and allocated to key workers (engineers, teacher, managers) as a social reward and similarly to communist party members (Szelenyi, 1983). Towards the end of the 1960s it was apparent that the Hungarian government's building targets were not being met by the state system on its own. Flats were therefore sold to applicants on a separate owner-occupier waiting list, so that there were two parallel lists. Applicants were required to make large cash deposits in the state bank (OTP) and take out a long mortgage with the bank. This method of finance was also extended to self-builders of common houses in urban areas. ('Common houses' were a familiar form of building at this time, being similar to English maisonettes; properties with three or four households under one roof). Both measures were clearly intended to inject private capital and savings into the building programme.

It was also acknowledged by the central state that the 'deep-subsidy' system (focused only on the state programme) had created imbalances with limited alternatives to households outside this system (actually the vast majority of the population). A severe difficulty during the 1970s was the growth of a large-scale private market *inside* the state rental system. This was a system of face-to-face exchanges, often involving hard currencies, and which the state was powerless to control. The logic of what happened was partly inherent in the 'Stalin' model of housing. The Stalin model was based around an idealized Soviet housing form in which the aim was to use housing to create ideal 'Soviet' men and women. This was more than the architectural determinism of the English Garden City movement and other utopian schools (e.g. the Bauhaus movement) for it was designed to create a new species of humankind. The key features of this model were: the collective built form – high-rise blocks, communal facilities; large state-owned building companies; very low rents (typically less than 3 per cent of income); the intention that everyone should have a flat; once allocated, a very secure form of tenancy. Families were able to inherit these tenancies once granted and shared in this and other ways in a bundle of property rights not dissimilar to owner occupation. The distinction between 'owning' and 'renting' was rather blurred. The problem in Hungary was that an inflationary spiral inside this housing system threatened the whole housing system and the government was forced belatedly to intervene, acknowledging – as part of a wider economic liberalization at the time – the reality of these markets. A housing reform in 1980 abolished the deep-subsidy and set up an openly market-oriented subsidy system which gave support not only to the state sector but the mass of self-builders who until then had solved their housing needs on their own.

Was There an 'East European Model'?

It is readily apparent that even in these two cases the differences cannot be explained away as 'insignificant model variations' according to the East European Model. In Hungary, the state committed large resources to a deeply subsidized state rental sector. The financial gains to those inside this system were enormous because rents were low and the total effect of the system was socially highly regressive. In Bulgaria, the timing, the purpose and the tenure were completely different. The subsidy was very shallow, involving a much lower financial commitment, a low standard of building and a form of state controlled owner occupation. In fact, the overarching factor that united these two societies through the period of communist government was not so much the state housing system but that these were the countries with the highest proportion of owner occupation in the communist bloc: about 70 per cent in Hungary and over 90 per cent in Bulgaria, figures that are high even by 'Western' standards. Needless to say, this form of owner occupation was not comparable to north and west European nations. There was no private building industry, no regulated mortgage institutions, a large part of the new housing stock was self-built and both countries had a large number of 'second homes'. These were very different scripts, and not the product of a ubiquitous 'model', albeit that communist government exerted a decisive influence over people's lives. It should also be noted that the scale of state-built rental property in the housing stock of these CEE nations was in the early 1990s about 25 per cent of all housing types, about the same as Britain, the Netherlands and Sweden. The picture of a monolithic, state-run housing system for the majority of the population applies only to the USSR, where the communist government came to power in 1917.

The Changing Pattern of East and Central European Housing since 1990

Table 9.3 which is taken from a working paper of the HABITAT housing indicators research, provides an overview of the tenure structure of the European communist states (those outside the former USSR) as they were at the time of the collapse of communism and in 1994.

The overall impression from Table 9.3 is that there have *not* been any really major changes to the structure of the housing systems of this group of countries. If anything they became *less* like their north and west European neighbours over the five years between 1990 and 1994. There are some key points to note:

- The most significant change has been the decline of the state rental sectors through the process of *privatization*. Table 9.3 shows a net change since 1990 of 8.3 per cent between state rented housing and owner occupation measured across the whole group. This was the biggest development in the tenure structure and more recent evidence suggests that this trend continued for another two–four years and had largely halted by 1999. But it should be noted that rapid privatization occurred in Hungary, Slovenia, Albania, Croatia and Romania but not in the Czech Republic, Slovakia, Poland and Bulgaria

Table 9.3   **Tenure structure of 'transitional' countries, 1990–4**

	Public rental		Private rental		Owner occupied		Other	
	1990	**1994**	**1990**	**1994**	**1990**	**1994**	**1990**	**1994**
CEES[a]								
Czech Rep.	29.6	27.6	0.9	4.7	40.3	42.2	29.2	25.5
Hungary	22.0	13.0	0.5	1.0	77.5	86.0	0.0	0.0
Poland	29.7	25.4	5.2	5.2	40.2	41.7	24.9	27.7
Slovakia	27.3	26.0	0.0	0.5	50.2	51.6	22.5	21.9
Slovenia	31.6	8.9	3.0	3.4	65.4	87.7	0.0	0.0
Total	**28.2**	**23.1**	**3.0**	**3.9**	**48.5**	**52.0**	**20.3**	**21.0**
SEES[a]								
Albania	35.4	2.0	0.0	0.0	64.6	98.0	0.0	0.0
Bulgaria	6.6	6.8	1.5	3.2	91.7	89.7	0.2	0.3
Croatia	25.5	10.6	NAV	3.7	69.6	84.5	4.9	1.2
Romania	21.1	NAV	1.0	3.0	76.1	88.9	1.8	0.4
Total	**18.7**	**7.6**	**1.1**	**3.1**	**78.7**	**89.1**	**1.7**	**0.5**
Total	**27.0**	**18.6**	**2.1**	**3.8**	**56.0**	**64.2**	**14.9**	**13.4**

Note: [a] CEES – 'Central' East European State; SEES – 'Southern' East European State
Source: Hegedüs, Mayo and Tosics (1996: 15).

(although Bulgaria, as we have seen, already had a mainly privately owned housing stock). In the countries where privatization has occurred, the pattern was for the best-quality housing to be sold at very discounted prices leaving behind a residue of poor-quality, inner city or peripheral housing, inhabited by families living in poverty. Thus the Czech Republic, Slovakia and Poland emerged as very distinctive in retaining a more balanced and less 'Anglo-Saxon'-looking housing system. Here the conditions are much more those associated with the social market countries such as Germany and the Netherlands.

- The *size of the owner occupied sector at the end* of the communist period was 56 per cent, higher than many west European countries at the time. This is partly a legacy of the pre-war situation (although private renting was the most common housing tenure in the 1930s, especially in urban areas), partly a consequence of the rural nature of most of these countries and the large scale of self-build activity. The case of Bulgaria, as we have seen, was exceptional. Excluding the Czech Republic, Slovakia and Poland the average for owner occupation in 1994 was 89 per cent, made up of the already high ownership levels and the newly privatized state rental stock. The average for owner occupation in the EU countries in the mid-1990s was 62 per cent. The highest EU nation was Ireland at 81 per cent (Priemus, 1997: 550).

- The PRS *clearly played very little role*, and this was the most enduring legacy of the communist 'Model'. As Mandic observed, 'What distinguishes this group from West European countries is its undersized private rental sector and its grossly oversized owner-occupied sector, which is nearly 85 per cent of the stock' (Mandic, 2000). In most countries private landlords were nationalized or repressed under the communist system although informal private renting continued to play a significant role owing to the practice of sub-letting. Despite the privatization programmes in some countries and the growth of owner occupation there has been no return to the historic housing tenure that was the foundation stone of nineteenth-century urbanization in all the major cities of Europe. The average for the PRS in the EU nations is currently about 20 per cent. But after a decade of exposure to the 'free market' it shows no signs of a revival in Eastern Europe (Lowe, 2000).

Thus the idea of a 'transition to the market' in housing does not equate with the data. Two quite distinct clusters have already emerged in relation to the post-communist housing situation – the Czech Republic, Slovakia and Poland (structurally similar to how they were before the overthrow of communism and comparable to the corporatist European nations) and a cluster of super-home owning societies, Bulgaria, Hungary, Slovenia, Albania, Croatia and Romania. The consequence of this analysis is to show that far from becoming more like the west European nations, nearly all these countries have, at least in terms if their housing tenures become *less* like their 'Western' neighbours.

It is very clear that households that were inside the privileged state rental sectors (newly built flats in central locations) enjoyed the greatest gains from the privatization sales, acquiring property at knock-down prices. Self-building continues in some countries as an important means for families to solve their housing needs. The residualization of the public rental housing stock is perhaps the most similar development to west European cities: households too poor to buy the property even with hugely discounted prices. Ironically it is the heavily depleted size, and attendant social problems, of the residual public housing sectors that is the main parallel with west European cities, especially the case of the UK. It is also comparable with the UK that the state built very little during the 1990s. At any rate it is hardly the point of a transition from state communism to liberal free markets that east European public housing should come to emulate the worst features of their Western neighbours. Home ownership has brought gains to those already in the system but the housing market, despite the very large scale of the owner occupied sectors, creates barriers to mobility and problems of access for first-time buyers because the home owning sector is poorly supported by the mortgage institutions (finance is available but at Western, 'hard currency' prices which are unaffordable), there are under-developed estate agency systems and a general lack of state support for the housing system. For most people most of the time very little has really changed in their housing experience compared to the communist period.

The Role of Housing in the Transition to the Market Economy

As has been shown throughout the text, housing does possess a number of characteristics which are different from other socially provided services. We noted particularly how housing has a key macroeconomic impact but also at the personal level fulfils important functions in building ontological security and basic social formation. It was spoken of as having a meso-level role in linking the wider economic sphere and the realm of the personal, notably through the intensely important process of 'home' building. In the transitional period in Central and Eastern Europe these features of housing have played a key role in stabilizing societies traumatized by the exposure of their economies to world competition.

With limited resources at their disposal, these post-communist governments sought to divest themselves from commitments to expensive housing subsidies inherited from the previous system. Privatization and decentralization are part and parcel of this process. It was common in the early 1990s for the central state to devolve responsibility for the state rental housing stock to local authorities. In their turn, the local authorities were compelled to enter into give-away privatizations because of their own lack of resources to support even the most basic management and maintenance structures. Most rented dwellings were sold in Hungary at 15 per cent of their market value (Hegedüs and Varhegyi, 2000). These were desperate times and desperate measures were needed.

This is reminiscent of the situation after the Second World War, when housing was taken for granted in the drive for rapid industrialization.

During the process of macroeconomic adjustment in the 1990s housing played a key role in stabilizing the wider social formation by providing *continuities* between the two systems. Its role was to moderate the hardships, acting as a 'shock-absorber' in highly volatile economies (Struyk, 1996). It was the one area in which the government could accede to popular demands for reform without any great budgetary implications. Privatization also had an important ideological role in demonstrating that the paradigm shift from communism to the market was actually happening, even if its effect concerned a relatively small proportion of the total population. In key places, its impact was often very considerable. For example, 114,000 flats were sold in Budapest up to 1997, which represented about 15 per cent of the total housing stock in the city. It was a visible symbol of what was much more difficult to demonstrate in the wider economy. However, the irony of this was that, in the process, east European housing became rather less like the rest of the European core states, and where there were similarities it is in the marginalization and social exclusion of the residual public rental housing stock, the very feature of housing which most west European governments are battling to rid themselves.

The ability of housing to perform this key social role arises from the sense of the embeddedness of housing in people's daily lives *despite* changes in other aspects of life. It is this that gives housing a stabilizing influence on social formation, particularly during a period of rapid economic change and social reconstruction. It should not be forgotten that for many people, whatever was happening beyond the front door, very little if anything changed in their home environments. Utility charges rose sharply, but in most cases the place where families lived in 1989 was probably the same home in 1990 or 2000. Here they are surrounded by the same familiar utilities, clutter and possessions which constitute a significant part of the sense of 'home'. Even though in some cases the form of tenure may have changed and over-crowding increased, the physical dwelling is the same. The key feature, therefore, which helps explain the 'difference' of housing is the discourse around its embeddedness in social formation – its rooted location, its longevity and above all the stabilization effect it can potentially create. As was mentioned in Chapter 3, Bachelard reminds us that 'our house is our corner of the world' (Bachelard, 1964: 28). During periods of rapid or indeed traumatic social change people will cling to their sense of 'home' even more firmly.

Other features that run in parallel with the narrative of west European housing in the 1990s are the influence of housing on welfare state re-structuring and urban form. It is premature to make too many connections on either front, but it might be noted that the influence of the International Monetary Fund (IMF) and World Bank agenda is much more keenly felt in the development of social security and health policies than in 'housing' policy. In those areas, the dominant influence has been the neo-liberal agenda of economic reform. There is no doubt that the state has withdrawn from full-employment, 'cradle-to-the-grave' welfare provision that was the essence of the 'Stalin Model' of social development. A survey of all the CEE nations has shown that the provision of health care has everywhere been decentralized and large elements of privatization introduced. Pharmacy services have been completely privatized whereas secondary and tertiary health care facilities have been much less affected by private solutions. In virtually every case, the role of central government in the management of health care has been reduced. Social insurance policy and pensions have also changed, although both have been dogged by problems of non-compliance, tax evasion and the continuing impact of the 'second' economies (which operate mainly for cash outside the formal economic sphere) Pensions management was described as weak and under-developed. This study concludes: 'Ironically, as the systems appear to have got better on macro-economic and labour market issues so they have been somewhat weaker at the other side [i.e. social policies]. To that extent there has been a transition from 'relative security to relative insecurity' (EC Phare, Consensus Programme, 2000: 156). This very under-stated view nevertheless does point to the persistence of widespread poverty and the fracturing of society between a *nouveau riche* able to opt out of all welfare reforms, a compliant middle class protected to an extent by self-provisioning and enterprise, and a large mass of ordinary households below survival income dependent on flat-rate, means-tested benefits. There has been a shift in welfare to 'weaker' forms of provision, workfare solutions and targeted social assistance, all factors that are congruent with neo-liberal western home owning societies. The super-owner occupied societies created in the post-communist 'transition' have indeed spawned minimalist welfare states.

The urban built environment has also undergone dramatic changes, but this varies from country to country. For example, on the outskirts of Tirana (Albania) self-building of single family houses has created a completely new countryside landscape, with plots staked out randomly across the fields. Often unsupported by utilities and dependent for electricity on illegally tapping into supply cables, this form of housing is more akin to a Third World solution than to the mainstream of Europe.

The urban infrastructure which was designed to accommodate 250,000 people now houses over 750,000 (Slootweg, 1999). The city has been ravaged by speculative development and most urban open space in the city disappeared in the years 1995–2000.

High-rise state built apartments are no longer being constructed anywhere across the region, although some of the technology is still used in venture capital, real estate developments. Speculative capitalists have, indeed, made an impact in the built form of many cities. For example, in Sofia the suburbanization of the *nouveau riche* has created the appearance of large fortified mansions in some areas.

Thus during the major changes to the macroeconomies and social reconstruction of the 1990s, 'housing' played a very particular role. Partly it was responsible for the transfer of the advantages of privileged access during the communist period into the market economic era, partly the privatization programme was a symbol of the new ideologies of free enterprise which were difficult to demonstrate elsewhere in the economy – Struyk's (1996) 'shock-absorber' effect – and partly it was the simple embeddedness in people's daily lives that gave housing a special role in bridging the pre and post–communist eras. At the risk of over-generalizing, the informal market with its reliance on family support, neighbourhood and occupational networks, cash exchanges and self-building continue (mainly in the poorer countries) to be the main ways of solving housing needs *just as they were in the communist period*. The conclusion from this analysis of the social processes at work and from the crude tenure comparison is that in overall profile the post-communist nations of Europe have become *less* like the EU nations and OECD member states than they were under the old system. In very broad terms, there would also appear to be a divergence between the two clusters outlined above – the super-owner occupied countries and those adhering to a social market approach and where rather less has changed than in the other countries (Czech Republic, Slovakia and Poland). In general, however, there is no real foundation for conceptualizing post-communist housing as being in the process of 'transition' – that is to say, transition to an ideal-type 'western' model of housing. Housing, to coin Torgersen's (1987) phrase, has been and remains a very 'wobbly pillar' under wobbly states.

Neither should it be forgotten that there is also a sense of nightmare in some people's homes, echoing the House of Doom from Chapter 3. Households in their millions wage a permanent battle against poverty. Minimum wage levels have been set at incredibly low levels and by indexing social security payments to minimum wages a great mass of people across the region have been driven into abject poverty. Guy Standing cites the chilling statistic that male life expectancy in Russia in 1995 was only fifty-eight years, having fallen by seven years since the overthrow of communism. Discussing with a government minister why the people did not fight back against such problems Standing cites the minister as saying 'They are just going into their homes and dying' (Standing, 1996).

Conclusion

The comparative housing literature has burgeoned over recent years, reflecting the effects of globalization. Learning to read this literature presents considerable problems because of its sheer scale. Without a conceptual 'map' as a guide it is difficult to make sense of its real meaning, and there is a danger of simply taking at face value 'facts' with little or no comparative analysis. The additional danger here is that the reader's or researcher's own country becomes the norm by which they judge all other cases. At the other extreme, very generalist theory tends to fit data or historical interpretation into a pre-existing thesis. Such juxtapositional or reductionist approaches do not do justice to the richness of the comparative approach, based on middle-range theory with its need for a sensitive understanding of cultural and historical foundations. This approach also strongly challenges the convergence logic, which is implicit in both the particularist and the generalist models. The case of British housing also makes much more sense when read in the light of a conceptualized comparative housing literature. Britain and home owning are by no means a norm by which to judge the other nations of Europe and the explanation that the growth of home ownership in Europe resulted from neo-liberal cross-fertilization (a form of policy transfer – see Chapter 10) in the 1980s needs to be qualified. The evidence in any case does not sustain the idea of a large-scale growth of home owning in Europe, with the exception of some (but not all) the post-communist nations of East and Central Europe. Indeed given the growth of incomes in the Western nations of Europe since 1945 it might be thought surprising that home ownership grew *so little*.

FURTHER READING

Barlow, J. and Duncan, S. (1994) *Success and Failure in Housing Provision: European Systems Compared*, London, Pergamon.

Doling, J. (1997) *Comparative Housing Policy*, Basingstoke, Macmillan Press.

Harloe, M. (1995) *The People's Home: Social Rented Housing in Europe and America*, Oxford, Blackwell.

Kemeny, J. (1992) *Housing and Social Theory*, London, Routledge.

Kemeny, J. and Lowe, S. (1998) 'Schools of comparative housing research: from convergence to divergence', *Housing Studies*, 13(2), 161–76.

Struyk, R. J. (ed.) (1996) *Economic Restructuring of the Former Soviet Bloc: The Case of Housing*, Washington, DC, Urban Institute Press.

10
The Significance of Housing

CHAPTER AIMS

- To show the significance of housing in shaping societies and welfare states
- To show the importance of institutionalism to the interpretation of housing as a social science field of enquiry
- To discuss the neglect of housing in the welfare state literature
- To sum up on the impact of the policy analysis approach in the evaluation of housing.

Introduction

This chapter draws together evidence and ideas scattered across the book as to how we can understand British housing policy, how it is made and delivered and how the British case should be 'read' in relation to comparable societies. It was readily apparent in Chapter 9 that there were significant differences between even the housing systems of the wider European nations, EU and non-EU countries, although it was possible to discern underlying patterns which group nations together and help explain how – and, crucially, why – they differ or where they fit into a wider family of nations or cluster. Perhaps above all else the evidence from this book shows that purely state centred approaches to explaining these divergences are no longer tenable. A major theme of the book has been that globalization processes have increasingly impacted on the configuration of housing systems, in part because the state, certainly the British state, has been restructured under these new circumstances. As we saw in Chapter 2, the 'hollowing out' of the state under the impact of the transnational economic order was a major task and accomplishment of the Thatcher/Major and Blair governments. The new institutional literature is defined by its capacity to capture this wide-ranging agenda and is especially suited to help explain why different policies develop in different societies. As was shown in Chapter 9, middle-range social theory helps overcome the limitations of juxtapositional research in which the focus is boiled down to the lowest common denominator. It is precisely because institutionalist approaches engage with the wider social context of the policy-making process that it is so powerful.

Institutions differ from organizations because they provide the underlying 'rules of the game' and include a wide range of bodies and agencies – political parties, the wider executive, intergovernmental arrangements, key economic groups (Thelen and Steinmo, 1992) and include the 'welfare' state (Pierson, 2001b). Institutions also include culturally shaped social norms and may be thought to incorporate class structures. These policy structures and actors create and develop the policy process and are the focal points of decision-making. New institutionalists focus also on the sources and distribution of power within these agencies, as Thelen and Steinmo suggest:

> Institutionalists are interested in the whole range of state and societal institutions that shape how political actors define their interests and that structure their relations of power within groups. (Thelen and Steinmo, 1992: 2)

The emergence of new institutionalism since the 1970s was strongly influenced by the recognition of globalization as a key analytical concept in making sense of the growing repertory of comparative studies. How and why do societies differ under the conditions of a globe increasingly integrated by the transnational economy? The outcomes of globalization were not predictable at a policy level, and this could very largely be ascribed to the institutional arrangements in different countries.

Schools of Institutionalist Thought

Although united by the aim of seeking to explain, 'the role that institutions play in the determination of social and political outcomes' (Hall and

Taylor, 1996: 936), new institutionalism has burgeoned into such a vast literature that it is possible already to discern different schools of thought. Hall and Taylor point to three distinct strands. 'Rational choice' or public choice theorists, emanating from an economic perspective with roots in eighteenth-century political economy and nineteenth-century utilitarianism, have argued the centrality of institutional settings in shaping options and the interactions between actors. The assumption here is that every player attempts to maximize their own position by calculating what is their best interest and most rational given the constraints of institutional structures. This line of thought has been criticized from a number of perspectives, not least long-standing ideas emanating from Lindblom and Herbert Simon, discussed in Chapter 1, who pointed to the qualified, unpredictable, 'muddling through' quality of political life and its essentially *incremental* character (Lindblom, 1979) which limits the scope of political choice and rationality.

If rational choice institutionalism emerges essentially from an economic perspective, a sociological strand of institutionalism emphasizes, however, that rational choice is itself a socially constructed concept. As Hall and Taylor point out:

> if rational choice theorists often posit a world of individuals or organizations seeking to maximize their material well-being, sociologists frequently posit a world of individuals or organizations seeking to define and express their identity in socially appropriate ways. (Hall and Taylor, 1996: 949)

According to this more sociologically influenced institutionalist school, policy-making actors (agents) have identities and see reality from a point of view shaped by core social values, leading to shared definitions of what policy options are most likely to succeed given their own and society's key reference points. The wider *cultural context* for decision-making is thus crucial. Developing this position in a new wave of literature from the 1970s 'historical institutionalists' argued that policy is normally the outcome not only of preferences that are socially and politically shaped but that are constructed from within existing historical contexts, often involving conflict between groups and agencies with pre-existing interests. Skcopol's (1995) work, for example, indicated not only that the 'state should be brought back in' but that a *long* historical view was needed to fully comprehend the outcomes of contemporary policy processes. Indeed, as has been argued at several places in the book, the cultural/historical framework is above all else the factor that the policy analysis approach supports as the key to knowledge of modern social development. It is clear, in answer to a dominant strand of economically influenced thinking in the comparative housing and welfare state litera- tures, that economic development does not fundamentally determine policy outcomes. If nothing else, the discussion of the history and develop- ment of British housing policy showed that 'politics matters', and that this lesson was equally true for thinking through the comparative housing literature.

State centred approaches were thus enhanced by a school of research that drew attention to the role of wider social institutions in working out the logic behind policy choices and the divergence of policies across nations that enjoy comparable economic development. As Thelen and Steinmo (1992) argue, it is in bridging between state centred and society centred approaches that historical institutionalists have advanced policy analysis. Its strength is that it links broad-brush ('grand theory') explanations to more focused, often empirically based one-country studies. Historical institutionalism thus points away from ethnocentrism – the focus on one's own, well-known case which by default becomes a norm by which other cases are often (mistakenly) judged. As Thelen and Steinmo argue:

> This approach has been applied in a wide range of empirical settings, but in each case what has made this approach so attractive is the theoretical lever- age it has provided for understanding policy continuities over time within countries and policy variations across countries. (Thelen and Steinmo, 1992: 10)

Hall and Taylor (1996) showed that historical institutionalism is distinctive because of its focus on the 'path dependency' of institutional change. They draw attention to the *unintended consequences* of strategic action and the uneven distribution of power between social groups and interests. They argue that given the same operative forces – economic, social and political – it would be logical to suppose that outcomes would be broadly the same everywhere. Of course, it is simply not the case in reality that we find such path dependency. The 'effect of such forces will be medi- ated by the contextual features of a given situation often inherited from the past' (Hall and Taylor, 1996: 941).

Historical institutionalism is well suited to an analysis of change over time, as we saw in Chapter 6, in the explanation of the restructuring of British housing tenure during the course of the twentieth century. It was shown that the idea of *critical junctures* is an important development inside this approach, broadly dividing history into normal periods and critical junctures, or turning point moments when significant institutional change occurs. These moments are often found in periods of crisis – or, as in this case, arise from marginal advantages enjoyed by one solution or policy direction over another (Hall and Taylor, 1996). Crises offer new opportunities for change and the possibility of new ideas being embedded in the institutional structure. The idea of 'punctuated equilibrium' usefully suggests that periods of rapid change and crisis are then followed by a time of consolidation (Krasner, 1984) and this also is illustrated in British housing policy.

Historical institutionalism also focuses on the power of *ideas* to mediate and structure policy change. Hay and Wincott (1998), for example, draw attention to the way in which political ideas filter down through institutions causing re-thinking of policy and even the re-structuring of institutions themselves. In turn, this gives rise to a focus on the spread of ideas, especially given the speed of communication through the powerful new information and communications technologies (ICTs) that have swept the globe. How ideas and new policy are diffused from one setting to another has been the focus of a major stand of institutionalist research, which collectively has become known as 'policy transfer'.

Policy Transfer

Connected to the new governance agenda through the 'network society' (Castells, 1996, 1997a, 1997b) national and international political institutions have become increasingly engaged in the process of policy transfer. Policy transfer refers to:

> a process in which knowledge about institutions, policies or delivery systems at one sector or level of governance is used in the development of institutions, policies or delivery systems at another sector or level of governance. (Evans with McComb, 1999: 30)

A wide range of concepts and ideas fall under the umbrella of policy transfer including bandwagoning, diffusion, harmonization, convergence/ divergence, etc., mostly in relation to comparative studies. An early version of this was the idea of lesson-drawing, which showed that despite every place, up-to a point, being unique with its own problems it was increasingly apparent that policies and programmes that were effective in one place could be copied in another (Rose, 1991). These sorts of ideas can be used to show how and why some policies succeed or fail and the source of the ideas that underpinned the policy itself. Policy ideas from other countries or other sectors of the economy or administration compete with alternatives from inside the political structures. Policy transfer is thus best understood as part of the broad policy process and not as an independent process in its own right (Wolman, 1992). There has been as a result increasing interest in how ideas for new policy evolve and why similarities in policy development occur in different countries, notably the adoption in Britain of American workfare social policies in the 1980s and 1990s (Wolman, 1992; Dolowitz, 1997, Deacon, 2000).

Recent versions of the policy transfer literature have also re-asserted the salience of policy networks as the key explanation for how the modern state functions. Networks are the 'engine-room' of the modern polity – or, more correctly, policy network analysis provides the empirical tools for understanding interorganizational politics (Evans, 1999). As we saw in Chapter 2 the breakdown of the post-war unitary state has given rise to a much more differentiated polity. This more fragmented form of governance is characterized as a series of interlocking policy networks with a high degree of autonomy. The central state provides a broad steer to the direction of policy but the 'rowing' has mainly fallen into the hands of unaccountable agencies and quasi-governmental bodies. Such policy communities are characterized by their limited access points and exclusionary structure (Marsh and Rhodes, 1992) and have similarities to what Adler and Haas refer to as 'epistemic communities' – professionals, scientists and policy analysts who share common perceptions of 'their' subject's territory and promote it into the policy-making level. These knowledge-based, epistemic communities are thus important to the evolution of new policy and increasingly important to the successful adoption of 'intelligent' policy (Adler and Haas, 1992). In the case of British housing policy, such types of policy community are readily apparent, although is significantly more diverse than in the past, with social housing increasingly run by quasi-businesses, overlooked by a burgeoning research community and encompassing a much more plural housing system of governance. Network analysis thus implies a significant ceding of delivery to regionally based elites and professionals despite the central government's rhetoric of stakeholdership and open government. Policy network analysis is a key to the evaluation of the new governance of housing.

New and greater knowledge of policies has been spread across the planet with ever-increasing velocity and frequency. A new policy transfer literature has grown equally rapidly in response to this development and has already shown not only the benefits of such information exchanges but also the very real problems that arise when policies nurtured in a specific cultural context are applied to an unsuitable policy environment. Equally it has been shown that such transfers often reflect the hegemonic ambitions of one society or interest against another, so that once again the issue of the *uneven diffusion of power*, which is a central tenet of the institutionalist approach, comes to the fore. There are numerous other ideas and nuances of approach in this literature but the key to it all is understanding that political and social institutions are at the centre of the policy process, and that 'history matters'.

Implementation Analysis

The book has touched on number of other strands in the policy analysis literature, following the agenda set out by Parsons (1995) (see Chapter 1). The decision analysis literature has played a relatively minor role in this discussion of housing analysis but it has was deployed in Chapter 4 in relation to measuring housing needs. For example, classic cost-benefit analysis is central to the determination of the building programme and frames the debate about relative advantages and disadvantages of building more housing in the overheated southern housing market. To what extent should governments adjust policy to account for known problems caused by the house price cycle? Through forecasting procedures, involving complex needs measurement, decisions have to be made about the size of the building programme, the balance of dwellings to households and the standard of accommodation suitable to the standards of the day. As we saw, however, these technical measurements in fact conceal highly political questions about what share of public spending should be spent on housing ('resource constraints') and how the housing programme should be used to influence wider regional economic policy.

An important set of issues for housing was also drawn from the delivery analysis or implementation literature. A focus here was on the role of 'street-level bureaucrats' in shaping the outcome of policy at the moment of delivery. Homelessness officers have a great deal of influence on the treatment of homeless people despite highly prescriptive codes arising from the legislation and case law. In a similar vein, the role of the planning system in directing the building programme has been a key restraint on achieving increases in the building programme, which is currently at its lowest level since the mid-1920s. The simple question of whether there is enough housing of the right quality and in the right places to meet housing needs is a key delivery issue. Wider issues here involve the extent to which housing professionals should be compelled to cede power to tenants and customers. As we saw, this raises important issues of top down/bottom up influences on the policy process and decision-making. 'Who decides?' is the classic question of the policy analysis literature. Finally, policy review and evaluation represent the end-game of the policy cycle; have past policies worked, in this case to supply the right quantity and quality of housing where it is needed and, if not, what should change to ensure improvements? Once again, however, attention returns to the policy network literature because in each of these cases (homelessness and the relationship between housing and planning) it is increasingly apparent that the 'housing' policy community has evolved a distinctive character over the last few decades. Institutionalist methodologies, particularly network analysis and the cultural/historical approach, have enabled a complex policy arena to be understood and, above all, explained.

Housing as the 'Wobbly Pillar under the Welfare State'

This section draws together and explores the distinctive features of the 'housing' case. The new pattern of governance in Britain has already been discussed, but there are wider issues than this for which it is necessary to pick up the themes from Chapter 9 where British housing was put into its wider, comparative context. In the discussion of comparative housing in Chapter 9, the point was made that housing has a major influence in the patterning of societies, particularly in the way in which it helps to define differences between countries and clusters of countries. As Kemeny has pointed out, housing has a significant influence on social formation, more so than is generally acknowledged in the social sciences (Kemeny, 1981). In the British case, we have seen in earlier chapters that the progressive conversion to home ownership was one of the major developments in society over nearly a century. This quiet social revolution had a major impact on the built environment and landscape of the country, on the division of the social classes geographically, as we saw in Chapter 7 was a major factor in equalizing wealth distribution and was at the forefront of public policy through the building of millions of council houses. Throughout the twentieth century housing policy was a focal point of social advance. The world wars, however, caused a major setback in the frequently stated aim of housing policy to provide a decent house for every household. In each case, the wars provoked large-scale state intervention as the population demanded social improvement after the traumas of the war years. After the Second World War the acute shortage of housing, worse than at any stage in the twentieth century in the equation of dwellings to households, led to a massive programme of state house building which lasted for over three decades and took its place alongside the three other pillars of the Beveridge welfare state: health, education and social security. Public housing was a pillar of the welfare state, with nearly one-third of the population living in council housing by the mid-1970s.

After this, however, public housing was subjected to massive cuts in its spending programme alongside the privatization of the council stock and its transfer to new types of landlord. The explanation for this, as was argued in Chapter 6, is connected to the maturation crisis of this stock, with the idea that it might become increasingly attractive compared to the private sector owing to its low rent structure. It is also clear that it has been possible to subject state housing to this regime of retrenchment and privatization because of a number of distinctive features of 'housing' *per se*. Indeed these characteristics have led to its status as a true pillar of the welfare state to be questioned. Principal among these, as Torgersen has shown, is the fact that housing is a very capital-intensive form of social provision, whereas the other pillars of welfare are much more labour-intensive – or, in the case of social security, essentially a form of income transfer between different social groups (Torgersen, 1987). Capital-intensive housing programmes made housing vulnerable to cuts in public expenditure and much of the story of British public housing during the twentieth century was of programmes of investment followed by retrenchment as national expenditure faltered.

A second general characteristic identified by Torgersen was that housing has normally been considered as a universal entitlement. Providing 'decent' housing according to the standard of the day became and remains a core objective of British housing policy. The difficulty in realizing this aim has been that provision has predominantly been in the form of privately supplied and privately owned housing with large-scale state subsidies in the form of tax reliefs to home owners and a separate programme of council housing. Latterly, state housing was supported by the housing benefit system – once the historic cost, 'bricks and mortar' form of subsidy was abandoned due to the maturation crisis. Since the advent of the Beveridge welfare state, housing in Britain has thus been somewhat ambiguously placed alongside health, education and social security. Because of its vulnerability to public expenditure cuts and the difficulty of establishing housing as a universal right in market economies Torgersen suggested that housing has been 'the wobbly pillar under the welfare state.'

The Neglect of Housing in the Welfare State Literature

One of the consequences of the ambiguity and 'difference' of housing spoken of by Torgersen is that housing is generally ignored by the comparative welfare state literature. Comparativists find housing either too difficult, or too unlike the other pillars of the welfare state, to incorporate into their analysis. As Kemeny argues, this is somewhat surprising given the *significance* of housing in social formation and in the general patterning of social life, as has been discussed throughout this text (Kemeny, 1999). Some scholars are quite explicit about this exclusion. Wilensky, for example, argued that housing was too complicated to include in comparative analysis, despite collecting data on it for his original study of twenty-one countries. He suggested this was due to the inter-relationship between housing and other issues such as road building and transport, but particularly because of the complexity of housing finance – subsidies, taxation and interest rate policy. Wilensky concluded that: 'A bewildering array of fiscal, monetary and other policies that affect housing directly and indirectly – even remotely – have made the task of comparative analysis of public spending in this area nearly impossible' (Wilensky, 1975: 7) Similarly, as we saw in Chapter 9, housing data was collected for Esping-Andersen's *The Three Worlds of Welfare Capitalism* study, but because the data did not fit with his basic proposition housing was excluded from the study. Kemeny argued that the neglect of housing in the comparative welfare state literature was principally a conceptual question, arising from what he called 'epistemic drift' away from social theory in the social studies literature. In other words, new insights into housing made by social theorists – such as Rex and Moore, Castells, Saunders et al – were not absorbed or developed by students of housing so that, 'the concepts eventually lose their theoretical anchorage and degenerate into descriptive categories' (Kemeny, 1999: 6). There is, despite its neglect, no reason to marginalize housing in this way.

It could equally be the case that what makes housing a 'wobbly pillar' of welfare might be a reason for paying special attention to it, rather than ignoring it. It might be supposed, for example, that housing could be a 'litmus test' because housing's 'difference' could be the key to explaining why welfare states (and wider society) differ from each other. As Kemeny argues housing is especially important precisely because it is different (Kemeny, 1999). This would seem to be compounded by reference back to the discussion in Chapter 3 about the role housing plays in creating social identity. It will be recalled that developing Goffman's sociology of place Giddens showed that the home is a 'locale' in which social life is sustained and above all *reproduced*. This is the same idea developed by Kemeny, that housing indicates differences between societies precisely because it is so socially embedded in social structure (what Giddens calls time–space pathways), in which the day-to-day activity of domestic life creates and sustains knowledge of our place in society; when we can predict with some certainty how people will behave, and how we are expected to respond. It is this set of ideas that underpin the view outlined in Chapter 3 about individualization as the opposite pole (Giddens calls it the 'personal pole'), in the face of the globalization agenda: the question of self-identity, of who are we in this world of infinite choice and personal risk. In the language of the policy analysis approach, the idea of 'home' is a key meso-level concept – that is to say, it acts as the *link* between the globalization and individualization agendas. The concept of 'home' is thus not an eclectic and disparate idea written about by sociologists, architects, psychologists *et al.* but, for housing studies, a central and fundamental concept. It is one of the windows through which orthodox, policy-focused, 'housing studies' needs to look out onto the wider world and engage with the fact that housing is a key feature of social formation and is *not separate from society*.

The 'End of Housing Policy' Thesis

Not only, therefore, do welfare state theorists – Wilensky, Esping-Andersen, Heidemheimer, Castles – tend to downplay the role and significance of housing in the shaping of welfare states, but the converse problem is also apparent in the housing studies literature, which tends to treat housing as an autonomous field unconnected to the wider welfare state. One example of this in the recent housing studies literature is the claim by some writers that housing policy has lost its relevance. The source of this idea was the response of some scholars to the globalization agenda, writing essentially from a convergence perspective. The realization that housing policies were not converging led them to imagine that housing policy *per se* was withering away. As the era of post-war shortages came to an end so the need for housing policy receded and was replaced by 'niche' markets or special needs and localized issues.

Another 'end of housing policy' argument was that most people now rely on unsubsidized housing markets for supplying their housing needs, so the extent to which these people are affected by 'housing policy' is quite limited (Malpass, 1999). Yet another variant of 'the end of housing policy' thesis argued that housing policy had become subsumed into urban regeneration or a generalized assault on poverty and social exclusion. Rising incomes and the crisis of welfare state spending have both led to state spending on housing being cut back. As Kleinman argued, 'Housing policy, in the sense in which the term was understood at the zenith of the post-war welfare state, has collapsed, or is collapsing' (Kleinman, 1998: 251). Whether in Britain, France or Germany, Kleinman argues, this trend is clear. Policy is either about dealing with poverty or about creating the conditions in which the affluent majority become property owners.

These 'end of housing policy' ideas, however, have over-dramatized what are precisely those characteristics of 'housing' which led Torgersen to describe housing as 'the wobbly pillar under the welfare state': the vulnerability of state housing to expenditure cuts and the difficulty of supplying housing as a universal right in a market economy. Most of these 'end of housing policy' authors equate the apparent demise of policy with increasing levels of owner occupation. As we saw in Chapter 9, the evidence for this on a European-wide basis is not convincing. As Stephens, Burns and MacKay show from their study of six European countries, 'There is no evidence of an inexorable rise of homeownership…there have been falls since 1990 in Denmark and Finland' (Stephens, Burns and MacKay, 2002: 3). Not only does this 'growth of home owning' thesis misconstrue the empirical evidence but the explanation for why there has been a growth, which is most commonly associated with the spread of the political ideology of the Reagan/Thatcher 'New Right', is implausible. Although there is widely documented evidence of a policy transfer from the USA to Britain of workfare ideas and policies housing, as we have seen, has been on a long path of catch–up spanning many decades through the twentieth century. Moreover this view misattends to the long historical sweep of policy as it is encapsulated in the 'balance of households to dwellings' narrative.

Policy does not suddenly come to an end because the era of mass shortages is over or because Britain has matured as a nation of home-owners. Instead, it adapts to the new conditions set by the globalization agenda. It is true that housing is no longer such a major plank of policy as it was in the decades after 1945. But this is by no means the whole story and in the European non-profit housing systems policy remains at the centre of the system's structure by guiding rent setting and investment. Housing remains at the centre of the wider configuration of welfare state development and social change, even though its salience in policy might have declined. It can be read as a case of 'punctuated equilibrium', of a period of change followed by long period of consolidation. (Krasner, 1984).

Resonances from Pierson's idea of path dependency is clearly relevant to the contrast between Britain and the Continental European housing systems. By following particular 'paths' different countries gradually diverged, with positive policy feedback effects consolidating the direction of the path being followed. 'Comparative advantage is not simply given, it is often created through a sequence of events over time' (Pierson, 2000: 255). Pierson argued that these increasing returns were the answer to why countries with many apparent similarities evolved highly specialized welfare policy solutions (Pierson, 1993, 1994, 2000).

The 'end of housing policy' thesis is thus misconceived and results paradoxically from an exaggerated emphasis on 'policy', which we have seen is a major flaw in the narrowly focused housing studies field. It is a case of 'epistemic drift' as defined by Kemeny (1999), in which discourses without firm disciplinary roots tend to misattend to facts and jump to misleading conclusions. It may be that the influence of the English case has been exaggerated because of the rapid pace at which the growth of owner occupation has occurred since the 1990s. Such an Anglo-centric view is in danger of ascribing to other countries a version of events that was not theirs. While it is true that there has been a tendency in some west European countries for home ownership to grow in relation to the rental sectors, this is not a 'catch-up' scenario. Housing policy has not come to an end but has been transformed by events. Far from being marginalized, housing and housing policy continue to be highly significant.

The Significance of Housing Policy

What are the grounds for suggesting that housing has a much greater role in society and the shaping of other aspects of welfare provision than has been acknowledged in the literature? There are a number of clear pointers. The earliest attempt to grapple with this issue, and in many ways still the definitive statement, was Kemeny's (1981) study which showed that societies with a high percentage of home owners tended to have low welfare state spending and welfare regimes strongly reliant on private insurance and self-provisioning. On the other hand, countries with high proportions of cost-rental housing (i.e. non-profit) tend to have higher-spend welfare states. Even the built form of such societies differed, with home owning societies (the classic English-speaking family of nations) tending to be more suburbanized and characterized by sprawl compared to the cost-rental nations where urban structure is more contained with an emphasis on living in flats rather than detached or semi-detached houses. Kemeny cites the cases of Stockholm, where 70 per cent of dwellings are apartment flats compared to only 22 per cent in Sydney (Kemeny, 1981: 44). These characteristics, according to Kemeny, lead to different attitudes to public services. Sprawling owner occupied suburbs make it difficult to run economical bus services and so produce great reliance on car ownership compared to the more compact built environment of the European flat dwellers where public transit is cheap and efficient. These differences alone produce a significant divergence in social attitudes and create conditions in which individualist and collectivist attitudes flourish.

Other examples of the microeconomy of home ownership and welfare state development were discussed in Chapter 7. There we saw how there is potential inside the housing market to generate large-scale spending opportunities which might directly sponsor access to welfare opportunities and services. It was shown through the work of Holmans and Frosztega (1994) and Hamnett (1999) that housing equity was a key to the expansion in Britain of residential care of the elderly in the 1980s and 1990s. The multi-billion pound scale of over-mortgaging and re-mortgaging, inheritances of housing equity, etc. produces for homeowners and their relatives access to a massive source of cash, sponsoring private transport, access to private medical care, private schools and care needs in old age. While the research evidence is at the moment limited, it needs no great stretch of the imagination to see how the huge resources generated for millions of households might filter into sustaining the costs of private solutions to welfare needs (while at the same time excluding the state dependent minority, reliant on residual state services).

By comparison, countries with a cultural imperative and economic and political foundations rooted in the European social market tradition operate according to a very different logic. Countries with a strong social democratic base, such as the Scandinavian group and those with a corporatist tradition, such as Italy, France, Austria and Germany (note that the distinction between these two types is not very clear cut), have more plural housing systems and do not generate such huge potential for equity leakage or personal wealth creation. This issue was discussed in Chapter 7, where it was shown that home ownership tends to force-feed a situation of 'low-tax/low-spend' because of the high costs of owner occupation, especially in the early years of the household life cycle. Room for manoeuvre in tax policy is restrained by the high costs of home ownership, which depletes household income. Later on, these costs give way to access to housing equity withdrawal which supplements household income. Castles and Ferrera's study of the OECD nations clearly showed that countries with high levels of home ownership had the lowest levels of state pensions and the central European cluster with unitary rental housing markets all had much higher levels of pension provision (Castles and Ferrera, 1996: 163). The reason for this is not very difficult to discern because most elderly owner-occupiers have paid off their mortgages and with reduced housing costs and equity stored in the property might be thought of as being favourably placed. On the other hand entitlements built up over years of high taxation provide the elderly population of the social market economies with higher pension provision but potentially higher housing costs. Paying mortgages over twenty or twenty-five years or paying rent and high taxes over a working life time lead to very different outcomes for care needs in old age.

One further explanation for the divergence between the home owning family of nations and the European social economy cluster is the pattern of post-war inflation. The pattern of state versus private spending on housing is clearly correlated with high versus low inflationary economies. Home owning became a popular choice in countries in which inflation not only increased the value of property quite rapidly but also decreased the real level of mortgage payments, thus ameliorating the 'front-loading' problem (of high mortgage-to-income payments at the beginning of the purchase). Castles observed in the OECD countries that it was the countries with the highest sustained levels of post-war inflation – Britain, Ireland and Italy – that had the greatest increases in home ownership, whereas the countries with the lowest inflation levels – Japan and Switzerland – had the least change, in fact, decreases (Castles, 1998: 257).

In short, there is compelling evidence for different narratives to unfold comparing home owning Britain and the European social market nations. In the former case, through its cultural imperatives, through its low-tax/low-spend fiscal logic and through the huge scale of equity generated from property ownership and filtered down though families and between the generations, homeownership indelibly imprints itself on welfare state policy. These processes and resources have aided the deconstruction of the Beveridge welfare state and helped clear the way for the residual workfare state. On the other hand, in the social market societies long-standing adherence to the principles of the social market, incorporating high-spend welfare systems and non-profit 'unitary' rental housing systems stand in considerable contrast.

'Home Owning' versus 'Social Market' Housing Systems

There is other evidence outside the purely welfare state literature which supports the contention of divergence between the home owning and the social market housing systems. It is important to review this briefly because there is a conceptual lesson here – namely, that while housing is significant, it is not determinant. While claiming a high profile for housing in comparative welfare state theory it should not *over-determine* the results of the analysis. The underlying economy, of course, matters a great deal. It will be recalled from Chapter 9 that the retention by Germany of a substantial manufacturing base to its economy was in marked contrast to the British case which underwent a dramatic loss of its core manufacturing from the 1970s onwards and its replacement by service-based industries (with high levels of part-time, female employment). The suburbanization processes which accompanied this restructuring was a key reason for the expansion of home ownership from the 1970s onwards.

A very important element in this development was the breakdown of the traditional association between left-wing political incumbency and support for state housing provision. As the need for housing to accommodate a mass industrial workforce declined and as the electorate incorporated high proportions of owner occupiers so the Labour Party found it necessary to re-brand itself. In contrast to the home owning nations, societies with long-term commitments to high public spending and a consequent high-tax/high-spend regime tend to have a more balanced housing economy incorporating cost-rental housing. These systems operate in the context of what has been referred to as a 'unitary rental market' in which the public and private rental housing sectors broadly work in the context of a common housing market, mediated by municipal government (Kemeny, 1995). Later on, as incomes grew, home ownership became gradually more affordable and expanded to varying degrees with better-off households able to afford both high taxation and the costs of owner occupation. This would seem to be the case in countries such as Austria, Belgium and France (see Table 9.3, p. 239), but less so in Germany where the influence of the manufacturing base continued to over-ride this factor and owner occupation remained at modest levels (see Chapter 9). But none of these countries has become 'home owning' societies.

As we saw in Chapter 9, there is also a strong cultural underpinning of this situation that can be traced back to the European Reformation and how these countries broke with feudalism. At the very least, there is a strong case to be made for an association between the predominantly Catholic societies and social market economies against the Protestant home owning nations. From within the historical institutionalist perspective the argument is thus that there are strong cultural/historical foundations to the development of welfare state clusters, with the litmus test of housing becoming increasingly significant in the twentieth century when the issue of how to house the new working classes figured prominently on the social policy agendas of all industrialized societies. Low-tax/low-spend approaches to welfare and the structural connection to home ownership and the converse high-tax/high-spend regime is thus sustained by strong cultural predilections, with roots buried in deep history. The social market approach persisted in the Germanic-influenced nations even after the post-war housing shortages came to an end. So that as the need for the state to be involved in housing provision abated, the non-profit, unitary rental market continued to shape the basic pattern of housing. There is clear path dependency logic in this situation. State directed building programmes have wound down in recent decades, but the logic of 'social market' housing has persisted.

There is nothing surprising in this or the reduced activity of the state since the 1970s. As post-war subsidies came to an end, through a process similar to Kemeny's 'maturation' process, so state funding of housing declined quite naturally and, contrary to the supporters of ideological explanations, was nothing to do with the gathering momentum of 'New Right' ideas. State withdrawal from housing subsidies in Europe is perfectly explicable on a longer-term view of events, and had little or nothing to do with rising rates of home ownership in Britain.

Table 10.1 sums up some of the key contrasts between the home owning societies and those with a strong social market tradition, the latter all European, the former spread across the globe but strongly connected by language and cultural/historical roots. The table is indicative only, but does show that there is a significant set of structural differences between these two broad-brush clusters of nations. Housing may be thought of as a meso-level function which both defines differences and to an extent shapes patterns of change. It plays an intermediary role with a significant degree of autonomy in shaping social outcomes and the patterns of social formation, which are the ways in which countries diverge from each other.

The nations which make up the 'social market' housing cluster are connected by a history of high-tax/high-spend welfare policy built round a distinctive European social market philosophy. These countries have retained housing systems with a balanced tenure structure incorporating

Table 10.1   **Characteristics of home-owning and rental market societies**

	Home-owning societies The 'English-speaking family'	Unitary rental societies Germany/Austria/Denmark Sweden/Belgium/the Netherlands/ Switzerland
Economic structure	Service-based	Mixed with strong manufacturing base
Tax system	Low	High
The state	'Steering not rowing', decentralization of delivery	Strong central management
Welfare state	Residual, low state pensions, workfare, safety net social housing	Comprehensive, high state pensions, strong employment rights, socially mixed non-profit rental housing
Economic policy	Free market	Social market
Built environment	Strongly suburbanized in houses	Urban/collective flats
Cultural/religious context	Protestant	Catholic majorities
Housing tenure	High owner occupation, clearly demarcated public and private renting	Medium owner occupation, harmonized public/private rental market
Political incumbency	Conservative	Social Democratic/Christian Democratic

non-profit rental housing and private rented housing in a commonly organized rental market. The state in these cases is not benign, but steers policy using a range of policies, but all with the aim of producing a balanced housing system. A key feature since the 1970s has been the extent to which these countries have defended their manufacturing base supported by strong labour movements and associated employment rights. Suburbanization has been much less a feature of these countries, and consequently there has been a lower imperative towards home ownership.

The new service economies have clearly supported a more suburbanized built environment and life styles, which are essentially about home ownership. In parallel, the welfare states of these countries share the very distinctive trait of being low-tax/low-spend, with the lowest levels of state pensions, residualized state housing and workfare employment policies. Long-term political incumbency built around Conservative parties have also added to the mix, although opposition parties have decoupled from strong support for state housing as the owner occupier vote swamped traditional working class allegiances.

Table 10.1 shows that it is the *configuration* of factors that creates the distinctive clusters around the home owning and social market housing systems. 'Housing' can thus be seen to be at the centre of social formation and although is justifiably thought of as a 'wobbly pillar' of the welfare state, nevertheless in the home owning societies it provides an anchor for the creation of workfare states, characterized by private insurance welfare solutions, self-funding and equity-based resources. In social market societies, the unitary rental market (Kemeny, 1995) buttresses strong welfare states. In both cases, housing is far from insignificant, shaping and reacting to events national and global, and arguably a major catalyst in defining the path dependency of different societies encapsulated, as we have seen in the European context, in two distinct housing types.

The Future for Britain

A new economy of 'footloose' service industries has emerged, located in science and business parks, generally on greenfield sites and with the accompaniment of waves of 'Barratt box' houses, exclusively owner occupied. These suburbanization processes underpin and to a large extent define the patterns of social life in the twenty-first century. Home ownership has been a major statement in the social formation and the new geography of Britain's services-based economy. The opposite pole of this dynamic, as was discussed in Chapter 5, was the depopulation and social residualization of the old industrial cities, formerly the hub of the manufacturing economy. The problem of low demand for housing in the inner cities, and the consequent spiralling down of community life, are the antithesis of the new suburban economy. Because housing is at the centre of people's lives and it is their home, the consequences and the dynamics involved in economic restructuring are profoundly and inherently shaped by 'housing'.

As has been argued throughout the book, the British case is an interesting one in which there has been a 'catch-up' history during the twentieth century, so that one of the explanations for the conditions favourable to the low-spend mixed economy of welfare, and ultimately New Labour's workfare state, is the gradual conversion of Britain to the status of a fully-fledged home owning society. The British case exemplifies precisely what would be predicted, even with the legacy of the Beveridge welfare

state, in a society originally composed of renters. During its modernization it has become an owner occupied society, unambiguously a fully-
fledged member of the home owning 'family of nations'. This trajectory
of change is what makes the British case 'different' and interesting in
the context of how welfare states evolve. Properly conceptualized, there
is no need to read British housing as an oddity (with the implication
that it is unique and can only be juxtaposed with but not compared to
other comparable nations) or 'peculiar', but as one particular case shaped
by its economic, political and cultural contexts. Britain is 'different' but
not peculiar. Thus read through the lens of the policy analysis literature
and informed by the ideas of new institutionalist political science there
is no need to imagine that we are at the end of housing policy, or that
housing does not 'fit', or is so difficult that it is should be ignored.
Instead it is best understood as a powerful agent of social development
and change and leads to a much clearer understanding of the differences
between societies.

What of the future? Having come to the end of the long catch-up era
the UK stabilized as a nation of homeowners during the early 1990s.
Attention then came to focus on the break-up of council housing. This
leaves Britain looking in two quite distinct directions. On the one hand,
there is the creation of a more plural social rental housing system, in
which housing associations, co-ops and other forms of company land-
lordship and 'social businesses' are distinctly European in orientation
and the funding regime which accompanies this change shares elements
of European practice. However, there has been no relaxation of the rules
that count local authority borrowing as part of public sector spending.
(In most European countries, only the subsidies received by housing
associations and other social housing providers counts as public spending,
allowing them to raise private finance more easily and with no direct
implications for the public purse.) The British government has made it
clear there is unlikely to be any change in this position, partly because
it has already been factored into the convergence criteria for British
membership of the European Single Currency. Moreover, most European
countries do not treat their social rental sectors as safety nets for the
very poorest households (Stephens, Burns and MacKay, 2002).

The implications of these different housing systems for the wider
political and economic relationship with Europe are far-reaching. In
particular, if home ownership does underpin a low-tax/low-spend
welfare orientation, convergence with EU social policies, predominantly
(though by no means exclusively) based on high-tax-and-spend welfare
states, might be difficult. Having become a fully-fledged member of the

home-owning English-speaking 'family of nations', Britain's relationship with her European cousins contains a central contradiction based around their very different housing systems. Housing might well be the thorn in the flesh of European integration.

FURTHER READING

Hall, P. A. and Taylor, C. R. (1996) 'Political science and the three new institutionalisms', *Political Studies*, 44. (5), 936–57.

Kemeny, J. (1995) *From Public Housing to the Social Market*, London, Routledge.

Pierson, P. (ed.) (2001) *The New Politics of the Welfare State*, Oxford, Oxford University Press.

Steinmo, S., Thelen, K. and Longstreth, F. (eds) (1992) *Structuring Politics: Historical Institutionalism in Comparative Politics*, Cambridge, Cambridge University Press.

Bibliography

Adler, E. and Haas, P. (1992) 'Conclusion: epistemic communities, world order and the creation of a reflective research program', in P. Hass (ed.), 'Knowledge, Power and International Policy Co-ordination', special edition of *International Organisation*.

Anderson, I., Kemp, P. and Quilgars, D. (1993) *Single Homeless People*, London, HMSO.

Anderson, I. and Sims, D. (2000) *Social Exclusion and Housing: Contexts and Challenges*, Coventry, Chartered Institute of Housing.

Ashby, J. (1997) 'The Inquiry into Housing Association Governance: (an inside view)', in P. Malpass (ed.), *Ownership, Control and Accountability: The New Governance of Housing*, Coventry, Chartered Institute of Housing.

Audit Commission (1992) *Developing Local Authority Housing Strategies*, London, HMSO.

Audit Commission (2002) *Public Services in Wales: Delivering a Better Wales*, London, Audit Commission.

Bachelard, G. (1964) 'The phenomenology of the dwelling – the house protects the dreamer', *Landscape*, Winter.

Bachrach, P. S. and Baratz, M. S. (1970) *Power and Poverty, Theory and Practice*, New York, Oxford University Press.

Balchin, P. (1996) *Housing Policy in Europe*, London, Routledge.

Ball, M., Harloe, M. and Martens, M. (1988) *Housing and Social Change in Europe and the USA*, London, Routledge.

Bank of England (1992) 'Negative equity in the housing market', *Bank of England Quarterly Bulletin*, 266–9.

Barlow, J. and Duncan, S. (1994) *Success and Failure in Housing Provision: European Systems Compared*, London, Pergamon.

Barnett, R., Bradshaw, J. and Lowe, S. (1988) *Not Meeting Housing Need*, monograph published by a Northern Group of Housing Associations and the University of York.

Barnett, R. and Lowe, S. (1988) 'Measuring housing need and the provision of social housing', *Housing Studies*, 5(3).

Barrett, S. and Fudge, C. (1981) *Policy and Action*, London, Methuen.

Bate, R., Best, R. and Holmans, A. E. (eds) (2000) *On the Move: The Housing Consequences of Migration*, York. Joseph Rowntree Foundation.

Beck, U. (1999) *What is Globalization?*, Bristol, Polity Press.

Best, R. (1991) 'Housing Associations: 1890–1990', in S. Lowe and D. Hughes (eds), *A New Century of Social Housing*, Leicester, Leicester University Press.

Boddy, M. (1980) *The Building Societies*, Basingstoke, Macmillan.

Booth, P. and Crook, T. (eds) (1986) *Low Cost Home Ownership*, Aldershot, Gower.

Bosanquet, N. (1980) 'Labour and public expenditure: an overview', in N. Bosanquet and P. Townsend (eds), *Labour and Inequality*, London, Heinemann.

Bowley, M. (1945) *Housing and the State 1919–1944*, London, Allen & Unwin.

Bramley, G. (1989a) 'The demand for social housing in England in the 1980s', *Housing Studies*, 4(1).

Bramley, G. (1989b) *Meeting Housing Need*, London, Association of District Councils.

Bramley, G. (1991) *Bridging the Affordability Gap in 1990*, London, Association of District Councils/House Builders Federation.

Bramley, G. (1996) *Housing with Hindsight: Household Growth, Housing Need and Housing Development in the 1980s*, London, Council for the Protection of Rural England.

Bramley, G. (1998) 'Housing surpluses and housing need', in S. Lowe, S. Spences and P. Keenan (eds), *Housing Abandonment in Britain: Studies in the Causes and Effects of Low Demand Housing*, York, Centre for Housing Policy, Conference Papers.

Bramley, G. and Pawson, H. (2000) 'Understanding recent trends in residential mobility in council housing in England', *Urban Studies*, 37(8)

Bramley, G., Pawson, H., Satsangi, M. and Third, H. (1998) *Local Housing Needs Assessment: A Review of Current Practice and the Need for Guidance*, London, DETR.

Bramley, G., Pawson, H., Third, H. and Porker, J. (2000) *Low Demand Housing and Unpopular Neighbourhoods*, London, DETR.

Bryan, J. (1999) *Local Housing Needs Surveys: An Evaluation of Current Practice*, Newcastle, Northern Consortium of Housing Associations for Housing Corporation North Eastern.

Burnett, J. (1986) *A Social History of Housing*, 2nd edn, London, Methuen.

Burrows, R. (1997a) 'The social distribution of the experience of homelessness', in R. Burrows, N. Pleace and D. Quilgars (eds), *Homelessness and Social Policy*, London, Routledge.

Burrows, R. (1997b) *Contemporary Patterns of Residential Mobility in Relation to Social Housing in England*, York, Centre for Housing Policy, University of York.

Burrows, R. (1998) 'Mortgage Indebtedness in England: An Epidemiology', in *Housing Studies* 13(1), 5–22

Burrows, R., Ford, J. and Wilcox, S. (2000) 'Half the poor? Policy responses to the growth of low-income home-ownership', in S. Wilcox (ed.), *Housing Finance Review 2000/2001*, York, Joseph Rowntree Foundation.

Burrows, R., Pleace, N. and Quilgars, D. (eds) (1997) *Homelessness and Social Policy*, London, Routledge.

Butler, K., Carlisle, B. and Lloyd, R. (1994) *Homelessness in the 1990s: Local Authority Practice*, London, Shelter.

Campbell, J. (1987) *Nye Bevan and the Mirage of British Socialism*, London, Weidenfeld & Nicolson.

Carruth, A. and Henley, A. (1990) 'The Housing Market and Consumer Spending', in *Fiscal Studies*, 11, 27–38.

Castells, M. (1977) *The Urban Question*, London, Edward Arnold.

Castells, M. (1983) *The City and the Grassroots*, London, Edward Arnold.

Castells, M. (1996) *The Rise of the Network Society, The Information Age: Economy, Society and Culture, I*, Cambridge, MA, and Oxford, Blackwell.

Castells, M. (1997a) *The Power of Identity, The Information Age: Economy, Society and Culture, II*, Cambridge, MA, and Oxford, Blackwell.

Castells, M. (1997b) *The End of Millennium, The Information Age: Economy, Society and Culture, III*, Cambridge, MA, and Oxford, Blackwell.

Castles, F. G. (1998) *Comparative Public Policy: Patterns of Post-War Transformation*, Cheltenham, Edward Elgar.

Castles, F. G. and Ferrera, M. (1996) 'Home ownership and the welfare state: is Southern Europe different?', *South European Society and Politics*, 1(2), 163–85.

Cerny, P. G. (1999) 'Restructuring the political arena: globalization and the paradoxes of the competition state', in G. Randell, *Globalization and its Critics*, London, Macmillan.

Cerny, P. G. and Evans, M. (1999) 'New Labour, globalization and the competition state', unpublished paper.

Chapman, T. and Hockey, J. (eds) (1999) *Ideal Homes? Social Change and Domestic Life*, London, Routledge.

CIH (Chartered Institute of Housing) (1998) *Low Demand in Housing*, Coventry, Chartered Institute of Housing.

Clapham, D., Hegedüs, J., Kintrea, K. and Tosics, I: (eds) (1996) *Housing Privatisation in Eastern Europe*, London, Greenwood Press.

Clapham, D. and Kintrea, K. (2000) 'Community-based housing organisations and the local governance debate', *Housing Studies*, 15(4), 533–59.

Cochrane, A. and Clarke, J. (eds) (1993) *Comparing Welfare States: Britain in International Context*, London, Sage.

Cohen, M. J., March, J. G. and Olsen, J. (1972) 'A garbage can model of organisational choice', *Administrative Science Quarterly*, 17, 1–25.

Cole, I., Robinson, D. and Slocombe, L. (2001) *Housing in the Regions: A Review and Evaluation of Regional Housing Statements*, Sheffield, Centre for Regional Economic and Social Research, Sheffield Hallam University.

Cole, I., Robinson, D. and Slocombe, L. (2002) 'Housing, planning and economic development in the English regions: strategy co-ordination – or confusion?', in S. Wilcox (ed.), *Housing Policy Review 2002/3*, York, Joseph Rowntree Foundation.

Cooper-Marcus, C. (1995) *House as a Mirror of Self: Exploring the Deeper Meanings of Home*, Berkeley, CA, Conari Press.

Coote, A., Harman, H. and Hewitt, P. (1990) *The Family Way: A New Approach to Policy Making*, London, Institute for Public Policy Research.

Cope, H. (1999) *Housing Associations: Policy and Practice*, Basingstoke, Macmillan.

Council of Mortgage Lenders (2003) Press release on 11/03 at www.cml.org.uk

Cowans, D. (2001) 'Harassment and unlawful eviction in the private rented sector – a study of law in action', *The Conveyancer and Property Lawyer*, 65, 249–64.

Crenson, M. A. (1971) *The Unpolitics of Air Pollution: A Study of Non-decision Making in the Cities*, Baltimore, MD, Johns Hopkins University Press.

Crook, A. D. H. (2002a) 'Private renting in the 21st century', in S. Lowe and D. Hughes (eds), *The Private Rented Sector in a New Century: Revival or False Dawn?*, Bristol, Policy Press.

Crook, A. D. H. (2002b) 'Housing conditions in the private rented sector within a market framework', in S. Lowe and D. Hughes (eds), *The Private Rented Sector in a New Century: Revival or False Dawn?*, Bristol, Policy Press.

Crook, A. D. H. and Hughes, J. E. T. (2001) 'Market signals and disrepair in privately rented housing', *Journal of Property Research*, 18(1), 21–50.

Crook, A. D. H., Hughes, J. E. T. and Kemp, P. (1995) *The Supply of Privately Rented Homes*, York, Joseph Rowntree Foundation.

Crook, A. D. H. and Kemp, P. (1996) *Private Landlords in England*, London, HMSO.

Crook, A. D. H. *et al*. (1991) *Tax Incentives and the Revival of Private Renting*, York, Cloister Press.

Currie, H. (2002) 'The Scottish system of licensing houses in multiple occupation', in S. Lowe and D. Hughes (eds), *The Private Rented Sector in a New Century: Revival or False Dawn?*, Bristol, Policy Press.

Daunton, M. J. (1987) *A Property-Owning Democracy – Housing in Britain*, London, Faber & Faber.

Daunton, M. J. (1990) *Housing the Workers*, Leicester, Leicester University Press.

Davis, M. and Hughes, D. (2002) 'Changing Rooms: the legal and policy implications of a burgeoning student housing market in Leicester,' in S. Lowe and D. Hughes (eds), *The Private Rented Sector in a New-Century: Revival or False Down?* Bristol, The Policy Press.

Deacon, A. (2000) 'Learning from the US? The influence of American ideas upon "New Labour" thinking on welfare reform', *Policy and Politics*, 28(1), 5–18.

DETR (Department of the Environment, Transport and the Regions) (1997) *An Economic Model of the Demand and Need for Social Housing*, London, DETR.

DETR (Department of the Environment, Transport and the Regions) (1998) *English House Conditions Survey, 1996*, London, The Stationery Office.

DETR (Department of the Environment, Transport and the Regions) (1999a) *Statistics of Local Authority Activities under the Homelessness Legislation: England, Third Quarter of 1998*, London, DETR.

DETR (Department of the Environment, Transport and the Regions) (1999b) *Housing in England 1998/99, Survey of English Housing*, London, DETR.

DETR (Department of the Environment, Transport and the Regions) (1999c) *Annual Report on Rough Sleeping*, London, DETR.

DETR (Department of the Environment, Transport and the Regions) (2000a) web-site, at www.odpm.gov.uk

DETR (Department of the Environment, Transport and the Regions) (2000b) *Quality and Choice: A Decent Home for All. The Housing Green Paper*, London, The Stationery Office.

DETR (Department of the Environment, Transport and the Regions) (2000c) *Coming in from the Cold: Progress Report on the Government's Strategy on Rough Sleeping (Summer 2000)*, London, The Stationery Office.

DETR (Department of the Environment, Transport and the Regions) (2001) *Best Value in Housing Framework*, London, DETR.

DHSS (Department of Health and Social Security) (1985) *Residential Accommodation for the elderly out younger physically handicapped people as at 31st March 1984*, London, HMSO.

Dickens, P., Duncan, S., Goodwin, M. and Gray, F. (1985) *State, Housing and Localities*, London, Methuen.

Diski, J. (1997) *Skating to Antarctica*, London, Granta.

DoE (Department of the Environment) *Housing Policy: A Consultative Document*, Cmnd 6851, HMSO, 1977.

DoE (Department of the Environment) (1987) *Housing Policy: The Government's Proposals*, Cmnd 214, London, HMSO.

DoE (Department of the Environment) (1993) *English House Conditions Survey 1991*, London, HMSO.

DoE (Department of the Environment) (1994) *Access to Local Authority and Housing Association Tenancies*, London, HMSO.

DoE (Department of the Environment) (1995a) *Our Future Homes: Opportunity, Choice and Responsibility* (The Housing Green Paper), Cmnd 2901, London, HMSO.

DoE (Department of the Environment) (1995b) *Survey of English Housing*, London, HMSO.

Doling, J. (1997) *Comparative Housing Policy*, Basingstoke, Macmillan.

Dolowitz, D. (1997) 'British employment policy in the 1980s: learning from the American experience', *Governance* 10, 32–42.

Donnison, D. (1967) *The Government of Housing*, Harmondsworth, Penguin.

Dorling, D. and Cornford, J. (1995) 'Who has negative equity? How house, price falls in Britain have hit different groups of home buyers', *Housing Studies*, 10(2) 151–78.

Drucker, P. F. (1954) *The Practice of Management*, London, Heinemann.

Drucker, P. F. (1990) *Managing the Non-Profit Organisation*, Oxford, Butterworth-Heinemann.

DTLR (Department of Transport, Local Government and the Regions) (2002a) *Homelessness Strategies – a Good Practice Handbook*, London, DTLR.

DTLR (2002b) *Your Region, Your Choice: Revitalising the English Regions – White Paper on Regional Governance*, London, DTLR.

Dunleavy, P. (1979) 'Some political implications of sectoral cleavoges and the growth of state employment', in *Political Studies*, 27.

Dunleavy, P. (1981a) 'Professions and policy change: notes towards a model of ideological corporatism', *Public Administration Bulletin*, 36, 3–16.

Dunleavy, P. (1981b) *The Politics of Mass Housing in Britain, 1945–1975: A Study of Corporate Power and Professional Influence in the Welfare State*, Oxford, Clarendon Press.

Dunleavy, P. (1991) *Democracy, Bureaucracy and Public Choice*, London, Harvester/Wheatsheaf.

Dunsire, A. (1978) *Implementation in a Bureaucracy*, Oxford, Martin Robertson.

Durant, R. (1939) *Watling: A Survey of Social Life on a New Housing Estate*, London, P. S. King.

EC Phare (2000) *Change and Choice in Social Protection – The Experience of Central and Eastern Europe*, EC Phare Consensus Programme, York, Pantheon, University of York.

Edelman, M. (1977) *Political Language: Words that Succeed and Policies that Fail*, New York, Institute for the Study of Poverty.

Edelman, M. (1988) *Constructing the Political Spectacle*, Chicago, Chicago University Press.

EHCS (*English House Conditions Survey*) (1998).

Elander, I. (1991) 'Good dwellings for all: the case of social rented housing in Sweden', *Housing Studies*, 6(1), 29–43.

Ellison, M. (2002) 'Room for improvement: the impact of the local authority grant system', in S. Lowe and D. Hughes (eds), *The Private Rented Sector in a New Century*, Bristol, Policy Press.

Elmore, R. (1979) 'Backward mapping', *Political Science Quarterly*, 94, 601–16

Emms, P. (1990) *Social Housing: A Social Dilemma?*, Bristol, School for Advanced Urban Studies, University of Bristol.

Esping-Andersen, G. (1990) *The Three Worlds of Welfare Capitalism*, Cambridge, Polity Press.

Evans, M. with McComb, P. (1999) 'Policy transfer networks and collaborative government: the case of social security fraud', *Public Policy and Administration*, 14(2), 30–48.

Finer, S. E. (1952) *The Life and Times of Sir Edwin Chadwick*, London, Methuen.

Fitzpatrick, S. (2001) *Young Homeless People*, Basingstoke, Macmillan.

Fitzpatrick, S., Kemp, P. and Klinker, S. (2000) *Single Homelessness: An Overview of Research in Britain*, Bristol, Policy Press.

Fitzpatrick, S. and Klinker, S. (2000) *Research on Single Homelessness in Britain*, 'Findings' 410, York, Joseph Rowntree Foundation.

Ford, J. and Seavers, J. (1998) *Housing Associations and Rent Arrears: Attitudes, Beliefs and Behaviour*, Coventry, Chartered Institute of Housing.

Ford, J., Kempson, E. and Wilson, M. (1995) *Mortgage Arrears and Possessions: Perspectives from borrowers, lenders and the courts*, London, HMSO.

Forrest, R., Kennett, P. and Leather, P. (1999) *Home Ownership in Crisis?*, Aldershot, Ashgate.

Forrest, R. and Murie, A. (1988) *Selling the Welfare State – The Privatisation of Council Housing*, London, Routledge.

Forrest, R., Kennett, P. and Leather, P. (1997) *New Problems on the Periphery? Have Owners on New Estates in the 1990s*, Bristol, Policy Press.

Forrest, R., Murie, A. and Williams, P. (1990) *Home Ownership: Differentiation and Fragmentation*, London, Unwin Hyman.

Forster, E. M. (1910) *Howards End*, London, Edward Arnold; various edns, Harmondsworth, Penguin.

Gaskell, E (1848) *Mary Barton: A Tale of Manchester Life*, London, Penguin Classics.

Gaskell, E. (1855) *North and South*, London, Penguin Classics.

Gauldie, E. (1974) *Cruel Habitations*, London, George Allen & Unwin.

Gemmell, N. (ed.) (1995) 'Wagner's Law and Musgrave's Hypotheses' in Gemmell, N. (ed.), *The Growth of the Public Sector: Theories and International Evidence*, Aldershot, Edward Elgar.

Gershuny, J. (1983) *Social Innovation and the Division of Labour*, Oxford, Oxford University Press.

Giddens, A. (1984) *The Constitution of Society*, Cambridge, Polity Press.

Giddens, A. (1989) *Sociology*, Oxford, Polity Press.

Glastonbury, B. (1971) *Homeless Near a Thousand Homes*, London, George Allen & Unwin.

Goffman, I. (1959) *The Presentation of the Self in Everyday Life*, Harmondsworth, Penguin.

Gregson, N. and Lowe, M. (1994) *Servicing the Middle Classes: Class, Gender and Waged Domestic Labour in Contemporary Britain*, London, Routledge.

Greve, J. (1964) *London's Homeless*, London, The Codicote Press.

Greve, J. (1991) *Homelessness in Britain*, York, Joseph Rowntree Foundation.

Greve, J. *et al.*, (1971) *Homelessness in London*, Edinburgh, Scottish Academic Press.

Grier, K. (1988) *Culture and Comfort: People, Parlours and Upholstery: 1850–1950*, Rochester, NY, The Strong Museum.

Gurney, C. and Means, R. (1993) 'The meaning of home in later life', in S. Arber and M. Evandrou (eds), *Ageing, Independence and the Life Course*, London, Jessica Kingsley.

Hall, R. H. (1977) *Organizations, Structure and Process*, Englewood Cliffs, NJ, Prentice-Hall.

Hall, P. A. and Taylor, C. R. (1996) 'Political science and the three new institutionalisms', *Political Studies*, 44(5): 936–57.

Hamnett, C. (1999) *Winners and Losers – Home Ownership in Modern Britain*, London, UCL Press.

Hantrais, L. and Letablier, M. T. (1996) *Families and Family Policies in Europe*, London, Addison Wesley Longman.

Harloe, M. (1985) *Private Rented Housing in the United States and Europe*, London, Routledge.

Harloe, M. (1995) *The People's Home: Social Rented Housing in Europe and America*, Oxford, Blackwell.

Hartwell, R. M. (1989) 'The political economy of policy formation: the case of England', in A. Gamble *et al.*, *Ideas, Interests and Consequences*, London, Institute of Economic Affairs.

Hay, C. and Wincott, D. (1998) 'Structure, agency and historical institutionalism', *Political Studies*, 46(5), 951–57.

Heclo, H. (1978) 'Issue networks and the executive establishment', in A. King (ed.) *The New American Political System*, Washington, DC, American Enterprise Institute.

Heclo, H. and Wildavsky, A. (1974) *The Private Government of Public Money*, London, Macmillan.

Hegedüs, J., Mayo, S. and Tosics, I. (1996) *Transition of the Housing Sector in East-Central European Countries*, Budapest, Metropolitan Research Institute.

Hegedüs, J. and Varhegyi, E. (2000) 'The crisis in housing finance in Hungary in the 1990s', *Urban Studies*, 37(9), 1619–41.

Hegedüs, J. *et al.*, (1996) 'Disintegration of the East-European Housing Model', in D. Clapham, J. Hegedüs and I. Tosics (eds), *Housing Privatisation in Eastern Europe*, London, Greenwood Press.

Held, D. and McGrew, A. (eds) (2000) *The Global Transformations Reader*, Cambridge, Polity Press.

Held, D., McGrew, A., Goldblatt, D. and Perraton, J. (1999), *Global Transformations*, Cambridge, Polity Press.

Hepworth, M. (1999) 'Privacy, security and respectability: the ideal Victorian home', in T. Chapman and J. Hockey (eds), *Ideal Homes? Social Change and Domestic Life*, London, Routledge

Hill, M. (1997) *The Policy Process in the Modern State*, 3rd edn, London, Prentice-Hall/Harvester Wheatsheaf.

Hills, J. (1998) 'Housing: a decent home within the reach of every family', in H. Glennerster and J. Hills (eds), *The State of Welfare*, Oxford, Oxford University Press.

Hirschman, A. O. (1970) *Exit, Voice and Loyalty*, Cambridge, MA, Harvard University Press.

Hirschman, A. O. (1983) *Shifting Involvements*, Oxford, Blackwell.

Hirst, P. and Thompson, G. (1999) *Globalization in Question*, 2nd edn, Cambridge, Polity Press.

Hockey, J. (1999) 'Houses of doom', in T. Chapman and J. Hockey (eds), *Ideal Homes? Social Change and Domestic Life*, London, Routledge.

Hofferbert, R. (1974) *The Study of Public Policy*, Indianapolis, Bobbs-Merrill.

Hoggett, P. (1996) 'New modes of control in the public service', *Public Administration*, 74, 9–32.

Hogwood, B. W. and Gunn, L. A. (1984) *Policy Analysis for the Real World*, London, Oxford University Press.

Holmans, A. E. (1987) *Housing Policy in Britain*, London, Croom Helm.

Holmans, A. E. (1991) 'Estimates of housing equity withdrawal by owner occupiers in the United Kingdom 1970–1990', *Government Economic Service Working Paper*, No. 116, London, DoE.

Holmans, A. E. (1995) *Housing Demand and Need 1991–2011*, York, Joseph Rowntree Foundation.

Holmans, A. (2000a) 'British housing in the twentieth century: an end-of-century overview', in S. Wilcox (ed.), *Housing Finance Review 1999–2000*, York, Chartered Institute of Housing and the Council of Mortgage Lenders for the Joseph Rowntree Foundation.

Holmans, A. E. (2000b) *Divorce, Remarriage and Housing*, London, DETR.

Holmans, A. E. and Frosztega, M. (1994) *House Property and Inheritance in the UK*, London, HMSO.

Holmans, A. E. and Frosztega, M. (1996) *Negative Equity*, London DoE.

Holmans, A. E., Morrison, N. and Whitehead, C. (1998) *How Many Houses will we Need? The Need for Affordable Housing in England*, London, Shelter.

Holmans, A. E. and Simpson, M. (1999) *Low Demand: Separating Fact from Fiction*, Coventry, Chartered Institute of Housing for the Joseph Rowntree Foundation.

Homeless Network (1997) *Central London Street Monitor*, London, Homeless Network.

Hood, C. (1991) 'A public management for all seasons', *Public Administration*, 69(1), 3–19.

Hood, C. (1995) 'Contemporary public management: a new global paradigm?', in *Public Policy and Administration*, 10(2), 104–17.

Housing Corporation (2001) *Registered Social Landlords in 2000 Profile of the RSL Sector*, Source Research, 47, London, Housing Corporation.

Housing Services Agency (1998) *The Outreach Directory Annual Statistics 1996–97*, London, Housing Services Agency and Homeless Network.

Hughes, D. (1991) 'Tenants' rights', in S. Lowe and D. Hughes (eds), *A New Century of Social Housing*, Leicester, Leicester University Press.

Hughes, D. and Lowe, S. (2002) 'New law, new policy', in S. Lowe and D. Hughes (eds), *The Private Rented Sector in a New Century: Revival or False Dawn?*, Bristol, Policy Press.

Hutton, W. (1995) *The State We're In*, London, Jonathan Cape.

Jaffe, A. and Fisher, L. (2000) 'Restitution in transition countries', *Housing and the Built Environment*, 15(3), 233–48.

Jackson, S. (1998) *Britain's Population: Demographic Issues in Contemporary Society*, London, Routledge.

Jessop, B. (1990) *State Theory: Putting Capitalist States in their Place*, Cambridge, Polity Press.

Karn, V. (1993) 'Remodelling a HAT', in P. Malpass and R. Means (eds), *Implementing Housing Policy*, Buckingham, Open University Press.

Kavanagh, D. (1987) *Thatcherism and British Politics – The End of Consensus?*, Oxford, Oxford University Press.

Kearns, A. (1997) 'Housing Association Committees: dilemmas of composition', in P. Malpass (ed.), *Ownership, Control and Accountability: The New Governance of Housing*, Coventry, Chartered Institute of Housing.

Kearns, A. and Stevens, M. (1997) 'Building societies: changing markets, changing governance', in P. Malpass (ed.), *Ownership, Control and Accountability: The New Governance of Housing*, Coventry, Chartered Institute of Housing.

Keenan, P. (1998) 'Residential mobility and low demand: a case history from Newcastle', in S. Lowe, P. Keenan and S. Spencer (eds), *Housing Abandonment in Britain: Studies in the Causes and Effects of Low Demand Housing*, York, Centre for Housing Policy, University of York.

Kemeny, J. (1981) *The Myth of Home Ownership: Public versus Private Choices in Housing Tenure*, London, Routledge.

Kemeny, J. (1992) *Housing and Social Theory*, London, Routledge.

Kemeny, J. (1995) *From Public Housing to the Social Market*, London, Routledge.

Kemeny, J. (1999) 'Housing and the welfare state: wobbly pillar or hidden foundation?', paper for Workshop on Reconceptualising Welfare, Florence, European Union Institute.

Kemeny, J. and Lowe, S. (1998) 'Schools of comparative housing research: from convergence to divergence', *Housing Studies*, 13(2), 161–76.

Kemp, P. A. (1991) 'From solution to problem? Council housing and the development of national housing policy', in S. Lowe and D. Hughes (eds), *A New Century of Social Housing*, Leicester, Leicester University Press.

Kemp, P. A. (1992) 'Housing', in D. Marsh and R. A. W. Rhodes (eds), *Implementing Thatcherite Policies: Audit of an Era*, Buckingham, Open University Press.

Kemp, P. A. (1997) 'The characteristics of single homeless people in England', in R. Burrows, N. Pleace and D. Quilgars (eds), *Homelessness and Social Policy*, London, Routledge.

Kemp, P. A. (1998) *Housing Benefit: Time for Reform*, York, Joseph Rowntree Foundation.

Kemp, P. A. (1999) 'Housing policy under New Labour', in M. Powell (ed.), *New Labour, New Welfare State*, Bristol, Policy Press.

Kemp, P. and Keoghan, M. (2001) 'Movement into and out of the private rented sector in England', *Housing Studies*, 16(1), 21–7.

Kleinman, M. (1998) 'Western, European housing policies: convergence or collapse', in Kleinman, M., Matznetter, W. and Stephens, M. (eds), *European Integration and Housing Policy*, London, Routledge.

Kleinman, M., Matznetter, W. and Stephens, M. (eds) (1998) *European Integration and Housing Policy*, London, Routledge.

Krasner, S. D. (1970) 'Approaches to the state', *Comparative Politics*, 16(2), 223–46.

Kuhn, T. (1962) *The Structure of Scientific Revolutions*, Chicago, Chicago University Press.

Kwon, H. (1997) 'Beyond European welfare regimes: comparative perspectives on East Asian welfare systems', *Journal of Social Policy*, 26(4), 467–84.

Laing, R. D. (1966) *The Divided Self*, London, Penguin.

Laswell, H. D. (1951) 'The policy orientation', in D. Lerner and H. D. Laswell (eds), *The Policy Sciences*, Stanford, CA, Stanford University Press.

Laswell, H. D. (1956) *The Decision Process: Seven Categories of Functional Analysis*, College Park MD, University of Maryland Press.

Laswell, H. D. (1959) 'Strategies of inquiry: the rational use of observation', in D. Lerner (ed.), *The Human Meaning of the Social Sciences*, New York, Meridian Books.

Laswell, H. A. and Lerner, D. (eds) (1951) *The Policy Sciences*, Stanford, CA, Stanford University Press.

Law Commission (2001) *Reform of Housing Law: A Scoping Paper*, London, Law Commission.

Lee, P. and Murie, M. (1997) *Poverty, Housing Tenure and Social Exclusion*, Bristol, Policy Press.

Leibfried, S. (1991) *Towards a European Welfare State: On Integrating Poverty Regimes in the European Community*, Working Paper, 2/91, Centre for Social Policy Research, University of Bremen.

Lewin, F. A. (2001) 'The meaning of home among elderly immigrants: directions for future research and theoretical development', *Housing Studies*, 16(3), 353–70.

Lewis, J. (1992) 'Gender and the development of welfare regimes', *Journal of European Social Policy*, 2(3), 159–73.

Lindblom, C. E. (1959) 'The science of muddling through', *Public Administration Review*, 19, 78–8.

Lindblom, C. E. (1979) 'Still muddling through', *Public Administration Review*, 39(6), 516–25.

Lindblom, C. E. and Woodhouse, E. J. (1993) *The Policy-making Process*, 3rd edn, Englewood Cliffs, NJ, Prentice-Hall.

Lipsky, M. (1980) *Street-Level Bureaucrats*, New York, Russell Sage.

Lister, D. (2002) 'The nature of tenancy relationships – landlords and young people in the PRS', in S. Lowe and D. Hughes (eds), *The Private Rented Sector in a New Century*, Bristol, Policy Press.

Lowe, S. (1986) *Urban Social Movements: The City after Castells*, Basingstoke, Macmillan.

Lowe, S. (1988) 'New patterns of wealth: the growth of owner occupation', in Parker, G. and Walker, R. (eds) *Money Matters: Income, Wealth and Financial Welfare*, London, Sage.

Lowe, S. (1990) 'Capital accumulation in home ownership and family welfare', in N. Manning and C. Ungerson (eds), *Social Policy Review 1989–90*, Harlow, Longman.

Lowe, S. (1991), 'Introduction: one hundred years of social housing', in S. Lowe and D. Hughes, *A New Century of Social Housing*, Leicester, Leicester University Press.

Lowe, S. (1997a) 'Homelessness and the law', in R. Burrows, N. Pleace and D. Quilgars (eds), *Homelessness and Social Policy*, London, Routledge.

Lowe, S. (1997b) 'Homes and castles: was it inevitable that Britain became a nation of home-owners?', in J. Goodwin and C. Grant (eds), *Built to Last: Reflections on British Housing Policy*, London, Roof Magazine, Shelter.

Lowe, S. (2000) 'A tale of two cities – rental housing in Budapest and Sofia in the 1990s', *Housing and the Built Environment*, 15(3), 249–66.

Lowe, S., Keenan, P. and Spencer, S. (1998) *Housing Abandonment in Britain: Studies in the Causes and Effects of Low Demand Housing*, York, Centre for Housing Policy, University of York.

Lowe, S., Keenan, P. and Spencer, S. (1999) 'Housing abandonment in inner cities: the politics of low demand for housing', *Housing Studies*, 14(5), 703–16.

Lowe, S. and Hughes, D. (eds) (1991) *A New Century of Social Housing*, Leicester, Leicester University Press.

Lowe, S. and Hughes, D. (eds) (2002) *The Private Rented Sector in a New Century: Revival or False Dawn?*, Bristol, Policy Press.

Lowe, S. and Watson, S. (1990) *From First-Time Buyers to Lost-Time Sellers: An appraisal of equity withdrawal from the housing market between 1982 and 1988*, York, Department of Social Policy and Social Work, University of York.

Lukes, S. (1974) *Power: A Radical View*, London, Macmillan.

Lundquist, L. J., Elander, I. and Danermark, B. (1990) 'Housing policy in Sweden – still a success?', *International Journal of Urban and Regional Research*, 14, 445–67.

Lynch, P. (2002) *Scottish Government and Politics*, Edinburgh, Edinburgh University Press.

Malpass, P. (ed.) (1997) *Ownership, Control and Accountability: The New Governance of Housing*, Coventry, Chartered Institute of Housing.

Malpass, P. (1997) 'Introduction', in P. Malpass (ed.), *Ownership, Control and Accountability: The New Governance of Housing*, Coventry, Chartered Institute of Housing.

Malpass, P. (1990) *Reshaping Housing Policy: Subsidies, Rents and Residualisation*, London, Routledge.

Malpass, P. (1991) 'The financing of public housing', in S. Lowe and D. Hughes (eds), *A New Century of Social Housing*, Leicester, Leicester University Press.

Malpass, P. (1993) 'Housing policy and the housing system since 1979', in P. Malpass and R. Means (eds), *Implementing Housing Policy*, Buckingham, Open University Press.

Malpass, P. (1999) 'Housing policy: does it have a future?', *Policy and Politics*, 27(2), 217–28.

Malpass, P. (2000) *Housing Associations and Housing Policy*, Basingstoke, Macmillan.

Malpass, P. and Murie, A. (1987) *Housing Policy and Practice*, 3rd edn, Basingstoke, Macmillan.

Malpass, P. and Murie, A. (1999) *Housing Policy and Practice*, 5th edn, Basingstoke, Macmillan.

Mandic, S. (2000) 'Trends in Central and Eastern European rented sectors', *Housing and the Built Environment*, 15(3), 217–31.

March, J. G. and Olsen, J. P. (1989) *Rediscovering Institutions: The Organizational Basis of Politics*, New York, Free Press.

Marsh, A. and Mullins, D. (1998) 'The social exclusion perspective and housing studies: origins, applications and limitations', *Housing Studies*, 13(6), 749–60.

Marsh, A., Niner, P., Cowan, D., Forrest, R. and Kennett, P. (2000) *Harassment and Unlawful Eviction of Private Rented Sector Tenants and Park Home Residents*, London, DETR.

Marsh, D. and Rhodes, R. A. W. (1992) *Policy Networks in British Government*, Oxford, Oxford University Press.

McClusky, J. (1994) *Acting in Isolation: An Evaluation of the Effectiveness of the Children Act for Young Homeless People*, London, Campaign for the Homeless and Roofless.

McConaghy, M., Foster, K., Thomas, M., Grove, J. and Oliver, R. (2000) *Housing in England 1998/9* (Survey of English Housing 1998/9), London, The Stationery Office.

McCrone, G. and Stephens, M. (1995) *Housing Policy in Britain and Europe*, London, UCL Press.

McGrew, A. G. and Lewis, P. G. (1992) *Global Politics: Globalisation and the Nation-State*, Oxford, Polity Press.

McGuire, C. C. (1981) *International Housing Policies*, Lexington, MA, Lexington Books.

Mead, G. H. (1934) *Mind, Self and Society*, Chicago, Chicago University Press.

Merrett, S. (1979) *State Housing in Britain*, London, Routledge & Kegan Paul.

Merrett, S. (1982) *Owner Occupation in Britain*, London, Routledge & Kegan Paul.

Merton, R. K. (1957) *Social Theory and Social Structure*, Glencoe, Free Press.

Miller, P. and O'Leary, T. (1987) 'Accounting and the construction of the governable person', *Accounting, Organizations and Society* 12(3), 235–66.

Ministry of Housing and Local Government (1961) *Housing in England and Wales*, Cmnd. 1290, London, HMSO.

Ministry of Housing and Local Government (1965) *The Housing Programme 1965–70*, Cmnd 2838, London, HMSO.

Ministry of Housing and Local Government (1968) *Old Houses into New Homes*, Cmnd 3602, London, HMSO.

Morgan, J. (2002) 'Unlawful eviction and harassment', in D. Hughes and S. Lowe, *The Private Rented Sector in a New Century*, Bristol, Policy Press.

Morton, J. (1991) 'The 1890 Act and its aftermath – the era of the "new model dwellings"', in S. Lowe and D. Hughes (eds), *A New Century of Social Housing*, Leicester, Leicester University Press.

Muellbauer, J. (1990) *The Great British Housing Disaster and Economic Policy*, Economic Study, 5, London, Institute for Public Policy Research.

Mullins, D. and Riseborough, M. (2000) *What are Housing Associations Becoming?*, Birmingham, Centre for Urban and Regional Studies, University of Birmingham.

Munro, M. and Madigan, R. (1993) 'Privacy in the private sphere', *Housing Studies*, 8(1), 29–45.

Murie, A. (1983) *Housing Inequality and Deprivation*, London, Heineman.

Murie, A. (1997) 'The social rented sector, housing and the welfare state in the UK', *Housing Studies*, 12(3) 437–61.

Murie, A. (1997) 'Beyond state housing', in P. Williams (ed.), *Directions in Housing Policy* London, Paul Chapman.

Murie, A. and Jones, C. (1998) *Reviewing the Right to Buy*, Bristol, Policy Press.

Murie, A., Leather, P. and Levin, B. (1998) *Changing Demand and Unpopular Housing*, London, Housing Corporation.

Murray, C. (1990) *The Emerging British Underclass*, London, IEA Health and Welfare Unit.

Musgrave, R. A. (1959) *The Theory of Public Finance*, New York, McGraw-Hill.

Muziol-Weclawowicz, A (1996) 'Polish housing in transition, 1990–1994', in R. J. Struyk (ed.), *Economic Restructuring of the Former Soviet Bloc: The Case of Housing*, Washington, DC, Urban Institute Press.

National Federation of Housing Associations (1995) *Competence and Accountability: The Report of the Inquiry into Housing Association Governance*, London, National Federation of Housing Associations.

Needleman, L. (1965) *The Economics of Housing*, London, Staples Press.

Nelken, D. (1983) *The Limits of the Legal Process: A Study of Landlords, Law and Crime*, London Academic Press.

Nevin, B. (1999) *Local Housing Companies: Progress and Problems*, Coventry, Chartered Institute of Housing.

Nevitt, A. A. (1966) *Housing, Taxation and Subsidies*, London, Nelson.

Nolan Committee (1996) *Standards in Public Life: Local Public Spending Bodies*, Cm 3270–1, Second Report of the Committee on Standards in Public Life, London, HMSO.

ODPM (Office of the Deputy Prime Minister) (2003) website www.odpm.gov.uk (housing page).

Ohmae, K. (1990) *The Borderless World*, London, Collins.

OPCS (Office of Population, Censuses, and Surveys) (1996) *Social Trends*, London, HMSO.

Orwell, G. (1933) *Down and out in Paris and London*, London, Victor Gollancz.

Orwell, G. (1937) *The Road to Wigan Pier*, London, Victor Gollancz.

Orwell, G. (1954) 'Politics and the English language', in *The Collected Essays, Journalism and Letters* of *George Orwell*, Orwell, S. and Angus, I. (eds) (1970) Harmondsworth, Penguin.

Osborne, D. and Gaebler, T. (1992) *Reinventing Government: How the Entrepreneurial Spirit is Transforming the Public Sector*, Reading, MA, Addison-Wesley.

Ostrom, E. (1990) *Governing the Commons*, Cambridge, Cambridge University Press.

Page, D. (1993) *Building for Communities: A Study of New Housing Association Estates*, York, Joseph Rowntree Foundation.

Pahl, R. E. (1984) *Divisions of Labour*, Oxford, Blackwell.

Parsons, W. (1995) *Public Policy: An Introduction to the Theory and Practice of Policy Analysis*, Aldershot, Edward Elgar.

Pawson, H. (1999) 'The growth of residential instability and turnover', in S. Lowe, P. Keenan and S. Spencer (eds), *Housing Abandonment in Britain: Studies in the Causes and Effects of Low Demand Housing*, York, Centre for Housing Policy, University of York.

Pawson, H. and Bramley, G. (2000) 'Understanding recent trends in residential mobility in council housing in England', *Urban Studies,* 37(8), 1231–59.

Perkins, H. C. and Thorns, D. C. (1999) 'Housing and home and their interaction with changes in New Zealand's urban system', *Housing Theory and Society*, 16(3), 124–35.

Perry, J. (2000) 'The end of council housing?', in S. Wilcox (ed.), *Housing Finance Review 1999–2000*, York, Chartered Institute of Housing and the Council of Mortage Lenders for the Joseph Rowntree Foundation.

Peters, T. and Waterman, R. H. (1982) *In Search of Excellence*, New York, Harper & Row.

Pieda, (1996) *Third Survey of Consumer Preference in Housing*, Research Report No. 51, Edinburgh, Scottish Homes.

Pierson, P. (1993) 'When effect becomes cause: policy feedback and political change', *World Politics*, 45(4), 595–628.

Pierson, P. (1994) *Dismantling the Welfare State? Reagan, Thatcher, and the Politics of Retrenchment*, Cambridge, Cambridge University Press.

Pierson, P. (2000) 'Increasing returns, path dependency, and the study of politics', *American Political Science Review*, 94(2), 251–67.

Pierson, P. (2001a) 'Introduction: investigating the welfare state at century's end', in P. Pierson (ed.), *The New Politics of the Welfare State*, Oxford, Oxford University Press.

Pierson, P. (ed.), (2001b) *The New Politics of the Welfare State*, Oxford, Oxford University Press.

Pleace, N. (1997) 'Rehousing single homeless people', in R. Burrows, N. Pleace and D. Quilgars (eds), *Homelessness and Social Policy*, London, Routledge.

Pleace, N. and Quilgars, D. (1996) *Health and Homelessness in London: A Review*, London, The King's Fund.

Pleace, N., Burrows, R. and Quilgars, D. (1997) 'Homelessness in contemporary Britain: conceptualisation and measurement', in R. Burrows, N. Pleace and D. Quilgars (eds), *Homelessness and Social Policy*, London, Routledge.

Polsonby, N. (1963) *Community Power and Political Theory*, New Haven, CT, Yale University Press.

Power, A. and Mumford, K. (1999) *The Slow Death of Great Cities?*, York, Joseph Rowntree Foundation, York.

Power, M. (1994) *The Audit Explosion*, London, Demos.

Pressman, J. and Wildavsky, A. (1973) *Implementation*, Berkeley, CA, University of California Press, 2nd edn, 1984.

Priemus, H. (1995) 'How to abolish social housing? The Dutch case', *International Journal of Urban and Regional Research*, 19(1), 145–55.

Priemus, H. (1997) 'Growth and stagnation in social housing: what is "social" in the social rented sector?', *Housing Studies*, 12(4), 549–60.

Quah, D. (1999) 'The Weightless Economy in Economic Development', CEP Discussion Papers 0417, Centre for Economic Performance, London, London School of Economics (LSE).

Randolph, B. (1993) 'The reprivatisation of housing associations', in P. Malpass and R. Means (eds), *Implementing Housing Policy*, Milton Keynes, Open University.

Ravetz, A. with Turkington, R. (1995) *The Place of Home: English Domestic Environments, 1914–2000*, London, E. & F. N. Spon.

Ravetz, A. (2001) *Council Housing and Culture: The History of a Social Experiment*, London, Routledge.

Rhodes, R. A. W. (1985) 'Power-dependence, policy communities and intergovernmental networks', *Public Administration Bulletin*, 49, 4–29.

Rhodes, R. A. W. (1994) 'The hollowing out of the state', *Political Quarterly*, 65, 138–51.

Rhodes, R. A. W. (1997) *Understanding Governance: Policy Networks, Governance, Reflexivity and Accountability*, Buckingham, Open University Press.

Richardson, J. J. and Jordan, A. G. (1979) *Governing Under Pressure in a Post-Parliamentary Democracy*, Oxford, Martin Robertson, 2nd edn, 1985.

Robson, B. *et al.* (1994) *Assessing the Impact of Urban Policy*, London, HMSO.

Robson, P. and Poustie, M. (1996) *Homelessness and the Law in Britain*, 3rd edn, London, Butterworths/Planning Exchange.

Room, G. (1995) 'Poverty and social exclusion: the new European agenda for policy and research', in G. Room (ed.), *Beyond the Threshold: The Measurement and Analysis of Social Exclusion*, Bristol, Policy Press.

Rose, R. (1991) 'What is lesson drawing?', *Journal of Public Policy*, 11, 3–30.

Rothstein, B. (1996) 'Political institutions: an overview', in R. E. Goodin and H. Klingemann (eds), *A New Handbook of Political Science*, Oxford, Oxford University Press.

Rugg, J. and Burrows, R. (1999) 'Setting the scene: young people, housing and social policy', in J. Rugg (ed.), *Young People, Housing and Social Policy*, London, Routledge.

Rugg, J., Rhodes D. and Jones, A. (2000) *The Nature and Impact of Student Demand on Housing Markets*, York, Joseph Rowntree Foundation.

Rybczynski, W. (1986) *Home: A Short History of an Idea*, New York, Viking Penguin, paperback edn, Pocket Books, 2001.

Saunders, P. (1981) *Social Theory and the Urban Question*, London, Hutchinson.

Saunders, P. (1986) 'Comment on Dunleavy and Preteceille', *Environment and Planning A*, 4, 155–63.

Saunders, P. (1989) 'Beyond housing classes', in L. McDowell, P. Sarre and C. Hamnett (eds), *Divided Nation: Social and Cultural Change in Britain*, London, Open University Press.

Saunders, P. (1990) *A Nation of Home Owners*, London, Unwin Hyman.

Saunders, P. and Williams, P. (1988) 'The constitution of home', *Housing Studies*, 3(1).

Schattscheider, E. E. (1960) *The Semisovereign People*, New York, Holt, Rinehart & Winston.

Scottish Office (1999) *Investing in Modernisation – An Agenda for Scotland's Housing*, Green Paper, Cm 4272, The Scottish Office.

Skocpol, T. (1985). 'Bringing the state back in: strategies of analysis in current research', in P. B. Evans *et al.* (eds), *Bringing the State Back In*, Cambridge, Cambridge University Press.

Slootweg, S. (1999) 'The changing face of Tirana, Albania', unpublished paper for ENHR-MRI conference, Hungary, 25–29 August.

Social Exclusion Unit (SEU) (1998) *Rough Sleeping Report by the Social Exclusion Unit*, Cm 4008, London, HMSO.

Social Exclusion Unit (SEU) (1999) *Bringing Britain Together: A National Strategy for Neighbourhood Renewal*, Cm 4045, London, The Stationery Office.

Spicker, P. (1998) *Housing and Social Exclusion*, Edinburgh, Shelter Scotland.

Spiers, F. (1999) *Housing and Social Exclusion*, London, Jessica Kingsley.

Standing, G. (1996) 'Social protection in Central and Eastern Europe: a tale of slipping anchors and torn safety nets', in G. Esping-Andersen (ed.), *Welfare States in Transition*, London, Sage.

Steinmo, S., Thelen, K. and Longstreth, F. (eds) (1992) *Structuring Politics: Historical Institutionalism in Comparative Politics*, Cambridge, Cambridge University Press.

Stephens, M., Burns, N. and MacKay, L. (2002) *Social Market or Safety Net? British Social Rented Housing in a European Context*, Bristol, Policy Press.

Strong, A., Reiner, T. A. and Szyrmer, J. (1996) *Transitions in Land and Housing*, Basingstoke, Macmillan.

Struyk, R. J. (ed.) (1996) *Economic Restructuring of the Former Soviet Bloc: The Case of Housing*, Washington, DC, Urban Institute Press.

Struyk, R. and Kosareva, N. (1994) *Transition in the Russian Housing Sector 1990–1994*, Moscow, Institute of Urban Economics.

Swenarton, M. (1981) *Homes Fit For Heroes*, London, Heinemann.

Szelenyi, I. (1983) *Urban Inequalities under State Socialism*, Oxford, Oxford University Press.

Szelenyi, I. (1989) 'Housing policy in the emergent socialist mixed economy of Eastern Europe', *Housing Studies*, 4(3), 167–76

Taylor, M. (1999) 'Ten years of stock transfers', in S. Wilcox (ed.), *Scottish Housing Review 1988–1998*, Edinburgh.

Taylor, M. (2000) *Stock Transfer Past and Present: A Summary of Research Evidence*, Research Review, 6, Edinburgh, Scottish Homes.

Taylor, M. (2002) 'Housing's place in post-devolution Scotland', in S. Wilcox (ed.), *Housing Policy Review 2002–3*, York, Joseph Rowntree Foundation.

Taylor, M. and Sim, D. (2000) 'Social inclusion and housing policy in the Scottish Parliament: prospects', *Critical Social Policy*, 20(2), 183–210.

Thain, M. (1999) 'Back on the agenda: housing policy and devolution in Scotland', in S. Wilcox (ed.), *Housing Finance Review 1999–2000*, York, Joseph Rowntree Foundation.

Thelen, K. and Steinmo, S. (1992) 'Historical institutionalism in comparative politics', in S. Steinmo, K. Thelen and F. Longstreth (eds), *Structuring Politics: Historical Institutionalism in Comparative Politics*, Cambridge, Cambridge University Press.

Thomas, A., Snape, D., Duldig, W., Keegan, J. and Ward, K. (1995) *In from the Cold – Working with the Private Landlord*, London, DoE.

Thompson, F. M. L. (1988) *The Rise of Respectable Society: A Social History of Victorian Britain 1830–1900*, London, Fontana.

Torgersen, U. (1987) 'Housing: the wobbly pillar under the welfare state', in B. Turner, J. Kemeny and L. Lundqvist (eds), *Between State and Market: Housing in the Post-Industrial Era*, Stockholm, Almqvist & Wicksell.

Townsend, P. (1964) *The Last Refuge*, London, Routledge.

Turner, B., Hegedüs, J. and Tosics, I. (eds) (1992) *The Reform of Housing in Eastern Europe and the Soviet Union*, London, Routledge.

Turok, I. and Edge, N. (1999) *The Jobs Gap in Britain's Cities: Employment Loss and Labour Market Consequences*, Bristol, Policy Press.

Utting, D. (1995) *Family and Parenthood: Supporting families, preventing breakdown; a guide to the debate*, York, Joseph Rowntree Foundation.

van Weesep, J. and van Kempen, R. (1993) 'Low income and housing in the Dutch welfare state', in G. Hallet, *The New Housing Shortage: Housing Affordability in Europe and the USA*, London, Routledge.

Warnes, A.M. and Crane, M. (2000) *Meeting Homeless People's Needs: service development and practice for the older excluded*, London, The King's Fund.

Watchman, P. and Robson, P. (1983) *Homelessness and the Law in Britain*, Glasgow, Planning Exchange.

Webster, D. (1998) 'Employment change, housing abandonment and sustainable development: structural processes and structural issues', in S. Lowe, P. Keenan and S. Spencer, (eds), *Housing Abandonment in Britain: Studies in the Causes and Effects of Low Demand Housing*, York, Centre for Housing Policy, University of York.

Whelan, B. and Whelan, C. (1995) 'In what sense is poverty multidimensional?', in G. Room (ed.), *Beyond the Threshold: The Measurement and Analysis of Social Exclusion*, Bristol, Policy Press.

Whitehead, C. and Kleinman, M. (1991) *A Review of Housing Needs Assessment*, London, The Housing Corporation.

Whyley, C. and Warren, T. (1999) *Wealth in Britain: A Lifecycle Perspective*, London, Policy Studies Institute.

Wilcox, S. (1990) *The Need for Social Rented Housing in England in the 1990s*, Coventry, Institute of Housing, mimeo.

Wilcox, S. (1997) 'Local housing companies', in P. Malpass (ed.), *Ownership, Control and Accountability: The New Governance of Housing*, Coventry, Chartered Institute of Housing.

Wilcox, S. (1998) *Housing Finance Review 1997–1998*, York, Joseph Rowntree Foundation.

Wilcox, S. (1999) *Housing Finance Review 1999–2000*, York, Joseph Rowntree Foundation.

Wilcox, S. (2000) *Housing Finance Review 2000–2001*, York, Joseph Rowntree Foundation.

Wilcox, S. (2001) *Thirty per cent Fall in Private Tenants Getting Housing Benefit*, Findings, 451, York, Joseph Rowntree Foundation, April.

Wilcox, S. (2002a) 'Housing benefit and social security', in S. Lowe and D. Hughes (eds), *The Private Rented Sector in a New Century*, Bristol, Policy Press.

Wilcox, S. (2002b) 'Border tensions: devolution, rents and housing benefit', in S. Wilcox (ed.), *Housing Policy Review 2002–2003*, Joseph Rowntree Foundation.

Wilcox, S. *et al.* (1993) *Local Housing Companies: New Opportunities for Council Housing*, York, Joseph Rowntree Foundation in association with the Chartered Institute of Housing.

Wildavsky, A. (1975) *Budgeting: A Comparative Theory of Budgetary Processes*, Boston, Mass., Little, Brown.

Wildavsky, A. (1980) *The Art and Craft of Policy Analysis*, London, Macmillan.

Wilensky, H. L. (1975) *The Welfare State and Equality: Structural and Ideological Roots of Public Expenditure*, Berkeley, CA, University of California Press.

Williams, P. (2002) 'Stand and deliver! Tackling the housing challenges in post-devolution Wales', in S. Wilcox (ed.), *Housing Policy Review 2002–2003*, York, Joseph Rowntree Foundation.

Wohl, A. S. (1977) *The Eternal Slum: Housing and Social Policy in Victorian London*, London, Edward Arnold.

Wolman, H. (1992) 'Understanding cross-national policy transfers: the case of Britain and the United States', *Governance*, 5, 27–45.

Index